FROM EMBARGO TO OSTPOLITIK

SOVIET AND EAST EUROPEAN STUDIES

FROM EMBARGO TO OSTPOLITIK

THE POLITICAL ECONOMY OF WEST GERMAN-SOVIET RELATIONS, 1955-1980

ANGELA STENT

GEORGETOWN UNIVERSITY

CAMBRIDGE UNIVERSITY PRESS

CAMBRIDGE

LONDON   NEW YORK   NEW ROCHELLE
MELBOURNE   SYDNEY

Published by the Press Syndicate of the University of Cambridge
The Pitt Building, Trumpington Street, Cambridge CB2 1RP
32 East 57th Street, New York, NY 10022, USA
296 Beaconsfield Parade, Middle Park, Melbourne 3206, Australia

First published 1981

Printed in the United States of America

Library of Congress Cataloging in Publication Data
Stent, Angela.
From embargo to ostpolitik.
(Soviet and East European studies)
Bibliography: p.
Includes index.
1. Germany (West) – Foreign economic relations –
Soviet Union. 2. Soviet Union – Foreign economic
relations – Germany (West) 3. Germany (West) –
Commerce – Soviet Union. 4. Soviet Union – Commerce
– Germany (West) I. Title. II. Series.
HF1546.15.S63S73 337.43047 81-2407
ISBN 0 521 23667 3 AACR2

To my parents,
GABRIELE *and* RONALD STENT
who survived and gave so much

Contents

Tables

Preface

The Soviet invasion of Afghanistan and the crisis in Poland have raised two unresolved and controversial issues in East–West relations. First, what is the utility of applying Western economic sanctions to change Soviet behavior? Second, the recent labor unrest in Poland has highlighted many divisive issues in relations between the two Germanies and the USSR, and has reminded the world that the German question has not entirely been resolved.

This book deals with questions at the heart of these two issues – the politics of East–West trade and the German problem. The treatment is partly historical, but the subject remains of great importance today. The book addresses a number of key themes that will continue to determine East–West relations for the foreseeable future.

The United States and the Federal Republic once agreed on the imperative of using East–West trade as a political instrument to elicit concessions from the Soviet Union. Why did West Germany alter its policy and cease to view East–West trade as primarily a political lever? The book examines in detail the German government's historical attempts to change Soviet policy through the use of economic weapons and explains why, when the Social Democratic–Free Democratic coalition came to power in 1969, it ceased to use trade as a primarily political instrument. The Soviet side of this equation is discussed in equal detail, in particular why the USSR has not historically responded to Western use of the trade weapon.

Prior to the detente era, Bonn and Moscow disagreed on the definition of the German problem and its possible resolution. Trade was used as one form of negotiation in discussions on Germany. The election of Chancellor Willy Brandt in 1969 and the change in West German Ostpolitik heralded a new era in Soviet–West German relations. In the past decade, ties between the two countries have undoubtedly improved; yet the German problem remains unsolved. Why is it that Brandt's Ostpolitik and Brezhnev's Westpolitik have not yet resolved the ultimate question of the future of Germany? This issue is examined from both the Soviet and German sides. It will continue to play an important role in European politics for many years. It is ultimately both a political and an economic question; moreover, economic relations are also at the core of intra-German contacts and the triangular Soviet relationship with both Germanies.

The relationship between the two Germanies has become an increasingly important determinant of West German Ostpolitik, and has given Bonn a considerable stake in maintaining detente in Europe. This commitment is not necessarily shared by the United States, as events since the invasion of Afghanistan have shown. This book discusses the origins of the divergences between American and German policies toward the Soviet Union in the early 1960s, and the development of these conflicts since detente. America and Germany share fundamental security goals toward the USSR; yet they disagree on how to achieve these ends, and on the ranking of their interests in East-West relations. In particular, they differ over the politics of East-West trade and the utility of punitive economic sanctions. The Reagan administration's opposition to Germany's participation in the Yamburg natural gas pipeline from the USSR and the disagreement between Washington and Bonn over the imposition of high technology and grain embargoes against the USSR under President Carter are reminiscent of the Adenauer-Kennedy conflicts over the pipe embargo and wheat sales to the USSR. The difference is that in 1980, unlike in 1963, Germany was not willing to follow the American agenda and reduce trade with the USSR. Meanwhile, the Soviet Union has consistently sought to capitalize on German-American disagreements over economic relations with the USSR. The German-American discord over East-West trade, and the Soviet reaction to it, form another theme of this book.

The 1970s began with great expectations for East-West relations. The 1980s have begun on a more sober and pessimistic note. As we move into an age of greater uncertainty, Soviet-West German relations will continue to play a pivotal role in determining and regulating the structure of the uneasy postwar coexistence between East and West.

Acknowledgments

I am greatly indebted to my colleagues and former teachers at Harvard for giving me advice and stimulating my thoughts on this book in its earlier incarnation. I would particularly like to thank Professor Adam B. Ulam, director of the Harvard Russian Research Center, for helping me to appreciate the subtleties of Soviet politics. The many mornings spent with him and other Center members as we attempted to penetrate the labyrinth of Soviet foreign policy brought both insight and understanding to this intricate subject.

I would also like to thank Professor Abram Bergson, who taught me most of what I know about the Soviet economy; Professor Stanley Hoffmann, for providing me with a more differentiated and broader perspective on international politics; Dr. Barrington Moore, for stimulating my interest in the social context of foreign policy making; and Professor Joseph Nye, for enabling me to understand the complexities of international political economy.

I have also profited from the advice of the following people who read all or part of the manuscript: Dr. Karen Dawisha, Mr. Bruno Friedrich, Professor William Griffith, Dr. John Hardt, Professor Michael Kaser, Dr. Edwina Moreton, and Mr. Ronald Stent.

I also express thanks to the more than thirty German government officials and businessmen who talked with me over a period of five years about this topic. Some asked not to be named, but I am grateful for their frankness and willingness to share information.

The Harvard Russian Research Center provided a congenial and supportive atmosphere for me during the research and writing of this book. I thank the Center for giving me financial assistance during its writing and revision. I gratefully acknowledge the financial assistance of the British Council, for supporting me for five months in Moscow; the American Association of University Women; the Harvard Center for European Studies; and the Deutscher Akademischer Austauschdienst for supporting the final update of the book in Germany.

I am indebted to a number of libraries and librarians who assisted me – most of all to Susan Jo Gardos of the Russian Research Center library, who has given me much bibliographical help over the years. The libraries at the Royal Institute of International Affairs in London, the Deutsche Gesellschaft fuer Auswaertige Politik in Bonn, the John F. Kennedy Memorial Library in Boston, and the Radio Liberty Library in Munich were all invaluable resources. I would particularly like to thank the Kennedy Library for declassifying so many documents concerned with the pipe embargo and for patiently giving me counsel on how to deal with recalcitrant government declassifiers.

A special word of thanks is also due to Professor Karl Kaiser, who provided me on several occasions with office space and advice at the Deutsche Gesellschaft fuer Auswaertige Politik in Bonn.

I would like to thank Brenda Sens, Mary Towle, Rose di Benedetto, Karina Forster, and Suzanne Schmidt for their expert and skillful typing of the manuscript.

Finally, I would like to thank Daniel Yergin for his encouragement throughout this project, for his insights into the subject, and for his good-humored and patient support over many years.

1

The German problem and linkage politics

I say, as Voltaire said of God, that if there were no Germans we should have to invent them, since nothing so successfully unites the Slavs as a rooted hatred of Germans.   Mikhail Bakunin, 1865[1]

[I]f war is too important to be left to the generals, surely commerce is, in this context, too salient to be left to bankers and businessmen. . . . Another misconception is that the potential for economic leverage, even if it exists, cannot be translated into effective pressure against the Soviets, because they will not make political concessions for economic purposes. In fact, however, only rarely have Western countries attempted to use economic leverage against them.

Samuel P. Huntington, 1978[2]

The German problem has been a major source of instability in European and world politics for over a century. Although it has been resolved for the time being since the normalization of relations between the Federal Republic of Germany (FRG) and its Eastern neighbors in the early 1970s, it could once again become a source of international tension. It is a central issue for Soviet foreign policy. The relationship between Germany and the USSR remains one of the most important determinants of East–West security today. It is therefore vital to understand the process of postwar Soviet–German conflict and rapprochement to outline future developments in East–West relations. Although political questions have dominated the evolution of West German Ostpolitik and Soviet Westpolitik, the economic aspects of the relationship have at times played a significant role in the development of German–Soviet detente, interacting with political issues. This book examines the importance of economic de-

1

terminants in shaping Soviet and West German foreign policy toward each other.

Unlike Soviet relations with other Western European countries, postwar Soviet–West German relations are unique in that until 1969 neither side would even agree on a common agenda for the conduct of relations or on what the parameters of their relationship should be. As long as the FRG refused to recognize the German Democratic Republic's existence, Soviet–West German relations were particularly strained and complicated, because West Germany's Ostpolitik was largely a function of its *Deutschlandpolitik* (policy toward East Germany). Detente has involved a process of normalizing East–West relations in Europe. Because of the prior hostile state of Soviet–West German contacts, the Soviet–FRG relationship has altered more dramatically than have Soviet relations with other West European countries. Relations with the FRG have always determined Soviet policy toward Western Europe. Hence the special significance of Soviet–West German contacts in the detente era. Moscow's improved ties with Bonn have involved major policy shifts on both sides since 1969 and changes in power relations that are particularly important for the future Soviet presence in Western Europe. Prior to 1969, the USSR and the FRG did not agree on what the rules of their bilateral game should be. Now their relationship is directed toward securing and modifying the rules of that game.

The history of West German–Soviet relations since 1955 is a chronicle of clashes over solutions to the German problem. Traditionally, the German problem prior to 1871 was defined by Germany's weakness and hence its inability to prevent domination by others. After 1871 the main problem was Germany's strength – it was either too strong to be contained by its neighbors or not strong enough to impose its hegemony on the continent.[3] In the cold war era, the German problem had centered on four main questions. First, what was the proper *geographical* location for Germany in Europe? Should it have remained truncated or should it have expanded eastward and recouped its territories of 1937? Second, there was the *division* of Germany. Should it have remained divided or if it were to have been reunified, what kind of government should it have had? Third, there was the role of *Berlin*. Should West Berlin have been linked to the FRG and if so, in what way? Fourth, there was the question of West Germany's role in the *international* system and its relations with both parts of Europe. By 1973, all four aspects of the problem had been resolved in international treaties, and the nature of the German question was materially altered.

In the formulation and implementation of foreign policy, states have limited resources at their disposal. As part of their attempt to influence outcomes in their favor, states will use whatever bargaining levers they possess. In an asymmetrical relationship, such as that prevailing between the USSR and the FRG after 1949, economic levers have had a special significance for West Germany. The FRG was by far the weaker country in terms of traditional measures of political and strategic power; yet economically it was often in a stronger bargaining position than was the USSR. The normalization of Soviet-West German relations in the last decade involved agreements on the core political questions of the cold war. Although the goals were political, the FRG sometimes used economic means in the process of negotiating with the Soviet Union. This book analyzes the extent to which Bonn succeeded in modifying Soviet foreign policy through the use of economic levers by focusing on three main themes.

Soviet-West German relations: background

The first theme is the development of German Ostpolitik and Soviet Westpolitik since 1955. Soviet-German relations were determined by the political and geographical situation in Europe at the end of the Second World War. Josef Stalin's prime concern after 1945 was to guarantee that Germany could never again threaten the Soviet Union. In his search for security, Stalin was convinced of the need to create a series of loyal buffer states between Germany and the USSR. He was willing to accept a Western sphere of influence in Europe but was intent on controlling the governments of Eastern Europe to ensure their compliance with Soviet goals. Without embarking on a discussion of the origins of the cold war, which have been extensively analyzed elsewhere,[4] suffice it to say that the USSR's definition of spheres of influence was different from that of the West. The United States and Britain considered the Soviet imposition of communist government in Eastern Europe a breach of the Yalta and Potsdam agreements.

There is some evidence that Stalin was undecided about what Germany's fate should be in 1945. By 1949, however, the USSR believed that the division of Europe could be secured only by the division of Germany into two halves, one of which had to be in the Soviet sphere. In redrawing the postwar map of Europe, the USSR moved westward, annexing parts of what had formerly been East Prussia, and Poland gained parts of Silesia and Pomerania, previously under the German Reich. The boundary of Poland was drawn at the Oder–Neisse line. Altogether, Germany lost 13,205 square kilometers of its territory to the USSR and 101,091 square kilometers to Poland. Apart from losing 24.3 percent of its prewar (1937) territory, Germany was divided into two halves. Berlin was also divided, although it remained under Four-Power control. The main point of contention between the USSR and the FRG after 1949 was the legitimacy of the postwar status quo. The West Germans rejected both the political legitimacy of the German Democratic Republic (GDR) and the geographical legitimacy of Poland's and the USSR's incorporation of territories belonging to the former Reich. They also insisted on maintaining links with West Berlin. The Soviet Union, on the other hand, sought German ratification of the status quo. In the absence of a peace treaty between the two sides, there were no bilaterally accepted rules of conduct.

There were three distinct West German Ostpolitiks in this period. The first was that of Chancellor Konrad Adenauer (1949–63) and was negative and passive until his final year in office. Adenauer's *Politik der Stärke* (policy of strength) was predicated on the premise that the FRG's integration into the West was the precondition for German reunification and also on an uncompromising stance toward the USSR. The issue of German reunification was certainly the most prominent in Adenauer's declaratory Ostpolitik, partly for domestic reasons. Every contact with the USSR in the early years was designed to induce the Kremlin to renounce its control over East Germany and allow Germany to be reunited. Reunification was upheld as the central goal. In his operational policy, however, Adenauer did not act as if reunification was his first priority. Germany's integration into the Western alliance was far more important for him. Mindful of his constant need to reassure the United States that the FRG was a reliable member of the Western alliance, Adenauer's Ostpolitik consisted largely of the periodic articulation of legal claims, such as self-determination for the "Soviet zone" (i.e., the GDR), free all-German elections, and the *Alleinvertretungsanspruch* – the claim of West Germany to speak for the whole of Germany, because East Germany was an illegitimate state. This became known as the Hallstein Doctrine, whereby the FRG refused to have diplomatic relations with any state that recognized the GDR. This placated domestic opinion, did not threaten the United States by appearing to be an autonomous policy, and was an alibi for prudent inaction.[5] The only concrete result of Adenauer's Ostpolitik was the reluctant establishment of diplomatic relations with the USSR. Adenauer's Ostpolitik was Moscow-oriented. He dealt only with the USSR and refused to pursue contacts with the Eastern European states, whose legitimacy he denied.

Under Chancellors Ludwig Erhard (1963–6) and Kurt Georg Kiesinger (1966–9), German Ostpolitik became more flexible. Bridge building and the "policy of movement" ultimately were unsuccessful in achieving their specific goals, but they implied a degree of reconciliation with the USSR. Instead of dealing only with Moscow, Erhard and Kiesinger tried to woo Eastern Europe. However, Germany refused to ratify the status quo in Europe and continued to deny the legitimacy of most of Eastern Europe's existence. The only concrete achievements of the more active Erhard–Kiesinger Ostpolitik were the establishment of trade missions in Eastern Europe and of diplomatic relations with Rumania. Under Chancellors Willy Brandt (1969–74) and Helmut Schmidt (1974–present), German Ostpolitik has changed dramatically. The FRG since 1969 has been willing to ratify the geographical status quo in Eastern Europe and to renounce its *Alleinvertretungsrecht*. Initially, Brandt realized that he had to revert to dealing only with Moscow. Subsequently, the FRG was able to establish relations with all Eastern European states, including the GDR, and although it retains an ultimate commitment to reunification, it recognizes the impossibility of achieving this goal in the near future.

Soviet Westpolitik since the death of Stalin has been more consistent than has German Ostpolitik. Prior to 1954, one could argue that the USSR was not sure about what course it wanted Germany to pursue or whether it should be reunified. There is evidence that Stalin was flexible on this issue, and yet the maintenance of a loyal East German buffer state was also considered a vital necessity. Although there are few data to support this claim, Khrushchev said in May 1963 that Beria in 1953 was willing to allow the FRG to absorb the GDR, and this was one of the reasons Khrushchev gave for his execution.[6]

Nineteen fifty-four was in some ways a watershed year for Soviet policy toward the FRG. Bitterly opposed to the Paris agreements by which the FRG joined the Western alliance, the USSR was reluctantly forced to accept Germany's membership of NATO as a fait accompli. Once the USSR had accepted the FRG's membership in the Western alliance and had secured German diplomatic recognition, its main goals were to obtain FRG diplomatic recognition of the GDR and the rest of Eastern Europe and an acknowledgment of the legitimacy of the postwar status quo in Europe. This remained a consistent Soviet stance during the regimes of Nikita Khrushchev (1954–64) and Leonid Brezhnev (1964–present). Apart from the 1958–62 Berlin crisis, the USSR has grudgingly been willing to accept that West Berlin has some links with the FRG. Soviet Westpolitik has largely achieved its aims, because the FRG by 1973 had acceded to all the main Soviet demands for ratification of the postwar status quo.

The USSR has had an advantage in the pursuit of its Westpolitik. Russia's Westpolitik was always oriented toward securing a legitimization of the status quo. Whereas the USSR sought ratification, however, the FRG's Ostpolitik was predicated on revisionism – on changing the status quo. In this sense, the Soviets, as the status quo (and the stronger) power, stood a greater chance of success than did the revisionist weaker Germans. The German issue was the main focus of Soviet policy toward Europe. The perceived need to prevent Germany from ever reaching the position in which it had the capability to threaten the USSR dictated Soviet policy toward Eastern Europe and exacerbated the differences that had been inherent in the wartime alliance with the West, that tenuous *marriage de convenance* that proved to be only too ephemeral. The Western Allies

- the United States, France, and Britain - felt equally constrained to supervise West German foreign policy for ten years, to ensure that West Germany could be reborn as a nation in which a commitment to a democratic system of government and an orientation toward the West were better rooted than they had been in the unfortunate Weimar Republic. It was only in 1955, when West Germany became a sovereign state, that the USSR and West Germany were able to begin to develop a bilateral relationship, albeit under the close supervision of the Western Allies.

Linkage politics

In their attempts to modify each other's policies, both the USSR and the FRG sought to link different aspects of their foreign policy. Linkage politics forms the second theme of this book.

Linkages arise when states decide that they can utilize levers and make an economic concession dependent on another state's granting a political quid pro quo, or vice versa. Since the Bolshevik revolution, Western states have tended to assume that, given the USSR's economic problems, it would be willing to make political concessions in return for trade. Linkage politics become particularly significant when obvious asymmetries in power arise between antagonistic nations. During much of the period that this book discusses, West Germany and the USSR were on opposite sides in the cold war and as such had mutually hostile relations. However, their economic contacts, meager though they were, implied a degree of normality and cooperation absent from their political relations. This asymmetrical situation of confrontational political relations and potentially cooperative economic relations was the environment that facilitated a policy of linkage. As unequal antagonists, both the USSR and West Germany were able to use reward power.[7] In a dynamic relationship that includes both political and economic contacts, linkage involves changing interactions between different levels of interstate relations. The possibility of linkage was always there, but the character of linkage altered as relations became normalized.

An analysis of the politics of West German–Soviet economic relations is comprehensible only in the context of the general environment in which they operated. West German–Soviet trade was largely determined by general East–West economic interactions. East–West economic relations are distinguished by four basic features that differentiate them from all other international economic transactions. First, they have taken place between two antagonistic, hegemonic political blocs confronting each other as ideological adversaries. Although they were initially dedicated to each other's overthrow in the early years of the cold war, their enmity has somewhat dissipated, although both sides remain wary of each other's future goals both inside and outside Europe. The era of detente has signaled a willingness to cooperate in some areas but by no means an end to the basic enmity. Second, not only have the political systems in the East and the West been antagonistic, but their economic systems have been very differently organized, creating problems. Capitalism, based on the more or less free play of the market and with some commitment to free trade, has faced socialism, in its guise of state-controlled economies, with rigid centralized planning and pricing policies that bear little relation to cost factors. Third, there has been a great asymmetry between the economic development of the two blocs, such that East–West trade has always been and continues to be mostly complementary, involving the exchange of raw materials for advanced Western technology. Fourth, despite the antagonism between the two blocs, the existence of a nuclear stalemate has meant that hostilities have had to be conducted by methods other than outright war. In much of the cold war era, trade was the continuation of politics by other means.

Soviet–West German relations are a particularly salient example of the interrelation of politics and economics because of their prior history of economic interdependence. The long tradition of economic relations between the two countries meant that both economies were oriented toward trade with each other, and there was a certain complementarity of interests. Even when political relations were bad in the prewar days, economic relations were relatively good. A few statistics will show how important trade with Germany was to Russia (it was always more important to Russia). From 1858 to 1862, imports from Germany formed 28 percent of Russian imports, and exports to Germany formed 16 percent of Russian exports. From 1868 to 1872, the figures were 44 and 24 percent, respectively. In 1914 – the best year – the figures were 47 and 29 percent. In 1923, they were 25 and 30 percent; and in 1932 they were 47 and 18 percent.[8] By contrast, 5.3 percent of the USSR's trade was with the FRG in 1979.[9] There was a tradition of Soviet admiration for German achievements, particularly in the field of economics.[10] German–Soviet trade has always been characterized by the export of advanced industrial goods from Germany in exchange for raw materials from Russia. There have also been the special asymmetries of a medium-sized, highly developed country, for which foreign trade is an important part of its GNP (roughly 30 percent), trading with a large, relatively backward country for which foreign trade forms only 5 percent of the GNP. This asymmetry has had both advantages and disadvantages for Germany. On the one hand, Germany has greater leverage in international trade than does the USSR. On the other hand, it is more susceptible to economic pressure from the outside.[11]

These are the reasons why linkage politics were both possible and feasible in FRG–Soviet relations. Based on these premises, it is possible to analyze the dynamics of German–Soviet relations in terms of four linkage strategies. These are four different ways of describing the possible uses of economic and political levers in a bilateral relationship, and they have all been used at various times during the 1955–80 period.

1. The first strategy is negative economic linkage, involving the use of *negative economic means* in the pursuit of political goals. In other words, country A indicates to country B that it will not sell B a particular commodity, or not trade at all with B because it disapproves of B's foreign policy. Trade denial is the most usual form of negative economic linkage. This linkage can be either general or specific. In other words, country A can deny country B some economic good because it disapproves of B's general policy, or it can deny the trade because of some specific foreign policy act by B, for instance, the U.S. technology embargo following the Soviet invasion of Afghanistan. The negative linkage could also be a response to domestic political developments in B, such as the U.S. Congress's denial of Most Favored Nation status to the USSR because of its Jewish emigration policy.

2. The second strategy is positive economic linkage, involving

the use of *positive economic means* in the pursuit of political goals. In this situation, country A uses trade inducement – offering country B something it wants – in the expectation that this will persuade B to modify aspects of its policies. Again, this linkage can be general or tied to a specific political quid pro quo, and could be directed toward country B's modifying its foreign or domestic policies.

3. The third possible strategy is negative political linkage, involving the use of *negative political means* in the pursuit of economic goals. In this scenario, country A pursues a more hostile policy toward country B than heretofore because it disapproves of B's foreign economic policies. The linkage can be general or specific.

4. The fourth strategy is the opposite of this. It is positive political linkage, involving the use of *positive political means* in the pursuit of economic goals. In this case, country A agrees to make a concession in its foreign policy toward country B in return for B's altering its foreign trade policy. The concessions can be general or specific.

This book will describe how all of these categories have applied at one time or another during the period and will explain why different strategies were valid at different times. On the basis of the evidence, it will suggest the environment in which similar situations might arise again, and it will evaluate the success of the use of these various negative and positive political and economic levers. Of course, trade and politics can develop as separate processes even if trade is politically motivated. Linkage occurs only when a country explicitly makes economics and politics interdependent. Moreover, economic and political relations can affect each other without conscious linkage strategies.

There is a major caveat involved in attempting to differentiate between negative and positive levers. The interaction of economic and political factors is complex, and it is not always easy to distinguish unambiguously between cases in which a lever is used negatively or positively. Linkage, like beauty, is often in the eye of the beholder, and the same lever can be interpreted as either positive or negative depending on the particular perceptions involved. We shall try, wherever possible, to differentiate between trade inducements and trade denial in specific instances, but sometimes the intricacies of the situation will blur fine distinctions. On occasion, the USSR and the FRG have used similar levers in mirror-image fashion, and the identification of negative or positive levers depends on discovering who initiated the linkage strategy.

In any discussion of the use of linkage strategies, one of the most important questions is who sets the agenda. Before we can develop a viable analysis of the use of levers in foreign policy, we must ascertain which country has the power to define the framework in which the linkage is made and can initiate such linkage. The kind of linkage that is used will be determined by the environment that establishes the terms of the relationship. In the case of West German–Soviet relations, the question of agenda setting is complex and involves various levels. The bilateral FRG–USSR relationship for much of the period operated within a larger three-party game. Until Willy Brandt's accession to power, German foreign policy, particularly its Ostpolitik, was subject to American control, and any initiatives were taken only with American approval. It was often the U.S.–Soviet relationship that set the agenda for the West German–Soviet relationship, most strikingly in the case of the pipe embargo of 1962, it was the United States that initially made the issue of trading with the USSR so controversial for the West.

To understand how trade becomes politicized, we can imagine a situation in which country A is in a position of power over country B. That is, it is less interested in trading with B than vice versa, from which it derives this power. *Primary* politicization occurs when A determines in what way it might utilize B's desire to trade with it by demanding certain political concessions from B. Politicization, in this sense, means placing economic issues on the political agenda between A and B. The situation may alter and B may subsequently become less interested in trade with A, but once A has set the agenda, B will probably react to subsequent situations essentially in the form spelled out by A's initial definition of the parameters of politicization. Thus, it is likely that, even if B is now in a position to link economic relations to political concessions from A, it may well define politicization – in this case, *secondary* politicization – in terms that are derived from those set by A. Thus, A has begun a chain reaction in which the initiative in the politicization of economic relations may shift from A to B, but in which the stakes involved in the politicization are likely to derive from the initial agenda setter. This places the actor who first politicizes trade in a strategically advantageous position.

Primary and secondary politicization are important aspects of agenda setting in international politics. However, domestic politics also influence agenda setting. Foreign policy consists of two discrete processes – policy formulation and policy implementation. In a pluralist society, the process of policy formulation is complex and involves inputs from many different domestic groups. In communist societies we have evidence that bargaining among various sectors of the leadership also exists, but it is far harder to document this process. However, the agenda for linkage, involving as it does both government and business in pluralist societies, is often determined as a result of domestic bargaining. The domestic group that has the most power will probably set the agenda, but different groups will predominate depending on whether it is economic or political levers that are being used in the pursuit of foreign policy goals. In this sense, trade can be politicized when the government interferes with the business sector. Agenda setting is therefore both an *international* and a *domestic* issue.

During the period covered by this book, West Germany enjoyed predominant economic bargaining power over the USSR and was generally the initiator of economic linkage strategies. For this reason, the USSR sought to avoid any such linkage because it had to respond to Bonn's policies. On the other hand, the USSR, as the predominant political power, initiated political linkage strategies to which Bonn had to respond. Thus, both sides preferred to operate in an environment in which they could be the initiator of, rather than the respondent to, a linkage strategy.

The domestic roots of linkage

The question of domestic politics of linkage forms the third main theme of this book. The book examines the problem that all pluralist societies face in pursuing a foreign policy of linkage, whether negative or positive, political or economic. There is a limit to how much any Western government can tell its business community what to do. We shall discuss the relationship of West

German business and government in the linkage question and examine the role of economic and political interest groups in formulating foreign policy and setting the agenda. There will be an asymmetry, however, in considering the role of various participants in the FRG. There will be a tendency to disregard the role of nongovernment actors in political questions and to examine them more closely in economic transactions. The reason is that for most of the time covered by the book, the political climate between East and West was so hostile that there was little room for nongovernment actors to exercise any influence.

As Arnold Wolfers has indicated, "the closer nations are drawn to the pole of complete compulsion, the more they can be expected to . . . act in a way that corresponds to the deductions made from the states-as-actors model."[12] It seems that nongovernment actors can play a more significant role when political relations are flexible enough to permit a variety of contacts. In the East–West situation, only after a relative relaxation of central political controls could these actors have more leeway. In an environment of intense ideological and political antagonism, the room for maneuvering was far smaller.

Although it is comparatively easy to identify West German transnational and nongovernment actors, any discussion of nongovernment Soviet actors is fraught with difficulties. This is not to say that Soviet society is a monolith. Since Stalin's death, there is increasing evidence of disagreements within the Soviet elite, and yet any attempt to identify specific interest groups or pluralist enclaves within Soviet society is difficult and remains largely within the realm of speculation. Political participation in the USSR is largely directed from above and does not represent genuine popular initiative. It is consequently problematic to identify autonomous sources of power or interest coalitions. Furthermore, although interelite bargaining undoubtedly takes place, these elites do not amount to interest groups in the Western sense of the word. These groups lack the necessary sanctions or "clout" to make their opinions felt if these views are opposed to those of the party leaders. The USSR remains a closed society, hierarchically controlled and organized, and unfortunately we lack systematic evidence on differences of opinion on foreign policy between specific groups, although anecdotes abound.[13]

There have been a variety of East–West nongovernment contacts in the cultural and economic spheres – trade union delegations, student and cultural exchanges, various friendship societies and discussion groups, and delegations of Western businessmen to the USSR. It is unclear what, if any, political significance these kinds of exchanges have had, although they may have had some economic importance. In terms of Soviet society, one cannot call these groups independent nongovernment actors. Because all official Soviet delegations that have contact with foreigners are carefully chosen by the party organs, it is debatable whether these formally nongovernment actors are indeed distinguishable from the government (and by implication the Communist Party) in the views that they put forward and in the freedom of maneuver and access to channels of influence that they have. In a society as highly centralized and stratified as the USSR, when insulation from foreigners until the detente period was fairly complete, the number of channels open for nongovernment foreign contacts were severely limited.

Although there will therefore be some asymmetry in considering the actors in Soviet–West German relations, we shall discuss the growing importance of economic interest groups in the formulation of West German foreign policy. As economic relations have become depoliticized since detente, the government has relaxed its control over business groups' freedom to negotiate economic contacts with the USSR. Certain economic groups in the FRG have come to play a more important role as foreign policy actors and have sought to insulate trade policy from negative political influences.

In the last decade, the economic content of Soviet foreign policy has become more marked, and it is generally agreed that economic determinants have grown in relative importance in the formulation of Soviet policy toward Europe. This increasing salience of economics in foreign policy has been matched by what appears to be the growing influence of the "managerial-technologist" group on Soviet policy.[14] The evidence suggests that the economic elite has been pressing for normalization of relations with the FRG and, like its Western counterparts, has sought to insulate trade from political interference.[15]

There is a central irony in any comparison of the feasibility of implementing linkage strategies in socialist and capitalist societies. It is structurally far easier for the Soviet government to enforce linkage strategies domestically than it is for the German administration. Because Brezhnev does not have to deal with an independent economic sector, he can more perfectly control the economic and political components of his foreign policy. There is no question that Stankoimport, for example, will obey his orders. Yet the USSR has made sparing use of its institutional advantage in using coercive economic power against the West, maybe because of its relatively limited involvement in international trade.[16] Moreover, despite the structural advantage that Moscow has in implementing linkage strategies, it has rarely possessed the economic power to do so in its relations with Bonn.

It is much harder structurally for the German government to utilize economic leverage because trade with the USSR is by and large the preserve of the private sector. Helmut Schmidt cannot order Krupp to do what he wants, and Adenauer did it with great difficulty, as we shall see. From an institutional point of view, it would have been easier for Bonn to use political leverage because the government would not have had to deal with the business community. However, as it was the weaker political power vis-à-vis Russia, this was never a practical possibility. Within Germany, the foreign trade agenda evolves through a process of bargaining between different groups. Only in the pipe embargo was the German government able to forbid private companies from selling to the USSR, at considerable political cost to the country. Otherwise, the German government can control trade with the USSR only to the extent that it negotiates trade treaties or determines whether credits can be subsidized. A further complication arises from the split between the executive and legislature in the FRG. The German government has to contend both with business and with the Bundestag if it wants to implement a linkage strategy. However, despite institutional disadvantages, West Germany is the stronger power economically in its relations with the USSR, and pragmatically it has been easier for the FRG to utilize economic leverage. Germany has tended to use economic levers, whereas the Soviets have usually used political levers. Agenda setting and the potential to initiate linkage depend on who has the predominant power, in what area, and how many actors – domestic and international – are involved.

The terms of the debate

Before we begin our discussion of the politics of West German–Soviet economic relations, we must tackle a few definitional issues. Although it is theoretically possible to differentiate between economics and politics, the two are so often intertwined that any all-encompassing methodological definition would be too abstract for the purposes of this analysis. Rather, when we discuss specific issues in German–Soviet relations, we shall distinguish between economic and political levers in a concrete context. The impossibility of developing a general theory that differentiates precisely between political and economic means and ends has been elegantly explained by one of the foremost scholars in this area:

On the one hand, it appears that the number of connections between economics and politics is limited only by the ability of social scientists to detect them. On the other hand, it seems quite unlikely that there exists somewhere a master key which would bring into view the usually hidden political dimensions of economic relationship or characteristics in some more or less automatic or systematic manner. Each time it seems to be a matter of specific ad hoc discovery.[17]

The use of Western political and economic definitions in specific contexts is compatible with Soviet writings on this subject. Soviet leaders are quite capable of differentiating between political and economic criteria on an ad hoc basis, irrespective of more theoretical Marxist–Leninist ideology. Factors such as the most advantageous price for goods and a desire to maximize profits are just as keenly appreciated by the Soviets as by their Western counterparts. Because the Russians have entered the world market on capitalist terms and use capitalist-determined world market prices, they are quite capable of dealing with the capitalists and appreciating capitalist economic criteria. According to an eminent Hungarian economist, "We can admit without shame ... that so far socialism has found no acceptable concept of its own covering the questions of foreign trade and international economic relations."[18]

When we analyze the politics of foreign policy making, we cannot talk about political and economic goals without differentiating between various levels. Beneath these two concepts lie many gradations of importance. Political goals, in the German case, ranged from German reunification to the release of

10,000 German prisoners of war from the USSR. Similarly, the USSR has pursued a variety of major and minor political and economic goals vis-à-vis the FRG. We can distinguish between *core* political values and *secondary* goals. Core political goals involve such vital interests as national security, territorial integrity, national survival, and, in some instances, prestige. They include both national goals and the preservation of alliances deemed essential to national security. Core values can involve practical or more symbolic matters. Secondary values are those concerned not with survival or prestige but with increasing influence, altering the international environment in one's favor, or satisfying domestic political groups. They are important at the margin of politics. Likewise, core economic goals involve questions of economic survival and maintaining present standards of living or access to vital raw materials such as oil. Secondary economic goals are concerned with more marginal issues. The success of linkage strategies depends on the kinds of goals involved. It is important to identify the kinds of foreign policy goals involved in order to ascertain the effectiveness of linkage strategies. Both West Germany and the USSR tried to utilize leverage in situations involving core political values, but linkage was in fact most successful where secondary goals were at stake and where the economic and political goals were symmetrical.

This book will examine the changing dynamics of Soviet–German relations by investigating a series of questions. First, from the West German side, we shall examine to what extent the German government consciously used economic incentives to encourage political concessions from the USSR and to what extent it used economic veto power when these political concessions were not forthcoming. Second, we shall discuss the differences between the government leaders, the various ministries (particularly the Foreign Office and the Economics Ministry), and the business community over the role of economic relations with the USSR. We will examine the kinds of interest group coalitions that were formed and how they evolved over time. Third, we will analyze to what degree the FRG's economic relations with the USSR have become relatively depoliticized in the years following the Brandt Ostpolitik and how the interaction of politics and economics has altered. If economic factors have become more important for the Germans, then we will examine what economic problems have arisen from less politicized contacts and how they have affected the formation of interest groups. We shall also discuss whether stronger economic ties have in any way improved political relations. Finally, we shall analyze to what extent a country can use economic levers successfully in the pursuit of political goals when dealing with an adversary, and the lessons that German policy makers have drawn from this practice.

From the Soviet side, we shall discuss first whether the Soviet interest in trade with the FRG was always more economic than was the German interest. Second, we shall examine the evidence of differences between various ministries, foreign trade organizations, and scholarly institutes on the question of economic ties with the FRG and whether one can infer any consistent pattern from these differences. Third, we shall discuss to what extent the Soviet response to Ostpolitik was predicated on specific Soviet economic needs. We shall ∖xamine alterations in the structure of Soviet trade with the FRG for clues about the relative importance of foreign trade with West Germany over time. Finally, we shall discuss to what extent Soviet leaders have been willing to make political concessions in return for economic benefits, and to what degree they have changed their ideas on this problem over the past few years.

This book deals with the politics of East–West trade. One of the main themes is that the use of economic and political means in the pursuit of foreign policy goals has altered as a result of the changing international situation and changing domestic economic conditions. The normalization of relations represented the key turning point in the use of levers. From the West German point of view, economic incentives and disincentives were used in the pre-Brandt period in an attempt to modify Soviet behavior on the German question but were largely unsuccessful. Since Brandt's Ostpolitik, there have been fewer attempts to utilize economic levers in political bargaining. From the Soviet side, there were some attempts in the post-1969 period to use political levers to gain economic concessions, but the Russians were mainly interested in keeping economic and political goals separate and avoiding linkage because they wanted to import from the FRG irrespective of the political climate. One cannot talk about the USSR using economic means in the pursuit of political goals because it was at a relative disadvantage economically and thus not in a position to manipulate economic levers.

Because detente has involved the process of normalizing previously hostile relations, the book will examine what happens to economic relations as political contacts become less hostile. In a period of general disillusion with detente, it may well turn out that the economic dimensions of East-West relations will be the more stable element in the delicate East-West equation, particularly in the German-Soviet relationship. However, the book will show that, based on the West German experience, it is in general illusory to believe that the West can significantly change Soviet political behavior through the use of economic levers.

2

The long road to Moscow: the origins of linkage, 1955

Bismarck spoke about his nightmare of coalitions against Germany. I have my own nightmare: its name is Potsdam.

Konrad Adenauer, 1953[1]

Chancellor Konrad Adenauer arrived in Moscow in September 1955, in response to a Soviet invitation, to begin negotiating with Soviet Premier Khrushchev. The talks were partly conducted out of a railway carriage, symbolizing the fact that West German–Soviet relations were still in their glacial phase.[2] The Soviet experience with Germany during World War Two had left a legacy of profound mistrust and fear of Germany among both the leadership and the Soviet people. From the German side, Adenauer, *Der Alte,* was preoccupied with proving Germany's loyalty to the West. In many ways West Germany was a beneficiary of the origins of the cold war. Had the USSR not become the United States's main antagonist immediately after the Second World War ended, West Germany would have found rehabilitation more difficult. As it was, the denazification program was soon scaled down, and the FRG became one of the bulwarks of the Western alliance. After the USSR and the FRG established diplomatic relations in 1955, Soviet–West German relations improved marginally but remained antagonistic. Adenauer's visit to Moscow marked the beginning of a new era in Soviet–German relations.

Background to the summit

In analyzing Soviet political goals toward West Germany prior to the 1955 summit, it is essential to bear in mind that, until Germany became a member of NATO and was granted full sovereignty in May 1955, there was some optimism on both sides of the iron curtain that a solution to the German problem could be found, other than its permanent division and incorporation into two antagonistic power blocs. Indeed, after the end of the Korean War, the Russians decided to initiate what was in retrospect seen by some as a major effort to find a solution to the German problem. It is probable that, at least until 1949, Stalin did not have a blueprint for Germany, and he was partly sounding out the other Allies to determine the geographical and political shape of a future united Germany. In his 1952 work *Economic Problems of Socialism in the USSR*, Stalin predicted that Germany would rise again as a great power and that, as a consequence of attempting to "break out of American bondage," Germany would bring on a new war.[3] His views in this book underline his concern to prevent a resurgent Germany from turning its aggression against the USSR.

Although the division of Germany appeared to be a fait accompli, Stalin sent the Western powers a note in March 1952 proposing a reunited, neutralized Germany. Unlike all previous Soviet proposals, this was the first to admit that a reunited Germany could have a national army.[4] This note was sent during the period when the Western powers were trying to agree on giving the FRG a greater measure of sovereignty and including it in a European Defense Community (EDC). In fact, the note was sent just prior to the signing of the EDC treaty in May. The main Soviet purpose behind this note was to forestall that development, because Russia now considered the strengthening of the Western alliance and the FRG's integration into it more of a menace than the possibility of a reunited armed Germany. In addition, because the opposition party, the German Social Democrats (SPD), vigorously opposed the inclusion of the FRG in an EDC because it would make reunification more difficult, the Kremlin decided to exploit these differences within Germany.[5] After a seven-month heated exchange of diplomatic notes, the Soviet proposal foundered on an irreconcilability of views.[6] The Western powers insisted that reunification be predicated on free elections in both parts of Germany, and the Russians countered that this was a diversionary tactic employed by the West to obscure the real purpose of the Soviet note. In an authoritative Soviet book about the German question, the weight of blame for the failure of the Soviet proposal was ascribed to the United States; however, Adenauer was also severely criticized.[7] Although the Soviets failed to prevent voting on the formation of an EDC, the French ultimately vetoed it because they feared a loss of sovereignty. Many years later, the theory of "lost opportunities" became popularized in the West. Some analysts believed that the USSR had genuinely been interested in German reunification in 1952 and that the Western powers had passed over this unique opportunity to solve the German problem. It is highly debatable, however, whether these Soviet moves were anything more than a delaying tactic by Stalin to prevent the solidifying of the Atlantic Alliance and the rearming of West Germany in the EDC. Perhaps they were both a delaying tactic and a serious negotiation bid. Ultimately, one will never know to what extent the Russians were prepared to put up with a reunited Germany, communist or capitalist.[8]

The death of Stalin and the accession to power of Khrushchev, Malenkov, and Molotov had an immediate effect on Soviet policy toward Germany. Although Khrushchev probably did not have complete control over foreign policy until he had ousted the "anti-party" group in 1957, his views on crucial foreign policy issues influenced the definition of Soviet goals toward Germany, together with those of his colleagues. There is a paradox about Khrushchev's German policy. He is in general known for his relatively flexible foreign policy, in contrast to the more rigid policies of Stalin. Both in style and in substance, Khrushchev saw the opportunities offered to the USSR of a world metamorphized by decolonization. However, in his German policy, Khrushchev was, if anything, less flexible, more hard-line, and more status quo oriented than was Stalin. This was largely the result of developments within the GDR, which necessitated a firm choice on the part of the Soviet leadership.

Toward the end of his life, Stalin was primarily preoccupied with the *West* German aspect of Soviet policy toward Germany, in that he sought to prevent the FRG's incorporation into the North Atlantic Treaty Organization (NATO) alliance by keeping options on reunification open. As long as Stalin was alive, GDR leader Walter Ulbricht seemed firmly ensconced. Shortly after Stalin's death, in the crucial succession period, the uprising in East Berlin on June 17, 1953, forced the new Soviet leadership to choose between the stability of the Ulbricht regime (and by implication the security of the Eastern bloc) and keeping reunification options open. The riots were caused by Ulbricht's insistence on raising work norms, despite the relaxation of Stalinist standards both in the USSR and in other Eastern European countries. Khrushchev and his colleagues realized that, if they did not provide firm backing for Ulbricht, domestic turmoil within the GDR might lead to the disintegration of the key Soviet buffer state. Because there was no viable alternative to the loyal but unpopular Ulbricht, the USSR had little choice but to keep him in power. Soviet troops quelled the riots in East Berlin, and this decisively showed that from now on, the stability of the East German government, backed permanently by Soviet troops, was the key determinant of Soviet German policy and took precedence over the attempt to make a deal with the FRG. Although the USSR continued to discuss the prospects of German reunification with the Western powers until the FRG's entry into NATO, the emphasis of Soviet policy had shifted. In the future, the preservation of East Germany, and not the wooing of West Germany, determined Soviet policy until the building of the Berlin Wall.

The failure of the West to come to the aid of the East German opposition in the abortive uprising of 1953 in some ways diluted the alleged Western commitment to "liberate" the GDR and strengthened the Soviet position. Although the Russians had secured the survival of the GDR in their sphere of influence, they failed to prevent the FRG's accession to NATO by the Paris Agreements in October 1954 and the bestowing of full sovereignty on it. Until the very last moment, the Soviet government tried to persuade the FRG to renounce its membership in NATO, but to no avail. The Soviet response to these developments was the creation of the Warsaw Pact on May 14, 1955, to counter the inevitable rearming of West Germany within NATO.[9]

Despite the solidifying of the Western and Eastern alliances, the international atmosphere improved prior to the Moscow summit. The signing of the Austrian Peace Treaty on May 15 indicated a Soviet willingness to compromise and create a neutralized Austria free of Soviet troops. The Kremlin had previously insisted that there would be no Austrian Peace Treaty until the German problem was solved. However, in 1955 the Russians changed their mind. Under the terms of the treaty, the USSR – in return for permanent Austrian neutrality – terminated its occupation of Austria and agreed to the complete withdrawal of all foreign troops. This renunciation of a forward military base in Europe was unprecedented, and it has been suggested that the leadership overruled the probable advice of the Soviet General Staff on this subject. On the other hand, although it had withdrawn from an important area, the USSR could reap the strategic benefit of creating a neutral wedge some 500 miles deep between West Germany and Italy. This in effect split the Western defense area. In return for their withdrawal, the Soviets were to be rewarded. Austrian goods would compensate them for the properties that the USSR had seized as German-owned and that it now returned to the Austrians.[10]

Some scholars have pointed to the Austrian treaty as a counterargument to the theory that the USSR was intent on controlling all the territories in Eastern Europe that it had occupied at the end of the war. They cite the Austrian case as an indication that the USSR was not inexorably committed to the cold war. Perhaps, if the United States had behaved differently, the argument goes, Poland, Hungary, and the rest of Eastern Europe could have had "Austrian" solutions. The reply to this view might be that, far from having Austria as a possible example for Eastern Europe to follow, the USSR would have preferred Western Europe, in particular the FRG, to have an Austrian solution. Indeed, Molotov, at the signing of the treaty, intimated that West Germany might like to follow the Austrian precedent.[11] Although the FRG was by now in NATO, the USSR was still holding out the possibility of an alternative settlement.

It is more likely that Austria was a unique example, the result of a special combination of circumstances. Austria was militarily and industrially insignificant, it had been declared a liberated rather than an enemy territory, and no communist regime had been placed in the Soviet zone. Thus, through a particular series of events, Austria was spared the fate of Eastern Europe and the USSR appeared to be magnanimous.[12] Because the FRG was already in NATO, there was little to be gained by delaying a solution to the Austrian problem.

The generally optimistic atmosphere of 1955 climaxed at the

Geneva summit, where declarations of peaceful intentions and friendship belied the unresolved tensions behind the superficially amicable exterior. It was as part of what came to be known as the "spirit of Geneva" that the Soviet government sent the West German government a note offering to hold talks on the establishment of diplomatic, cultural, and economic relations. The Soviet political motivation in inviting Chancellor Adenauer to Moscow was part of its new post-Stalin Westpolitik that eschewed any support for German reunification and showed that Moscow had by now accepted the two-state theory. Having battled for so long to prevent the FRG from joining NATO, Moscow realized that the only way to deal with this fait accompli was to reorient its German policy and secure West German diplomatic recognition and the ratification of the status quo in Eastern Europe. The USSR set the political agenda for the FRG. At a minimum, the presence of ambassadors from two German states in Moscow would, in Soviet eyes, contribute to the legitimization of the GDR and enhance Soviet prestige in the international arena. At a maximum, the USSR may have hoped that, if it were able to improve its relations with the FRG, it might be able to influence West German policy within the Atlantic Alliance and possibly encourage its independence from the United States. The attempt to divide the FRG from the U.S. has been a consistent Soviet goal since 1955. A *Pravda* editorial on the eve of the Moscow talks emphasized the good relations that the two countries had had in the past and minimized the historical enmity between them. However, it made it quite clear that the FRG's entry into NATO complicated the issue of German reunification, although the USSR supported reunification in principle.[13] The normalization of relations could not be conditional on the reunification issue, which Moscow had no intention of discussing. Its main political goal was to establish diplomatic relations with the FRG.

Because West Germany's foreign policy was controlled by the Western Allies prior to May 1955, the definition of German political goals toward the USSR was in part a product of U.S., British, and French influence. The United States established the political bargaining agenda for the FRG in Bonn's negotiations with Moscow. At the beginning of his chancellorship in 1949, Adenauer had defined his policy toward the USSR. He emphatically eschewed the prewar policy, the so-called *Schaukelpolitik* ("see-saw" policy) whereby Germany had balanced its commitments between East and West. He strove instead to prove his unshakable loyalty to the Western alliance.[14] Within this context of priorities, Adenauer's Ostpolitik was definitely secondary to his Westpolitik because he wanted to dispel any possible Western suspicion about where Germany's sympathies lay.

Konrad Adenauer's Ostpolitik in 1955 was in many ways a continuation of the policies he had espoused in the 1920s. As a Rhineland Catholic, Adenauer had never liked Prussia or the Bismarckian Reich. Under the Weimar Republic he disagreed with the policies of his contemporary, Foreign Minister Gustav Stresemann, who, as a Protestant Prussian, felt ambivalently toward Western Europe and believed that Germany should pursue a *Schaukelpolitik* between Russia and the West. While mayor of Cologne in the 1920s, Adenauer favored closer economic ties between Germany and France and opposed the trend toward rapprochement with Russia (as exemplified in the 1922 Rapallo Treaty) because it smacked of expansionist German nationalism. He was, from the beginning, a firm believer in Western European unity based on Franco–German reconciliation.[15]

Adenauer's policy toward the USSR was constitutionally determined by the Basic Law, in its preamble and in Article 146, which bound the Federal Republic to strive for reunification.[16] The main feature of his Ostpolitik was to deal only with the USSR and not recognize the legitimacy of the Eastern European states, including East Germany. The GDR was always referred to as the "Soviet occupation zone," and in a characteristic speech in Berlin, he proclaimed: "We must remove any doubt that Germany will ever get accustomed to the existence of two separate German states."[17] An essential part of this policy of nonrecognition of the GDR was the emphasis on West Berlin's links with the FRG. The only way that Germany could be reunited, in Adenauer's view, was on the basis of free all-German elections, and thus all Soviet proposals were unacceptable because they did not include free elections. Adenauer was largely supported by the opposition SPD in his policy of not recognizing the GDR, but they opposed his efforts to promote West Germany's integration into the Western alliance, claiming that this would impede the cause of German unity. Until the granting of sovereignty to the

FRG, Adenauer was opposed to any dealings with the USSR. He rejected an offer to go to Moscow in January 1955 to negotiate diplomatic relations, saying this was a trick designed to break the Western alliance.[18]

However, once West Germany became a fully sovereign state on May 5, 1955, Adenauer indicated his willingness to begin talks with the Soviet leaders, albeit with the understanding that this would further the cause of reunification.[19] Given this commitment, it is instructive to examine his aims prior to his Moscow journey.

In discussing the German government's political goals in agreeing to talk to the Soviets, one must distinguish between declaratory and operational policy. Adenauer was limited in his freedom of maneuver because of his need to dispel the specter of Rapallo for the United States, Britain, and France, and to prove that, in its first major independent negotiations since becoming a sovereign state, the FRG would be a responsible ally. The chancellor consulted with Eisenhower, Dulles, and Eden before he accepted the Soviet invitation.[20] According to one source, he assured the Allies prior to going to Moscow that he would not establish diplomatic relations with the USSR unless the Kremlin made significant concessions on reunification.[21] Adenauer claimed that he would do nothing in Moscow to weaken the position of the West in the upcoming October Foreign Ministers Conference in Geneva, and there were suggestions that the talks were to be treated only as exploratory in view of the Geneva conference.[22] In an interview before his departure, Adenauer claimed that the Soviet desire for conversation was "a success for the consistent and determined policy of the West."[23] Despite the reunification rhetoric, Adenauer's political goals were more limited – the release of German prisoners of war still held in the USSR.

The economic situation

The most striking aspect of Germany's postwar economic development was its rapid recovery from the ruins of war, so that by 1958, the FRG could boast the world's third largest GNP. This phenomenal economic recovery was largely the result of the application of the *Soziale Marktwirtschaft* (social market economy), a theory popularized by Economics Minister Erhard. The object of the social market economy was to create a truly competitive market, free from domination by the state or by private monopolies. The market was allowed to operate freely, subject to such conditions as would ensure all-round and "social" development instead of one based solely on private profit.[24] The outstanding achievement of this philosophy, which was above all responsible for Germany's *Wirtschaftswunder* (economic miracle), was the phenomenal growth of foreign trade. The Marshall Plan and the building of new plants were also significant. From 1952 to 1957, the rise in the volume of exports was equal to more than 25 percent of the growth in GNP, providing a stimulus to economic expansion.[25] The spectacular increase in exports was in part a product of extensive liberalization measures, both internationally and within Germany, that ensured West Germany a continuous export surplus in this period.[26] Thus foreign trade was a vital component of Germany's economic recovery.

Germany's export structure played a key role in the *Wirtschaftswunder*. Germany's export strength lay in its manufactured goods, in particular capital goods from the engineering sector. These were, of course, goods that the USSR wanted to buy, but the FRG radically altered the direction of its trade flows in the postwar era as a result of the political situation. Whereas trade with the East had been very important in the prewar era, after the war Western Europe became the chief market for German manufactures, with only 5 percent of its trade going to the East.[27]

Germany's import needs changed considerably after the war as it became a highly industrialized nation. In the prewar period, the FRG's import dependence – imports as a percentage of national income – was well over 20 percent, but after the war it became less dependent on imports. In particular, it became more self-sufficient in foodstuffs, some of which it had imported from the USSR in prewar days. After the creation of the European Economic Community (EEC) in 1957, the FRG imported most of its foodstuffs from the EEC area; thus it had little need for Soviet imports in this sector. The most important structural change in imports in the postwar period, however, was the fact that manufactured goods became an increasingly significant import item. It is characteristic of more industrialized countries to conduct the bulk of their business with each other by exchanging

Table 1. *West German trade with the USSR, 1952–7 (in millions of US dollars)*

Year	Imports	Exports	Total
1952	4.0	0.2	4.2
1953	15.6	1.7	17.3
1954	22.2	12.6	34.8
1955	35.9	26.7	62.6
1956	53.2	68.8	122.0
1957	97.4	59.6	157.0

Source: United Nations, *Yearbook of International Trade Statistics,* 1958 (New York, 1959).

industrial goods for industrial goods. Germany began to import textiles, chemicals, and the products of the engineering industry in the postwar years (see Table 2).[28] Although the USSR would have liked to export manufactured goods and machinery to the FRG, Soviet manufactures could not compete in quality with those from the West.

West Germany's trade with the USSR had risen from $4.2 million in 1952 to $62.6 million in 1955 (see Table 1), but even in 1955 only 0.35 percent of its foreign trade was with the USSR. However, some of its trade with East Germany undoubtedly went to the USSR. Trade with East Germany was known as Interzonal Trade and was conducted by a Trusteeship for Interzonal Trade (*Treuhandstelle für den Interzonenhandel*) under the aegis of the German Chamber of Commerce and Industry (Deutsche Industrie und Handelstag, or DIHT) to preserve the legal position that Bonn did not officially recognize the GDR. In 1953, Interzonal Trade was $123.3 million and in 1955 it was $270.5 million.[29] Whereas trade with East Germany was quantitatively and politically important for the FRG, its trade with the USSR was in this period peripheral.

A cursory examination of Soviet foreign trade would give the initial impression that the USSR would be far less susceptible to economic pressures from other countries than would the FRG. Although it is true that for the USSR foreign trade is far less important than it is for West Germany, there are nevertheless countervailing factors that suggest that Russia is, in certain sec-

Table 2. *Commodity composition of West German foreign trade, 1952-7 (in millions of US dollars)*

		Imports			
Year	Food	Crude materials, including fuel	Manufactures	Machinery	Total
1952	1155.5	1628.8	522.7	123.2	3814.1
1953	1076.3	1556.2	610.5	126.3	3771.0
1954	1344.4	1756.1	812.5	172.0	4570.8
1955	1423.2	2351.5	1190.6	268.6	5793.4
1956	1745.3	2637.0	1257.4	331.4	6616.5
1957	1909.5	3016.3	1369.0	440.8	7499.0
		Exports			
1952	68.0	577.3	1244.1	1459.2	4001.6
1953	83.5	611.4	1165.0	1673.0	4389.1
1954	90.3	695.4	1340.5	2041.2	5247.6
1955	126.9	707.5	1581.3	2456.5	6134.7
1956	158.7	792.1	1956.6	2974.4	7357.7
1957	149.3	870.9	2304.7	3560.4	8574.7

Source: United Nations, *Yearbook of International Trade Statistics,* 1958 (New York, 1959).

tors involving the import of technology, more dependent on foreign trade than the latter's overall contribution to its GNP would imply. Like the FRG's, the USSR's main task in the immediate postwar years was to build up an economy severely damaged by war, and it did this largely by harnessing the economic capacity of Eastern Europe, extracting sizeable reparations, neglecting the consumer goods sector, and continuing the Stalinist strategy of unbalanced growth. Whereas its prewar trade with Germany had been a significant factor in the Soviet industrialization drive, in the postwar years the exigencies of the political situation compelled Russia to reorient its trade toward Eastern Europe. In the early 1950s, over 75 percent of Soviet trade was with Eastern Europe. The rapid rate of growth of Eastern European foreign trade in the postwar years exceeded that of world trade in general, and the trade turnover of the USSR increased by more than 120 percent between 1950 and 1956.[30] Thus, foreign trade became relatively more important for the USSR in the postwar years, although it was predominantly an autarkic nation.

An analysis of the commodity composition and direction of Soviet trade reveals that trade with the West played a subordinate role in Russia's foreign trade. The USSR's export surplus of foodstuffs diminished, and in 1956, 55 percent of its exports were of fuels and raw materials.[31] However, all of the fuels or raw materials were products that the FRG could purchase elsewhere. Machinery formed about 15 percent of Soviet exports, but this machinery was not of sufficiently high quality for the FRG to import it. About 1 percent of Soviet trade was with the FRG in this period (see Table 3) and thus was an unimportant part of its total exports.

The USSR's interest in trade with the FRG was relatively more significant on the import side. Although until Stalin's death autarky was the desired goal, imports of foreign machinery were important, and in the mid-1950s, 30 percent of Soviet imports were of machinery. Nevertheless, the USSR could obtain most of its machinery imports from Eastern Europe, although the most advanced technology was still to be had in the West. Imports from the FRG increased from 0.78 percent to 1.89 percent of its total imports between 1955 and 1956 but still were only a small part of total Soviet imports. Thus, from the point of view of both commodity composition and the direction of foreign trade, the USSR was also substantially impervious to economic pressure from the FRG.

West German–Soviet economic relations before 1955 were in large part determined by activities of the United States that were beyond Bonn's influence. America set the agenda for German–Soviet economic relations. Under the terms of the 1951 Battle Act, the U.S. was authorized to cut off economic and military aid to West European countries if they failed to comply with the embargo. Until the Paris agreements of October 1954, Germany's foreign trade was controlled by the Allied Joint Export and Import Agency, which, on behalf of the FRG, negotiated trade agreements with all of the Eastern European states except the USSR, Rumania, and Albania.[32] Of more direct impact on the conduct of Germany's trade with the USSR was the American-inspired Consultative Group-Coordinating Committee (CoCom) set up in 1949 to administer the strategic embargo

Table 3. *Soviet-West German trade as a percentage of total Soviet trade, 1953–7 (in millions of rubles)*

Year	Total foreign trade	Trade with FRG	% of total trade
1953	5145.1	4.6	0.09
1954	5824.2	19.9	0.34
1955	5838.5	47.7	0.82
1956	6504.9	98.9	1.52
1957	7487.3	120.2	1.61

Source: Roger A. Clarke, *Soviet Economic Facts, 1917–70* (London: Macmillan, 1972).

that the U.S. had instigated against the Soviet bloc in 1948.[33] The CoCom embargo lists, which were particularly stringent during the Korean War, were revised and modified in 1954, but they placed restrictions on a large variety of goods that were construed as of "strategic" value to the communist bloc. There were three lists – munitions, atomic energy, and industrial/commercial. There were three types of embargoed goods – those totally embargoed, those permitted in limited quantities, and those to be kept under surveillance. In May 1950, Bonn had been nominally coopted into the joint embargo decision-making process.[34] However, there were some people in West Germany who opposed the embargo policy because they thought it was counterproductive to the cause of German reunification. They also objected to the fact that, until 1952, West Germany was affected much more heavily by the export controls than any other nation.[35] Indeed, there were violations of the CoCom rules on the part of West German businessmen. Of a particularly controversial nature was the American attempt to prevent the German mainly state-owned shipping company, Howaldtwerke, from selling fishing vessels to the USSR. The Americans, after much German pressure, compromised by saying that the Russians had to sell Germany strategic goods in return.[36]

The theory behind the strategic embargo represented the quintessence of negative economic leverage and implied a departure from a policy designed to maximize a nation's economic welfare. In the pursuit of national security, countries were willing to sacrifice current consumption in return for reducing what they perceived as the uncertainty involved in future consumption.[37] The West responded to what it perceived as Soviet economic warfare with its own version of it. Some economists have argued that the Allied embargo policy was counterproductive for the West because it speeded up the process of the economic integration of the Soviet bloc and forced the Russians to develop an autonomous productive capacity that they might not have had to develop had there been no embargo, making them more independent of the West. Although it is difficult to obtain precise data on the impact of the embargo on the Soviet system, a few tentative conclusions are possible. First, the embargo undoubtedly imposed some costs on the Soviet system. Nevertheless, given the high rate of Soviet GNP growth in the 1960s, these costs were certainly not crippling. As against the modest gains of the embargo, the West also incurred considerable costs. The U.S. and its allies forewent some of the productivity gains resulting from foreign trade, and differences of opinion between the U.S. and its Western allies over the political use of trade denial caused considerable intra-CoCom tensions.[38]

The desire to mitigate the effects of the CoCom embargo was one of the factors that motivated the Russians to begin a new trade offensive with the West after 1953. The cornerstone of Malenkov's "new course" was that, based on the successful creation of a powerful heavy industry, the USSR could and should accelerate its growth in the output of consumer goods. These goods were to be manufactured at a rate even faster than that of producer goods. At the same time, the USSR normalized its trade relations with Eastern Europe, placing them on a less exploitative foundation and basing the trade on world market (i.e., capitalist) prices.[39] Although Stalin had initiated the bid for more Western trade, the main aim of this policy had been to import Western machinery to increase Soviet self-sufficiency. Under Malenkov and Khrushchev, the USSR's interest in trade with the West was broader. It was still primarily oriented toward imports of capital goods, but there was also a desire to increase Soviet exports to these countries. Needless to say, there was also political motivation behind this policy, above all a hope of weakening the Western alliance by encouraging Western European independence of the U.S. in trade matters.

This Soviet drive was implemented by a series of initiatives to negotiate with Western businessmen. Marshall Plan aid had been terminated in 1953, and the 1952–54 recession in Western Europe revived interest in new foreign trade markets. Sensing this new opportunity, and the possibility of exploiting "contradictions in the capitalist camp," the USSR tried to increase the interest of Western businessmen in the Soviet market. Russia, in April 1952, organized the International Economic Conference in Moscow, whose theme was "peaceful coexistence through means of world trade"; it was attended by a German delegation. Large orders were placed by the Soviets with individual Western businessmen, although Western governments decried it as a propaganda move. The Russians described the strategic embargo as "a senseless manifestation of aggressive policy."[40] In August, representatives of the West German steel industry met with the deputy Soviet foreign trade minister in Copenhagen. Although these negotiations were unproductive, the Soviet initiatives were successful in the longer-term perspective. Nineteen fifty-two saw the beginning of a modest trade between the two countries.[41]

In 1953, at the Economic Commission for Europe (ECE) conference in Geneva, the first official contacts were made between West German and Soviet representatives, although these talks too were not particularly productive because the Russians wanted firmer commitments than the Germans were willing to give.[42] Indeed, as early as 1953, the Soviets wanted to negotiate a trade agreement with the FRG government, but the Germans declined, saying that any agreement had to go through the ECE and have U.S. approval. Thus, the first Soviet attempt to encourage German independence from its allies in matters of trade failed.[43]

Given Soviet import needs and financial problems, West Germany had a relative advantage in economic diplomacy, because there was nothing the USSR wanted to sell to the FRG that Germany could not purchase elsewhere. Furthermore, Germany did not lack export markets in the West. However, although the FRG had this relative advantage and was in a better position to use economic levers than was the USSR, in the early 1950s Germany's capacity to exert economic pressure on the USSR was limited by the small share that it had in Soviet trade, by the Soviet desire to avoid dependence on Western markets, by the differences in economic systems, and by U.S. control.[44] Both the Soviet and West German markets were oriented away from each other, and both could have survived without the other. However, politics is sometimes played at the margin, and therefore, as soon as Moscow and Bonn entered into economic relations, the potential for German use of economic levers existed.

The domestic German lineup on trade

Within the FRG, the debate about the efficacy of the *Russland-handel* (trade with Russia) revolved around two central questions: first, was it politically judicious – that is, would more intense economic contacts facilitate or hinder the core political goal of reunification – and second, was it economically desirable – in other words, to what extent would it enhance West Germany's economic welfare and enable businessmen to make more profits? Often the protagonists on both sides of the issue were themselves unable to make a clear distinction between the two, and would use one to rationalize the other. In general, those who were against any great extension of trade with the USSR argued from the point of view of its political inadvisability and then brought in as proof of this essentially political argument various economic data to show how relatively unprofitable it was. This was true of the government in particular. For those who favored an increase in trade – namely, certain sections of the business community and the SPD – the main argument was that it was economically beneficial for the FRG, and in support of this they pointed out that it could have favorable political results.

Chancellor Adenauer and his supporters derived their position on trade with the USSR from the political dictates of the time. The government, because of its delicate political position and its need to demonstrate its loyalty to the Western powers, supported the CoCom embargo policy and rebuffed Soviet moves for a greater trade volume. The political opposition, however, strenuously opposed this policy. In 1951, the SPD tabled a motion in the Bundestag demanding an end to the embargo policies and an increase in East-West trade.[45] In their view, this would facilitate reunification. In the debate that followed, the Bundestag adopted a resolution demanding a normalization of trade with the communist countries and identical restrictions among all Western European countries.[46] At a cabinet meeting called to discuss the Bundestag resolution, the government went on record as practically agreeing – albeit somewhat ambiguously – with this position.[47]

The government's attitude toward trade with the USSR was most explicitly outlined in a statement by the head of the trade division of the Foreign Ministry. Admitting that "no area of German foreign trade policy is so symbolic of foreign policy as East–West trade," he emphasized the economic limitations of East–West trade. Even if there were no embargo restrictions, he claimed that it was doubtful whether Germany would be exporting much more to the East than it was at the present time. The crux of the matter was not the unwillingness of Germany to export to the East but the inability of the East to deliver goods of interest to Germany. The prewar situation, when trade between the two countries had been so much greater, was not to be repeated.[48]

Within the German government there were also differences of emphasis on the question of East–West trade between the Economics Ministry and the Foreign Ministry. However, the origins of these differences were institutional rather than substantive. From the early fifties on, it was clear that the West German government viewed trade with the East as primarily a political problem. In 1951, a general department for East–West trade was established within the German Economics Ministry, but in 1953 the Foreign Ministry took over the Economics Ministry's responsibility for determining guidelines for the embargo policies and left the Economics Ministry with responsibility for only the purely technical details of trade. The Foreign Ministry challenged the competence of the Economics Ministry in *Ost-handel* (trade with the East), a fact that irked Economics Ministry officials. A prominent German advocate of East–West trade concluded in 1954 that a depoliticization of this trade was inconceivable in the near future.[49]

The conflict between the two ministries became clear when the question of Adenauer's advisors for the summit arose, specifically whether Economics Minister Erhard should form part of the delegation to Moscow. On the one hand, Economics Ministry officials and some businessmen argued that his presence in Moscow would signal a genuine willingness on the part of the

FRG to conclude a trade agreement with the USSR. On the other hand, it was argued that Erhard's presence would overemphasize the FRG's interest in trade with the USSR and that it would detract from the significance of the political questions. After an acrimonious debate, it was decided that Erhard would not go to Moscow, to impress on the Kremlin that for Bonn, political questions were paramount in these negotiations.[50] Both Foreign Minister Brentano and Hallstein, the state secretary, downplayed the possibilities of extending German–Soviet trade.[51] Thus, in 1955, it was clear that the Foreign Ministry, with the support of Chancellor Adenauer, had prevailed over the Economics Ministry on the question of responsibility for trade policy toward the USSR.

Because the German government could not officially negotiate matters of East–West trade, it had created, on the initiative of Economics Minister Erhard, an organization of businessmen to coordinate East–West trade. The Ostausschuss der deutschen Wirtschaft (Eastern Committee), under the sponsorship of the BDI (Bundesverband der deutschen Industrie, Federation of German Industry), was formed in 1952. Its purpose was to coordinate trade with the communist countries in close cooperation with the government. It was officially recognized as the sole representative of businessmen on questions of trade with the East and brought to the attention of the government the wishes and needs of industry in trade with the Soviet bloc. The committee's power and prestige were indicated by the fact that unlike other BDI committees, it was made up of industrialists and important bankers. Its executive committee included directors of many of the largest Ruhr firms.[52]

In the absence of diplomatic relations with the communist bloc, the Ostausschuss conducted negotiations with trade officials from Eastern Europe. There was also some confusion as to what its exact status was, because it was variously described as an "independent" and a "semi-official" organization. The limits of its independence became clear in 1954. As a result of the 1954 Geneva Conference on East–West trade, the Ostausschuss, led by Otto Wolff von Amerongen,[53] was scheduled to go to Moscow and negotiate a trade agreement with the Russians.[54] At the last moment, the Foreign Office called off the trip for "technical reasons." Inquiries into these reasons aroused such confusion and anxiety in the Foreign Ministry that it was assumed that the reasons were political rather than technical.[55] This episode indicates that, although there were differences of opinion between the Ostausschuss and the government over the degree to which the former should promote trade with the USSR, in the final analysis, the Ostausschuss deferred to the government and did not publicly disagree with it. Nevertheless, the Ostausschuss continued to press for liberalization of the embargo regulations and for more trade with the East, within certain limits.

A 1954 survey by Gabriel Almond found that, on the question of trade with the East,

it remains interesting that the business community in Germany is relatively unaware of the priority of political factors in communist policy-making. Only government officials and some leaders of business pressure-groups seem to see this point. Few of the industrialists, even in the largest establishments, are aware of it. Their thinking about the possibilities of the communist market is dominated by simple, apolitical economic calculation.[56]

Almond's survey highlighted the fact that, like the SPD and the Free Democratic Party (FDP), considerable sections of the business community opposed the limitations on trade with the East from a primarily economic standpoint. When Adenauer was re-elected in 1953, the German Chamber of Commerce and Industry (Deutsche Industrie und Handelstag) drew up a memorandum to him that they suggested he consider in formulating his new economic policies: "The trade and political efforts of the Federal Republic should not be restricted to the Western world. It is necessary to reestablish the traditional trade relations with the countries behind the iron curtain."[57] Many German commentators began to urge more trade with the East, because it would help businessmen to diversify their markets and insure themselves against the effects of a recession. They also claimed, as an important byproduct, that a normalization of trade with the East would improve political relations.[58]

The economic argument for more trade with the USSR was not based on immediate need but rather on longer-term factors. Businessmen believed that rather than have such a heavy dependence on Western markets, Germany should diversify its foreign trade. There was also considerable resentment over the fact that Germany was discriminated against in the embargo regulations, and it was precisely Germany that had been the

East's main industrial supplier in prewar times. There was some nostalgia for the Rapallo era and the memory of Russian orders for machine tools that helped Germany during the Depression. Some industrialists also asserted that a planned economy was a more reliable trade partner. Finally, many businessmen, aware of the chronic shortage of consumer goods in the USSR, believed that massive orders for these goods would soon be forthcoming. Almond, in criticizing the views of these businessmen, points to their lack of understanding of the structural changes in both the Soviet and German economies that rendered these hopes of large-scale Soviet orders chimerical.

A section of the West German business community in the early fifties believed that the prewar Russo–German trade pattern could successfully be revived. Perhaps this overestimation of the trade potential of the USSR was in part a result of lack of contact with the Soviet market for ten years, a situation that encouraged false expectations.

The businessmen who favored more trade with the USSR were supported both by the opposition political parties and by sectors of the public. For instance, in 1954, in answer to the question, "Should trade between the Federal Republic and Soviet Russia be strengthened or should it be reduced as much as possible?" a public opinion survey in the FRG showed that 56 percent of the people felt it should be increased as much as possible, 18 percent felt it should be eliminated altogether, and 13 percent felt it should be maintained or held to a minimum.[59] An FDP deputy, Pfliederer, suggested that the FRG return to its Rapallo diplomacy and send a Bundestag delegation to Moscow to initiate contacts on trade with the USSR.[60] Prewar Chancellors Brüning, Luther, and Wirth came out strongly for more economic ties with the East, to balance what they considered Germany's injudicious one-sided commitment to the West. They were severely criticized by Adenauer and the BDI for these views.[61] Thus, on the eve of Adenauer's departure, there were three main groupings on the question of trade with the USSR. On the one hand, Adenauer and most of the Christian Democratic Party (CDU) argued against any significant increase in trade because it would make Germany politically more vulnerable. On the other hand, certain sections of the business community claimed that the economic prospects for trade with the

USSR were so promising that they must be exploited, and it was hoped that they would also improve political relations. Finally, a third group, composed of the Ostausschuss, some businessmen, and politicians, argued for some increase in trade but pointed to the inherent economic problems, irrespective of political developments.

The Soviet view of trade

In the early post-Stalin years, it was difficult to detect any differences of opinion within the USSR on the issue of trade with the FRG – or indeed, on the question of Soviet policy toward the German problem. This is because it was such a sensitive subject that no public airing of differences was permitted, particularly in the transition period before Khrushchev had secured his position, when the USSR was groping to find a new political modus vivendi. Nevertheless, it is instructive to examine the way in which the Russians expressed their views on trade with the FRG. As Marxists, Soviet commentators stressed the interdependence of economics and politics, saying that more trade would promote better political relations. Soviet commentators expressed their support for more trade with the FRG in political terms, although their motivation was often economic. Thus Soviet articles in the early 1950s that dealt with the issue of trade with the West generally said that its prime purpose was to strengthen the cause of peaceful coexistence.

The Soviet motivation in attempting to increase trade with the FRG in 1954 was partly political, a move to prevent what seemed inevitable – Germany's entry into NATO as a fully sovereign power. By tempting the government with economic bait and promises of reunification, the USSR somehow hoped that it might forestall this event. *Pravda* and *Izvestiia* published articles stressing how much German businessmen wanted to trade with the USSR, and Molotov singled out West Germany as the country with which the Russians would like to trade.[62] *Neues Deutschland* also emphasized the German business community's desire for more trade with the USSR and said how profitable it would be.[63] The communist press reiterated the conflicts that existed between the FRG government and the political opposition and business community over the issue of trade with the USSR, using this partly to encourage those elements of opposition in Germany. This also served to make the USSR appear more reasonable in its dealings with the FRG because it could justifiably say that it wanted to improve relations, whereas the Germans did not.

Despite this political element in the Soviet drive for more trade with the West, there was also a strong economic component that, on the basis of the prevailing Soviet economic difficulties, seems to have been predominant. Because of its unwillingness to admit economic problems, the USSR generally used the device of emphasizing how much German industrialists wanted to increase their economic contacts with Russia. A *Pravda* article in June 1955 stressed that German industrialists were very interested in the Adenauer invitation to Moscow because of the economic possibilities they saw in it.[64] Other articles described the work of the Ostausschuss and its enthusiasm for trade with the USSR.[65] One writer claimed that "the more far-sighted West German industrialists understand that normal relations between the Federal Republic and the USSR ... would considerably overcome the difficulties in foreign trade with which the GFR is beset."[66]

These articles, which were to become a Soviet pattern, all stressed the Rapallo connection and the fact that it was Germany's extensive economic relations with the USSR in the twenties and thirties that had saved Germany from the worst effects of the Depression. Emphasizing Germany's current "economic difficulties," Soviet commentators assured the Germans that more trade with the USSR would solve their "export problem" and that "trade strengthens peace."[67] The Russians clearly were exaggerating the desire of German businessmen to trade with the USSR and the extent of Germany's economic problems – indeed, the German economy was booming. Nevertheless, they realized that there were businessmen in the FRG who were responsive to Soviet overtures. The Soviet moves were part of the general Stalinist and post-Stalinist "peace offensive" and were motivated by the need for Western machinery to promote the further industrialization of the Soviet economy.

When Adenauer left for Moscow, the German and Russian governments appeared to have taken irreconcilable positions. The Soviets, for both economic and political reasons, wanted to

increase their trade with Germany, and the German government, because of largely political exigencies, would not take any
practical steps to do this.

The Moscow summit

The arrival of Marshal Bulganin's note of June 7, 1955, at the
German embassy in Paris was apparently something of a surprise.[68] The note declared that "the interests of peace and European security . . . demand a normalization of relations between
the Soviet Union and the German Federal Republic." Citing the
mutually beneficial economic relations that had prevailed in the
past between the two countries, the note, *inter alia,* stressed the
great importance that the USSR attached to improving economic relations with the FRG.[69] Although the note was primarily
concerned with the need to normalize and improve political relations, the desire to increase trade was apparent. In his short
reply of June 30, Adenauer agreed in principle to discuss these
issues but demanded further clarification of the problems involved.[70] The Russians, in their August 3 reply, reiterated their
desire to establish diplomatic relations and conclude a trade
treaty but made it clear that these issues had to be discussed
unconditionally.[71] The German reply countered that the discussion of these issues had to be conducted within the context of
other important political questions, in particular German
reunification, European security, and the release of Germans
still held in the territory of the USSR.[72] The Soviet reply of
August 19 agreed to discuss all these issues, although it noted
that the Soviet position on the question of German reunification
was "well known" to the Bonn government.[73]

As we have argued above, although Adenauer had to pay lip
service to German reunification as the main aim of his
Ostpolitik, he realized that this goal was hardly obtainable and
was more concerned to integrate the FRG into the Western alliance. In his memoirs he stresses that he approached the
Moscow negotiations "without illusions" and "sceptical . . . about
whether the Soviet Union would make offers on the question of
German reunification which could be seriously discussed." His
stated aim was to secure the release of German prisoners of war
who had been kept in the USSR for ten years.[74]

There were some suggestions that Adenauer should use economic incentives to extract Soviet political concessions, although the precise nature of these concessions was never articulated. Some businessmen claimed that expanding trade with the Russians might make them more amenable politically.[75] Others hoped that the United States might offer to finance German industrial projects in the USSR in return for reunification.[76] However, there is no evidence that Adenauer shared these expectations, nor that he was interested in the economic dimension of these talks. His main aim – the release of prisoners of war – was political, whereas the Soviet government was clearly as interested in economic as in political questions. The key Soviet political goal was the establishment of diplomatic relations with the FRG.

Adenauer's five-day visit to Moscow was punctuated by periods of high drama.[77] After an exchange of pleasantries about the need for closer understanding between the two nations, the discussions became quite acrimonious at times. Soviet references to Hitler and the sins of the German people prompted Adenauer to inquire politely of Molotov, "Who actually concluded the agreement with Hitler, you or I?" Adenauer's criticism of the behavior of Soviet troops in Germany after the war brought outraged denials from Khrushchev, who claimed that Soviet troops had comported themselves impeccably. Discussions on German reunification and the status of the GDR proved to be fruitless, and thus Adenauer focused on his main aim – the release of 9,628 German prisoners of war. For four days, the Russians insisted that there were no prisoners of war, only "war criminals" in the USSR. Finally, the course of negotiations became so intolerable that Adenauer ordered his plane ready to take him home. When the Russians realized that they would obtain nothing from these talks if Adenauer left abruptly, they changed their tactics at the last moment and agreed to release the prisoners of war in exchange for diplomatic relations. However, Foreign Secretary von Brentano and State Secretary Hallstein were categorically opposed to diplomatic recognition without Russian concessions or reunification. Adenauer overrode their objections and agreed to recognize the USSR.[78] According to Khrushchev, it was Charles Bohlen, the U.S. ambassador, who tried to prevent the signing of the treaty, and the Russians would have been quite prepared for the Germans to leave, but the Germans changed their mind and persuaded the Soviets to sign the treaty.[79] This view is corroborated by Bohlen himself, who criticized Adenauer for his actions.[80]

Although the bulk of the negotiations dealt with political questions, it is instructive to survey the economic content of the talks, because they bring out the differing approaches to the question of trade.[81] In his speech welcoming Adenauer, Bulganin referred to the fact that West German–Soviet trade was very limited and expressed the hope that both sides would discuss the mutually beneficial broadening of economic contacts during the talks. In reply, Adenauer agreed that economic relations between the two countries could develop advantageously, but his references were vague. Khrushchev stressed how good the conditions for trade were and said that the USSR was a most attractive economic partner. However, with his characteristic mercurial turn of phrase, he reminded the Germans in the next sentence that if they did not want to trade with the USSR, that was a matter of indifference to him: "We can wait, we have strong nerves and our economy can continue to develop without the German economy."[82]

The only time that the German delegation made an official statement about trade was when Hallstein, pointing out that good trade relations depended on a favorable political climate, said that trade relations had been broken so long between the two countries that insufficient information was available about the levels of production and availability of goods. Although the Federal Government hoped for better economic relations with the USSR, this was not the time to discuss this issue and trade talks would have to take place at a later date.[83] According to Adenauer, Khrushchev asked for a clarification of the German position, questioning whether it would be possible to discuss trade relations at that time. Adenauer reiterated Hallstein's viewpoint, that trade talks would have to take place at a later date, and, according to the chancellor, Bulganin looked disappointed. As Adenauer was departing, Khrushchev repeated that he hoped economic ties would be strengthened, because closer trade relations could improve the political climate between the two countries. He emphasized that the political aspect of trade was the most important to him.[84] Indeed, the Russians had hoped to conclude a five-year trade agreement during the course of the talks.[85] Needless to say, when one compares Khrushchev's to Adenauer's account, one receives a somewhat different picture. Khrushchev believed that Adenauer had come to Moscow

> hoping to use economic leverage against us. West Germany had already gained considerable economic might and was in a position to extend credits to the Soviet Union – money we badly needed in order to buy modern industrial equipment that was available neither in our own country nor from any other socialist state.[86]

Khrushchev also claimed that, because of pressure from German capitalists, Adenauer offered the USSR credits and more reparations. He offered, so said Khrushchev, 500 million deutsche marks in return for the GDR, which he wanted to incorporate into a capitalist Germany. Khrushchev congratulated himself on increasing trade with the FRG as a result of the treaty and said he was "able to break the American blockade because the prospect of our commercial contract appealed to German business interests."[87]

The final communiqué stated that trade talks would be held in the near future but dealt mainly with the establishment of diplomatic relations. It also formalized what later became known as the Hallstein Doctrine. In a letter to Bulganin accompanying the communiqué, Adenauer made it clear that the establishment of diplomatic relations between the FRG and the USSR in no way constituted a recognition of the GDR. Germany continued to assert its *Alleinvertretungsrecht*.[88]

There was disappointment among some German businessmen, who had hoped that there would be a discussion of economic matters.[89] However, while the conference was taking place, Hilgar von Scherpenberg, head of the Foreign Trade Department of the West German Foreign Ministry, had private exploratory talks with Alexander Saburov, a Politburo member and head of Gosplan (The State Planning Office), and Ivan Kabanov, minister of foreign trade. German officials considered that a trade volume of 250 million marks per year both ways – more than double the 1954 volume – would be a realistic beginning, with medium-term credits to be arranged by banks.[90] During these private talks the Russians offered to export timber, cotton, manganese ore, chrome ore, petroleum, and some chemicals. They expressed the wish to purchase from the FRG ships, machinery, diesel engines, technical apparatus, and pharmaceutical materials.[91] In addition, it was reported that one week after the Moscow negotiations ended, Soviet economic officials began extending numerous invitations to Bundestag members to come to Moscow for economic talks.[92] Skepticism about the potentialities of trade with the USSR remained, however, and Carlo Schmid, vice-president of the Bundestag, reminded the Germans that they could not expect political concessions to follow from economic concessions.[93]

After the conclusion of the talks, Bulganin sent a letter to Adenauer reminding him of the importance of holding talks on trade in the near future, showing that the Kremlin attached importance to these talks.[94] An *Izvestiia* article answered German criticism of the inability of the USSR to supply Germany with needed goods and emphasized Russia's great export potential.[95] Other articles used the traditional tactics of stressing how much German businessmen wanted to trade with the USSR.[96] When the German prisoners of war were repatriated, the Soviet press referred to them as "war criminals," thus reasserting the USSR's refusal to make any political compromises.[97]

Most of the West German reaction to the Moscow talks centered on the political issue of whether Adenauer had "walked into a Soviet trap" in Moscow because by establishing diplomatic relations he had appeared to accept the Soviet claim that there were two German states, both represented in Moscow, and that only their two governments could negotiate reunification. There was also the question of whether it was right to increase Soviet prestige by extending diplomatic recognition to the Moscow regime in international law in exchange for a few thousand prisoners of war. A poll taken after Adenauer's return, however, showed that 48 percent of the population considered his trip an unqualified success and 31 percent thought it a qualified success, with only 9 percent saying it was a failure. The presence of a West German ambassador in Moscow and a Soviet ambassador in Bonn enhanced both countries' bargaining power.[98]

The bulk of the criticism of Adenauer on the economic front came from the expellee party, the Bund der Heimatvertriebenen und Entrechteten (BHE), a small group in the Bundestag. In the Bundestag debate of September 22, Adenauer had said that his delegation deliberately held back on the issue of trade talks because political questions had been uppermost, but that trade talks would come later.[99] In the ensuing discussion, an expellee deputy criticized Adenauer for not discussing trade with the Russians, because their domestic economic situation was so precarious that he was convinced that the Kremlin would be willing to make concessions on reunification if they were offered economic gains in return. Indeed, he was sure that the USSR would prefer the economic might of a reunified Germany to give it economic assistance, and he urged that trade talks begin immediately with this in mind.[100] The right-wing groups such as the BHE were more convinced of the efficacy of economic–political tradeoffs than were their centrist opponents, because for them the urgency of reunification was greater than the need to placate the West or maintain national prestige.

In 1955, it was impossible to utilize levers from two separate spheres of relations in the pursuit of foreign policy goals. There were two main reasons for this. First, economic contacts were too meager to provide the wherewithal for manipulating trade in the service of politics. Subsequent developments demonstrated that there had to be a certain level of economic contacts before the use of linkage was possible. Where political suspicion was so great, the promise of more trade – without any strategic materials – was inadequate to elicit political compromises. This leads to the second reason for the independence of trade and politics at this stage. The asymmetry between the economic and political stakes involved in these negotiations was too great to make linkage a viable policy. The use of economic levers in the pursuit of political ends, or vice versa, can be successful only when there is some equivalence between the magnitude of the economic and political stakes.

3

From diplomacy to trade: 1955-1958

We are not of the opinion that we must conduct a political policy for the sake of business. [Eastern] markets are *political markets*. How we shape our relations is a political and not an economic question.

Heinrich von Brentano, 1956[1]

We would rather go down in the dust than make political concessions to capitalists. I can say to all who combine trade with political concessions that they will be eaten by worms before we will crawl to them.

Nikita Khrushchev, 1964[2]

The international situation immediately following Adenauer's visit to the USSR was not auspicious for the development of Soviet-West German relations. The Geneva meeting of the foreign ministers of the Big Four in October proved to be yet another "exercise in public relations" at which contacts seemed good on a superficial level.[3] Adenauer and his government realized, however, that beneath the declarations of good intent, the Russians were as uncompromising as ever on the issue of German reunification.[4] The deadlock over the future of Germany was complete.[5] The Suez crisis and the Soviet intervention in Hungary in the autumn of 1956 marked the conclusive end to the period of the Geneva thaw.[6]

The FRG, now firmly ensconced as a member of NATO, continued to assert its commitment to German reunification while reintroducing conscription and taking measures to strengthen its integration into the Western bloc.[7]

Although the main priority of Khrushchev's German policy was the continued stability of the Ulbricht regime, he began to pursue a more active policy toward the FRG. The United States and West Germany could not match this Soviet strategy with a similarly active policy toward East Germany, because their position

48

on the GDR was negative – to deal with the GDR implied a legitimization of its existence. In this period, Soviet policy in regard to the FRG was directed partly toward the stimulation of anti-German feeling in other NATO countries and partly toward achieving arms limitation in Europe, which would also create tension between Germany and its allies.[8]

Khrushchev's policies in this period reflected a variety of interests. At the Twentieth Party Congress, he rejected Stalin's two-camp theory of international relations and announced a new policy of peaceful coexistence. The main goal of this policy was to avoid nuclear war and seek improved relations with the West while continuing to support the international class struggle and to aid national liberation movements. Khrushchev engineered a rapprochement with Marshal Tito, Stalin's bête noir, and thus mended his fences with one former enemy. He asserted his strength by meeting the challenges to Soviet foreign policy posed by the unexpected destabilizing consequences of destalinization policies in Poland and Hungary. One of his most notable successes occurred when he impressed the world with Soviet prowess by launching the Sputnik. He also continued to promote divisions between Western Europe and America.[9] The U.S. decision to permit access to tactical nuclear weapons for the European NATO forces, particularly the Bundeswehr, aroused Soviet fears. By the end of 1956, the FRG had acquired access to dual-purpose nuclear delivery systems whose warheads remained under exclusive U.S. control. One response to this situation was the Polish Rapacki Plan, calling for a "denuclearized zone in Central Europe." There is some question about whether this was a Soviet-inspired proposal or represented an independent Polish initiative.[10] Soviet–West German altercations about nuclear weapons increased, and the FRG for the first time concretely implemented the Hallstein Doctrine when it broke off diplomatic relations with Yugoslavia in October 1957 after the latter recognized the GDR.

For Adenauer, 1957 was an election year, and charges by the opposition that his Ostpolitik was in a cul-de-sac prompted him to pursue a more active strategy toward the communist world within the limits of the NATO alliance. In both the FRG and the USSR, domestic exigencies suggested a more flexible policy. Whereas West Germany was preparing itself for an election, the

USSR was experiencing a period of relative domestic turmoil. Khrushchev's denunciation of Stalin at the 1956 Twentieth Party Congress had a devastating effect, both domestically and abroad.[11] Barely had the USSR recovered from this fundamental questioning of the past thirty years when Khrushchev himself was faced with dismissal. In 1957 he consolidated his rule by purging the "anti-party" group that had tried to fire him and introduced innovative – but ultimately unsuccessful – economic policies.[12] Given the domestic need for foreign policy success, there was some incentive on both sides to pursue more conciliatory foreign policies toward each other. It was against this background that the Russians invited the Germans to negotiate a trade agreement.

The 1957–8 talks represented the first time that linkage strategies were consciously used in Soviet–West German postwar relations and reveal some important aspects of the interrelationship of economics and politics. In these negotiations, the use of economic and political means in the pursuit of specific goals was a stated object of both sides. The negotiating room is a uniquely valuable laboratory in which to examine the explicit use of these different levers. There were to be no bilateral negotiations on this scale until 1969, and in the intervening years, the use of political and economic means in the pursuit of different goals tended to be more diffuse and less explicit.

Because the main Soviet aim in inviting the Germans to negotiate was to secure the conclusion of a trade agreement, it is instructive to outline briefly the issues involved in the conclusion of such an agreement. The main focus of the debate over German–Soviet trade had shifted from *whether* to trade to *how* to trade, because both sides had by now accepted that a relatively small amount of bilateral trade had become the norm. Economic relations had grown to the point where some form of linkage was possible. It became increasingly important for the USSR to conclude a trade agreement, such as it had at that time with various capitalist countries. The typical East–West trade agreement stipulated the overall value of trade and broad classes of goods for periods ranging from two to six years and also regulated the method of payment, application of tariffs, exchange of trade missions, and other technicalities. The Kremlin's motivation in concluding a trade agreement was both political and economic. Politically, the conclusion of such an agreement would further enhance Soviet claims to the legitimacy of the GDR by securing another legal document with West German signatures and would increase Soviet prestige. However, the economic incentives for seeking a trade agreement were also important. With a bilateral agreement, imports and exports could be more concretely planned and integrated into the overall economic structure. The Soviet desire to conclude a trade treaty was part of Khrushchev's new foreign policy, which recognized the importance of economics and the link between the economic and political aspects of foreign policy more than had Stalin's policy.

The political disadvantages for the Germans of concluding a trade agreement with the Russians stemmed from exactly the same cause as the Soviet political advantages – namely, reinforcing the FRG's independent existence, implying that the GDR too was equally separate and autonomous. In addition, the Germans considered that traditional trade treaties were impossible to arrange with political enemies and also thought that less formal agreements were inappropriate. However, there were mitigating economic factors. A trade agreement would formalize the Bonn government's role in trade with the USSR, thereby enabling it to exert more control over the business community. It also had the advantage of allowing the FRG to regulate Moscow's dealings with private traders and prevent indiscriminate market disruption. Because trade agreements are not legally binding, they could also be less than fully honored. There was not much to be lost by concluding a modest agreement.

The German perspective on trade

The debate about trade with the USSR became more intense in West Germany during 1956, and for some time both sides hardened their positions. In general, those who were against more trade continued to argue from a primarily political standpoint, and those who were in favor of a trade agreement and more trade argued from a basically economic position. The debate became more complex because both sides realized that their case would be strengthened if they could adduce economic arguments against greater trade or political reasons suggesting the judiciousness of more trade. It was partly as a result of the modification of these arguments that the German government agreed to enter into trade negotiations with the USSR.

There was a general hardening of Adenauer's position on trade with the USSR after the end of the Geneva Foreign Ministers Conference and a reversion to the stand he had taken before his visit to Moscow. He adopted the position, to be reiterated many times throughout 1956, that a trade agreement between the USSR and the FRG could be concluded only after their relations had been normalized. As long as two-fifths of Germany's soil was occupied by the Russians, there would be no trade agreement.[13] Foreign Minister von Brentano claimed that the Russians were pressing economic negotiations not because they were interested in peaceful trade but because they wanted the strategic embargo to be lifted. He cited economic difficulties that would impede trade with the USSR and said that the FRG had no intention of discussing a trade agreement or the strategic embargo with the USSR until the political situation improved. Brentano emphasized that the Soviet trade offensive was the key to the new Russian foreign policy in the underdeveloped countries whose success lay in the favorable economic conditions granted by the USSR.[14] The FRG should in no way give economic assistance to a communist country trying to woo the new states with economic aid while at the same time demanding similar aid from the FRG. The furthest he was prepared to go was to say that the government might consider a partial trade agreement with the USSR. Economics Minister Erhard concurred with these views.

The government, therefore, continued to argue from an initially political standpoint. However, there were also more specific fears about the interrelation of the political and economic disadvantages of greater economic contacts with the USSR. According to some sources, the German government feared that a bilateral trade agreement would open the doors to the Soviet infiltration of West German industry, which could result in an organized German business lobby against Bonn's pro-American foreign policy. There was also concern in the United States that Soviet leaders wanted to "persuade German industrialists that alliance with the Atlantic community simply doesn't pay."[15]

The Social Democrats disagreed with the government's view. The SPD, whose prime focus was Ostpolitik and not Westpolitik, had consistently adopted the position that economic concessions to the USSR would induce the Soviet leadership to reconsider the issue of German reunification. They favored the use of positive economic levers.

The issue of trade with the communist countries came to a head in December 1956, when the SPD, frustrated over the lack of progress in German reunification, pressed for a debate on the *Osthandel.* This debate, the most comprehensive discussion about trade with the East that the Bundestag had ever held, outlined the differing points of view. The debate was prompted by the events in Poland and Hungary and the realization that even though the Hungarian rebellion had been crushed by Soviet tanks, the very fact that both countries had attempted to assert their independence showed that Eastern Europe was no longer a monolith. Its main focus was on the question of establishing trade missions in Eastern Europe as a substitute for diplomatic missions, thereby seeking to encourage the autonomy of Eastern Europe in opposition to the USSR. This would be done only in the 1960s, but the discussion foreshadowed the "bridge building" era. Although much of the debate concerned Eastern Europe, the SPD began by directing some of its remarks to trade with the USSR, asserting that trade with the East was part of the general problem of the FRG's relations with the communist world, the main aim of which was to secure the reunification of Germany. The SPD criticized the strategic embargo and demanded that the FRG not comply with it, and they pressed the government to explain why there was no trade agreement with the USSR. The lack of an agreement placed West Germany in a disadvantaged financial position compared to those Western countries that did have trade agreements with the USSR.[16] The FDP, supporting the SPD stand, claimed that the policy of withholding trade from the USSR had had no political results and said that it would be good for Germany's economy to diversify its markets. Both parties believed that more trade with the USSR would improve political relations.

Foreign Minister Brentano, in his reply, reminded the Bundestag that his party "understood the difference between politics and economics, and we do not believe that we can subordinate politics to economics." He defended the strategic embargo as a political necessity but said that despite it, trade between the

USSR and the FRG had grown 130 percent since Adenauer's visit to Moscow.[17] He claimed that in its final communiqué with the USSR after the September talks, the government had deliberately used vague wording about the conclusion of a trade agreement and had promised nothing. The government did not give any ground on its stand that trade talks with the Russians were predicated on an improved Soviet attitude on the question of German reunification and reiterated its support for the NATO strategic embargo. It is also instructive that the foreign minister, and not the economics minister, spoke in the debate, emphasizing the primacy of politics. The German government was not yet ready to use economic incentives in the pursuit of its political goals with the USSR and saw this position as a cornerstone of its "policy of strength." Only negative linkage was permissible. In this debate, both sides exaggerated the significance and effects of West German–Soviet trade. The symbolic value of this trade to both sides was greater than its commercial value.

The business community in Germany was still divided over the desirability of increasing trade with the USSR and tended to stress the need for caution. One group of industrialists, after studying the possibilities, concluded that the necessary economic conditions no longer existed for a strong return to the Soviet market. West German industrial production was primarily committed to customers in the West, and the pattern of trade between the USSR and the FRG had altered sufficiently to make businessmen question what the USSR wanted to buy from them. Total trade between the two countries had risen from $62.6 million to $122.0 million from 1955 to 1956; but this was still a very small fraction of Germany's total $14,021.30 million foreign trade.[18] The USSR continued to purchase steel from Germany, and a Soviet delegation spent some time studying automotive manufacturing at the Daimler-Benz company.

The Ostausschuss continued to press quietly, firmly, and realistically for expanded trade on a more legal basis. In August 1957, *Handelsblatt* published the first of what were to become an annual series of trade supplements on the *Osthandel,* to which German and East European authors contributed. Its main aim was to provide information and an advertising forum for encouraging more trade. In the first issue, Otto Wolff von

Amerongen admitted that trade between the FRG and the East suffered from politicization, called for a depoliticization of trade, and was relatively optimistic about its future.[19] It is possible that, under government pressure, business's full desire for more trade with the USSR did not receive commensurate publicity because the business community continued to advocate a trade treaty with the USSR behind the scenes.

The Soviet perspective on trade

The Soviet pressure to conclude a trade agreement with the FRG was part of a broader strategy aimed at intensifying economic relations with the West. At the Twentieth Party Congress, Khrushchev emphasized the desirability of trade with capitalist countries.[20] The sixth Five-Year Plan was announced at the conference, and among its most important elements was the decision to create a "third metallurgical base" in Siberia and Kazakhstan to produce more pig iron, a commodity in demand in the West.[21] The plan was abandoned a year later for a new Seven-Year Plan. It appeared that by 1956 Khrushchev had renounced the Stalinist conception of foreign trade as an adjunct to autarky and looked upon economic relations with the West in a longer-term, more favorable light as an essential component of the further industrialization of the USSR.[22]

Soviet writers continued to stress the link between trade and politics, claiming that "international trade and the development of business contacts encourage the weakening of international tensions and the normalization of relations."[23] They condemned the NATO embargo, said that it had failed, and proposed the slogan "Let's trade" as the beginning of a more peaceful world.[24] Khrushchev also emphasized that "ideological differences are in no way an obstacle to the development of mutually profitable trade between socialist and capitalist countries."[25] Indeed, the Russians deliberately minimized the economic motivation in their trade drive by claiming that the USSR was primarily interested in trade for the political benefits of peaceful coexistence.[26]

Peaceful coexistence was both a political and an economic strategy, and it is difficult to establish precisely the division between its two faces. Khrushchev was genuinely interested in minimizing the possibilities of a nuclear war, and at the same time he hoped that improved political relations would lead to an intensification of East–West trade. He envisaged, however, the amelioration of East–West political and economic relations while maintaining an uncompromising position on the German question.

One might question whether the Russians really believed that a greater volume of international trade would improve political relations. The attempt to infer motivation from Soviet foreign policy statements is fraught with difficulties. In the absence of concrete evidence to the contrary, one can assume that official explanations of Soviet foreign policy to some extent reflect genuine concerns or inter-elite communication. A related question is the extent to which Soviet leaders genuinely believe their ideology or the degree to which one must discount ideological pronouncements as explanations of foreign policy actions. Because we do not possess mind-reading instruments, a more fruitful way of posing this question is to ask to what extent ideology determines Soviet foreign policy today. Soviet ideology has historically served four main purposes in relation to policy: interpretive, predictive, legitimizing, and cohesive. Marxist–Leninist ideology was probably much more important as an interpretive and predictive tool of Soviet foreign policy under Lenin. Today, it is used much more to legitimize policies motivated by pragmatic needs. However, one cannot always separate ideology from practice so neatly. Even if ideology does not serve as an everyday guide to foreign policy actions, there is a fundamental sense in which the leadership in the USSR is influenced by Marxism–Leninism despite the prevalence of Realpolitik determinants.[27]

In seeking to evaluate whether the Soviet leaders really believed that a greater volume of international trade would improve political relations, one is faced with a specific example of the more general problem of inferring motivation from official explanations of Soviet foreign policy. Lenin and his successors have undoubtedly appreciated the economic utility to the USSR of trading with the West. However, as Marxist–Leninists, they must also have been aware of the interconnection between economics and politics in East–West relations, and both Lenin and Khrushchev may have believed that trade with the West would both help the Soviet economy and promote better political relations. Moreover, in Soviet relations with West Germany, Marxist-Leninist ideology reinforced prior perceptions arrived at as a result of historical experience, political culture, and practical considerations. The Kremlin leaders may genuinely have believed the Leninist maxim that trade promotes peace even if they were also aware of their more immediate pragmatic economic motivation in seeking more trade with the West. If the first consistent theme of Soviet writing was the desire to increase trade with the capitalist countries in the interests of peaceful coexistence, the second was to stress the extent to which German businessmen wanted to trade with the USSR. There was continuing comment in the Soviet press about how much German businessmen supported by the SPD wanted to regularize and increase their trade with the USSR.[28] Throughout 1956, Soviet foreign trade organizations invited German firms to enter into discussions about concluding business deals. This fueled American fears about the Russians trying to woo German businessmen to lobby the government.

The Soviets also made attempts to approach the government on the question of trade. As soon as Valerian Zorin, the first Soviet ambassador to the Federal Republic, arrived in Bonn on December 20, 1955, he began to press for negotiations leading to a trade treaty, citing Adenauer's commitment to these talks at the Moscow conference, but all his efforts were rebuffed. The minister of foreign trade, Ivan Kabanov, although reiterating that the USSR did not need the trade treaty and could do very well on its own, criticized the failure to hold talks and warned of the deleterious economic consequences.[29] In reply to the German note of September 1956 on the question of reunification, the Soviet government demanded to know why trade talks had not yet been held.[30]

The Russians also increased the use of historical parallels. For instance, they claimed that trade with the East could help Western countries overcome their economic difficulties, as it had in the 1930s.[31] Soviet commentators, in academic journals, popular journals, and the daily press, increased their emphasis on the historical trade links between the two countries. The scholarly *International Affairs* published a series of documents from captured German archives, consisting of memoranda from leading German businessmen to the chancellor advocating more trade

with the USSR in the twenties and also asking for large credits to
the USSR. The documents included a strong request from Foreign Minister Stresemann for a substantial credit to the USSR,
which was granted to prevent competitors from cornering the
Soviet market.[32] The more popular *New Times,* recalling how the
Rapallo Treaty had benefited the Soviet and German economies
during the world depression, claimed that "with the situation
altered, much that was important in the Rapallo Treaty now
belongs to history. But the *underlying principles* of that treaty
have lost none of their validity; and to ignore that would be a
dangerous error."[33] The message behind these frequent historical allusions was hard to miss. *Neues Deutschland* even went so far
as to cite the 1649 treaty between Brandenburg and Russia as an
example to be followed.[34]

The Soviet treatment of the German business community,
however, had two distinct faces. On the one hand, Moscow
stressed how much "far-sighted" German businessmen wanted
to trade with the USSR, but on the other hand it constantly
harped on the "revanchist" and "militarist" proclivities of West
German monopoly capitalism.[35] One might question whether
the constant criticism of German monopoly capitalism was not
counterproductive to Soviet economic goals, but it seems that
most German businessmen accepted it as part of standard Soviet
operating procedure and were convinced of the Soviet desire to
trade with the FRG.[36]

It is also possible, although we have little concrete evidence for
it, that there were divisions within the Soviet bureaucracy over
increasing trade with the FRG and that the moderates encouraged contacts with German businessmen, whereas the more conservative politicians insisted on an uncompromising attitude toward German capitalism. Thus the conflicting press comments
possibly reflected at least two distinct groups within the Soviet
hierarchy.

The Russians combined the drive for a trade agreement with
unremitting criticism of German politics in both scholarly and
popular publications. Khrushchev, although reiterating that
only the two German states could decide on their reunification,
claimed that in the FRG "the Hitler techniques are being
vigorously applied and democratic freedom suppressed."[37] The
Kremlin was also incensed by what it considered the German

volte face on the issue of trade. *Pravda* and *Izvestiia* attacked von Brentano, stressing that his refusal to discuss a trade treaty was against the interest of most West German businessmen.[38] In a reply to the *Izvestiia* article, the German government *Bulletin* ridiculed the Russian suggestion that German businessmen were opposed to their government's policy because they wanted more trade and confirmed that the normalization of trade relations was dependent on an improvement in the political situation.[39] The attempt to profit from and fuel conflicts over East–West trade between Western governments and their business sectors has been a consistent Soviet tactic since the Revolution. By the end of 1956 both sides had adopted what they claimed were immutable positions. The FRG refused to discuss trade unless there was progress on the reunification issue, and the Russians demanded to hold trade talks but refused to discuss reunification, saying that it was a matter for the two German states to arrange between themselves. Six months later, trade talks began, and both sides were willing to manipulate political and economic means and goals.

The trade and repatriation negotiations

Bulganin's note of February 6, 1957, represented a major initiative on the Soviet side after over a year of icy relations with West Germany. Saying that he and his colleagues were "not satisfied with the way the relations between our countries have developed since the establishment of diplomatic relations" and discussing at great length the political problems of German foreign policy, particularly the issue of atomic weapons, he alluded to the "tremendous possibilities for a large-scale development of overall economic contacts between the Soviet Union and the Federal Republic of Germany, to the mutual advantage of both sides." He suggested that trade talks begin, because better economic relations could provide "a firm foundation for improving the political relations between states."[40] The motivations behind this Soviet note were both political and economic. On the one hand, the Kremlin was seeking to break out of the diplomatic isolation in which it had found itself since the intervention in Hungary.[41] Conciliatory moves toward the FRG were part of a larger policy designed to improve Russia's image in the West. On the other hand, the more intense interest in trade negotiations was connected to the progress made toward the organization of the EEC and the European free trade area.[42] The Russians feared that, in the absence of a trade agreement, they might be subject to further economic discrimination once the EEC was fully organized.

It is also possible that the Kremlin had decided to link closer economic relations to specific political issues. One problem between the FRG and the USSR that had remained unresolved was that of the repatriation of Germans from the USSR and of Soviet citizens from Germany. In October 1955, about half of the German prisoners of war were returned, but then the repatriation stopped suddenly for two months. The holdup was attributed to delays in the Soviet–German talks on setting up their respective embassies and to Soviet demands for the repatriation of 100,000 Soviet nationals allegedly held in the FRG.[43] The issue was naturally of some importance to West Germany, and it is conceivable that Moscow had decided to use this as a bargaining device to extract economic concessions. Bulganin's note had hinted that an improvement in consular and trade relations could expedite the repatriation of Germans in the USSR.

The German reaction to the note was cautiously receptive. In his memoirs, Adenauer explains that in his opinion, the reason for the Soviet note was the difficult economic position in which the USSR found itself.[44] Publicly, Adenauer welcomed the note, refuted the Soviet stand on the existence of two German states, but admitted that some points of the letter could profitably be discussed. There was general agreement among all German political groups, from the SPD to the right-wing Deutsche Partei, that the note was considerably more moderate in tone than previous Kremlin pronouncements and could provide a basis for useful talks. Soviet Ambassador Smirnov had a lengthy discussion with Economics Minister Erhard, in which "political questions . . . were not discussed."[45]

Adenauer's reply represented a change in the German government's position. Reiterating his views on the issue of reunification, he nevertheless alluded to the favorable increase in Soviet–West German trade and proposed early intergovernment talks on trade, because better trade conditions could facilitate an improvement in the political atmosphere.[46] Adenauer's reason for changing his position on the FRG's willingness to discuss

trade in the absence of reunification proposals was partly a result of the need, in an election year, to show that he was willing
to compromise in order to make some progress in his Ostpolitik.
His more immediate practical objective, however, was to secure
the release of some 100,000 German nationals who were estimated to be in the USSR. The chancellor had also agreed to the
talks because of pressure from the parliamentary opposition and
some business circles to improve economic relations with the
USSR.[47] Thus, for the first time, the German government was
reluctantly prepared to use positive economic incentives to secure political goals – albeit limited – because the release of Germans in the USSR was clearly more important to Adenauer than
was the negotiation of a German trade agreement with Russia.

The difficulties in agreeing to start the trade and repatriation
talks demonstrated the extreme reluctance with which both sides
committed themselves to their respective bargaining levers and
indicated that neither side would make a concession without
commensurate payoffs. The preparedness to use such levers was
in itself a tacit admission that the previous policies – on both
sides – had failed. The German government had twice delayed
beginning the talks because of Soviet intransigence over the repatriation issue. It refused to accede to the Russian demand that
the talks be at the ministerial level, and the preceding acerbic
exchange of notes on atomic rearmament and German reunification had not softened the atmosphere. The USSR continually
harped on Bonn's atomic weapons and used this theme to
popularize its call for the conclusion of a European security
treaty, that is, a multilateral ratification of the postwar status
quo. The German government did not want to negotiate a formal trade treaty and was only prepared to make informal arrangements. It also had no desire to increase the volume of trade
to the extent proposed by the Russians and only wanted to conclude a one-year agreement on trade.[48] The Russians, on the
other side, accused the Germans of wanting to make "political
capital" on the eve of German elections and denied the existence
of the repatriation issue.[49] They countered German demands
with their own request for the compulsory repatriation of Soviet
citizens in Germany – the great majority of whom had no desire
to return to the USSR and could be classed as political refugees.
The Kremlin's main aim was to conclude a long-term formal

trade treaty and a treaty on consular rights. Thus, when Ambassador Rolf Lahr, from the foreign trade division of the German Foreign Ministry, arrived in Moscow with his delegation of twenty-five, the auspices for a successful conclusion of negotiations were not good.

The negotiations were difficult, and by the end each side had made use of bargaining devices and conceded important elements of its original position; yet each side achieved its minimum goals. The Soviet delegation was led by Deputy Foreign Minister Vladimir Semyenov, a former political advisor to the Soviet control commission in the GDR and later Soviet ambassador to East Germany. He was considered one of the top Soviet experts and a tough negotiator. The appointment of such a high-ranking political expert suggested to some that Semyenov was told to sound out the German delegation on the possibility of the FRG's agreeing to the Soviet plan for a loose federation of the two German states as a step toward reunification.[50] The institutional structure of these talks reinforced the interconnection of the political and the economic. There were three parallel sets of negotiations in Moscow – on repatriation, trade, and consular matters – and each set had its own negotiators. Although the discussions were conducted separately, there was linkage among all three, and ultimately progress could not be made in one area if another area were stalled. The Soviets tried to separate the economic from the political negotiations, but the Germans insisted on linking them.

The repatriation negotiations were by far the most difficult. The central issue was not the return of the prisoners of war whose release had been agreed upon in 1955 but the release of a far broader category of Germans. Indeed, the German claim that there were up to 100,000 German nationals in the USSR from Memel, the Baltic, East Prussia, and Bessarabia was open to question. The Germans fell into three categories. The first, and smallest, were those who had German nationality before the war – living in what is now East Germany or those parts of prewar Germany now incorporated into Poland or the USSR. The second category, which was much larger (about 20,000), were known as "treaty resettlers" and consisted of those "racial Germans" who, under the Molotov–Ribbentrop pact of 1939 were removed from their former domiciles in the Baltic states and parts of prewar Poland and Rumania, given German nationality, and resettled in territories incorporated into the German Reich. The third group, known as "administrative resettlers," consisted of 70,000 racial Germans to whom the policy of Germanization and resettlement was unilaterally applied by the German administration in occupied Russia between 1941 and 1944.[51] Not surprisingly, the Russians rejected the assertion that these people were really Germans, particularly because these FRG claims revived some of the worst memories of Hitler's racial policies.

The first phase of the talks, which lasted from July 23 to 31, resulted in deadlock, with the Russians refusing to admit the problem of repatriation. Foreign Minister Gromyko accused the Germans of artificially creating the repatriation problem for propaganda purposes instead of concentrating on economic questions, which were the core of the negotiations.[52] The Germans, surprised by this Soviet volte face, recalled Lahr and sent a note to the Soviet government admitting that for the FRG government, "humanitarian questions are more important than political ones" and asking why the USSR had reneged on its agreement to discuss repatriation.[53]

When the talks resumed two weeks later, the Soviet press published articles citing letters by Soviet citizens of German extraction who claimed they were very happy as Soviet citizens in the land of "peace and progress" and had absolutely no desire to return to Germany.[54] The second round broke down on the question of repatriation, although the Russians made one slight concession by agreeing to discuss "individual" cases.[55] On one list of 1,000 names submitted by the West Germans, all but a dozen were claimed as citizens of the USSR. The USSR's position remained that all the so-called Germans whose names were on German lists were now Soviet citizens.

For two months, the talks were suspended, with neither side willing to sever them completely. Adenauer was reelected under the slogan of "No Experiments" by the Bundestag in September, and the Christian Democratic Union–Christian Social Union (CDU–CSU) increased its majority by winning 270 out of the 497 Bundestag seats.[56] Finally, when it became clear to the Soviets that the Germans would refuse to conclude a trade agreement unless there were concessions on the repatriation problem, they decided to concede part of the issue. Although they were willing to jeopardize to some extent the economic side of the negotiations for the sake of their political prestige, the Russians must have realized that ultimately their uncompromising position on the repatriation issue would be counterproductive because they would not achieve their economic goals. They finally agreed to the repatriation of Germans in the USSR who possessed German nationality before June 21, 1941, and said they would consider individual cases of other people of German extraction. This was their political concession. In return, the Germans had to compromise by dropping their request for the repatriation of people naturalized after Hitler's invasion of the USSR. The Germans also had to agree that the Russians would not publish their declaration explaining the terms of repatriation in the USSR, thus making it difficult for Germans in the USSR to find out that they would leave. Apparently the German delegation prolonged the negotiations over this point but had to concede it in the end. Thus, both sides made compromises on the political issue, but the Germans achieved most of their initial political goals.[57]

The economic negotiations were much easier than the political, because the political issues involved symbols of national prestige for Germany and the USSR, whereas the economic issues were less delicate. The Russians, under the direction of Deputy Trade Minister Pavel Kumykin, initially offered the Germans a five-year trade agreement authorizing the exchange of 6.5 billion rubles (about 7 billion marks) in goods between 1957 and 1961. The main Russian imports would be machinery and chemical products, and the main German imports would be oil products, ores, linens, and other goods. The Germans countered with an offer for a three-year trade agreement worth 3,900,000 marks.[58]

There were four main problem areas. The Russians wanted a five-year trade agreement with five times the trade volume of the initially proposed three-year German treaty. Moscow wanted import quotas fixed item by item, whereas the Germans preferred overall quotas. The USSR asked for the strict application of Most Favored Nation treatment, and the Germans were reluctant to grant this. The Soviets were prepared to pay in limited convertible deutsche marks but wanted clearing account credits to be mutually granted at an agreed upon rate of interest. The Bundesbank, having recently abolished this policy of "swing credits," did not want to restore this bilateral arrangement. There were also problems about specific items – for instance, oil. The Germans wanted to purchase more Soviet oil than the Russians wanted to sell, and the Soviets were wary of divulging information on oil prices.[59] Both sides compromised on all these economic issues. They agreed on a three-year treaty, which would double the volume of Soviet-West German trade, a total exchange of 3,150 million marks between 1957 and 1960. Thus, the Russians achieved their aim of concluding an official trade agreement, but the Germans were able to veto the signing of a long-term trade treaty similar to those the USSR had with the West. The Soviet negotiators were able to secure quotas fixed by item.[60] Only 0.08 percent of goods desired by the Russians had to be denied because of the CoCom embargo restrictions. The Germans had wanted to sell more consumer goods than the Soviets were willing to buy, so a compromise was reached whereby a certain percentage of the German export quotas (8–10 percent) was reserved for consumer goods, a higher proportion than existed in most Western arrangements with the USSR.[61]

The Soviet negotiators succeeded in securing limited Most Favored Nation treatment – much against German wishes – with reference to customs and other matters connected with the import and export of merchandise, and not in the broader sense in which such privileges were afforded Germany's Western partners. Because Germany was a member of the EEC, it was limited in the extent to which it could grant Most Favored Nation status.[62] On the payments issue, the Germans refused to accept a strictly bilateral clearing system. Thus, the Russians were to pay primarily in convertible deutsche marks,[63] but the payments agreement permitted the contracting parties some maneuverability on the question of credit and payment in other currencies.[64] As for the third element of the negotiations – the consular agreement – the Russians had wanted to open a number of additional consulates in German cities other than Bonn to promote more extensive economic relations. They were finally permitted to set up one additional consulate – in Cologne – to serve primarily as a trade information center.

The Russians hailed the agreement as a victory for their policy of peaceful coexistence and stressed its economic value for both sides. Repeating their contention that the German economy was suffering, Soviet commentators stressed how beneficial the treaty would be for German businessmen and for international trade as a whole.[65] They also, however, warned that the "so-called Common Market" would bring considerable harm to international trade.[66] The Soviets reiterated that the repatriation problem "did not exist," although "a businesslike discussion of questions took place at the talks concerning individual Germans who for some reason or the other remained on USSR territory."[67] Finally, the Soviet press stressed the politically beneficial aspects of the trade agreement, which would improve overall political relations.[68] The Kremlin had achieved its main economic objective – to regularize trade between the two countries and ensure that it would expand, at the same time strengthening its position on the validity of the existence of two German states.

The Germans also achieved their main objectives in the negotiations. Ambassador Lahr, describing them as "not only the most difficult and the most tense, but also the most unusual of the many economic negotiations that I have conducted in twenty years of professional life," indicated that he still accepted the theory that the USSR viewed trade with the West only as a short-term stopgap measure.[69]

During the 1957–8 negotiations, both sides utilized positive linkage strategies involving secondary political and economic stakes. It is possible to differentiate between economic and political means and ends in these negotiations and to identify the linkage strategies because the tradeoffs were explicit. For both the FRG and the USSR, the repatriation issue represented a secondary political goal, involving questions of international prestige and national pride rather than security. Likewise, the trade treaty involved secondary economic goals and was not a matter of economic survival for either side. The Germans initiated the strategy of positive economic linkage by tying the negotiation of a trade treaty to the repatriation of Germans. The Russians were forced to respond to this German politicization strategy, although they would have preferred to avoid linkage altogether, by offering to repatriate Germans in return for a trade treaty.

Unlike the situation in 1955, although economic contacts were still modest, the expectation of increased trade and the growth of political contacts between the two societies meant that a sufficient basis for the implementation of low-level linkage strategies had been created. No *basic* political or economic goals or compromises were involved. Linkage would not have worked over issues such as German reunification; it was feasible only because limited goals were involved, because there was some degree of symmetry between the economic and political stakes.

4

Trade and the Berlin Crisis: 1958–1961

The Soviet Government seeks to have the necessary change in Berlin's situation take place in a cold atmosphere, without haste, and unnecessary friction, with maximum possible consideration for the interests of the parties concerned.

Soviet ultimatum, November 27, 1958[1]

The Berliners have a right to know how the land lies. The people of this city are strong enough to stand the truth. The Soviet Union has given its mastiff Ulbricht a slightly longer leash. This city desires peace but it will not capitulate . . . But peace has never been saved by weakness. There is a point when you have to recognize that you cannot retreat one step. This point has been reached.   Willy Brandt, 1961[2]

Scarcely had the Soviet–German agreement been signed than the Kremlin challenged its newly established modus vivendi with Bonn and initiated a new crisis in East–West relations that sought to alter the status quo. During this conflict, which lasted until the resolution of the Cuban missle crisis in 1962, the focus of East–West tension shifted to West Berlin, whose links to the Federal Republic and protection by the Western Allies became the focus of the unresolved German question. For us to analyze the importance of Soviet–West German relations during the Berlin crisis, it is necessary to examine the disparity in the significance of West Berlin for the two countries. The USSR and the FRG had conflicting interests in Berlin, and both viewed the status of West Berlin as a central issue in their bilateral relations. The Soviet Union sought to incorporate West Berlin into the GDR, whereas the FRG, backed by the United States, Britain, and France, insisted that West Berlin was part of the Federal Republic.

The Berlin crisis

The preservation of West Berlin's links with the FRG was a core political value for West Germany. One can distinguish between two kinds of core values: those concerned with the physical security of a state and those involved in the symbolic legitimacy of a nation or government. Physically, the Federal Republic could have survived economically and politically within the Western alliance without its links with West Berlin. Indeed, it would have been better off economically without West Berlin. It was a continuous effort for Bonn to support the precarious economy of West Berlin, which was surrounded by the GDR and cut off from normal trade relations. The trauma of the division of Germany, however, had influenced the FRG to view its ties with West Berlin as an essential component of West Germany's legitimacy as a nation–state. It had imbued its nonterritorial links with West Berlin with values normally associated with issues of national survival and territorial integrity. West Berlin was a symbol of the unresolved German question, of the FRG's security in the Western alliance, and of its commitment to reunification. Furthermore, support for West Berlin's integrity was perceived as a litmus test of U.S. reliability. Any questioning of West Berlin's links to the FRG was defined as a direct attack on the security of West Germany. Adenauer's unswerving and uncompromising commitment to the freedom of West Berlin and to the FRG's right to represent it internationally contrasts to his strong declaratory but weak operational policy on reunification. This was partly because the defense of West Berlin's position represented a West German acceptance of the postwar status quo, whereas reunification would have meant a major change in the status quo.

West Berlin's status was also a core political issue for the USSR, but more indirectly than it was for the FRG. West Berlin per se was directly crucial to Bonn, but what concerned Moscow was not the city itself but the indirect implications of West Berlin's position for the GDR. The Kremlin responded to the West's insistence on retaining ties to West Berlin by denying the legitimacy of these links. The status of West Berlin was a core value for the Soviets because West Berlin represented a concrete threat to the stability of the Ulbricht government. The fundamental issue was the permanence of the division of Europe, which was predicated on the division of Germany. The West refused to ratify this division, and under President Eisenhower and Secretary of State Dulles there was a commitment to "roll back" the iron curtain, although the failure of the United States to assist the Hungarian freedom fighters in 1956 revealed that this policy was more rhetorical than real.

Khrushchev in 1958 was using Berlin as a lever in his pursuit of the basic Soviet goal of securing Western recognition of the division of Germany. Berlin was always more a symptom than a cause of Soviet policy toward Germany. It was a convenient pressure point with which to draw attention to Soviet demands, but the central issue was the larger one of Germany rather than the narrower one of Berlin, in particular, the survival of the Ulbricht regime and its continuing loyalty to the USSR. West Berlin not only represented an annoying testimony to the economic and political advantages of life in the West; it was a concrete threat because, as long as the border between East and West Berlin was open, it presented an escape route to the West, thereby challenging the stability of the GDR. Because the USSR had defined its security in terms of the maintenance of stable Eastern European allies, West Berlin's status was indirectly linked to the survival of the postwar Soviet sphere of influence and control.

. Although West Berlin was more directly important for Bonn's legitimacy than for Moscow's, the FRG had far less control over events in the beleaguered city than did the USSR. This was because of the peculiar situation in West Berlin, where the four Allied nations had jurisdiction over the city and West Germany had none. West Berlin was both a domestic and an international issue for the FRG, whereas it was only an international question for the USSR. Russia and Germany held irreconcilable views on the legitimacy of East Germany and on the right of West Berlin to maintain its links to the West. The Berlin crisis, although it did not initially impinge on economic relations between the two sides, ultimately had economic repercussions that highlighted the role of economic bargaining in a time of political hostility. It also showed clearly the limits of economic leverage in an acute political crisis.

The 1958 Berlin crisis (known as the "second Berlin crisis" to distinguish it from the 1948–9 crisis) began when Khrushchev stunned the Western powers by issuing an ultimatum on the status of West Berlin. His threats were foreshadowed by Ulbricht in two speeches in which the leader of the GDR insisted on a normalization of the situation in Berlin, hinting that West Berlin lay within the territory of the GDR.[3] Khrushchev took up this theme in a speech to the Polish United Worker's Party in Moscow on November 10, when he declared: "The time has obviously come for the signatories of the Potsdam agreement to renounce the remnants of the occupation regime in Berlin and thereby make it possible to create a normal situation in the German Democratic Republic."[4] The formal ultimatum came in the form of a Soviet note to the United States, Britain, France, and Germany on November 27, 1958. Claiming that the Western powers had forfeited their occupation rights in West Berlin because they had "grossly violated" the Potsdam agreements, he insisted that they must withdraw from West Berlin. Instead of incorporating West Berlin into the GDR, Khrushchev said he was willing to make a compromise:

The Soviet government on its part would consider it possible to solve the West Berlin question at the present time by the conversion of West Berlin into an independent political unit, a free city, without any state, including both existing German states, interfering in its life. Specifically, it might be possible to agree that the territory of the free city be demilitarized and that no armed forces be contained therein.[5]

Making it clear that he would negotiate on no other basis than that of a free city, Khrushchev gave the Western powers six months in which to work out the details of their withdrawal, warning that "if the above-mentioned period is not utilized to reach an adequate agreement, the Soviet Union will then carry out the planned measures through an agreement with the GDR."[6] Thus the note contained two distinct ultimata: first, the immediate threat of a separate peace agreement with the GDR, which would permit it to control Western access to Berlin, and second, the free city demand.[7]

The Soviet note was both menacing and ambiguous on the specifics of the neutralized city plan for West Berlin, all of which raised questions about Soviet motivation. Perhaps one should begin with the Soviet explanations for the precipitation of a new crisis. Khrushchev, in a press conference justifying his action, described West Berlin as a "kind of cancerous tumor," saying that it was being used by the Western powers as a launching pad for their aggressive policies against the GDR.[8] More sober academic accounts reiterated the same point. The Federal Republic was trying to change the balance of forces in favor of imperialism within Germany and was threatening the peace and security of Europe.[9] Another account, claiming that "the German question is a peculiar barometer of the political weather," said that the West German militarists and revanchists were using West Berlin consciously to overthrow the East German government.[10] Indeed, Soviet writers claimed that, whereas the USSR had put forward a modest compromise proposal for Berlin, it was the Western powers that had twisted the proposal around and had used it as an excuse to reinforce their occupation of West Berlin.[11]

In analyzing Soviet motives in provoking the Berlin crisis, one must avoid the assumption that there was one continuous, consistent cause. One must also separate Soviet concerns about the specific German problem from its policies related to broader international developments. From the ambiguous and erratic nature of Soviet behavior throughout the crisis, it appears that the causes were diffuse. They had to do with developments within both the GDR and the FRG. The German question itself remained an unresolved irritation for Khrushchev. Having failed to prevent the FRG's entry into NATO, he was still trying to persuade the Germans to renounce their access to nuclear weapons. Undoubtedly, Khrushchev also thought that in trying to make political capital out of the USSR's recent technological successes – particularly the Sputnik – he would weaken West German security and increase East German security by forcing the West out of Berlin. By creating a new crisis, he might also slow down the process of West European integration and increase his stature in Eastern Europe. The economic and political consequences of the constant stream of East Germans "voting with their feet" and leaving for West Germany through Berlin also influenced his decision. Khrushchev's primary focus in his German policy remained the stability of the Ulbricht government. Although the GDR leader had purged his main opponents, the so-called Harich group in 1956 and others in 1958, his regime remained unpopular, and the exodus from the GDR challenged the survival of his government.

Extra-European factors may also have been significant in the Soviet decision to provoke a Berlin crisis. Sino–Soviet relations were deteriorating and collapsed in 1959. Perhaps the USSR wanted to solicit China's support in a gamble before the alliance completely broke down.[12] Soviet motives were partly determined by the situation in Berlin and the GDR and within West Germany, but they were also the product of more wide-ranging foreign policy goals that were directed toward changing the balance of power within Europe and possibly outside of Europe.[13]

The Western response to the Soviet note was firm and uncompromising. The three powers refused to cede any of their rights in West Berlin and stressed that the USSR had no right to put such conditions on them.[14] For the moment, we will discuss Western reactions in general and will consider West Germany's policies in a later section. This is because, on the issue of Berlin, the USSR was primarily dealing with France, Britain, and the United States. There were, of course, differences among the Western powers as to the Soviet motivation and what the appropriate response should be, but they managed to present a more or less united front to the USSR.[15]

The strategy of pressurizing Berlin as a way of attacking the wider German problem became clear when Khrushchev sent a note to the United States in January 1959 proposing a draft peace treaty for Germany. Reiterating many of the points of the November note, it also implicitly gave up the six-month ultimatum.[16] Khrushchev threatened to sign a separate peace treaty with the GDR – that would also give it the right to control Berlin – if the Western powers did not resolve the German issue.[17] There was little mention of Berlin at the Twenty-first Party Congress in January, although this may have been the result of some divisions among the leaders.[18]

The Geneva Conference of 1959 indicated the impasse on the German issue that both sides had reached. The Western powers attempted to link their proposals on Germany to a general European security system, as they had in 1955. Once again this failed, because it was impossible to have a European security system without incorporating the GDR, which they refused to do.[19] The Soviet draft peace treaty for Germany was one-sided and would have opened up West Germany to communist influence while barring any Western influence from the GDR.[20] The conference ended in deadlock, and Khrushchev's subsequent visit to the United States did nothing to ameliorate the situation. Indeed, the "spirit of Camp David" seems to have been born partly from a misunderstanding over Berlin.[21] Thus, by 1960 neither side had altered its position. The USSR demanded that the Western powers withdraw from West Berlin and agree to the German states forming a confederation under a new peace treaty. The West insisted on its rights in West Berlin and demanded free all-German elections.

It is conceivable that Khrushchev hoped to gain some ground in the Berlin issue at the Paris summit meeting in May 1960, but when he walked out of the conference following the U-2 incident, the German issue remained unresolved. Khrushchev may have broken up the conference because it had become clear that the West would not give way on Berlin, and he did not want to return home empty-handed. However, one could also argue that, given the public American justification of the U-2 flights, even if Khrushchev had returned from the summit empty-handed he could have blamed the lack of progress on the Berlin issue on American "cold war mongers." This leads to a second theory – namely, that Khrushchev's actions were prompted not by foreign policy considerations but by a domestic struggle for power, in which his opponents forced him to break off the summit. Based on the fact that Khrushchev had in January announced a major reduction in military manpower, this theory holds that the opposition, led by Marshal Malinovsky, forced him to return to Moscow after he had arrived at the Paris summit prepared to take part in it.[22] Whatever the reason for his dramatic volte face at the conference, Khrushchev's refusal to negotiate did nothing to alleviate the German problem and the Berlin situation.

Throughout 1960, domestic exigencies within both the GDR and Berlin continued to determine the development of the Berlin crisis. In January 1960, encouraged by the USSR, the East Germans resumed their drive for collectivization that they had abandoned in 1953. Between January and March, the entire GDR agricultural sector was collectivized and the peasants were all put on LPGs (*Landesproduktionsgenossenschaften*), the East German collective farms. The campaign savored of the worst of the Stalinist excesses during Soviet collectivization, with widespread trials, deaths, and suicides. Presumably, the Ulbricht government collectivized on the assumption that it would soon gain full control over its frontier through the peace treaty that Khrushchev had promised it in Berlin on his way back from Paris.[23] Unfortunately for the GDR, there was no treaty, and East Germans reacted to collectivization by fleeing in increasingly large numbers to the FRG. Because there was an open border in Berlin until the building of the wall, in the first six months of 1961, 103,000 persons left East Germany; in the following six weeks, 50,000, compared to a total of 194,000 refugees in 1960.[24] In the days preceding the erection of the Berlin Wall, 2,000 refugees were leaving every day. Clearly this spelled immediate economic and ultimate political disaster for the GDR regime.

After the failure of the Paris summit, the Berlin issue entered a relatively quiescent phase internationally. However, perhaps as a result of the domestic situation within the GDR, Khrushchev began to brandish the sword again. His moves may also have been prompted by the failure of the Bay of Pigs invasion, from which Khrushchev drew the conclusion that the new president of the United States would take no strong action in Germany. During his meeting with Kennedy in Vienna, he again threatened to sign a separate peace treaty with East Germany if the United States did not agree to his proposals for Berlin. Thereafter his threats increased, as did American resistance, and finally the Berlin Wall was erected on August 13. Western statements may have encouraged the Soviets to believe that their action would not provoke Western resistance. Most Western statesmen were concerned with the freedom of West Berlin, but not specifically with freedom of movement from one part of Berlin to another.[25] Intended primarily as a defensive measure to halt the stream of East German refugees into West Berlin, the wall ultimately had the effect of stabilizing the Ulbricht government and thus solving the Berlin crisis. It was subsequently clear that Ulbricht had played a major role in persuading Khrushchev to build the wall.[26]

Soviet explanations for the building of the Berlin Wall focused on the need to take defensive actions against Western aggression.[27] This was not only political but also economic, because, according to one author, the West was trying to destroy the economy of East Berlin and ultimately the economy of the GDR.[28] The Russians stressed that the "strengthening of the borders of the GDR" destroyed West Berlin's role as a NATO base and "demonstrated the change in the correlation of forces in Germany and the growth in the international authority and prestige of the GDR."[29] Undoubtedly, this last explanation sheds important light on Soviet motives in building the wall. Although the immediate cause was the need to stop the stream of refugees, this was a symptom of a much larger problem – the legitimacy and viability of the East German regime and the division of Germany. Ultimately, the building of the wall helped to consolidate the Ulbricht regime and ensure its survival with the tacit compliance of the West, which failed to take any measures against the wall.[30]

The second Berlin crisis entered a less acute phase on the night of August 13. The Russians resumed nuclear testing, and the war of words continued.[31] However, at the Twenty-second Party Congress, Khrushchev, despite his menacing rhetoric, had renounced the idea of the free city.

By removing the ultimatum, he was in fact admitting that the crisis no longer existed. Despite all his menacing posturing and his repeated threats, Khrushchev had not succeeded in changing the status of West Berlin; nor had he secured a peace treaty that would have meant Western recognition of the GDR. However, he had achieved one important gain – stabilizing the Ulbricht regime and ensuring its economic and political survival. He had also prevented the West from taking any measures to strengthen the position of West Berlin. This in itself was an important step on the road to a resolution of the German problem for the USSR.

West German policy during the crisis

The USSR tried at various points during the crisis to exploit the differences between the members of NATO over the Berlin crisis; in particular, it attempted to woo the British, who were more flexible than the Germans. Germany played an important role in this crisis as a source of pressure and defender of a special interest, with its veto power over certain Western policies. West Germany was initially in a disadvantageous position because the freedom of West Berlin was a more immediate core political goal for Bonn than for any of the other Western powers. However, it did hold one important political bargaining lever: It could ultimately threaten the West with neutralization or even defection to the Soviet bloc if the West did not protect its interests. Nevertheless, there were significant limits to German maneuverability and independence during this crisis. West Germany could do little to influence the USSR's actions because it had no legal rights in Berlin and because of the great disparity in power between the USSR and the FRG. However, Bonn calculated that there was one area in which the balance of power was in its favor. This was in the economic sphere, and in the later stages of the Berlin crisis Adenauer attempted to use what he considered to be his bargaining advantage over the Russians to exact a relatively minor, but nevertheless politically symbolic, concession from the USSR.

Adenauer's government adopted a rigid stance throughout the Berlin crisis: no compromise on either the status of West Berlin or the legitimacy of the GDR. The two were intimately connected in German perceptions. However, this situation was complicated by the apparent inconsistency between West Germany's own considerable dealings with the GDR – particularly in the trade field – and its disapproval of any Allied dealings with Ulbricht.[32] Adenauer believed that the FRG had the right to deal with the GDR on "technical" issues, but other Western countries did not.

Adenauer's attempt to exert political leverage on the Western Allies was ultimately successful, in that they did not recognize the GDR. However, although he realized that West Germany's survival was dependent on the Western Allies, he tried for some time to develop a closer bilateral relation with Khrushchev. Adenauer was trying to establish the legitimacy of Germany to develop its own political agenda within the framework established by the United States.

Before the beginning of the Berlin crisis, Adenauer had in March 1958 secretly proposed to Soviet Ambassador Smirnov that East Germany be neutralized and given the status of Austria, a proposal that Khrushchev rejected. By the end of 1958, State Secretary Hans Globke had drafted the "Globke Plan." This plan moved closer to the Soviet position by proposing a ten-year period during which East Germany would be liberalized and after which elections to decide the issue of reunification would be held. Khrushchev rejected the Globke Plan.[33] Adenauer unofficially was more flexible than in public. The official face of the FRG–Soviet dialogue was the correspondence between Adenauer and Khrushchev, initiated in August 1959, in which the two leaders tried to iron out some of the more pressing issues. According to Hans Kroll, the controversial German ambassador in Moscow, one of his main aims in encouraging this correspondence was to arrange a visit by Khrushchev to Germany, but Adenauer said the German people were not ready for this. In the letters, both sides discussed their views on Berlin and other questions.[34] Although the correspondence failed to achieve any substantive changes in either side's position, it was symbolically important in indicating a willingness on both sides to explore controversial topics.

Adenauer's Ostpolitik was not determined only by his relations with the United States. It was also part of his domestic policy. He challenged his Social Democrat opponents for being influenced by the communists, because they advocated a more flexible attitude toward the USSR. There was, however, a difference between Willy Brandt, the Social Democrat mayor of Berlin, and the rank and file of the SPD. Brandt adopted an uncompromising position on Berlin. He insisted on the integrity and freedom of West Berlin, and his views on East Germany were closer to those of the CDU than to some of his more radical SPD colleagues.[35] The head of the SPD, Erich Ollenhauer, for instance, met with Khrushchev in East Berlin in March 1959 and told Brandt about it only at the last moment. Although the meeting was inconclusive, the SPD chief was severely criticized in the German press for meeting with the Soviet leader in East Berlin, because it implied a de facto recognition of the city.[36] The Social Democrats put forward their own plan for German reunification involving a neutralized Germany that was rejected by the CDU, and a further meeting between Khrushchev and SPD leaders in Moscow produced no results.[37] After the Bad Godesberg Program of November 1959, when the SPD finally renounced Marxism and accepted democratic socialism as its credo, the Soviet press comments about the SPD became scathing.[38]

The Soviet attitude toward trade during the Berlin crisis

For much of the period under review, it had been in the Soviet interest to separate politics and economics in its relations with West Germany because Russia could gain little by politicizing economic issues. Because the Soviets were on the whole more interested in trade with the FRG than vice versa, there was little that they could achieve by using economic incentivies or veto power to extract political concessions from the Germans, who had the predominant economic power and initiative. Moscow wanted the economic benefits of trade with the FRG regardless of the political situation. There was thus a contradiction between Soviet economic and political goals. The incentive for increased trade with the FRG was a result of the Russian desire to maintain its growth rate and enhance its efficiency by importing capital and technology as well as by improving the quality of products it imported in daily commodity trade.[39] The USSR's economic goals dictated cooperative relations with the FRG. Yet its political goals were oriented toward confrontation with West Germany. No Soviet writer since Stalin has ever criticized the desirability of trading with the Federal Republic, although most Soviet commentators have denounced West German political activities.

Soviet–West German economic relations during the Berlin crisis indicated that politics and trade were conducted at different levels. Despite the mounting political tension, trade increased two and a half times between 1958 and 1961. It grew from $163 million in 1958 to $196 million in 1959, to $345 million in 1960, to $401 million in 1961.[40] Although this still formed only a fraction of the total trade of either side, and fell short of the original targets set in the 1958 agreement, it represented a definite increase in both the value and range of goods. German businessmen began to visit Moscow, and Soviet trade officials became more active in Cologne.

The Russians continued to point out that the volume of trade could grow more.[41] Khrushchev separated his political diatribes against Adenauer from his mildly optimistic remarks about the beneficial effects of West German–Soviet trade. His criticisms on economic issues were mainly directed toward the United States, which promoted the CoCom embargo. Khrushchev claimed that it was not the USSR but the United States that carried on politically motivated trade:

Some people might say that Khrushchev has a political approach to trade. I can reply: And what is the approach of the United States ruling circles to trade, when they put an embargo on trade with us and boycott the socialist countries? This is an exclusively political approach . . . Foreign trade has great economic and political importance; it can help to clear the political horizon and ease international tension.[42]

Soviet economists claimed that the USSR was not interested in autarky and that it believed in the international division of labor.[43] Despite occasional invective against militarist German monopoly capital, journalists distinguished between German capitalists who were in favor of progress and trade with the USSR and those reactionaries who were against trade with the Soviet Union.[44] Perhaps the most instructive functional demonstration of the separation between politics and economics can be illustrated by a speech that Anastas Mikoyan, known in the West for his expertise in East–West trade, gave on the forty-first anniversary of the Bolshevik revolution. Delivered four days before Khrushchev announced his Berlin ultimatum, it criticized the United States, France, and Britain but said nothing about Germany.[45] Mikoyan's role as a promoter of West German–Soviet trade became more apparent when, in May 1960, he published an article in *Handelsblatt* appealing for more trade between the two countries.[46] The Kremlin made a concerted effort to ensure that trade and politics were independent during the Berlin crisis because it wanted to maintain economic relations in as congenial an atmosphere as possible; even though trade with the FRG was only marginally significant to the USSR, it was important to keep those economic channels open and functioning in the best possible environment.

The economic situation in the USSR provides some explanation of the significance of trade with the FRG. Khrushchev had discarded the sixth Five-Year Plan (introduced in 1956) for a new Seven-Year Plan for 1959 to 1965. The main aim of the new plan was to speed up the growth of the relatively backward chemical industry and change the fuel balance of the USSR, which was too heavily oriented toward coal, to oil and natural gas.[47] The plan had no specific foreign trade quotas, although a minimum 6 percent annual rise in trade with other socialist countries was envisioned.[48] However, in the late fifties, the rate of growth of Soviet foreign trade began to decline and continued to drop into the early sixties.[49] The Russians continued to stress their desire to export more finished goods, particularly machinery.[50] Foreign trade still played a marginal role in the Soviet economy, although with the planned increase in oil and natural gas production, the USSR was intensifying its drive to become a leading exporter of energy to the rest of the world.

The German experience with Soviet trade

After the signing of the 1958 agreement, the issue of trade with the USSR more or less subsided as a controversial question in Germany. For two years, economic relations between the two countries remained relatively unpoliticized from the German side. The immediate modest political goals of the 1958 agreement were fulfilled, in that the USSR returned most of the Germans whose release it had originally promised.[51] However, on the economic side, there were problems that persuaded many German businessmen that their originally optimistic forecasts about trade with the USSR had been exaggerated.

The root of these economic disparities was the need for strict bilateralism because of Soviet currency inconvertibility. The Russians were eager to buy as many German investment goods and manufactures as possible, but they simply did not have enough to sell in return. It was this lack of suitable Soviet exports that proved to be the main hindrance in fulfilling the trade quotas. The Russians complained that the Germans were pursuing discriminatory practices against them in the import of raw materials. Apart from import restrictions on textiles that were designed to protect the German home market, the Soviets asserted that the Germans had calculated the cost of and had graded their grain exports in such a way that Soviet grain sold at a lower price in Germany than it deserved. Stressing that high-quality grain was one of the USSR's most attractive exports, the head of the foreign trading organization Exportkhleb, responsible for grain exports, said that because of the unfair import regulations and price assessments, the Soviets were being prevented from fulfilling their grain quotas for the FRG and therefore from purchasing more German goods.[52] Aside from the problem of importing Soviet raw materials, German–Soviet trade was hampered by the refusal of the FRG government to guarantee credits, and this made the extension of credits more problematic. The Russians could have bought more German goods had they been able to secure guaranteed German credits.

The German business community, although it differed over specific economic policies toward the USSR, was convinced that trade and politics should be separate. This was clearly demonstrated by two incidents that occurred shortly after the signing of the 1958 agreement. Berthold Beitz, managing director of Krupp, was invited by Anastas Mikoyan, on his visit to the FRG, to come to Moscow. At the end of May he made a ten-day visit there, "to re-establish contact with Soviet foreign trade organizations."[53] He traveled throughout the USSR and was given a lavish reception by Mikoyan, although he did not sign any agreements. Chancellor Adenauer, in a speech to industrialists, criticized Beitz for going to Moscow without prior discussion with the chancellor and questioned his "national reliability."[54] Alfred Krupp wrote a stiff letter to the chancellor for casting aspersions on Beitz's loyalties, and relations between the Krupp firm and the chancellor were not particularly cordial following the incident.[55]

Shortly after Beitz's return, a group of prominent West German industrialists from the Ruhr steel industry went to Moscow on what was termed a private visit.[56] Their departure happened to coincide with the anniversary of the 1953 East Berlin uprising and the day on which the news of the execution of Hungary's former leader, Imre Nagy, was made public. To compound these political developments, the Soviets chose to retaliate against a German demonstration that had been held outside the Soviet embassy in Bonn to protest against the death of Nagy. The Russians' "spontaneous" demonstration resulted in stones being hurled at the West German embassy in Moscow just as the industrialists were negotiating in the Kremlin. Adenauer then put out a public statement, saying, "I hope and wish that these gentlemen will return immediately." However, the industrialists did not interrupt their tour.[57]

Despite Adenauer's apparent disapproval of businessmen disregarding political factors in their relations with the USSR, his policy in this area was far from consistent. Indeed, when it suited him, he was quite willing to utilize these less political, and therefore less complex, contacts to his own political advantage. For instance, in December 1960 he sent Berthold Beitz of Krupp, whose activities in Moscow he had previously censured, to Poland to try to improve relations with the Warsaw government. The idea of the CDU at this point was to establish a permanent trade mission in Warsaw as a substitute for formal diplomatic relations, which were impossible because of the Hallstein Doctrine. Because of Beitz's background and his cordial relations with Polish leaders, he was considered to be the best man for the job.[58] Although his mission was ultimately unsuccessful – because the Poles refused to sign an agreement with the Germans unless they were willing to make a compromise declaration, as de Gaulle had done, on the recognition of the Oder–Neisse line – Beitz at this point was clearly regarded by the Adenauer administration as a man of considerable value.[59] Adenauer was quite willing to utilize businessmen for his own political ends, and he did not object in principle to their dealings with the USSR. However, the key factor here was control. He would not permit businessmen to pursue independent initiatives.

Despite these various efforts to link politics and economics, after the April 1958 agreement the issue of trade with the USSR was less often discussed in the German media and, despite the Berlin crisis, there was less pressure to try to couple the two. By the end of 1960, it seemed as if Adenauer, in the midst of his more conciliatory policy toward Khrushchev, was content to leave the conduct of trade to the businessmen without any government interference. Suddenly, however, trade once again became a highly political issue, and Adenauer intervened to link politics and economics. The reasons for this were largely domestic.

The 1960 crisis over trade and Berlin

Despite the USSR's inability to implement strategies of economic linkage, there was one area in which the Kremlin did exert some leverage – the renewal of trade agreements. There has been remarkable continuity in the Soviet policy on trade agreements with the Federal Republic. Moscow has continuously sought to exclude West Berlin from these treaties, claiming that it is a separate entity that should have its own trade treaty with the USSR. Indeed, the Soviets sought to exclude West Berlin even after the signing of the 1971 Four-Power agreement on Berlin. Trade treaties are both economic and political agreements, and it is difficult to establish the dividing line between these two aspects. Indeed, trade treaties had only limited economic impact. For instance, between 1963 and 1972, when there was no trade treaty between the two countries, trade grew at a modest rate and was influenced much more by the economic situation inside the FRG and the USSR than by any legal agreement. Trade treaties, rather than determining economic relations, were more a reflection of the political situation. When political relations deteriorated, this had an impact on the USSR's willingness to conclude an economic agreement.[60]

One of the paradoxes of Soviet–West German economic relations between 1958 and 1961 had been the Soviets' tacit agreement to include West Berlin in their trade with the FRG while publicly denying its right to political links with the Federal Republic. In the original 1958 agreement there was no explicit Soviet agreement to include West Berlin, but the Russians were prepared to trade with the city because this did not affect the stability of the GDR.[61] In 1952, it had been agreed that West Berlin could be included in all of the FRG's international treaties. In 1952 the mayor of Berlin and Adenauer had exchanged letters stipulating that West Berlin would be included in the currency sphere of the FRG's trade treaties with Western nations. A 1957 Federal bank law had stated that West Berlin was de jure part of the deutsche mark (D mark) currency area. The Russians in 1958 had verbally agreed to trade with the D mark area but had refused to sign a written agreement on this.[62] Although it might have been possible to continue this way, events in the GDR changed the German government's attitude toward this aspect of the Berlin question.

In the fall of 1960, the East German authorities, in what in retrospect was the beginning of measures that culminated in the building of the Berlin Wall, instituted travel restrictions for West Berliners entering East Berlin. The reply of the Bonn government, after much debate, was to threaten to break off all trade relations with the GDR within three months unless the restrictions were withdrawn. Economics Minister Erhard explained these moves by declaring that "interzonal trade for the Federal Republic is the most uninteresting thing there is." He added that the only reason the FRG traded with the GDR was to assist the threatened population of West Berlin. However, he claimed that the best answer to communist aggression for the West would be a total trade embargo against the East.[63] The Soviets denounced this "provocative" step and stressed that it was not in the interests of German businessmen to break off trade relations with the GDR. They reiterated that of course, as was well known, West Berlin was not part of the FRG and could trade independently with the GDR.[64] The West German position, however, remained that the GDR wanted to trade with the FRG and would ultimately make some political concessions over the freedom of movement of West Berliners in order to secure the economic benefits of interzonal trade. The East Germans then demanded a separate trade agreement with West Berlin, although in previous interzonal agreements West Berlin had been treated as part of the FRG. The disagreement finally ended with a compromise solution at the end of the year, in which the GDR included West Berlin in the new agreement and lifted the travel restrictions, thus restoring the status quo.[65]

While these problems were being worked out, the Soviets and West Germans began talks about concluding another trade agreement, because the 1958 agreement was about to expire. The time was certainly not propitious, given the situation in Berlin and the troubles with interzonal trade. In view of the tense political situation, these trade negotiations were seen by many West German officials as a test that would show how effective Adenauer's attempts at a rapprochement with Moscow had been. A West German official explained the degree to which the government was consciously pursuing a policy of keeping trade and politics independent at the start of the talks:

Precisely because the political situation is not favorable, we feel we should do our best to maintain good relations with the Soviet Union in other fields, such as trade. If we were to extend the struggle over Berlin by breaking off trade with the Soviet Union as well, we would be called too aggressive by the very same people who are criticizing us today for negotiating at all with the Russians.[66]

As the negotiations dragged on, it became clear that the issues involved were not purely economic. Willy Brandt, mayor of Berlin, had hinted as early as the beginning of October that Berlin must be included in any new agreement with the Soviets. A Foreign Ministry spokesman virtually agreed that this was the official government position. In reply to these statements, Sergei Borisov, the deputy foreign trade minister who was leading the Soviet delegation, said these were political issues that he was not competent to negotiate and that West Berlin had nothing to do with a Soviet–West German trade agreement.[67] Despite the somewhat contradictory statements made by German officials about the inclusion of a West Berlin clause in the new agreement, the economic details of the negotiations were satisfactorily worked out. The Germans had agreed to some concessions on credits. The new agreement was to have the same basic format as the previous one, with higher import quotas for some goods, particularly Soviet oil. On December 9, the head of the German delegation, Hilgar von Scherpenberg, a state secretary in the Foreign Ministry, announced that all technical details had been worked out and that the signing would take place on December 12. In retrospect, this was a move by the Germans to force the issue, because the Berlin question had clearly not been resolved. On the morning preceding the signing, von Scherpenberg and State Secretary Carstens consulted with Adenauer over the Berlin question. At 8 o'clock that evening, the ceremonial room in the Foreign Ministry was prepared for the signing; eighty members of the press corps were there, the waiters with glasses of champagne and the Soviet negotiator, Borisov, in an ebullient mood. When von Scherpenberg arrived, he presented the Russians with a letter that he expected them to sign. Although it did not mention West Berlin by name, the letter said that the trade agreement would apply to the same area as previously, namely, the entire D mark area. The Soviets, who apparently were taken by surprise, proceeded to argue with the Germans for two more hours and then left the Foreign Ministry with the trade agreement unsigned.[68]

The Soviets expressed outrage at this last-minute attempt to force their hand on the Berlin issue: "This was a gross attempt to subordinate the development of trade relations between the Soviet Union and the FRG to Bonn's political goals, an attempt that is utterly alien to normal trade relations practice and is directed against an amelioration of the political atmosphere in

Europe." Claiming that the USSR "has believed and still believes that trade is an excellent instrument for establishing good relations among states," *Izvestiia* went on to explain that the USSR could not include West Berlin in its trade agreements because "as is well known, West Berlin is not FRG territory."[69] *Neues Deutschland*, condemning the West German move, tied it to the problems over the new interzonal trade agreement.[70] The Soviets were taken by surprise, and their comments on the incident reflected their basic attitude toward trade and politics – namely, that although trade could improve political relations between nations, it was wrong to link specifically economic contacts to political purposes.

The question that arises from this incident is why the Federal government chose to make an issue out of Berlin at this point. There is considerable evidence that the alignment on this issue was the reverse of previous German divisions of opinion on trade with the USSR. Adenauer himself was quite content to have the trade agreement concluded without an explicit clause including West Berlin. The Soviets were aware of pressures on Adenauer to become tough on the Berlin issue. They assumed, with their limited comprehension of parliamentary politics, that Adenauer would be able to override all opposition to his stand. Adenauer's response to the breaking off of the negotiations implied his disagreement with the tactics chosen. He said he had not interfered with the final stages of the negotiations, although he had been kept informed about the negotiations. The tone of the announcement was somewhat distant.[71] The real question, therefore, is why Adenauer responded to the pressures on him to adopt an uncompromising stand on the Berlin issue.

The Berlin crisis had enhanced the significance and the influence of West Berlin during the three years in which it was under threat from the USSR. Whereas in quieter periods West Berlin faded from public attention, during this crisis it acquired more leverage over West German policies because it was both the symbol and the immediate cause of the FRG's commitment to stand up to the USSR. Willy Brandt, Adenauer's opponent in the forthcoming parliamentary elections, had taken a very determined stand on the issue of including West Berlin in any trade treaty. He publicly insisted that all trade be broken off with the USSR unless Berlin were formally included in the agreement.[72]

It was not enough, Brandt stressed, to renew old informal arrangements whereby the USSR did in fact include Berlin. Senator Klein, who represented West Berlin in Bonn, had complained in 1958 about the lack of a Berlin clause in the agreement, but this time he received an assurance from Foreign Minister Brentano that no agreement would be signed without an explicit Berlin clause.[73] Adenauer was not only under domestic pressure from political interests in West Berlin but realized the international significance of the issue. Bonn was pressuring the other Western powers to take an uncompromising stand toward the USSR on Berlin and to be ready, if necessary, to fight for West Berlin. The FRG, therefore, had to demonstrate its willingness to sacrifice a trade agreement for the sake of Berlin.

Because the treaty had to be ratified in the Bundestag, Adenauer also had to take into account the views of the opposition parties. Thus, the German legislature played a role in setting the political agenda. The SPD took an extremely hard line on the Berlin issue and reversed its normal policy of being more lenient on issues of East–West trade than the CDU. Berlin was a Social Democratic city and was also an important component of the SPD's plan for a reunified Germany. The SPD accused the Bonn government of "abandoning the interests of the West Berliners" and said it would not ratify the agreement if Berlin were not included because this would represent a victory for the Soviet free city proposal.[74] After the breakdown of the talks, the SPD praised the government's stand. The USSR, said the SPD announcement, would not necessarily honor a verbal or vague written agreement about the D mark area if it did not suit its political purpose. Only if all parties in Germany took a united and firm stand could Berlin be protected.[75]

The SPD was only one group that had to ratify the agreement. The Bundestag Foreign Affairs Committee made it clear to Adenauer that it could not ratify a treaty without a specific Berlin clause.[76] The FDP concurred with this, although it criticized the "exhibitionist" way in which the government had gone about "attempting to embarrass the Soviets into signing."[77] There was also some conflict between the Economics Ministry and the Foreign Ministry on the Berlin issue that may have had some influence on Adenauer's decision. Although the Economics Ministry had laid the groundwork for the economic side of the negotiations, the Foreign Ministry negotiated the details of the agreement, and it was the Foreign Ministry that interjected the Berlin demand. The Economics Ministry thus felt that it had been excluded from what were, in its opinion, primarily economic negotiations because of political factors.[78]

All three political parties, therefore, were agreed on the principle that West Berlin should be included specifically in the new trade agreement, but there were differences of opinion on how this should be done. The way in which the point was made – announcing the ceremony and ensuring full publicity for what would inevitably be a last-minute failure, given the fact that the Russians had made their views on this subject explicit – indicates that there was some disagreement and bargaining beforehand. Until the last moment, Adenauer resisted pressuring the Soviets into including West Berlin in the trade agreement. When it became clear that Soviet recalcitrance on this issue was unswerving, Adenauer was persuaded by his political opponents and by the negotiators in the Foreign Ministry to take a firmer stand. Domestic pressures were the main reason for the Adenauer change of line.

After the initial breakdown of the talks, it emerged that, despite von Brentano's statement that no trade agreement would be signed unless it contained a Berlin clause, the German government was willing to work out a compromise agreement with the Russians once it had taken a firm public stand.[79] The crucial issue was to stress the importance of West Berlin. A prominent West Berlin industrialist conducted private negotiations with the Soviets and devised a formula that was acceptable to the Kremlin – a *Geltungsbereich,* or range over which an agreement is valid, that would enable the Soviets to accept the inclusion of West Berlin without mentioning it by name.

The first public announcement that a compromise had been reached came after Soviet Ambassador Smirnov (and not the economic negotiator, Borisov) visited Chancellor Adenauer on December 28, three days before the 1958 trade agreement was to have expired. The foreign secretary, von Brentano, was on vacation, and thus the chancellor, who would not normally have been involved in such negotiations, met with Smirnov. This was an indication of the urgency that he felt the situation demanded. The meeting was called at the request of the Soviets, who, despite their earlier intransigence on the Berlin issue, were obviously concerned about concluding a new trade agreement. This meeting followed a conciliatory speech to the Supreme Soviet by Andrei Gromyko, who stressed the Soviet desire to improve its relations with the West, which some commentators thought was aimed at impressing the newly elected President Kennedy. During their meeting, the chancellor and the ambassador worked out the final details of the compromise formula and announced that the agreement would be signed on December 31.[80] The signing ceremony took place with no publicity. The Russians accepted a letter in which the Germans claimed that the new agreement would have the same *Anwendungsbereich* – area of applicability (not of validity, as was earlier agreed upon) – as the previous agreement.[81]

The German government's action was greeted with general approval by all parties. The CDU claimed that the successful conclusion of the trade agreement and the agreement over the interzonal treaty with the GDR showed that it was possible to work out the most important questions in German–Soviet relations. The SPD said that the agreement showed that the USSR had no more doubts that "the Federal Republic takes its duties as a representative in international law of West Berlin very seriously." The FDP agreed at the conclusion of the treaty that even difficult political situations could lead to a good result through the pursuit of an active policy. Willy Brandt, reiterating that the FRG had an international legal obligation to represent West Berlin, said that the compromise agreement showed that the international representation of Berlin was "a problem of vital significance." Indeed, the solution to the trade agreement ensured that the FRG and the GDR would be able to work out their differences over the interzonal agreement.[82] The official announcement explained the government position:

It was not the intention of the Federal Government in these economic negotiations to create or solve a political problem that falls within the jurisdiction of the four powers. But the area of application of the agreement had to be clarified and anything which prejudiced the legal situation of Berlin in any way, even if only through silence, had to be avoided.[83]

The trade agreement, which was to run from 1961 to 1963, stipulated only a modest increase in West German–Soviet trade. During the 1958–61 agreement, trade between the two countries had totaled 1,600 million deutsche marks each way. This was to be increased by 20 percent in the new agreement to a total of 1,820 million deutsche marks each way. The main German exports to the USSR were to be machinery and equipment, some metals, consumer goods, and finished and semifinished manufactures. The main Soviet exports were to be grain, oil, coal, and other raw materials.[84]

The 1960 compromise on the trade agreement was represented in the German press as a success for the FRG, but it is doubtful that this was an accurate description of the outcome. The Federal Republic had resorted to this negative linkage for specific political purposes. It achieved a minor political goal, namely, that the USSR was willing to include West Berlin in the trade agreement. However, it is doubtful whether this was ever in dispute. The only issue that the Russians contested was the matter of explicitly agreeing to include West Berlin, and this they did not do in the final draft, thus refusing to make the linkage.

The first question about Soviet behavior during the episode concerns the initial Soviet unwillingness to accept the letter presented at the original signing. Given the Kremlin's attempts to sever all ties between the FRG and West Berlin, it could not formally accept a letter containing the D mark area clause. On the other hand, there is no indication that the Russians would not have continued to trade with West Berlin. Their main objection was to making a public issue out of so sensitive a question, which touched on the legitimacy of the GDR. However, it is also evident that the Soviets were not willing to forego the trade agreement altogether, as their efforts to find a compromise show. Khrushchev said that the main cause of Soviet willingness to conclude the treaty was to maintain the possibility of better relations with the FRG. The economic aspects of the treaty were, of course, important, but the political significance was even more important. The USSR did not want to forego the supply of West German machinery and equipment. Because the successful conclusion of a West German–Soviet trade agreement was tied to the renewal of the interzonal economic agreement, the USSR may have been under pressure from East Germany and Eastern Europe to ensure the renewal of both of these agreements.

Although we can point to both political and economic motivation for the Soviet willingness to compromise, we can also question to what degree the Russians made a compromise at all. The final letter that they accepted was extremely vague, and as their subsequent actions showed, the acceptance of the letter made not one iota of difference to their Berlin policy. In May, the Russians refused to renew a cultural agreement with the FRG because the Germans asked for assurances on West Berlin's inclusion, a policy that they continued until 1980. In criticizing the German policy, *Pravda* reiterated that "West Berlin, as is known, is not part of the FRG and, consequently, no agreement can extend to it."[85] In May the Russians also proposed setting up a trade mission in West Berlin as a step toward normalizing relations with it. The Germans, claiming that this was a violation of the 1961 agreement, refused to allow it, although they did permit an Intourist bureau to be established.[86]

In this episode, the USSR changed the political agenda on West Berlin, and the FRG politicized economic relations by demanding a return to the status quo of the 1958 treaty. Within West Germany, the Bundestag politicized the trade issue and Adenauer was forced to respond. During the December 1960 trade negotiations, the German government utilized specific negative economic linkage by refusing to sign a trade treaty without a Berlin clause. The Soviets responded to the German linkage strategy by informally making a specific positive political concession.

They did not, however, publicly compromise, and they would probably have included West Berlin de facto in the treaty. The 1960 negotiations represent a modified form of negative economic linkage in which the immediate bilateral economic stakes involved were modest, but the larger symbolic political issue of Berlin was significant. It is doubtful that this represented a success for German linkage strategy because the Soviet concession was minimal.

5

The pipe embargo: 1962–1963

From the standpoint of the U.S., the [CoCom embargo] system has been intricately interwoven into our overall strategic thinking about the cold war and in our overall cold war posture. Trade denial is looked upon as an effective weapon of cold war regardless of how large or how small the quantities of goods involved may be, on the simple assumption that since the U.S. is richer than the USSR any trade between the two must necessarily help the USSR more than the U.S. and hence must improve the relative power position of the USSR. Trade denial has also come to be an important symbol of our cold war resolve and purpose and of our moral disapproval of the USSR.   Walt Whitman Rostow, 1963[1]

Of course, anything one pleases can be regarded as strategic material, even a button, because it can be sewn onto a soldier's pants. A soldier will not wear pants without buttons, since otherwise he would have to hold them up with his hands. And then what can he do with his weapon? If one reasons thus, then buttons also are a particularly strategic material. But if buttons really had such great importance and we could find no substitute for them, then I am sure that our soldiers would even learn to keep their pants up with their teeth, so that their hands would be free to hold weapons.

Nikita S. Khrushchev, 1963[2]

The most controversial example of negative linkage in West German–Soviet relations prior to 1980 was an American order forbidding the Germans to honor a sales contract to sell large-diameter pipe to the USSR. The NATO pipe embargo, more than any other single incident, highlighted the U.S.'s primary role both in the establishment of the East–West trade agenda and in the politicization of specific economic issues. The Federal Republic had proven its loyalty to the Western alliance, and the assumption was that Adenauer could not act independently in his dealings with the USSR. Even if bilateral German–Soviet relations deteriorated significantly as a result of U.S. actions, the German government was in no position to challenge the U.S. prerogatives in these issues because of Bonn's strategic dependence on the United States. Until 1969, the FRG's autonomy in foreign policy was restricted, and it had to heed Washington.

The United States, through the formation of CoCom, had determined the general parameters of East–West trade and indirectly influenced Soviet–German trade, yet it did not often intervene directly in any specific German–Soviet bilateral economic relations after 1953. The pipe embargo of 1962–3 involved a politicization of economic relations different from previous policies. This linkage was much more concerned with U.S.-Soviet and U.S.-European relations than with the strictly bilateral German–Soviet dimension, although there were considerable repercussions from the pipe embargo on German–Soviet relations. The pipe embargo represented an American attempt to coordinate and alter the East–West trade policies of its European allies.

The U.S.-inspired strategic embargo was based on the premise that all economic transactions between East and West were a function of political relations. In reply to a question by President Kennedy on whether the strategic embargo policy should be reconsidered, the head of the Policy Planning Staff, Walt Rostow, wrote in a memorandum:

The major issues of our trade control policy are political – not strategic, economic or commercial. From the standpoint of the USSR, the political significance of the U.S. restrictive policies has been out of all proportion to their impact on the Soviet economy or strategic position. The principal reason for this is that they serve as a symbol of U.S. unwillingness to grant the USSR full respectability as an equal in the postwar world order, a symbol that the U.S. dares to discriminate against the USSR under contemporary conditions.[3]

The U.S. view was that any technology export to the USSR was dangerous because it might help the Soviet Union increase its economic and military power. As far as strategic goods were concerned, politics and economics could not be separated.[4]

Although Germany had been particularly hard hit by the CoCom embargo lists in the early days, by the mid-1950s there did not appear to be much discrimination against the FRG in what it was entitled to export to the USSR. The CoCom embargo lists had been radically revised and shortened in 1954 and 1958.[5]

East-West trade continued to grow, and despite Soviet criticism of the strategic embargo, CoCom rules did not adversely affect West German-Soviet trade. In order to understand the U.S. decision to reimpose an embargo on the export of large-diameter steel pipes to the USSR, we must therefore briefly examine political and economic developments in late 1962.

The political preconditions of the embargo

The U.S. decision to impose an embargo on the export of large-diameter pipe to the Soviet Union was taken a month after the Cuban missile crisis. Although it is generally agreed that the ultimate outcome of that showdown was to facilitate detente, in the immediate aftermath relations between the United States and USSR were strained. As far as U.S. relations with its Western European allies was concerned, there was much friction over de Gaulle's concept of Europe and continued American resistance to his demands for more autonomy. The Franco–German treaty of January 22, 1963, was important in the evolution of the pipe embargo.[6] The United States interpreted Adenauer's signing of the treaty as an anti-American act because it emphasized the desire of Germany and of France for greater independence from the United States. The treaty followed de Gaulle's rejection of Britain's application to join the EEC one week earlier. American leaders considered these moves a concerted attempt on the part of the two West European powers to assert their autonomy.[7] Nevertheless, in a secret memorandum shortly after the treaty, Secretary of State Dean Rusk wrote:

The most fundamental [of our objectives] has always been to deny Europe to Communist control – European unity . . . [is] the most effective framework within which to contain and provide a creative outlet for West Germany which might be tempted to seek reunification with East Germany through bilateral arrangements with Moscow. . . . We should not make an attempt to prevent ratification of the Franco–German treaty. We should, on the other hand, make absolutely clear to Adenauer . . . that the stability of U.S.–German relations requires unambiguous German commitment, in words and deeds to: 1. NATO; 2. the multilateral force . . . and 3. British accession to the Common Market.[8]

Events in 1963 showed that the Germans still took the American rather than the French side in all matters of great international importance – the multilateral force (MLF), the test ban

treaty, and preparations for the Kennedy round of trade negotiations. Nevertheless, in the first months of 1963 there was considerable German–U.S. tension, and the Adenauer regime felt constrained to placate the U.S. government.

The United States was not the only superpower that disliked
the Franco–German treaty. The USSR protested strongly
against "the facade of bombastic words about a 'historic reconciliation' [which] merely conceals a detailed program for merging
the armed forces of the Federal Republic and France." Another
reason why the USSR objected to the treaty was the inclusion of
West Berlin in all its provisions.[9] Replying to the Soviet note, the
German government assured the Russians that "this treaty is
directed against no nation and no state" but stated that "Berlin is
a part of Germany."[10] Thus, the FRG had alienated both the
United States and the USSR with its treaty with de Gaulle.

In the aftermath of the building of the Berlin Wall, Bonn and
Moscow had resumed their dialogue, but with limited results.
There was a furor in early 1962 when Erich Mende, leader of
the Free Democrats, advocated separate German–Soviet talks
concurrent with those being conducted by the United States and
the USSR. The Christian Democrats clashed with their Free
Democrat Coalition partners over pursuing a more flexible policy toward Moscow.[11] Adenauer's insistence on continuing his
"policy of strength" was demonstrated most clearly in the Kroll
affair in March 1962. The controversial ambassador's attempts
to improve Soviet–German relations single handedly were recounted in the previous chapter. The final straw came when
Kroll, who had previously proposed a meeting between
Khrushchev and Adenauer, reportedly advocated major concessions to the Kremlin. The Springer-owned *Bild-Zeitung* and *Die
Welt* said that Kroll had outlined a plan that included Bonn's
renunciation of the former German territories in the East; the
recognition of the existence of two German states and the political separation of West Berlin from West Germany; and a loan of
$2.5 billion to the USSR. Kroll denied that he ever said this, but
he was called home and transferred elsewhere.[12] The Russians
supported Kroll's efforts to promote talks between Germany
and the USSR.[13] Kroll may well have been dismissed because of
his breaches of diplomatic protocol and his overly independent
line, and not only because of the specific content of his policies.

However, what is important for us is that any hint that Germany should recognize Eastern Europe diplomatically created an uproar in the FRG. In 1962, any talk of such compromise was totally unacceptable and traitorous. By 1969, the situation had completely changed.

Although relations with the USSR remained strained, Adenauer's new foreign minister, Gerhard Schroeder, had begun to pursue a more flexible and imaginative policy toward the other states of Eastern Europe. He had launched a more active Ostpolitik and, when he took over from Brentano in October 1961, advocated improved relations with Eastern Europe. He envisioned establishing trade missions as the first step and as a substitute for diplomatic recognition.[14] Schroeder's "policy of movement" was a product of ideas developed by the "flexible Atlanticist" politicians who favored greater West German contacts with Eastern Europe.[15] It was a precursor of the bridge-building policy of the Johnson era. Eschewing any change in the Hallstein Doctrine because it would enhance the international status of the GDR, Schroeder's strategy was to institutionalize official contacts while avoiding diplomatic relations and continuing to isolate the GDR. He sought to achieve this by establishing West German trade missions without consular rights in East European capitals, thereby breaking the East German monopoly on representation in Eastern Europe. West German policy was successful in establishing trade missions in Poland (March 1963), Rumania (October 1963), Hungary (November 1963), and Bulgaria (March 1964). However, these trade missions did little to improve political contacts in the mid-1960s. Adenauer gave these moves his qualified approval.[16] Thus, it was the official policy of the German government to promote expanded trade relations with Eastern Europe after 1961, and to remove as many economic barriers as possible to facilitate better political contacts without officially recognizing the European status quo. Moscow was wary of this policy, despite the implicit acceptance of East European relations with East Berlin, because it increased West German influence in Eastern Europe.

West Germany's trade with the USSR increased after the signing of the 1960 trade treaty. Trade rose from $196.5 million in 1959 to $345.4 million in 1960, to $401.5 million in 1961, to $422.3 million in 1962.[17] The Russians continued to press the

Germans to increase the quantity and variety of their economic exchanges, pointing out in various memoranda that the USSR was an "ocean-sized market" for the products of the "gifted" German people.[18] Trade developed so satisfactorily that negotiations on a new goods protocol that had been planned for the end of 1961 were ruled out as unnecessary.[19]

The embargo: antecedents and imposition

The U.S. decision to reimpose a ban on the export of large-diameter steel pipes to the USSR was a response both to political developments and to the state of the Western oil industry prior to the NATO decision. By mid-1962, there was a growing feeling within the United States that increasing Soviet oil exports represented an economic and political threat to the Western world. In 1958, 60 percent of Soviet energy needs were met by coal, 26 percent by oil, and 5.4 percent by natural gas. The corresponding figures for the United States were 28.8 percent, 36.6 percent, and 30.7 percent.[20] The Seven-Year Plan of 1959–65 had foreseen a considerable increase in the production of Soviet oil so that by 1965, oil was to constitute 32.7 percent of the total Soviet energy needs. In 1955, the USSR had exported to the West some 116,000 barrels of oil daily; in 1960 its exports rose to 486,000 barrels a day, and by 1965 to 1,020,000 barrels.[21] By 1961, Soviet crude oil exports formed about 4 percent of total world sales; 70 percent went to the West, with 40 percent of these exports going to Italy, Japan, and West Germany.[22] The Western oil companies claimed that the USSR was dumping oil, selling it to Germany at a price of $1.71 a barrel, whereas the going world market price was $2.56.[23] It was generally recognized that the Russians were selling crude oil in Western Europe at a price below that charged to East European countries because of their need to accumulate hard currency. However, because prices for Soviet oil varied depending on where the oil was extracted in the USSR, some observers argued that this was not dumping but merely a reflection of differing cost factors.[24]

Despite the fact that total Soviet crude exports formed only 4 percent of world sales, there was an outcry over the increasing Soviet production and sale of oil disproportionate to the economic importance of the issue. In July 1962, Senator Kenneth

Keating's subcommittee to investigate the administration of the Internal Security Act held a series of hearings on Soviet oil in East-West trade. The conclusion was ominous:

Ever since the Soviets came to power in 1917, they have looked for methods to undermine the free world. Economic warfare is especially well adapted to their aims of worldwide conquest. Khrushchev has threatened to bury us on more than one occasion.

It is now becoming increasingly evident that he would also like to drown us in a sea of oil if we let him get away with it. The Soviets are dumping oil at bargain prices throughout the world. This is not dumping for economic reasons but for political and military reasons. They are using oil to buy valuable machinery and know-how from the West. They have even succeeded in exchanging oil for the pipelines, valves and tankers which they must procure from free world sources in order to produce and distribute oil at a rapidly accelerating rate.

If these tactics continue to succeed, there is danger that Western countries will become increasingly dependent on Soviet oil supplies for vital defense as well as industrial activities. The danger such a situation would pose to the security of the free world cannot be overstated.[25]

The hearings specifically cited the transportation problem that the Russians were overcoming by building pipelines with the help of imported Western pipe. The view of Soviet trade was the classical perception of economic warfare. The Russians, according to the testimony, did not trade for primarily economic reasons. All their exports were directed toward some overriding military-political aim. Despite its predictions of imminent dangerous Western dependence on Soviet oil, the testimony also said that importing Soviet oil made "no economic sense" because there was a surplus of oil in the West anyway. There was also the assumption that the main purpose of the Soviet "economic offensive" was to export, thereby creating dependencies, and that the need to import was secondary.[26] The report expressed the fear of the Soviet oil offensive leading to greater Russian penetration of the Third World.

The sentiments expressed in the Keating hearings were reiterated in a somewhat more sober form in an EEC report of 1962. "The Community" said the report, "cannot afford to ignore the danger which a suspension of these [Soviet oil] imports would represent for its supplies."[27] The urgency of the rhetoric, as expressed in the Keating hearings, seems discordant with the reality of the situation, given that Western Europe was not by any conventional definition dependent on Soviet oil. This leads to one of two possible explanations for the outcry over Soviet oil exports. Political factors, given the prevailing cold war climate, may have distorted perceptions of the economic significance of Soviet oil exports. Policy makers tended to see in every barrel of oil exported from the USSR a potentially sinister force for undermining the security of the West. The other explanation suggests that the Western oil companies, fearing price competition from the Russians, put pressure on the U.S. government to impose measures to curb Soviet oil exports to the West. The United States was aware of this latter charge, but the government denied it vigorously.[28]

The West German interest in Soviet oil had two main components. On the import side, Soviet oil and natural gas were increasingly being used in the FRG. However, the export side was more significant. The export of large-diameter (40-inch) steel pipes to the USSR for the construction of pipelines was important for the Ruhr steel industry, which after its expansion in the 1950s suffered from underutilized capacity. Soviet crude oil exports to the FRG had risen from 261.4 thousand tonnes in 1959 to 1,240.9 in 1960, to 1,572.3 in 1961, to 1,914.5 in 1962, to 2,214.6 in 1963.[29] In addition, discoveries of Soviet natural gas began to attract the West German gas industry, although its main suppliers were France via the French Sahara. In 1962, the Russians proposed building an oil refinery in West Germany to process Soviet oil exports to the FRG. This aroused fears in the United States and Germany that the building of the refinery by two Russian-controlled firms in Austria and France would further disrupt the Western oil market, particularly that of the Common Market, by enabling the Soviets to sell oil below existing price levels.[30] Despite the growth of Soviet oil exports, the quotas established in the 1960 trade agreement did not allow for any spectacular increase in Soviet oil exports to the FRG, and Germany continued to purchase most of its energy supplies from the Middle East and the West.

West Germany's interest in the Soviet oil and natural gas industry was focused much more on the export of steel pipe than on the import of oil. Transportation posed the most serious problem for the development of the Soviet oil industry. At no time in the postwar period was the USSR able to fulfill its annual plan for the construction of petroleum pipeline.[31]

The 1959–65 Soviet Seven-Year Plan required 2,100,000 tonnes of 40-inch pipe, of which 1,700,000 were for gas lines. Americans estimated that the Soviet output of 40-inch pipes through 1965 would be only 850 thousand tonnes. All in all, the Soviet deficit in this 40-inch pipe was estimated at about 703 thousand tonnes through 1965. This would delay the Soviet pipeline program from eight months to two years if additional imports of pipes, over and above existing contracts, were not available.[32]

The construction of 40-inch diameter pipes required a specialized technology, at which the Germans excelled. In the early sixties, the Soviets were engaged in building the so-called Friendship Pipeline connecting the Baku oil fields to Poland, Czechoslovakia, and East Germany, which was scheduled to be completed in 1963. However, in reports to the Supreme Soviet in 1962, Soviet officials conceded that steel pipes had become a bottleneck commodity.[33] The import of steel pipes was therefore a vital component in the development of the Soviet energy industry.

West Germany had begun to sell large-diameter pipes in greater quantities to the USSR after Washington prevented U.S. steel firms from exporting pipes to the USSR in 1959. Anastas Mikoyan had negotiated a deal in the United States, but the Department of Commerce refused the necessary export licenses. As a result, the Soviets, who had first purchased German pipes in 1956, placed an order with three Ruhr concerns. German exports of large-diameter steel pipes to the USSR rose from 3.2 thousand tonnes in 1958, to 150.5 in 1959, to 179.5 in 1960, to 207.5 in 1961, to 255.4 in 1962.[34] In 1962, the West German steel industry was experiencing some difficulties because of the falling export price of steel. It was hoped that the exports of steel pipe to the USSR, which would be used to construct the 26,000 kilometers of pipe foreseen in the Soviet Seven-Year Plan, would alleviate some of the difficulties of the German steel industry. On October 5, 1962, three giant Ruhr concerns, Mannesmann, Hoesch, and Phoenix-Rheinrohr, signed a contract to supply the USSR with 163,000 tonnes of 40-inch steel pipe valued at $28 million. Because of the USSR's difficulties in paying for the pipe, the deal stipulated that the Russians would export the pig iron to Germany, where it would then be converted into steel, a classic compensation agreement.[35] It seemed, in the fall of 1962, that the Soviet–West German trade in steel pipes was one of the more promising areas of economic contact between the two countries.

In July 1961, the United States had attempted to secure a NATO agreement on embargoing large-diameter pipe. Unknown to the German steel firms, the NATO Council in Paris had secretly adopted a resolution forbidding the export of large-diameter steel pipe to the Soviet bloc by member states on November 21, 1962. According to *World Petroleum,* "the first demand to use NATO and U.S. diplomatic channels to restrict trade in oil between the West and the USSR had been made in November 1960 . . . by President Brockett of Gulf Oil and then President of Standard Oil Co. (N.J.), Mr. Rathbone."[36] The text of the 1962 resolution was never released. It stated: "Member countries, on their own responsibility, should to the extent possible: (1) stop deliveries of large-diameter pipe (over 19 inches) to the Soviet bloc under existing contracts; and (2) prevent new contracts for such deliveries. The Committee will keep the situation under observation and review as appropriate."[37] There was much discussion as to whether the NATO resolution was a recommendation or an order, but it seems that it was a recommendation. The real question is why the United States chose the NATO forum to make a ruling on strategic exports rather than using the more appropriate CoCom machinery. The answer was that the CoCom method required unanimous agreement by fifteen countries (the members of NATO plus Japan, minus Iceland).

When the United States had tried to introduce the matter in CoCom, the British indicated that they would vote against it.[38] The Americans, claiming that the pipe would be used to supply Red Army divisions with fuel in the GDR, used the NATO forum to pass their resolution because it did not require unanimous consent. The United Kingdom, however, "which did not concur in SHAPE estimates of the military importance of the CMEA (Council for Mutual Economic Assistance) pipeline to the Soviets . . . only reluctantly permitted the NATO resolution to be adopted."[39] Although both American and German officials claimed that the decision was unanimous, the British were resolutely opposed to the embargo because they had never supported the concept of economic warfare against the USSR to achieve political concessions.[40]

The Americans had used NATO to impose an embargo on pipe exports because building pipelines to supply the Red Army was not an enterprise in which Western countries should be involved. The State Department claimed that the Friendship Pipeline would improve the USSR's military position, facilitate supplying Red Army troups in Europe, and intensify the Soviet oil offensive against nonbloc countries.[41] The resolution demanded no political concessions from the Russians; it merely forbade exporting pipes. However, the Red Army had survived tolerably well without the Friendship Pipeline to supply it with fuel, and it was hard to argue that the refusal to sell pipes would in any way impair the performance of the Soviet military. Indeed, the State Department, in one memorandum, admitted that

the effect of the NATO resolution, provided it continues to be implemented, will probably be to delay construction by about a year of the Soviet Union's large-diameter gas and oil truck lines. However, it is possible that the much-publicized CMEA oil line, the principal objective of the NATO restriction, could be completed on schedule at the end of 1963, or sometime in 1964.[42]

Although preventing the construction of the Friendship Pipeline may have been the immediate objective of the U.S. NATO action, imposing the embargo had wider implications. The United States realized that most West European countries did not share its views on restricting trade with the USSR, and it imposed this ban partly as a matter of principle, to assert its predominance in the Western alliance in matters of East–West trade.

Some observers and scholars have argued that the real reason for the American apprehension about the new Soviet oil pipeline was economic and not political. It was fear of future Soviet competition with Western oil. Once the Friendship Pipeline was built, the Russians would be able to supply cheap oil to the West German border and beyond.[43] This was a realistic economic concern on the part of the U.S. oil companies, yet it was never publicly admitted. Instead, the move was rationalized solely in terms of the political–strategic danger of supplying the USSR with large-diameter pipes. State Department telegrams indicate that the U.S. government was aware that critics of the embargo – particularly in the FRG – considered that "the embargo is a result of pressure from U.S. oil companies to avoid increased competition." The State Department, however, insisted that the "strategic importance [of] these pipelines was [the] sole basis [of the] NATO decision."[44]

The pipe embargo's main effect was to delay the construction of the Friendship Pipeline by one year. However, it had a detrimental impact on U.S. relations with its allies, which suggests that the embargo was ultimately counterproductive for American foreign policy. Although there was undoubtedly some pressure on the government from the oil companies, the evidence suggests that economic motivation was not the main reason for the imposition of the embargo. The State Department felt that the development of the Soviet oil exporting industry represented a strategic–political threat, and it was also concerned about the cohesion of the NATO alliance on matters of East–West trade. The motivation for the imposition of the embargo was both economic and political, but political factors were predominant.

The imposition of the embargo in Bonn

Because the United States largely determined the framework of West German foreign policy, Bonn had little choice but to comply with the imposition of the embargo. German businessmen, however, objected to the retroactive nature of the embargo, and this was a source of friction between the government and industry. The United States may well have pressed for the embargo in late November because it was aware that the contracts had already been signed.

The NATO resolution had been foreshadowed by Senator Keating, who, at a meeting of the "Atlantic Bridge" in Berlin in mid-November, had strongly condemned the export of strategic materials to the USSR.[45] Because the USSR was importing two-thirds of its large-diameter steel pipe from the FRG, Germany was particularly affected by the NATO embargo. Economics Minister Erhard complied with the NATO recommendation by issuing an administrative order on December 19 requiring special permits for the export of all steel pipe to the East. The order was passed under a 1961 clause of the Foreign Trade Law stating that trade can be limited to guarantee the security of the FRG, but giving the Bundestag the right to cancel government embargo decisions within three months.[46] The order was passed over the opposition of both the SPD and the CDU coalition partner, the FDP. In order to emphasize the importance of the NATO decision, U.S. Secretary of State Dean Rusk met with the West German ambassador in Washington and insisted on literal compliance with the order. Indeed, the State Department was very concerned that the FRG might not apply the embargo fully. At the beginning of December, Bonn made it clear that, although it would prevent the future export of pipes, it might not cancel existing contracts. The State Department put considerable pressure on the German government to cancel existing contracts, citing the FRG's moral and political obligations to comply with U.S. wishes.[47] The State Department, however, realized that it had to give the Federal government a better legal basis for carrying out the embargo.[48] There was also some concern that, although the German ambassador in Moscow, Horst Groepper, was fully in favor of the embargo, "ex-Ambassador Kroll, who is [a] known protagonist of Soviet FRG trade . . . also remained in Act [i.e., trying to influence the German government]."[49]

The Soviet government, needless to say, had a strong objection to the German government's attempt to cancel the pipe orders. The Soviet commercial mission in Bonn, responding to the December 19 licensing controls, claimed that they were a violation of the 1960 trade agreement.[50] The Germans claimed that no violation of the trade agreement existed, because the agreement did not include the pipe deal. In an interview with the business newspaper *Industriekurier,* the head of the Soviet trade mission in Bonn, Pyotr Gritchin, denied that the cancellation of the deal would impair Soviet pipeline-building capacity, but his strong condemnation of German actions belied this supposed confidence in the USSR's pipe-building capacity.[51]

The crux of the question for the West German government was whether the contract that had been signed prior to the NATO resolution, in October, could be fulfilled. The three firms concerned claimed that the dimensions and specification of the pipes that they were to deliver showed clearly that they would not be used for building the Friendship Pipeline, but would be used to build a natural gas pipeline from Bukhara to Sverdlovsk. According to the managing director of Hoesch, Willy Ochel, the firms were warned that there might be an embargo on November 22, but they were not told about it formally until

December 19, when they applied for export permission. They were then informed that exports of steel pipe with a diameter of 19-inches or over would be made contingent on special licensing procedures, but they were not told that the embargo might be applied retroactively. In order to gain some clarification of this important matter, the three Ruhr firms sent eleven letters to the chancellor, the Ministry of Economics, and the Foreign Ministry requesting information, but received no replies. Indeed, on January 8, the Customs Office in Duesseldorf had granted them the necessary permits for the export of pipes.[52] Thus the government, or at least its CDU members, pursued a confusing policy following the December order, attempting to procastinate until the three months during which the embargo could be rescinded in the Bundestag had elapsed.

The U.S. State Department attempted to forestall any campaign by the three German firms involved. It advised the Bonn embassy to inform the firms "that [the] pipe resolution [is] based on NATO agreement, that such action [is] in [the] interest of all Free World countries and *not,* repeat *not,* [arising only] from U.S. intercession."[53] Despite these American attempts at persuasion, the German firms were not convinced. The director of Phoenix-Rheinrohr, Mommsen, visited the U.S. State Department and argued that his firm should be allowed to export the pipe. Representatives of all three firms went to Moscow, and the Soviet president of Promsyroimport suggested various ways of bypassing the embargo. The German firms felt that the Economics Ministry in Bonn was against the embargo, although the Foreign Office was in favor of it.[54]

Despite these bureaucratic differences within the German government, and despite the lobbying effort by the steel firms both at home and abroad, Adenauer continued to stress the validity of the embargo on the grounds of national security.

The German government's tactics failed to placate either the business community or the SPD and CDU. In the three months between December 19 and March 19, a complex series of negotiations was conducted, with the three firms trying to influence the Bundestag foreign trade committee to clarify the matter and the CDU trying to avoid a debate on the issue.[55] The foreign trade committee, supported by the SPD, the FDP, and certain CDU members, voted against applying the embargo retroactively, and the controversy intensified to the point where the government could no longer avoid a debate. The debate was finally held on March 18. The SPD argued that the government must recognize the validity of the principle *Pacta Sunt Servanda*. Because the contracts had been made prior to the NATO resolution, they could not now be retroactively broken. They had been made as part of a compensation agreement involving the import of Soviet pig iron. Because that iron had already been imported and was part of the trade treaty, the German government would be breaking its agreement. In addition, because both Britain and Italy had announced that they would continue to sell large-diameter pipe to the USSR, the opposition argued that the NATO resolution could not have been binding. In this case, why was the German government forcing firms to cancel their orders?[56]

In his reply, Foreign Minister Schroeder tried to argue from an economic point of view, claiming that the contracts were not part of a compensation agreement. However, the crux of his argument was political:

My heart is completely with the iron and steel industry, with full employment and the full utilization of our capacity. . . . But I must choose here between the interests of foreign policy and the interests of the economy. Thank God only in a limited sphere. So I am choosing foreign policy.[57]

The argument for the primacy of foreign policy was not persuasive, and it became clear to the CDU, as the debate wore on, that its coalition partners would desert it and it would not win the debate. The U.S. embassy in Bonn had taken the unusual step of approaching the Free Democrats but had been unable to persuade them. Finally, the CDU resorted to the only tactic it had left. In order to have a vote, a quorum of 250 members of the Bundestag was necessary. The CDU walked out at the end of the debate, leaving only 244 members in the chamber. There could therefore be no vote, and so the embargo ordinance went into force by default.[58]

There was a general outcry within Germany about what the *Economist* termed "parliamentary malarky."[59] The business paper *Handelsblatt* condemned the political implications of this move:

It is a question of the political conduct of the biggest German party that fills the citizens of the republic with displeasure and evokes memories of the last days of the Weimar Republic in which, through similar tricks which the CDU has seized upon, the efficacy of the parties in the Reichstag was impaired.[60]

Even the conservative *Die Welt* condemned the Bundestag vote because it violated the sanctity of contracts and, by applying a law retroactively, impaired the reputation of German business. Most German newspapers, of whatever political hue, were opposed to the imposition of the embargo retroactively. The way in which the embargo was imposed revealed significant evidence about the priorities of the various parties concerned. The CDU – or at least its leaders – failed to support industry, normally its chief ally, because it placed the necessity to show loyalty to the United States above its need to placate its domestic constituency. Many CDU deputies, particularly those representing industry, disagreed with the embargo but consented to the walkout because of party loyalty. The FDP, on the other hand, chose to court the breakdown of the government coalition rather than lose industrial support. The SPD, because it opposed the government, aligned itself with big business, not usually its ally. If one pursues the apparent surface inconsistencies a little further, their logic becomes clearer. The CDU leaders realized that because of their need to prove their loyalty to the United States in the aftermath of the Franco–German treaty, their commitment to industry would have to be subordinated to their overriding NATO obligations. Thus what were perceived as fundamental international necessities took precedence over domestic considerations. As the CDU defined it, the question had less to do with whether large-diameter pipes were a strategic good than with the FRG's international political obligations. Some CDU deputies did not agree with this interpretation and saw the question as fundamentally one of Germany's reliability as an international trade partner of the USSR. There were conflicting perceptions of what was the key concern – international political reliability or international economic reliability.[61]

The SPD's alliance with big business was also not unprecedented. In previous instances, particularly in the late fifties, the SPD had advocated an increase in trade with the USSR because of its economic and political implications. What differentiated the pipe embargo, however, from previous developments was that the SPD was specifically allied with Ruhr steel interests. Of course, part of the issue involved in the pipe debate was the employment of workers in the steel factories, and thus the SPD was defending the interests of the workers as much as those of management. The FDP stand is most interesting. On the one hand, the FDP had consistently advocated more trade with the East. On the other hand, its actions were a rebuff to its coalition partners and it seemed to consider its governmental obligations unimportant. Some observers argued that the FDP had used the pipe debate to create a government crisis, but these rumors disappeared when it soon became clear that there would not be a crisis.[62]

Domestic repercussions of the embargo

The pipe embargo caused considerable controversy within the FRG, among the NATO allies, and between the USSR and the FRG. These tensions had an important effect not only on the development of political and economic interest group coalitions within the FRG but also on attitudes toward the politicization of trade with the USSR. Although the German government complied with the embargo out of political loyalty to the United States, it alienated sectors of its domestic political constituency. Privately, some German officials conceded that increased Soviet mistrust of West Germany as a result of breaking the pipe contracts more than offset any Western strategic advantage from denial of pipe to the Soviets.[63] Thus, the political repercussions of the embargo on Soviet–West German relations were counterproductive for the West Germans because the pipe embargo stiffened Soviet resistance to the new Ostpolitik.

The pipe embargo shows more clearly than any other case the differences between the German government and certain sectors of German business. Although the United States had initiated the embargo, the German government found itself in the position of defending the right to impose the embargo retroactively against the Ruhr firms, which in this case had the support of some CDU members as well as the SPD and FDP. Indeed, the immediate cause of friction between the government and business did not involve questions of the advisability of trading with the USSR but was concerned with the more limited matter of government interference in business. The question was whether the government had the right to forbid businesses to carry out contracts that had already been signed and to which the government had not objected at the time. The Ruhr firms had made a concerted but ultimately unsuccessful attempt to influence the executive. The day before the Bundestag debate, Foreign Minister Schroeder met with representatives of the three firms and tried to persuade them to comply willingly with the embargo in the interests of German security. The day after the debate, Economics Minister Erhard, who was known to have been unhappy about the embargo decision, met with the three firms to tell them that they had been denied export licenses for the steel pipes. He refused to show them the text of the NATO resolution and said that whether all the NATO members had complied was irrelevant. What was important was that the FRG government put its loyalty to NATO above all domestic considerations.[64] Thus, the government and some segments of the business community were in conflict over the question of priorities. The government considered its loyalty to the United States paramount. Business, on the contrary, believed that its contractual obligations to the USSR were more important.

The immediate economic effects of the embargo on the three steel concerns were considerable. They lost almost three hundred thousand tonnes of pipe exports between 1962 and 1963.[65] Mannesmann alone, which had been selling steel pipe to the USSR since 1890, lost $25 million altogether, and its business suffered for some time afterward.[66] As a result of the embargo, the welding capacity at Mannesmann was cut by one-third and at Hoesch by two-thirds. In many ways, the steel workers suffered the most. Phoenix-Rheinrohr had to shut down one special plant as a result of the embargo.[67]

The USSR was Hoesch's most important purchaser of large-diameter steel pipes, and two-thirds of its capacity had been devoted to production for the USSR.[68] In addition, the Russians sued the three firms for breach of contract and the German government denied any responsibility in the suit.[69] There were reports that the firms tried to circumvent the regulation by transshipping pipe to the USSR through Austria and by forming a joint steel export firm with Sweden, which would then ship the pipe to the USSR.[70] However, these attempts were unsuccessful. Despite these deleterious economic consequences, the BDI and the DIHT, continuing their policy of absolute loyalty to the Adenauer regime, failed to mention the pipe embargo in their annual reports on East–West trade in 1963, indicating that they were unwilling to express their opposition to the embargo.[71]

Although the immediate domestic repercussions of the embargo exacerbated conflicts between the German government and business, ultimately they had some utility. Once they had accepted the fact of the embargo, leading sections of the German business community realized that, in order to prevent similar problems in the future, there had to be more coordination between government and business in East–West trade. The industrialists, whatever their particular views, agreed that the government should not interfere again in such a heavyhanded way. "There is no doubt that we will face the government as one man," a leading industrialist said of attempts by the business community to reach some modus vivendi with the government. After some months of delay, Adenauer agreed to meet with representatives of Germany's business community who were involved with trade with the USSR. There were two main issues to be discussed: future coordination between government and business to ensure that there would never again be a retroactive cancellation of orders, and more generally the rationale for pursuing any form of embargo policy toward the USSR.[72]

The long-awaited meeting finally took place in Bonn on July 19, 1963, when Adenauer, Schroeder, Erhard, and Finance Minister Dahlgruen met with eighteen leading businessmen.[73] A few days earlier, in a speech in East Berlin, Khrushchev had proposed greater Soviet–West German economic cooperation, and it was said that the industrialists wanted to discuss with the government specific proposals designed to stimulate trade with the USSR.[74] It was also the first time that the German government had ever met formally with business representatives to discuss the politics of East–West trade. The results, however, were disappointing. The businessmen, who wanted to talk about specific guidelines for future trade, were told by the government that trade with the USSR was "an extremely complicated political problem" that could not be discussed in a general way.[75] The only concession that the government made was to establish a foreign trade advisory committee attached to the Economics Ministry in July 1963. The committee consisted of twenty-six leading industrialists, among them some who were involved in trade with the USSR. However, the main function of this committee was to advise, not to make policy.[76] Thus, the business community failed to receive coherent guidelines about the politics of trade with the USSR from the government. Adenauer was not willing to commit himself to any specific policy or to give businessmen assurances about the future stability of their trade with the East, perhaps because he realized that the ultimate decisions on these questions lay with the United States.

The international repercussions

The pipe embargo not only caused some political strains within Germany but also created a furor among the NATO allies. Although they may have been united in their main political aim of resisting Soviet expansion, NATO members were seriously divided over the issue of trading with the USSR. Great Britain had always taken a more pragmatic attitude toward trading with the Communists because these economic contacts were viewed as having little detrimental political significance. A memorandum by U.S. Ambassador Lewellyn Thompson, specifically refuted the British view:

One argument used by the British that is largely phony is that trade offers an opportunity for contacts and for the development of friendship and understanding. Since the Soviets, however, in general, prevent contacts between their end-users and foreign exporters, and handle trade matters in a few central government offices, this is not, in fact, the case.[77]

The British government did not consider itself bound by the NATO resolution because of the resolution's ambiguous wording. It was a recommendation with which members could choose to comply, but it was not an order with any mandatory force.[78] The British continued to supply large-diameter pipe to the Russians, and the opposition to the embargo inside Germany cited the British example as proof of the German government's perfidy. In addition, the Italians interpreted the embargo as not being applicable retroactively, and they continued to supply steel pipes under contracts that had already been concluded prior to the embargo.[79] The embargo, therefore, caused strains within NATO. Thus a move that was initially intended to have deleterious economic and political effects on the USSR may have had even more disruptive short-term political effects on the Western alliance. East–West trade policy became a source of friction within the Western bloc. The immediate effect of the embargo was to complicate German relations with the USSR. The Russians initially denied that the embargo would affect their pipeline construction. In a press conference on March 14 designed to influence the German Bundestag vote, Yuri Bokserman, deputy chief of the State Committee for Gas Industry, claimed that despite the embargo, Soviet domestic capacity combined with foreign imports would enable the pipelines to be built on schedule.[80] However, Soviet comments immediately after the Bundestag vote belied the Russians' assertion of self-sufficiency.

The Kremlin reacted cautiously to the German decision at first and directed its complaints toward the United States. Khrushchev stressed that the United States was interfering with the relations of the USSR with third countries. The Soviets attributed the U.S. embargo to "American oil monopolies" that were worried about competition. The Soviets concluded:

It is not strategy or security of Western European or other countries but "strategy" and "security" of high profits of the American oil monopolies, their commercial interest . . . that is determining this policy of trade discrimination and limitations which the United States is attempting to impose on other countries.[81]

In response to this attack, the American government claimed that it had always believed that large-diameter pipes were strategic goods, and that the Western European nations had complied with the NATO recommendation because they considered it to be in their own strategic interest.[82]

Despite their initial caution in reacting to the German decision, the Soviets ultimately decided that they would hold the German government responsible, particularly because it was clear that not all NATO nations had complied with the resolution. Describing the German government's move as an "openly hostile act," a Russian note of April 6, 1963 accused Bonn of breaking its contracts with the USSR and reneging on its trade agreement. The action, said the note, was "a contravention of the fundamental principles of international law: the principle of adherence to treaties." The Germans had chosen to follow a U.S. directive motivated by the needs of the oil monopolies, and in breaking their treaty with the USSR, they called into question the most fundamental principles of international relations and trade. The Soviets did not need the pipes but had purchased them in the FRG to promote better contacts. The Russians reserved their right to take any appropriate retaliatory action.[83] The USSR also complained to the Germans that the embargo would have detrimental political consequences, to which the German ambassador replied, "What has the high level of West German trade with the Soviet Union accomplished to date with respect to the solution of our outstanding problems?"[84]

The West German reply was moderate in tone but stressed that the FRG had not reneged on the trade agreement. According to Bonn, the 1960 trade agreement did not guarantee that the FRG would export large-diameter pipes to the USSR, either in the quantity stipulated in the October contracts concluded between the three Ruhr firms and Moscow or as part of a compensation agreement whereby imported Soviet pig iron was specifically to be used for the manufacture of large-diameter pipes. The note denied that the embargo was in any way intended as a hostile act but said that it had been adopted because of Germany's most vital security interests. The decisive factor had been the presence of twenty Soviet divisions in East German territory, for whose supply in the event of war the Soviet network of pipelines was essential. The note then cited Soviet Marshal Sokolovskii's treatise *Voennaia Stragtegiia (Military Strategy)*, which stressed the importance of pipelines for fuel demands in offensive warfare. The note also pointed out that the Russians had not fulfilled their obligations under the 1960 trade treaty, because they had never imported as many consumer goods as they were obliged to under the agreement. It concluded by saying that "German–Soviet trade as a whole has a bright future."[85] The German government wanted to forestall any further deterioration of German–Soviet relations, but it would not admit that it had succumbed to U.S. pressure. Instead, it sought to portray its decision as a sovereign, autonomous act.

In May, the Russians announced the completion of a new pipe-making installation for an oil and gas network in the Ukraine.[86] One of the main economic effects of the embargo on the USSR was to stimulate the development of Soviet productive capacity for large-diameter pipes, although they were of inferior quality compared to German pipe. In 1961, the USSR produced no 40-inch pipes; by 1965, it was producing 600,000 tonnes.[87] The USSR admitted that the embargo had caused "some difficulties for a time,"[88] but by 1965, it was claimed that the USSR was now completely self-sufficient in large-diameter pipes.[89] The USSR stressed the unemployment within Germany resulting from the embargo and the anger of the business community.[90] There was much Soviet interest in the meeting between Adenauer and the industrialists and comment on the frustration of the businessmen.[91] The Soviets, as in previous instances, were stressing their common interests with German industrialists.

The embargo may have had detrimental short-term economic effects on the USSR, but ultimately its effect on the Soviet ability to construct pipelines was marginal because the Russians were able to continue importing pipes from Sweden and Japan. The United States was unable to persuade the Japanese to embargo large-diameter pipe because of the inability of achieving a unanimous vote in CoCom.

Immediately after the embargo, Berthold Beitz, managing director of Krupp, visited Moscow in his capacity both as a businessman and as an unofficial ambassador, and it seemed at the time that the embargo's effects had not been very marked.[92] Khrushchev was reported to have spoken in mild tones about the embargo when he received Beitz at the Kremlin. However, it was apparent that the embargo had had a greater psychological effect than the Russians were initially willing to admit.[93] Beitz's main purpose was to see how Krupp could expand its trade with the USSR and to work out ways of dealing with the difficult payments problem. While he was there, Khrushchev raised the possibility of Germany renewing and expanding its three-year trade agreement with the USSR, which was due to expire in December 1963.[94]

The German question and the fall of Khrushchev

It is impossible to determine the economic and political effects of the pipe embargo without analyzing them in the broader context of German–Soviet relations. Although relations between Bonn and Moscow were adversely affected by the embargo, there were countervailing political developments that mitigated its impact. In 1963 and 1964, there were signs within the Soviet leadership of conflict over policy toward Germany culminating in Khrushchev's projected visit to the FRG, which proved a major catalyst to his ouster. After the end of the Cuban missile crisis and the building of the Berlin Wall, Khrushchev revived his interest in detente.[95] The GDR, even though it continued to experience domestic problems, was more stable with the Berlin Wall in place. Khrushchev apparently decided to pursue a more flexible policy toward West Germany, although he was not supported in this endeavor by most of his colleagues.[96] Indeed, Khrushchev's overtures to the FRG prior to his fall remain one of the more intriguing aspects of his protean foreign policy.

In examining the statistics on Soviet–West German trade, the decisive downturn in the FRG's balance of trade with the USSR came after 1964, leading some to speculate that Khrushchev's fall may have affected German–Soviet economic relations as much as the pipe embargo.[97] The economic signals emanating from Moscow in 1964 were occasionally inconsistent. Despite Khrushchev's interest in renewing the trade agreement in January, the Soviet government sent the Germans an *aide-memoire* saying that it was not interested in negotiating a new trade agreement and that trade between the two countries should continue on the basis of the quotas worked out in the previous agreement, which had expired in December. The quota lists were those of December 1960, because no new lists had been drawn up since then.[98] No reason was given for the Soviet note, and the German government pressed its demand for new trade negotiations in order to work out a more up-to-date trading system. Throughout 1964, the Germans sent notes to the Russians suggesting that trade negotiations begin, and the Russians procrastinated for different reasons.[99] They claimed that the embargo violated the previous trade agreement and emphasized their displeasure by refusing to negotiate another one. The Soviets were always careful to differentiate between businessmen, whom they acknowledged wanted to trade with them, and the German government, which could not be trusted. Indeed, one German commentator suggested that the Russians hoped to induce businessmen to pressure the government to change its trade policy.[100]

Total Soviet–German trade fell from $422.3 million in 1962 to $362.4 million in 1963 (see Table 4), the first time bilateral

FRG–USSR trade had ever decreased in the postwar years. Also, for the first time, Germany had a negative balance of trade with the USSR in 1962, and from 1962 to 1966 its negative balance grew.[101] However, this decrease was caused by factors other than the pipe embargo, particularly the shortage of hard currency in the USSR and West German import restrictions.[102]

Within Germany, however, it was felt that the main reason for the Russian refusal to negotiate another trade agreement was economic. The Soviet economy, some commentators reasoned, was in difficulty, experiencing a falling rate of growth.[103] More specifically, they argued that the Russians could not enter into a trade agreement because they had little to export. Grain had previously been one of their main supplies to the FRG, but because of the agricultural crisis they could no longer export this commodity and were for the first time since 1945 importing grain.[104] Although Moscow was undoubtedly experiencing economic difficulties, at the same time as it rebuffed the Germans it concluded a new trade agreement with France on the basis of seven-year credits, and it was negotiating large credit deals with Britain, Japan, and Italy.[105] Another economic factor here was the German refusal to grant credits to the Soviets. However, there was also the issue of Berlin. The Russians had been embarrassed by the willingness with which the other Eastern European countries had signed trade agreements with the FRG which included West Berlin. Indeed, on two separate occasions, the Kremlin had proposed concluding a trade agreement with West Berlin independently and had issued a special invitation to West Berlin to exhibit at the Moscow Fair.[106] On balance, it seems that the Soviet anger over the pipe embargo, exacerbated by domestic agricultural difficulties and by the issues of credits and Berlin, combined to produce the Soviet rejection of any new trade agreement with the FRG. It is impossible to measure exactly what impact the pipe embargo had on economic relations.

The vacillations over the trade treaty were connected to broader political questions. At the beginning of 1964, there were contradictory signals emanating from the Kremlin indicating possible debates within the leadership about relations with Bonn. In March, there was a harsh exchange of notes in which the Soviets accused the Germans of being set on a "course of revenge."[107] Shortly thereafter, the economic counsellor of the

West German embassy in Moscow was expelled. The public Soviet attacks on the Germans were more vitriolic than previous statements and centered on the issue of a multilateral nuclear force within NATO. The main Soviet preoccupation was to prevent the FRG from obtaining nuclear weapons via the MLF.[108] However, privately, the Soviets began to have secret talks with the Germans in a much more conciliatory vein.[109] While Ambassador Smirnov began to sound out Chancellor Ludwig Erhard privately about a possible meeting with Khrushchev, the USSR finally signed its long-announced twenty-year treaty of friendship, mutual aid, and cooperation with the GDR. However, this treaty, although confirming the integrity of Ulbricht's regime, represented the lowest common denominator of agreement between the two states.[110] It fell far short of conferring the kind of sovereignty on the GDR that it desired because it retained Soviet Four-Power obligations in Berlin.[111] A few days before the signing of the treaty, while Ulbricht was being entertained in Moscow, the Kremlin put out a statement saying that Erhard would be welcome in Moscow too. This was the first public indication of a more conciliatory policy toward Bonn.[112] Erhard then declined to go to Moscow but said that Khrushchev was welcome to come to Bonn for a summit.[113] From June on, Khrushchev seemed to be making a concerted attempt to improve relations with West Germany.

The visit of Khrushchev's son-in-law, Alexei Adzhubei, the influential editor of *Izvestiia*, to the FRG in July was an exploratory foray to discuss the details of a Khrushchev visit. During his twelve-day tour, Adzhubei had a talk with Erhard at which the details of Khrushchev's trip were discussed. It was also reported that he conveyed to Erhard Khrushchev's willingness to sign a trade agreement that included a Berlin clause.[114] In various interviews and articles, Adzhubei made it clear that one reason for Khrushchev's visit was a desire to increase German–Soviet trade and establish economic contacts on a firmer and broader basis.[115] Indeed, German officials, although dubious that any meaningful political developments would emanate from the talks, thought that the future of Soviet–German trade was one of the few areas in which a visit from Khrushchev might produce tangible results.[116] Adzhubei conveyed the message that the Kremlin was now willing to draw up a list of goods for

1965. It was also assumed that the first secretary would press for long-term credits.[117] In August the Volga Germans were rehabilitated – another conciliatory gesture from Moscow.[118]

The German government put out an official announcement in September that Khrushchev was to visit Bonn in December, although this was never mentioned in the Soviet press. Given the fact that Khrushchev's son-in-law was the editor of *Izvestiia*, it is surprising that this was not announced in the Soviet press, indicating some opposition to his trip. The German statement stressed that "in Bonn, the personal meeting between the Soviet and German heads of government is viewed with sober realism. No-one anticipates any fundamental change in German–Soviet relations from the visit."[119] Khrushchev's acceptance of the invitation followed a series of top-level meetings with Eastern European leaders in Prague, where he had discussed West Germany with Czech, Bulgarian, Hungarian, and Polish ministers.[120] The German press was full of articles about exactly when Khrushchev would come to Bonn, until it suddenly became clear that there were complications. On September 6, a German engineer working at the Moscow embassy was attacked with mustard gas while attending a church service. The Germans protested against this attack, and the Russians replied that the technician was a spy.[121] Not wanting to jeopardize Khrushchev's visit, West Germany dispatched another note, and finally the Kremlin sent a conciliatory reply on October 13. A few hours later, Khrushchev was removed from office. His successors, Leonid Brezhnev and Alexei Kosygin, indefinitely postponed the trip.[122]

The bizarre series of events leading to Khrushchev's removal leaves many unanswered and interesting questions about the role of Germany in the fall of the first secretary. It is instructive to inquire, first, what might have been Khrushchev's motives for going to Germany. The Sino–Soviet split may have influenced Khrushchev to mend his fences with the West. In fact, the Chinese had accused Khrushchev of wanting to "sacrifice" the East Germans in a "criminal political deal" with West Germany. Peking claimed that he was going to turn Pankow over to Bonn in return for credits.[123] However, the main reason for Khrushchev's visit probably had more to do with Germany itself than with China. There are two possible explanations for this position. The first, a modest one that seems to have accorded with German perceptions of the summit, was that Khrushchev wanted to discuss the MLF, a source of great concern to Moscow, and other issues, including recognition of East Germany and concluding a new trade and cultural agreement in which West Berlin was included. However, there is also evidence of a second explanation – namely, that Khrushchev was planning to make some major concessions on German reunification and that this was one of the reasons for his downfall. During a visit to Scandinavia prior to his ouster, Khrushchev is reported to have favored a "quick solution" to the German problem.[124] There were some reports that Khrushchev had decided that a reunified, neutralized Germany might be preferable to the current status quo, and he was willing to make radical alterations in Soviet policy toward Germany.[125] Even if this is an exaggeration it seems that Khrushchev's German policy was the occasion of his downfall. The mustard gas attack may have been an independent KGB initiative, but the way in which it was carried out and the Russian response to the German protest suggest that it also could have been a deliberate high-level move by those Politburo members opposed to Khrushchev's softer line on Germany to discredit him. One week before Khrushchev's ouster, Brezhnev, who was instrumental in overthrowing his erstwhile patron, delivered a speech in East Berlin emphasizing that "the Soviet Union has always stood and will also in the future always stand by the side of the GDR."[126] His colleague Mikhail Suslov, who allegedly was Khrushchev's chief denouncer when he was ousted, declared the same week that friendly USSR–GDR relations "are not for sale, even if all the gold in the world were offered for them."[127] That such statements could be made indicates the degree of controversy and disagreement surrounding the issue. The degree of press coverage given to these statements also indicates that by this time Khrushchev may have lost control of the press.

This does not mean that Khrushchev's projected visit to Germany was the most important cause of his fall. Rather, it seems that, although the underlying reasons for discontent with Khrushchev were probably caused by his domestic social and economic policies, his overtures to Germany may well have provided the final straw for his opponents.[128] It is plausible that one of Khrushchev's main motives in coming to Germany was economic – to secure German credits in return for some minor political concessions such as the agreement to include West Berlin in the trade and cultural treaties. However, it seems that economic factors were secondary and that the prime motive was political – to improve relations with West Germany, perhaps at the expense of the GDR. It was well known that Ulbricht disliked Khrushchev and may well have pressured his opponents when he found out about Khrushchev's projected visit.[129] The abortive Khrushchev visit, however, probably does not belong to the "missed opportunities" category. Khrushchev would have been willing to reach a settlement with Bonn only on the basis of a West German acceptance of the postwar status quo. However, the Erhard government was not ready to do this in 1964 and remained committed, in Schroeder's words, to the "positive overcoming of the status quo."[130] Khrushchev's successors had little interest in improving either political or economic relations with the FRG, and the German problem remained unsolved. In 1964, any suggestion in the Soviet Union of a new approach to the German question other than on the basis of the current status quo was considered illegitimate.

The wheat deal

At the very end of Adenauer's tenure in office, a controversy arose that illustrated the chancellor's attitude toward the relationship between trade and politics and also showed how dependent Germany was on the United States for the definition of its concept of economic relations with the USSR. The wheat sale demonstrates the opposite of the pipe embargo, in that it was Adenauer who tried to impose a wheat embargo and the United States that overruled him. The wheat sale reinforced the fact that the United States was setting the East–West trade agenda.

A series of disastrous harvests, combined with Khrushchev's unsuccessful virgin lands scheme, forced the Russians to import wheat in large quantities in 1963. The Russians purchased eight and a half million tonnes of wheat from Australia and Canada.[131] The United States also agreed to sell wheat to the USSR in a decision that, at first glance, seems to represent a *volte face* in the American attitude toward trade with the East. There

is much evidence that, in the last few months of his administration, President Kennedy was considering significant modifications in the U.S. trade policy toward the East and was reexam-
ining the value of the strategic embargo controls. A few months
after the pipe embargo, a State Department memorandum suggested that "in dealing with the USSR, increased trade might
be included as a U.S. concession in a detente package."[132] Walt
Rostow, although admitting that "we cannot use trade to wring
basic concessions from the Soviets," advocated the use of trade
as a "lever with limited political goals."[133] Other government
officials suggested that

it would appear certain that a [wheat] sale by the U.S. would be advantageous to U.S. foreign policy interests. It would advertise the superiority of our agricultural system over the communist system in a most
dramatic fashion – it would be a further step toward reduction of
East–West tensions.[134]

Whereas the issue of pipelines was considered important
enough to use trade denial, the Kennedy administration believed that the disastrous Soviet grain harvest offered the United
States the opportunity to use positive economic levers in pursuit
of detente. A National Security Council meeting concluded that
"the purchase of U.S. wheat diverts Soviet resources from arms
to food."[135] A CIA report argued that one reason not to sell
wheat to the USSR was "the probable repercussions in Western
Europe, specifically Germany and France, where critics of the
U.S. are bound to point to the transaction as proof of a major
turn in U.S. policy."[136]

Despite these arguments, President Kennedy announced on
October 9 that the United States would sell 500,000 tonnes
of wheat to the USSR for gold and cash. He saw this as the
beginning of a policy of utilizing East–West trade to improve
East–West relations.[137] In a letter to Senator Mansfield one week
before his assassination, the president urged that the Senate
should permit the use of credit guarantees for trade to the
communist countries for the sake of the "American farmer, the
American exporter, the American citizen concerned with the
strength of our balance of payments position."[138]

The Soviets had also contracted to buy 300,000 tonnes of
wheat from Germany, 35,000 of which had received authorization.[139] The wheat sale would probably have continued out of
the public eye had the chancellor not intervened and invested

this commercial deal with great political significance. This last episode in Adenauer's career as chancellor is illustrative of his outlook on *Osthandel*. On hearing about the prospective wheat sale, Adenauer made a series of speeches throughout the country condemning it. In one speech, he said:

All Western countries which are now ready to help Soviet Russia to really become a dangerous enemy are making a serious mistake. Shall we demand that first the Russians demonstrate by acts their desire for peace, before the question of such assistance is even raised? To ask such a question is to answer it.[140]

In a speech in Munich, warning that "only the stupidest calves choose their own butcher," he termed the USSR's purchases of wheat "a political event of the greatest importance," because it gave the West an opportunity to influence Soviet policies. He elaborated on this theme more specifically in Berlin a week before his retirement. Grain should be delivered to the USSR, he asserted, only if Russia was willing to pay a political price – the destruction of the Berlin Wall.[141] Declaring that "I can't stand any more of this wretched talk of detente," Adenauer, in his denunciation of the wheat sales, probably made the most explicit linkage between politics and trade that he had ever made.[142] He was demanding fundamental and massive political concessions from the USSR, involving a complete change in its German policy, in exchange for 300,000 tonnes or $18,000,000 in wheat. There were considerable discrepancies between the means and the end.

The tables were turned on Adenauer in the wheat embargo, as opposed to the pipe embargo. In response to Adenauer's criticism of America for selling wheat to the USSR, Senator Mansfield retorted: "If we did need objective advice from abroad it would hardly come from West Germany. For there is in this comment of the Chancellor something of a hypocritical preachment: 'Do as I say but not as I do.' "[143] Mansfield's last sentence referred to Germany's $350 million trade with the USSR in 1961. One might argue that whereas the United States considered pipes to be strategic material, it considered grain to be strictly commercial and therefore resented the FRG's attempts to interfere with its freedom to export. On the other hand, one could equally argue that in the pipe embargo, a threat to the interests of the large oil companies was involved, but in the wheat deal, the United States grain exporters stood only to profit from exports to the USSR. Certainly, the American viewpoint was supported not only by the opposition within the FRG but also by most other members of the government. For instance, Foreign Minister Schroeder said it was unrealistic to believe that Soviet policy could be influenced by wheat flour. "If it is necessary, they will pull their belts tighter, but their policy will not change."[144] Schroeder's position had the support of the FDP and the SPD. Those CDU members who were connected with industry opposed Adenauer's stand and pointed out that the wheat sale was being conducted within the framework of the existing treaty, and an embargo on wheat would contravene the treaty. The FDP argued that it would be futile for the FRG to wage a "private economic war" against the USSR, and the SPD termed Adenauer's call for a wheat embargo "the senseless plan of an old man."[145] All those opposed to Adenauer considered that the gains involved in following a policy of tying wheat exports to specific political concessions would be minimal, but the risks resulting from such a policy might be great.

In order not to make Adenauer's last days in office more problematic, the German cabinet decided to refer the matter of wheat exports to the NATO council, in the hope that that body might issue clearer guidelines on trade policy with the East. On October 9, the United States government gave permission for wheat to be exported to the USSR.[146] On October 28, the new chancellor, Erhard, granted the export licenses for the sale of German wheat to the USSR. The United States lead had been decisive in the German decision. In his interview on *Face the Nation* shortly after becoming chancellor, Erhard said that he thought the possibilities for expanding trade with the East were very limited because the Russians had many demands but little to supply.[147] However, in his first press conference, he reiterated the Schroeder line of improving relations with Eastern Europe by setting up trade missions.[148] Erhard, even if he had doubts about the economic attractiveness of trade with the USSR, held different views on the degree to which it should be politicized.

The political economy of the pipe embargo

The pipe embargo was a quintessential example of negative economic linkage. The United States used a specific economic lever –

trade denial – because it disapproved of Soviet foreign policy. The Soviets did not respond because this was an asymmetrical linkage situation in which no concessions were demanded. In terms of the outcome – desired and actual – of the embargo, the results were mixed. If its purpose was to delay the completion of the Friendship Pipeline, it was only marginally and temporarily successful, because the USSR continued to import pipes from Britain, Sweden, and Japan and improved its domestic pipe-producing capacity. The embargo did not prevent the USSR from increasing its sales of oil to Europe. If its purpose was to reimpose United States control over its allies' policy on East–West trade, then it was only partly successful. The FRG complied, but Britain defied Washington. Nevertheless, the wheat deal shows that the United States did have an important role in designing the regime for East–West trade. Once America approved of a sale to the USSR, it was hard for any NATO member not to comply. The more politically dependent a country was on the United States – and surely West Germany was more directly dependent on the United States for its security than any other NATO member – the more it had to follow U.S. guidelines on East–West trade.

If we examine the political and economic stakes involved in the pipe embargo, it appears that, for the United States, the political goals were not core values. Although the embargo was directed at containing Soviet strength and reinforcing the NATO alliance, neither the building of the Friendship Pipeline nor Britain's nonadherence to the embargo threatened U.S. security. Likewise, for the USSR, although pipe was an important commodity, the embargo did not threaten Soviet economic security. However, for the FRG, the stakes in complying with the embargo were somewhat higher. The real political issue for Adenauer was loyalty to the United States, a core political goal, because only the United States could guarantee Germany's security and territorial integrity. By contrast, the perceived need to prevent the building of the Friendship Pipeline was only a secondary goal.

It is difficult to detect any gains to the West from this use of negative economic levers. The chief result was a general irritation both in East–West relations and in relations between the United States and its allies. Indeed, one could argue that the pipe embargo caused more damage to U.S.–European relations than to the Soviet economy. The United States belatedly realized that a total trade embargo against the USSR diminished its ability to utilize bargaining levers in negotiating with its adversary – hence the decision to sell wheat to the USSR as a positive lever. The pipe embargo indicated the futility of using negative linkage strategies.

6

The failure of linkage: 1964–1968

We are seriously interested in the intellectual discussions that are taking place in the Eastern bloc at this moment . . . Perhaps economic relations will later bring us close together. We shall continuously and carefully explore all the possibilities open to us.

Gerhard Schroeder, 1963[1]

The facts prove the connection between Bonn's "Ostpolitik," on the one hand, and its neocolonialist policy on the other hand. Although each foreign policy line of the FRG has its own problems, altogether they combine to form the aggressive course of German militarists, whose central role focuses on the fight against the European socialist countries.

M. Voslenskii, 1967[2]

The pipe embargo marked the end of an era for Bonn. It was one of the last explicit uses of negative economic leverage by Adenauer, whose "policy of strength" had achieved no concessions from the Russians on the central issues of reunification, Berlin, or the restoration of the prewar German eastern territories. The next two CDU chancellors and their foreign ministers pursued a somewhat more flexible Ostpolitik. The Erhard–Schroeder and later the Kiesinger–Brandt Ostpolitik eschewed the "Moscow-first" basis of Adenauer's Ostpolitik and sought to develop bilateral ties with Eastern Europe without granting diplomatic recognition. This German version of bridge building was based on two assumptions. The first was that the West German economy was bound in the long run to acquire a power and momentum that the countries of Eastern Europe would not be able to withstand. The second was that the FRG's negotiating position and its ability to exert influence were likely to increase with the spread of polycentrism in Eastern Europe.[3] Under the Grand Coalition (1966–69) there was a further modification in

127

policy when CDU Chancellor Kiesinger and SPD Foreign Minister Brandt realized that the Hallstein Doctrine limited their ability to adopt a more assertive policy toward Eastern Europe. Abandoning the Hallstein Doctrine, the Grand Coalition substituted for it the *Geburtsfehlertheorie* (birth defect theory). This stated that the Eastern European countries had never had any choice but to follow Moscow's orders when they recognized the GDR and withheld recognition from the FRG.

This eschewing of the Hallstein Doctrine meant that the FRG would contemplate diplomatic relations with all East European states except the GDR. This Ostpolitik did not ratify the status quo in Europe and was therefore unacceptable to the Kremlin. From the Soviet point of view, therefore, the more flexible Ostpolitik had to be resisted because of its destabilizing implications for the GDR and Eastern Europe. Moscow's policy toward Germany had three main goals: recognition of the two German states, signature of a peace treaty between the two states, and the independence of West Berlin. The new Brezhnev–Kosygin leadership in the USSR eschewed Khrushchev's innovative German policy and assumed a more intransigent stance toward the FRG until the issue of its role in Eastern Europe was resolved by the Czech invasion. In many ways German–Soviet relations became a dialogue of the deaf, with neither side willing to accept the other's preconditions for negotiations.

There were few negotiations in this era in which linkage was explicitly used. However, there were certain questions that dominated economic relations and facilitated diverse types of politicization. One was the question of renewal of the trade agreement, with its central political and economic problems – the status of Berlin and German import policies. Another closely connected problem was the unresolved issue of financing Soviet trade and the German unwillingness to grant credits. Both politically and economically, Soviet–West German relations had reached an impasse by the fall of 1968.

The Soviet–West German thaw freezes over, 1964–68

Chancellor Erhard attempted to maintain the perceptibly more cordial relations with the USSR that had been established in the last few months of Khrushchev's leadership after the "harebrained" first secretary had been removed. He immediately extended an invitation to visit the FRG to the new Soviet leaders and repeated Germany's desire to seek more fruitful relations with the Kremlin.[4] Although the main focus of West Germany's Ostpolitik under Erhard and Schroeder was Eastern Europe, Germany did not overlook the fact that in order to improve its relations with Eastern Europe it would also have to extend some feelers toward the USSR.[5] Germany appointed a new ambassador to Moscow who had better connections with the USSR and was expected to improve contacts, whereas the Russians appointed a new ambassador to Bonn who was less familiar with German politics.[6] Despite the Erhard government's overtures towards the USSR, Germany's basic policies toward Moscow remained unchanged. Reunification was still the declaratory goal, as Foreign Minister Schroeder reiterated:

From time to time it is suggested that we regard German reunification less as a basic requirement of our policy than as an historical process which should be left to the healing hand of time. This view seems to me unrealistic. Such a policy of resignation would dash the hopes of Germans living on the other side of the Iron Curtain; would help to consolidate the unnatural and unjust partition of our country without bringing peace and security to Europe; and would perpetuate a dangerous source of tension in Europe indefinitely.[7]

The Soviet response to the first German initiatives following Khrushchev's fall was reserved. The new leaders appeared not to favor any substantial change in their relations with Bonn, reinforcing the impression that Khrushchev's overtures had not enjoyed the support of his colleagues. In 1965, the Russians and East Germans stepped up their harassment of Western land and air communications with West Berlin, and this harder stance continued into 1966.[8] At the same time, the Russians began to develop the theory of a special "Bonn–Washington axis" within NATO, indicating that there were interests in common between the two countries that were injurious to those of the other members of NATO, thus seeking to exploit polycentrism within the Western alliance.[9] Soviet commentators denied that Erhard's policies were any different from those of his predecessor: "Talk of a 'new era,' a 'new Eastern Policy,' 'middle-of-the-road policy' and 'mutual understanding' which was in vogue – was apparently just so much phrase-mongering. Bonn rolls along the old tracks laid by Adenauer, without noticing the tracks have rusted."[10]

The West Germans, in the Soviet view, were as "revanchist" as before, and those hints of greater flexibility that had seeped into Soviet comments prior to Khrushchev's fall disappeared from the pages of *Pravda* as Soviet policy hardened.

There are various possible explanations for the tougher Soviet line. After Khrushchev's fall, his successors reverted to a more cautious foreign policy, whose aim was to consolidate Soviet influence rather than to expand and innovate. On the one hand, Khrushchev's policy of a rapprochement was unacceptable to the new Soviet leadership, perhaps because uncompromising hostility toward the FRG had for so long been one of the linchpins of Soviet foreign policy. It also served as the chief rationale for maintaining discipline in the Warsaw Pact. Ulbricht also influenced the hardening of Soviet policy because he could ultimately threaten the USSR with the possible disintegration of the GDR were there to be a rapprochement between Moscow and Bonn. Moreover, Polish leader Gomulka, also because of the tenuous legitimacy of his own regime, was a hard-liner on the German issue. It appears that the flexibility of the last few months prior to Khrushchev's fall had been an aberration and that the Brezhnev–Kosygin policy was a more predictable continuation of the traditional postwar Soviet stance toward the FRG. It is also conceivable that Soviet tactics altered because of the changed environment. In the period when the multilateral force had been a viable possibility, it had been in the Soviet interest to woo Bonn away from Washington, because Moscow feared that the MLF might entail an eventual acquisition of nuclear weapons by the Bundeswehr. Once the MLF plan was dropped late in 1964, the Soviets did not have to concern themselves with this issue. In the absence of any overriding need to court the Germans, the USSR reverted to its previous familiar antagonism toward the FRG.[11]

Soviet policy toward the FRG was more clearly spelled out in a series of exchanges with Bonn on the subject of the renunciation of force. In 1966, the FRG government, in what was publicized as a major foreign policy initiative, sent a "Peace Note" to all governments with which it had diplomatic relations. Asserting that "the German people desire to live on good terms with all, including their East European neighbors," the note offered what amounted to a series of nonaggression pacts with all countries that wished to enter into negotiations with Bonn.[12] The note included the first formal declaration that the Munich agreement was no longer valid. However, Bonn still claimed that the 1937 boundaries were the FRG's lawful ones, thus refusing to recognize the postwar status quo. The note was a belated German reply to the Rapacki Plan, and it offered to all East European states (apart from the GDR) the opportunity to conclude the renunciation of force agreements with the FRG. This West German initiative was undoubtedly intended to reduce the climate of hostility in Europe without changing the FRG position on the Oder–Neisse line or on recognition of the GDR.

The immediate Soviet response was to denounce the German note as "a gross attempt at propaganda" because Bonn's intentions were anything but peaceful. At the Twenty-third Party Congress, Brezhnev attacked West Germany in traditional Soviet phraseology, saying that the note showed that "the FRG intends to continue its aggressive and revenge-seeking policy."[13] Brezhnev attributed the initiative for the peace note to the United States, whereas later Soviet analyses claimed that it was a response to the frustration of realizing that the United States would not support any new initiative on the German question.[14] Whereas the East European replies to the Bonn note were less than hostile, the Soviet reply was uncompromising in its critique of German policies. Unless Germany changed its position on its boundaries and recognition of the GDR, there could be no renunciation of force.[15] There were other attempts within Germany to move on the Ostpolitik front. The SPD, responding to an East German initiative, attempted to arrange an "exchange of speakers" series of meetings with the ruling East German Socialist Unity Party (SED). However, this failed when the GDR, perhaps under pressure from the Kremlin, called the project off after the SPD's Dortmund Party Conference.[16] In 1966, therefore, Germany's attempts to extract itself from the *immobilisme* of its policy toward the USSR were thwarted by the Soviet insistence on a prior ratification of the status quo.

Whereas Soviet policy continued to criticize West Germany, domestic political developments within the FRG led to a change in government and in Ostpolitik. Erhard's cabinet resigned and the Grand Coalition was formed. With CDU Chancellor Kurt Georg Kiesinger at its head, the Grand Coalition gave the SPD its first role in government and the FDP left office. The crucial appointment was Willy Brandt, who became foreign minister and began to formulate a new Ostpolitik, one of *geregeltes Nebeneinander* (regulated coexistence), attempting to seek a more viable relationship with East Berlin and Moscow while at the same time courting Eastern Europe and trying to ameliorate the situation within the GDR. The SPD had always taken a more flexible attitude toward Eastern Europe than had the CDU. The essence of the SPD policy was *"Wandel durch Annäherung"* (change through rapprochement), whose main theoretician was Brandt's press chief, Egon Bahr. Enunciated by Bahr in 1963, this policy called for more compromises with the USSR and the GDR as a precondition for long-term change and eventual reunification.[17]

In his first major speech, Kiesinger reiterated his government's desire for eventual reunification but said that Germany would be willing to establish diplomatic relations with Eastern European states (although not with the GDR).[18] The Hallstein Doctrine was finally abandoned when, in the first and only major success of the new Ostpolitik, Bucharest and Bonn established relations in January 1967, much to Moscow's dismay.[19] In December 1967, Belgrade and Bonn reestablished relations.

The establishment of diplomatic relations between the FRG and Rumania represented the first major breach in East European solidarity on the German problem and was a significant setback for Moscow. The USSR's response to this success of the new Ostpolitik was to tighten cohesion within the Warsaw Pact. At the Twenty-third Party Congress, Brezhnev revived the concept of a European Security Conference, which had first been advocated by the Russians in 1954. The Soviet plan was formalized in a declaration issued by the Political Consultative Committee of the Warsaw Pact in Bucharest, appealing for a European Security Conference in June 1966, and was reiterated at the Karlovy Vary meeting of the European Communist parties in April 1967, although the latter appeal was more defensive than the former.[20] By utilizing this approach, the Russians could maintain their position that a European peace was desirable. The Karlovy Vary Conference was partly convened as a response to the new Ostpolitik, and Rumania and Yugoslavia refused to attend. The Karlovy Vary meeting issued a statement implying that no other member of the Warsaw Pact would establish diplomatic relations with the FRG until the GDR was officially recognized.[21]

Foreign Minister Brandt's main initiative toward the USSR was to begin discussions on the renunciation of force similar to the proposals that Germany had made in the 1966 Peace Note. The discussions seemed to be making progress when the Kremlin upped the ante and demanded a complete severance of Bonn's ties with Berlin as a precondition for a renunciation of force agreement.[22] Moscow was sufficiently disturbed by the destabilizing effects of Germany's overtures to Eastern Europe that it saw no advantage in improving relations with West Germany. Between January 1967 and the Soviet invasion of Czechoslovakia, the FRG tried to maintain a precarious balance between courting Eastern Europe and seeking a genuine reduction of tensions with Moscow. Its many offers to negotiate were ultimately rebuffed, and it was only after the invasion of Czechoslovakia that Bonn and Moscow were able to resume a more productive bilateral dialogue.[23] The renunciation of force talks failed because Germany would not depart from its traditional position on the need for German reunification and the nonrecognition of the GDR. Bonn conceived the renunciation of force agreement as a means of reducing tension while keeping open the status quo. Moscow, however, wanted to use these talks as a means of securing German recognition of the status quo.[24] Willy Brandt, in a *Foreign Affairs* article of 1968, claimed that Germany's position on reunification had changed. It was now prepared to wait until after a general settlement instead of making reunification a precondition for a treaty with the USSR. He also intimated that there would be compromises on the question of the Oder–Neisse boundary and the role of the Russians in West Berlin. However, the Soviets chose not to interpret these sentiments as representing any genuine departure from the policies of Adenauer.[25]

Throughout 1967 and 1968, Moscow repeated the same theme: The FRG was dominated by monopoly capitalists whose ideology was revanchism and militarism.[26] Kiesinger's Ostpolitik was no different from that of his predecessors,[27] and a new theme was added: The rise of the NPD (Neo-Nazi Party) showed that Nazism was once again a real danger in the FRG. In 1966 and 1967, the NPD won more than 8 percent of the vote in local elections and seats in the Landtage.[28] While the Russians were taking this uncompromising stand toward the FRG, events in Czechoslovakia were preoccupying the Kremlin, and the Sino-Soviet split increased the possibilities of polycentrism.

In the months preceding the invasion of Czechoslovakia, the Soviets pursued a dual policy toward West Germany. On the one hand, they established a common front with the GDR and Poland to counter Bonn's overtures to Eastern Europe. On the other hand, the USSR also pursued a bilateral policy of seeking to preempt the West German Ostpolitik by entering into renunciation of force talks.[29] In a speech to the Supreme Soviet in June 1968, Foreign Minister Gromyko, while criticizing Bonn's Ostpolitik, reiterated the Soviet willingness to discuss renunciation of force.[30]

Soviet-West German relations deteriorated in the months preceding the Warsaw Pact invasion of Czechoslovakia. Immediately after the invasion, the USSR cited West German activities in Czechoslovakia as one of the main reasons behind the Czech appeal for Soviet "fraternal assistance."[31] Although this explanation for the invasion was undoubtedly an ex post facto rationalization of actions determined largely by the internal situation in Czechoslovakia, there was a series of developments in FRG-Czech relations under the Dubcek government that were perceived as a threat to the stability of the Warsaw Pact and a challenge to Moscow's vital interests. Political relations between the two countries began to improve, with high-level visits by West German politicians to Prague. In their Action Program of April 1968, the Czech reformers took a more flexible stand on the FRG, supporting improved relations with "realistic" forces within West Germany. Nevertheless, both Kiesinger and Brandt were careful to avoid the impression of being too enthusiastic about developments in Prague.[32] In the aftermath of the invasion, the USSR claimed that it had the right, under articles 53 and 107 of the UN Charter, to invade West Germany should it deem it necessary for its security.[33] The West Germans strongly contested this allegation, but nevertheless it was a sober reminder of the FRG's vulnerability in Europe.[34] The Dubcek regime, the Soviet argument went, was encouraged by the FRG to break away from the USSR and join the revanchist Bonn drive.[35] This was particularly serious because Czechoslovakia was a vital "Northern Tier" state, a buffer between the FRG and the rest of Eastern Europe. Moreover, it was the only socialist state bordering the West without Soviet troops and therefore was solely responsible for its defense. Any defection of Czechoslovakia would have split the Warsaw Pact in two, although Dubcek, unlike Nagy in 1956, never tried to leave the Warsaw Pact. There is, needless to say, little evidence that the Germans were trying to wrest Czechoslovakia away from the Soviet bloc, although there were certain economic contacts that might have caused some anxiety to the USSR.

Not only were political developments perceived to threaten Moscow's interests; economic contacts between Bonn and Prague intensified during this period, leading to later Soviet charges of West German economic "penetration" of Czechoslovakia. The FRG and Czechoslovakia had finally signed a trade agreement in August 1967, after previous impasses over the inclusion of a Berlin clause. An important aspect of economic reform under Dubcek was a more flexible foreign trade policy and the search for more Western credits to improve the performance of the ailing Czech economy. In June 1968 various West German banks conducted talks about credits with Czech officials. In July, the president of the Federal Bank (Bundesbank), Blessing, ignoring Chancellor Kiesinger's advice, went to Prague and discussed the possibility of a $500 million loan to Czechoslovakia.[36] In retrospect, the nature and extent of German–Czech economic contacts do not appear to have posed any real threat of Czech economic dependence on the FRG; however, the active economic dialogue between the two countries was a further proof to Moscow of the dangerous effects of the new Ostpolitik.

The real motivation behind the Soviet invasion of Czechoslovakia had more to do with domestic developments within Czechoslovakia and with their implications for Eastern Europe. The USSR feared a loss of control over Czechoslovakia. Moreover, the potential attraction of the Czech liberalization movement and its model of Czech socialism threatened to destabilize not only the GDR and Poland but also the Soviet Ukraine, and ultimately to undermine Soviet hegemony in Eastern Europe. The Russians were terrified of losing control over Czech party cadres and the German threat was a convenient justification, although it did not provide the main Soviet explanation for the invasion.[37] Nevertheless, although the accusations against Germany were only an excuse, the Soviet invasion of Czechoslovakia was a substantial defeat for the Ostpolitik that Bonn had been pursuing since 1963. West Germany's overtures toward Czechoslovakia and the rest of Eastern Europe prompted Moscow to reassert its control over its sphere of influence. Bridge building in Eastern Europe had backfired on Germany. Ironically there is a sense in which the more flexible Kiesinger–Brandt Ostpolitik did influence Czech developments. It was not the threat of German revanchism but exactly the opposite – the German desire for rapprochement with Eastern Europe – that provided the less threatening international environment in which the Dubeck reform movement could flourish. It would have been more difficult for the Czech intelligentsia to embark on a reform program faced with an implacably hostile West German policy. The Soviet disquiet with the Prague spring was reinforced by constant pressure from East Berlin to adopt a harsher policy toward Bonn. Ultimately, although the invasion was a reflection of Moscow's weak position in Eastern Europe, it facilitated the creation of a stable environment in which the Kremlin would move toward rapprochement with Bonn.[38]

It was evident by the fall of 1968 that Bonn's Ostpolitik had ended in a cul-de-sac. During the years 1964–68, Bonn also unsuccessfully attempted to use the promise of economic benefits to wrest certain political concessions from the Russians.

Soviet–West German economic relations

Between 1963 and 1966, Germany's trade position vis-à-vis the USSR worsened (see Table 4). Although Germany remained the biggest NATO trader with Eastern Europe as a whole, it lost position in terms of its total share in the Soviet market (see Table 5). The most striking feature in this period was Germany's growing negative balance of trade with the USSR. Whereas in 1961 it had had a positive balance with the USSR, its negative balance grew steadily until 1966, and only in 1969 did its exports to the USSR exceed its imports from Russia (see Table 4). Machinery and ships remained the most important German exports to the

Table 4. *West German trade with the USSR, 1961–9 (in millions of US dollars)*

	Imports cif	Exports fob	Total	Balance
1961	142.9	204.0	346.9	+ 61.1
1962	186.8	206.8	393.6	+ 20.0
1963	163.7	153.6	317.3	− 10.1
1964	170.4	193.6	364.0	+ 23.2
1965	210.5	146.5	357.0	− 64.0
1966	245.3	135.3	380.6	− 110.0
1967	264.8	198.0	462.8	− 66.8
1968	292.3	273.4	565.7	− 18.9
1969	334.2	405.7	739.9	+ 71.5

Source: United Nations, *Yearbook of International Trade Statistics* (New York, 1963, 1969).

USSR, whereas petroleum products and wood products were the largest Soviet exports.[39]

The reasons for this pattern of trade were both political and economic. The pipe embargo and the lack of a trade agreement were factors hindering the development of German–Soviet trade. Domestic Soviet economic difficulties also had their effects. After the disastrous harvest of 1963, the USSR found it more difficult to pay for Western imports.[40] One reason other Western countries were able to increase their trade with the USSR at the expense of the FRG was that they offered more favorable credit terms (see Table 6). The Soviets were changing their import pattern and emphasizing the purchase of entire production plants on long-term credits from the West.

One of the most significant determinants of Soviet foreign trade in the period following 1963 was the Russian need to accumulate hard currency after spending a large proportion of their hard currency on the purchases of wheat. To counter the deficit, the Soviets took a series of steps to increase exports and decrease imports, selling large amounts of gold as a subsidiary measure. The Russians increased their sales of petroleum, and the pattern of their imports changed. After 1966, when the need to buy wheat diminished, machinery imports, which had fallen

Table 5. *FRG–Soviet trade as a percentage of total Soviet trade, 1958–68*

	Total foreign trade (million rubles)	Trade with the FRG (million rubles)	% of trade
1958	7,782.4	124.0	1.59
1959	9,462.6	188.4	1.99
1960	10,071.1	286.2	2.84
1961	10,643.3	268.3	2.52
1962	12,136.1	304.9	2.51
1963	12,898.1	252.1	1.95
1964	13,876.2	290.0	2.08
1965	14,609.7	248.5	1.70
1966	15,078.6	292.3	1.93
1967	16,370.1	319.1	1.95
1968	18,039.9	393.9	2.18

Source: Roger A. Clarke, *Soviet Economic Facts, 1917–1970,* pp. 44–5 (London: Macmillan, 1972).

since 1962, began to increase.[41] At the Twenty-third Party Congress, Kosygin called for "a reappraisal of the role of foreign trade," and there was an obvious concern to increase its effectiveness.[42]

In September 1965, the USSR introduced a series of economic reforms that Kosygin announced at a Central Committee Plenum in 1965.[43] Based on the theories of economist Evsei Liberman, they sought to modify the innovation-averse, overly centralized Stalinist economic system, in which performance was judged by the ability to fulfill quantitative output targets, and the erratic Khrushchev system of *Sovnarkhozy* (regional economic councils). Profit and quality were now to form part of the criteria for judging performance, and although more authority was placed in the hands of central ministries in Moscow, there was an attempt to decentralize and encourage more initiative at local management levels. Less far-reaching than similar economic reforms introduced in other East European countries, these reforms were never widely implemented in the USSR. Moreover, despite their flexible nature, these Kosygin reforms did not go far enough in encouraging viable decentralization and more innovation.[44]

Table 6. *Soviet trade with the FRG compared to Soviet trade with other Western countries (in millions of rubles)*

	1960	1961	1962	1963	1964	1965	1966	1967	1968
West Germany	286.2	268.3	304.9	252.1	290.0	248.5	292.3	319.1	393.9
Great Britain	270.5	319.5	296.6	310.4	307.6	398.8	449.0	450.5	575.7
France	183.3	179.9	214.6	157.0	157.6	202.4	261.4	299.6	388.4
Italy	173.7	203.6	207.0	245.5	209.5	224.7	225.5	348.3	396.5
Finland	264.1	251.0	355.9	384.5	349.6	408.3	426.7	461.9	458.9
Japan	123.9	161.6	232.9	260.4	322.1	326.1	416.6	466.8	518.6
U.S.	76.1	67.5	40.0	47.4	164.3	89.2	99.0	91.7	89.5
Canada	13.7	45.3	4.7	160.4	296.5	240.0	324.8	147.0	131.2
Australia	31.6	26.6	27.1	53.6	123.3	92.1	35.2	18.6	36.9

Source: *Vneshniaia Torgovlia SSSR za 1961–1968 god* (Moscow: Izdatel'stvo Statistika: 1964, 1967, 1969).

Whereas in the other Eastern European countries the economic reforms of the 1960s had considerable impact on the conduct of foreign trade, the Soviet economic reforms appear to have had little influence in the foreign trade sector, which remained highly centralized.[45] Despite the Soviet leaders' obvious reluctance to permit decentralization of the foreign trade sector, or to introduce a more flexible price structure in foreign trade, the concern to improve foreign trade performance was evident at the Twenty-third Party Congress. Kosygin said:

In the past five years, foreign trade has helped us to solve a number of important national-economic tasks. However, we are not yet making adequate use of the possibilities offered us by the development of foreign economic relations.

The time has come to evaluate the role of foreign trade in a somewhat different way. Workers in the foreign trade organizations frequently shut themselves up in their own sphere, failing to give sufficient consideration to the fact that their entire activity should be subordinated to the task of raising the effectiveness of the national economy as a whole... [W]orkers in industry often regard foreign trade as something secondary. This totally incorrect view must be changed, and businesslike contacts between industry and foreign trade must be strengthened.[46]

Although the Soviet Union continued to exchange raw materials for the products of Western technology, Soviet writers stressed the USSR's potential as an exporter of high-quality industrial goods. However, throughout this period the pattern of trade with the West reflected little Soviet success in selling more finished goods to the advanced capitalist countries.[47]

In their comments on trade with the FRG – which were relatively scarce in this period – Soviet writers emphasized their willingness to increase trade with the FRG but pointed out that "trade relations [between the USSR and the FRG] are characterized by complications and tensions connected with the discriminatory policies implemented by the West German government."[48] Russian authors also continued to distinguish between the German government, which followed the U.S. lead in imposing the strategic embargo, and the German business community, which favored more trade with the USSR. Indeed, one scholar claimed that the Ostpolitik under the Grand Coalition was primarily an economic search for new markets.[49]

The position of the West German government on trade with the USSR in this period remained somewhat inflexible. Al-

though the Schroeder policy of offering economic incentives to
Eastern Europe in return for a loosening of the ties that held the
Soviet bloc together continued, German economic policy toward
the USSR remained more rigid. The Federal government maintained that it would do nothing further to discourage trade with
the USSR, but on the other hand, it would do nothing to alleviate the competitive disadvantages from which German industry suffered in its trade with the USSR. The perceived need
to heed U.S. policy in the area of East–West trade was still one of
the most significant determinants of German economic relations
with the USSR. However, it was West Germany that insisted
that the pipe embargo be lifted in November 1966. Only after
NATO had formally lifted the embargo did the FRG permit its
firms to sell pipe to the USSR. The furthest that the FRG was
prepared to go was to pressure the United States to modify its
policies so that Germany could follow suit.[50]

Certain sections of the German business community, however,
continued to decry the government's restrictive policies on
Soviet trade. Indeed, in this period, business opposition to the
government's policies grew more vociferous and organized itself
around certain concrete issues that gave the opposition a more
coherent focal point. The Ostausschuss and prominent businessmen such as Krupp Managing Director Berthold Beitz acted
as coordinators between government and industry to some degree, yet ultimately the Ostausschuss represented the interests of
business rather than government. Most large steel, chemical,
and shipbuilding concerns continued to lobby for increased
trade with the USSR. Krupp, which had built numerous chemical factories in the USSR, became the first Western firm to have
its own permanent representative in Moscow, although two
years later the bureau was closed amidst increased Soviet propaganda against the firm.[51]

The 1961 trade agreement had expired in 1963, and the
Soviets stalled negotiations on another treaty. The Federal government had informed Moscow in April that the old commodity
lists would be valid up to mid-1964 and not, as originally requested by the Soviets, until the end of 1964. Meanwhile, German businessmen had begun unofficial preliminary talks with
Soviet officials on improved trade relations.[52] In November, the
Foreign Ministry announced that it had offered to begin talks

with Moscow.[53] It is instructive to recount the opinion of a prominent CDU MdB, (Member of the Bundestag) Kurt Birrenbach, whose firm, Thyssen, did a significant amount of trade with the USSR:

The motive behind the desire to conclude a trade agreement with the Soviet Union is political in nature . . . The Federal government hopes to activate the interest of the Soviet Union in an exchange of goods with the Federal Republic, and in the long run to create a basis which will make it possible to discuss questions of vital interest to the nation: the division of Germany.[54]

Throughout 1965, the Soviets refused to begin negotiations unless the FRG gave up insisting on the inclusion of a Berlin clause. As we have seen in Chapter 4, the inclusion of West Berlin explicitly in any such treaty was an important symbolic political statement for the West Germans. However, the Soviets informed the Germans that they would not explicitly include West Berlin in a trade treaty.[55] The perceived necessity to conclude a new trade agreement with the Soviets was important enough to influence Foreign Minister Schroeder to attempt to find a compromise formula. In a series of confidential memoranda, Schroeder proposed altering the 1952 convention whereby every treaty that the FRG signed contained a specific Berlin clause. Instead, the FRG would make a one-time general declaration, valid universally, that West Berlin was part of any agreement concluded between the FRG and any other power. The purpose of this was to prevent embarrassment for East European states every time they concluded trade treaties with the FRG, so that they would not appear explicitly disloyal to the GDR. However, the problem was that West Berlin was also governed by the Allied powers, and the Schroeder formula proved unacceptable to them.[56] The Soviets would not sign a trade treaty unless political issues were divorced from the negotiations. Furthermore, they demanded long-term credits and a clause promising compensation if a situation similar to the pipe embargo were to recur to be included in the treaty.

The political importance that the Germans attached to the trade treaty was demonstrated when the Bonn government used the occasion of an economic event in Moscow to send the highest-level German politician to the USSR since Adenauer's visit in 1955. In September 1965, there was a large International Chemical Fair in Moscow, in which 153 West German firms and

2,000 businessmen took part. The German government had decided to send Karl Carstens, state secretary at the Foreign Office, to Moscow, ostensibly to preside at the "German Day" in the chemical exhibition. Carstens expected to discuss German–Soviet economic and political relations with the Soviets, and they expressed a willingness to hold talks.[57] The Carstens visit was the brainchild of Schroeder, who could have sent Secretary Lahr, the man responsible for economic questions at the Foreign Ministry. However, Schroeder decided that the economic occasion of the fair could be used for both political and economic benefit.[58]

Carstens apparently offered the Soviets a new trade agreement for two to five years that included long-term credits.[59] In view of Bonn's past stand on credits, this was a major change. Carstens's plan was supported by the head of the Ostausschuss, who in a Moscow press conference said:

Trade can also continue without a trade treaty. But in Germany we believe that the conclusion of a new treaty will bring great advantages to both sides. The Federal Republic supplies mainly capital goods for the machine building industry to the Soviet Union which require long delivery times. For this reason a long-term treaty would offer both sides greater security.[60]

Despite the relatively friendly atmosphere of the talks, the Carstens visit produced no changes in Soviet policy. The economic carrots offered were not enough to offset the Soviet commitment not to include West Berlin in a trade treaty.

As Germany's trade balance with the USSR worsened and pressure from industry continued to mount, Bonn persevered in its attempts to begin trade negotiations. The Soviets finally relented. Before the talks began, German industry spokesmen appealed to them to conclude a trade agreement because it would lead to longer-term economic relations.[61] Both the government and industry wanted the trade agreement because it was economically desirable, and officials in Bonn expressed "cautious optimism" about the results. The FRG government realized that the Russians would not accept any written Berlin clause, but apparently they hoped that a compromise similar to that of 1961 could be arranged. Bonn also hoped to introduce new quota lists that would enable the Germans to increase their exports and redress their negative trade balance. The talks lasted for nine days and were conducted in a "friendly" climate. The chief point at issue was the Soviet desire to increase its export quotas for cotton and some chemicals and the question of German import liberalization. The Berlin problem was apparently not mentioned because the Soviets had refused to discuss it. The Soviet press, however, gave no coverage to the meetings, which were adjourned because the Russian team had to go to Finland to negotiate. Finally, because of the Bonn government crisis in November 1966, the Germans postponed the next round of discussions until a new government had taken office.[62]

The Grand Coalition, with its more active economic Ostpolitik, continued to press for the conclusion of a trade agreement. Willy Brandt recognized that one problem in the trade negotiations was the question of liberalizing imports.[63] In March 1966 the previous government had liberalized 60 percent of its imports of goods from Eastern Europe, but most of these import liberalizations had not applied to Soviet goods.[64] Brandt promised to relax some of the West German import restrictions on Soviet goods, particularly on oil products, timber, ores, and furs.[65] In January 1967, the new government had offered further liberalization of imports, but the Soviets countered by demanding full liberalization or nothing.[66]

Whereas both German government and industry pursued a consistent policy of seeking to conclude a trade agreement with the USSR, Soviet behavior was erratic. Initially, the Soviet ambassador in Bonn, Semyon Tsarapkin, called for greater trade between the USSR and the FRG, but only if German import regulations were liberalized and the Berlin clause dropped. The Soviet attitude was expressed in an interview that two Soviet officials gave to German correspondents in which they said that the USSR would be pleased to conclude a new trade agreement, but it could also live without trade with the FRG.[67]

In their daily contacts with German businessmen, the Soviets were enthusiastic about concluding deals. However, in their public pronouncements they went so far as to deny that any economic relations existed between the two countries.[68] The contradictory Soviet attitude toward trade with the FRG crystallized when Soviet Foreign Trade Minister Nikolai Patolichev announced that the USSR was no longer interested in concluding a trade agreement with the FRG. Harking back to the pipe embargo, he pointed out that the FRG was not a reliable trade partner and that the USSR's trade relations with Finland, Japan, and Western Europe were developing well. According to some commentators, the Russians wanted to secure freer import regulations from Germany so as to accumulate a hard currency surplus, which they would then spend elsewhere in Europe.[69]

The Soviet–West German conflicts over concluding a trade agreement illustrate several dimensions of the complex web of economic and political means and ends. A new trade treaty was perceived as part of Schroeder's policy of improving ties with Eastern Europe. The Soviets had the superior bargaining power, because the Germans were more interested in a trade treaty than were the Russians, and the latter could manipulate the situation within the agenda initiated by the FRG.

The Germans, it emerged, were increasingly willing to make some economic compromises – particularly on the credit issue – in order to secure the trade treaty, but they were not willing to make any major political concession on the Berlin clause, other than suggesting more general formulas for essentially the same principle. On the issue of the desirability of a trade treaty, government and business were more or less agreed. Because most of the other Eastern European countries had accepted Berlin clauses in their trade treaties with the FRG, the Berlin issue had become a symbol to the Soviets of Schroeder's successful Ostpolitik, which they saw as a direct threat to their control over Eastern Europe. This is why they were more intransigent on the Berlin clause in 1966 than they had been at the height of the crisis in 1961. Any compromise on that issue would have appeared as a major victory for Germany's Ostpolitik. Perhaps if the FRG had offered more attractive economic terms and the economic benefits had clearly outweighed the political payoffs, the Soviets might have accepted the treaty. However, the longer the negotiations dragged on, the more the Germans could have represented the ultimate conclusion of a treaty as a symbolic victory.

West Germany and the "credit war"

A major issue of contention between the FRG and the USSR was the credit question. Since the founding of the Soviet state, the question of whether to grant credits to the USSR had been one of the most heated controversies in East–West trade. Before the Second World War, Germany had been the first country to grant medium-term commercial credits to the USSR, and other European countries followed suit.[70] After the end of the war, the United States prohibited the granting of long-term credits to the USSR in the 1952 Battle Act, and until 1958 this pressure was quite effective.[71] However, the Soviets in 1958 made a concerted effort to obtain medium- and long-term credits to finance imports of capital goods. Their first success was a British credit for five years, followed by a German bank credit.[72] The Soviets stepped up their efforts to gain more long-term credits as they intensified their drive to import advanced technology, in particular the construction of chemical plants and methods of improving their agriculture. In 1964, they published one of Lenin's last letters justifying the use of Western assistance to help build up the Soviet economy, to give ideological legitimacy to their demands for increased technical ties with the West.[73] A later Soviet article explained that "the Soviet Union has always considered and considers that the granting of credits on mutually advantageous terms is a normal phenomenon in international trade; however, the terms of credit must be determined directly by the trading partners."[74] Given their shortage of hard currency and their desire to import complete installations, plants and other costly processes, the Soviets have consistently sought Western credits and since the fifties have not debated the ideological justification of taking capitalist money and paying it back with interest.

In the wake of the cold war, however, the Western countries, led by the United States, regarded the granting of credits as politically inadvisable. The foremost argument against credits was that they constituted a form of aid, and one should not aid one's political enemy. Additional arguments were that by giving credits for use in the civilian Soviet economy, the West would enable its adversary to free its resources for use in other parts of the economy – notably the military sector. Thus, credits would eventually enable the USSR to become a more formidable military foe.

International efforts to coordinate export credit practice antedate the cold war, going back to the formation of the Union d'Assureurs des Credits Internationaux, or the Berne Union, which was founded in 1934. The rules of the association amount to no more than a gentlemen's agreement without binding legal force. However, until 1958, the eighteen Western member countries agreed that commercial credits to the East should be limited to five years and be subject to an initial cash down payment of at least 20 percent of the purchase price. This was to prevent credits from becoming a source of financial aid.[75] In the United States, the five-year credit limit was written into law by the Johnson Act of 1934, although the U.S. government had never guaranteed any credits to the USSR.[76] However, the Berne Union has not been the main policy-making body to decide on credit restrictions against communist nations, but was rather used as an instrument for a policy that was decided by NATO.[77] Certainly, the Soviets claimed that it was NATO, led by the United States, that set the credit limits.[78]

West German credit policy toward the USSR was very restrictive prior to the Erhard regime. Despite the Berne Union rules permitting up to five-year credits, the government had refused to insure any credits to the USSR. Although the private sector was permitted to grant credits, in the absence of government backing for credits German industry was unable to guarantee substantial loans. German credits were insured through the Hermes Kreditversicherung AG, a private company that issues export guarantees on behalf of the German government and also operates as a credit insurer for its own account.[79] Until 1964, the express permission of the Bonn government (as opposed to the *Länder* authorities) was required for medium credits to all socialist countries. In 1959, the Soviets had requested West German credits, but only very limited facilities had been made available, although there were some bank-to-bank credits.[80] In general, the German position was similar to that of the United States. Because long-term credits were a form of economic aid, credits should not be granted in the absence of Soviet political concessions. Bonn also feared the possibility of a credit war between the Western states if there were no explicit rules on credit.

There are indications that Germany's credit policy, although initially determined by the United States, contained elements of independent formulation. In 1951, the United Kingdom had established a system of financial guarantees via the Export Credit Guarantee Department designed to provide long-term insurance and subsidized rates of interest for major projects such as plant and machinery installations in the USSR. Britain's adverse balance of trade with the USSR encouraged the government to take steps to liberalize credit policies toward the USSR, and the motivation seems to have been largely economic.[81] Germany became alarmed that other Western countries would break the Berne rules and that the FRG would be at a competitive disadvantage if it did not liberalize its own credit rules. Accordingly, in July 1963, the FRG proposed to the Economic Committee of NATO that the members of NATO harmonize their trade policies toward the East in the spheres of credits, patent rights, and artistic and literary property.[82] The FRG's proposals were discussed at a NATO meeting in November, with the United States insisting that the Berne rules be observed. The U.S. government was concerned "to obtain NATO support for a resolution that would prevent a credits race."[83] However, the FRG and the United States were ultimately defeated because of British resistance. The British argued that credits would facilitate the employment of British workers to build plants for Russia, and the USSR was much more likely to repay credits than were other, less developed countries. It was also pointed out that there was a logical inconsistency in permitting wheat sales to the USSR but refusing to give credits, which were a less overt form of aid.[84] The more pragmatic British approach found support in France and Italy. By 1964, French banks had extended credits totaling $322 million on ten-year terms to the USSR; the British provided $278 million on fifteen-year terms; and the Italians in 1966 extended $367 million in credit for the construction of a Fiat plant in Togliattigrad with a fourteen-year maturation. Needless to say, the USSR applauded these decisions.[85] Throughout the sixties, the FRG government made repeated calls for the coordination of Western credit policies through NATO and the EEC in order to limit the amount and duration of credits that other Western countries were granting to five years, as the Berne rules had originally envisioned.

At various times, the FRG government tried to use the EEC forum to work out a common credit policy.[86] At a meeting to discuss trade with the East, an official voiced skepticism about the ability of the EEC to unify its policies:

Without a coordination of credit policies a common trade policy of the EEC towards the state trading nations is neither possible nor desirable. Through Britain's and the prospective or already negotiated long-term credits granted by France and Italy, the chances for a unified credit policy towards the Eastern bloc have been sharply reduced.[87]

Even if the FRG had been able to unify government credit policies, however, the problem of controlling private credit insurance remained, making it impossible to ensure that both Western governments and banks would adhere to a five-year rule.[88]

The Federal government therefore pursued two strategies in its attempt to prevent the granting of long-term credits to the USSR. It tried to influence other countries, and it began to reappraise its own policies. Bonn also tried bilateral pressure to prevent German firms from being at a competitive disadvantage.

As soon as he took office, Erhard make it clear that he would not offer long-term credits to the USSR until the Russians had abandoned their "irreconcilable attitude towards Germany." This viewpoint was reiterated throughout the first half of 1964, when the other Western European countries were changing their credit rules. "Nothing should be done to strengthen the Soviet Union either economically or militarily," because the USSR was in a difficult economic situation. If the USSR would not make political concessions, why give it economic assistance?[89] Because the USSR was a supposedly developed state, which itself gave credit to the Third World, why should it receive low-interest credits from the West?[90] However, Foreign Minister Schroeder admitted that the offer of short-term credits to Eastern Europe (up to five years) "could possibly contribute to the improvement of West Germany's relations with these nations and also strengthen their national independence from Moscow or Peking."[91] Thus, although the German government defended the use of credit denial toward the USSR, it favored the positive use of credits as an incentive for Eastern European polycentrism.

The Erhard cabinet was eventually forced to make some concessions in the wake of the British and French deviations from the Berne convention and the pressure from industrialists that followed. In August 1964, the government repealed a 1955 edict and authorized the *Länder* governments and not Bonn to grant permits for suppliers' export credits to the USSR for periods of up to five years according to the Berne Union rules. Until then, companies granting such medium-term credits were forced to seek special government authorization. However, the effect of this partial liberalization was meager because the government still refused to sanction guarantees for these credits, and private export insurance was extremely expensive.[92] This decision on the *Länder* therefore did nothing to alter the situation by which the USSR was eligible for only six-month guaranteed credits.

Finally, in March 1965, the government announced that it would underwrite through Hermes commercial exports to Eastern European and Soviet purchasers for five years. In some cases, it would support export contracts specifying repayment in up to eight years. Thus, the problem of guaranteeing medium-term export credits to Eastern Europe was finally solved. A spokesman admitted that the government had changed its policy after failing to persuade its Western allies to join in a common position on credit. The Grand Coalition government that succeeded Erhard was equally intransigent on long-term credits to the USSR, although it was marginally more liberal in its credits to Eastern Europe.

The government faced continuous and growing opposition from many sections of the business community on its credit policy. The business community consistently argued for the granting of credits within the Berne Union rules. Moreover, some businessmen were apparently convinced of the political payoffs that the granting of credits might yield. Throughout 1964, there were persistent rumors that a group of prominent West German industrialists, some from Berlin, were pressuring the government to approve of a vast multi-billion-dollar West German credit loan program to the USSR for up to thirty years, in return for which the Russians would reconsider their reunification policy. Apparently, the plan was to grant the Russians credits and technical know-how in special fields, a sort of super Marshall Plan for the East. These plans, formulated before Khrushchev was scheduled to visit the FRG, were based on the premise that the Soviet first secretary's deteriorating relations with Ulbricht would influence him to accept the credits and make concessions at the expense of the GDR.[93] According to an Economics Ministry spokesman, there were a few prominent West Berlin industrialists who attempted to bring the chancellor around to their view, but he refused.[94] Moreover, in 1966, the then head of the CDU parliamentary caucus, Rainer Barzel, had proposed purchasing German reunification by increasing intra-German trade.[95]

The majority of businessmen, unlike the few cited previously, urged that credits be given for the simple economic reason that German industry was at a disadvantage compared to French, British, Italian, and Japanese firms.[96] Moreover, it was clear to them that the Russians would rather go without export credits than make any political concessions. The BDI changed its position and called for government guarantees on medium-term export credits to the USSR – that is, within the Berne Union rules. Moreover, after the pipe embargo, the Ostausschuss wanted to include in any credit guarantees insurance against another possible embargo. An Ostausschuss petition to the government in December 1964 spelled out this request in detail.[97] The Bundestag foreign trade committee recommended government backing for credits, as did the Free Democrats. Krupp was particularly persistent in its demands for a liberalization of credit rules, arguing that problems of financing East–West trade were becoming more urgent.[98]

It is undeniable that the government eventually compromised on guaranteeing five-year credits because of pressure from industry. Nevertheless, in view of the fact that France, Britain, and Italy were already granting long-term credits, the FRG government's compromise on medium-term credits did not represent a major victory for industry. It is also unlikely that the Federal government would have yielded to business pressure had that not coincided with its own political interests. The Schroeder policy of movement toward Eastern Europe enabled the government to justify the granting of medium-term credits to the USSR, a policy that would have been impossible under the Adenauer regime. Nevertheless, the Russians were not satisfied with this compromise and utilized the credit issue to justify their reluctance to increase their economic relations with the FRG.

Trade and politics in the 1960s

The main determinant of Soviet–West German trade relations in the mid-1960s was the unstable situation in Eastern Europe and the deteriorating German–Soviet political relationship. Trade and politics were often inseparable because the political situation inevitably influenced economic relations. Given the asymmetry between the economic and political stakes involved in bilateral German–Soviet relations, linkage was not effective in this period. In the presence of overwhelming political exigencies for the Kremlin, the economic dimension of relations receded into the background. The German economic initiatives were met with a negative Soviet response because the Kremlin was preoccupied with other issues.

Bonn's chief concern during this period was to pursue a more flexible Ostpolitik toward Eastern Europe, using economic incentives, and to increase political contacts without recognizing the status quo. However, this trade policy was not intended for the USSR, to which the FRG already had given diplomatic recognition. So as not to exacerbate Soviet fears of Bonn's exploiting East European polycentrism, the FRG used mild trade incentives to assuage Soviet doubts, and in this sense the repeated offers to conclude a trade treaty were symbolically important. However, this positive economic leverage was too insignificant to secure any Soviet political concessions, particularly over Berlin.

The Soviet Union's response to West German linkage policies was determined by the challenge of Bonn's Ostpolitik. Whereas Soviet *economic* needs in this period dictated closer economic ties with West Germany, the *political* need to control responses to Schroeder's and Brandt's Ostpolitik overrode economic considerations. The central Soviet preoccupation was to contain the changes taking place in Eastern Europe and to counter the instability caused partly by Bonn's conciliatory Ostpolitik and exacerbated by the establishment of German–Rumanian diplomatic relations. In the trade treaty negotiations, the economic incentives offered by the FRG were not enough to offset the political concessions that the Germans demanded. Had the Germans offered to rewrite their import quotas – in other words, had the economic incentive been great enough – the Soviets might have made a concession on Berlin. The German attempts to secure a political compromise on Berlin in return for granting the Soviets more attractive credit terms in the trade treaty failed because the political stakes proved too high for the Soviets and the economic recompense too meager.

The failure of the Germans to elicit any significant political concessions from the USSR through the use of economic levers in the mid-1960s was the result of the discrepancy between the economic incentives offered and the political concessions demanded. The invasion of Czechoslovakia indicated the irreconcilable contradictions of the Ostpolitik of Erhard and Kiesinger. This impasse was resolved only when the rules of the game were changed, that is, when the political and economic stakes, the parameters of politicization, and the uses of linkage were altered by the Ostpolitik of the Brandt administration.

7

Brandt's Ostpolitik and the Soviet Response: 1969-1970

In my opinion, Germany will not rise again and will not be able to maintain herself if she fails to find an adjustment with the East as well as the West, regardless of an East or West orientation.

Willy Brandt, 1949[1]

The Soviet-West German Renunciation of Force Treaty of August 1970 symbolized the waning of the cold war, the settlement of the unfinished postwar agenda, the inauguration of the detente era, and the achievement of a modus vivendi on the German question. Twenty-five years after the German surrender in the Second World War, the USSR and the FRG had accepted the reality of the European boundaries. However, whereas Moscow wanted a ratification of the status quo in order to make it more permanent, Bonn agreed to accept the status quo in order ultimately to change it.[2] Previous German Ostpolitiks were pursued within the framework of Germany's looking to the United States to define its policy. Under Chancellor Willy Brandt, however, Ostpolitik became more autonomous. After 1969 the United States ceased to determine the parameters of the German-Soviet relationship, and this altered the Kremlin's perceptions of the Federal Republic and the environment in which linkage could be used. The Soviet-West German rapprochement was possible because both sides modified their previous policies, although undoubtedly Bonn reoriented its policy more than did Moscow. Brandt's Ostpolitik represented a German acceptance of Soviet proposals. Moscow appreciated that because Bonn had redirected its Ostpolitik, it would be possible to permit some rapprochement between Eastern Europe and West Germany while maintaining Soviet control and minimizing societal instability that might result from an easing of tensions in Eastern Europe.

154

Although the Russians made some concessions in their Westpolitik, the architect of the German–Soviet rapprochement was undoubtedly the FRG, and in particular, Willy Brandt and Egon Bahr.[3] Brandt, the exile from Nazi Germany, whose views on Ostpolitik derived from his experience governing a divided Berlin, had for some years advocated a more flexible policy toward the East.[4] As mayor of Berlin, he adopted tough policies toward the USSR and the GDR that resembled those of his opponent, Konrad Adenauer, more than those of many of his SPD colleagues.[5] However, he developed a more conciliatory policy toward the USSR on becoming foreign minister in 1966. While reaffirming the primacy of the NATO alliance Brandt stressed that "for me, there is no separation between Westpolitik and Ostpolitik. What is called German Ostpolitik is for me only viable against the background of the Atlantic Alliance and West European integration."[6]

Brandt was willing to negotiate with Moscow and the GDR without making German reunification and a resolution of the status of West Berlin prior conditions for any agreement, although the Berlin issue was linked to ratification of the treaties. He was prepared to accept the postwar boundaries, leaving the issue of German reunification until some later date. Brandt realized that the refusal to legitimize Eastern Europe's existence had greatly weakened Germany's international bargaining power. He perceived the cul-de-sac into which German Ostpolitik had run and was determined to revitalize relations with Moscow by offering significant concessions on issues toward which Bonn had hitherto adopted an inflexible position.[7] His Ostpolitik was primarily defensive "to maintain the substance of the nation," that is, the common ties that existed between the two Germanies.[8] The key determinant of this Ostpolitik was the desire to improve intra-German relations. The unresolved issue of German national identity was the prism through which Brandt viewed relations with Moscow.

The political dimension of the Bonn–Moscow rapprochement

Although it is commonly assumed that Brandt's election as chancellor preceded the Soviet–West German rapprochement, the USSR had in fact put out feelers to Bonn for almost a year before his election, and the reasons for Moscow's change in Westpolitik go back to the period immediately following the invasion of Czechoslovakia. The invasion was an end rather than a beginning, a "detour on the road to detente," as Michel Debre called it. Having reasserted the Soviet right to determine and control the pace of polycentrism in Eastern Europe, the USSR now felt that it could adopt a more conciliatory policy toward West Germany. Indeed, the invasion emphasized for Brezhnev the need to secure an agreement with the West that would recognize the legitimacy of Soviet influence in Eastern Europe and thereby lessen the prospect of another Czechoslovakia.[9]

Soviet–West German relations deteriorated in the immediate aftermath of the Czech invasion. When it became clear to Moscow that it was going to be difficult to sustain the fiction that the Warsaw Pact intervention had been "requested" by the majority of the Czech leaders, the Russians intensified their criticism of West Germany, citing attempts by Bonn to launch a massive "politico-military operation" against the Czech Republic.[10] Bonn had learned the main lesson of the Czech invasion – namely, that the key to any future settlement of the German issue lay with Moscow and with no one else. Soviet–German relations were also strained by Bonn's continuing refusal to sign the nuclear nonproliferation treaty, a resolve that was strengthened by the Czech invasion.[11] Despite these tensions after the Czech invasion and the enunciation of the so-called Brezhnev doctrine of limited sovereignty, the Kremlin was willing to improve ties with the FRG.[12] At the beginning of October, Andrei Gromyko made a key conciliatory speech toward the West.[13] The Bonn government reacted with mild optimism to the speech, which had also suggested that the two governments resume their talks on the renunciation of force.[14] The more conciliatory Soviet attitude led to a surprise meeting between Brandt and Gromyko in New York, the first time since 1962 that a West German and a Soviet foreign minister had met. By the end of 1968, therefore, Soviet–German relations had improved somewhat.[15] The decision to ameliorate relations with Bonn had already been taken in the Kremlin as part of its strategy of pursuing a broader European detente policy. This policy may have represented another traditional Soviet goal – to encourage West European independence from the United States.

Soviet–West German detente was also, however, linked to the wider Russian goal of improving relations with the United States. Soviet concern about the growing arms race coupled with the election of President Richard Nixon enabled the US and the USSR to revitalize their dialogue, which had been in abeyance as a result of the Czech invasion. Nixon was concerned to secure Soviet assistance in ending the Vietnam War. Moscow's desire to improve relations with Washington was the prism through which it formulated the other elements of its detente policy.[16] The new Soviet detente policy was in practice less dynamic than the peaceful coexistence policy of Khrushchev, but it contained similar elements: It foresaw the political and economic benefits of diminished East–West tension while the USSR continued to increase its influence in the third world.

If relations with the US influenced the USSR to seek a rapprochement with West Germany, then another equally important determinant of Soviet Westpolitik was the intensification of the Sino–Soviet conflict. The decisive turning point, from the Soviet side, came in March 1969. In December 1968, the FRG had announced that it would hold the 1969 West German presidential elections in West Berlin, as it had done on three previous occasions. This move aroused strong protests in the GDR and the USSR. In February 1969, the GDR announced that it would bar all members of the *Bundesversammlung* (West German Federal Assembly), the body that elects the West German president, from traveling across the territory of the GDR until further notice. It took various other measures that ensured the harassment of all those connected with the election.

Pravda then followed with a strongly worded statement to the Bonn government. Emphasizing the fact that NPD (Neo-Nazi Party) members would be in Berlin, the note said:

The circles who advocate such schemes [i.e., the election in West Berlin] in the FRG are apparently very little concerned that such a gross violation of the Four-Power agreement determining the status of West Berlin and the terms for maintaining communications with it can have the most undesirable consequences in this area and likewise for the interests of the West Berlin population ... The illegal intrigues of the FRG in West Berlin have been and will be resolutely rebuffed by the Soviet Union as a manifestation of revanchism and aggressiveness.[17]

The Soviets followed up the stick with a carrot. In a series of meetings between Soviet Ambassador Tsarapkin and Chancellor

Kiesinger, the Soviets offered the Germans long-term passes for West Berliners to visit their relatives in East Berlin over Easter if the Germans moved the presidential election to another location.[18] It was a significant move in that the Russians had clearly overridden GDR leader Ulbricht in this matter. The FRG refused to move the site of the election, there were more Soviet protests, and the election was finally held on March 5, 1969. There was a definite deescalation of this Berlin crisis in the few days preceding the election.[19] The Soviets could have done much more to exacerbate the situation, and apart from some GDR harassment on the autobahn, there was relative restraint from the communists. The reasons for this volte face were to emerge only a week later, when the Soviets announced that there had been serious border clashes with the Chinese on the Ussuri River and Damansky Islands – just three days before the Berlin election.[20] In an unprecedented move, the Soviet ambassador had briefed the German chancellor on the clashes with the Chinese (indeed, Kiesinger was reportedly the first Western head of state to be informed), indicating the seriousness with which the Kremlin viewed these skirmishes.[21] Although the Russians never precisely spelled out this linkage, it seems that the Soviet leadership decided not to press the issue of the West Berlin elections because of the seriousness of the Sino–Soviet split. With such a potentially volatile situation on its Eastern flank, the Kremlin was constrained to maintain tolerably good relations on its Western flank. Thus, the Berlin issue suggests that one Soviet motivation for the pursuit of Westpolitik was a direct result of the absence – or impossibility – of a Soviet Ostpolitik toward the People's Republic of China.

However, the China problem was only one of several factors influencing Soviet policy toward the FRG, and one should not exaggerate its decisive impact. The evidence suggests that there had been some deescalation of the Berlin mini-crisis prior to the Sino–Soviet border clashes, implying that the Soviet change in policy preceded the fighting. Indeed, it has been suggested that the Soviets deliberately played up the border clashes (after all, there had been other Sino–Soviet skirmishes before) as a consequence of their prior decision to seek a rapprochement with Bonn. Because the threat of West German revanchism had been the rationale for disciplining the Warsaw Pact, it would have been impossible to pursue the new Westpolitik without finding a substitute external threat to maintain Warsaw Pact discipline, and the exaggerated Chinese danger provided this convenient rationale.[22] Although this explanation is probably too Machiavellian, the Sino–Soviet border fighting seems to have been a catalyst that reinforced the timing of Soviet detente moves toward West Germany, rather than the main reason for that policy.

The Kremlin, following the Ussuri River clashes, embarked on a concerted policy aimed at improving ties with Western Europe. An important Warsaw Pact Consultative Committee meeting in Budapest issued another call for a European Security Conference, a theme that persisted in Soviet pronouncements on the West.[23] In Gromyko's report to the Supreme Soviet, the Soviet foreign minister underscored the change in the Soviet attitude toward the FRG:

A turning point in our relations can occur – and we would like this – if the FRG follows the path of peace . . . Proceeding from this position, the Soviet government is ready to continue the exchange of opinions with the FRG on the renunciation of the use of force, up to and including the conclusion of an appropriate agreement.[24]

Another indication of Soviet interest in improving relations with the FRG was the declaration by Politburo ideologues Mikhail Suslov and Boris Ponomarev, at the March 1969 conference celebrating the fiftieth anniversary of the founding of the Comintern, in which they refuted the Stalinist theory that social democracy was the chief enemy of communism. Ulbricht, however, rejected this new line.[25] Soviet-West German talks continued into the summer, but the Russians were watching for the outcome of the September election. Brandt made it clear that, if he was elected chancellor, he would resume the dialogue with the USSR.[26] Both FDP and SPD deputies visited Moscow prior to the election, provoking criticism from the CDU.[27] The Soviets were attempting to sound out the two parties on their attitudes toward Ostpolitik, and some German politicans accused the Kremlin of interfering in the outcome of the election. It appears that the Soviets were already predisposed toward coming to an agreement with the FRG, but the precise way in which this might occur depended largely on who won the election. It was also becoming evident that Moscow might have to deal firmly with the GDR were Brandt elected. Ulbricht had expressed displeasure at the idea of an SPD victory, because a more conciliatory German policy might diminish the GDR's leverage over the USSR and might mean that Moscow would accept de facto recognition of the GDR instead of de jure, which Ulbricht demanded. As long as the German problem remained unsolved, East Berlin could make demands on Moscow that might carry less weight were there a reconciliation with Bonn.

The final political reason for the change in Soviet Westpolitik was the change in West German Ostpolitik. Willy Brandt's election as chancellor marked the beginning of a new phase in German–Soviet relations with the first SPD chancellor in postwar history. Before the election Brandt had begun unofficial discussions – unknown to the CDU – with the GDR and the USSR about improving relations. The Italian Communist Party had played an instrumental role in these exploratory talks.[28] In his first major foreign policy speech after his election, Brandt declared that his aim was to reach a modus vivendi with the GDR and also to continue talks with the USSR.[29] This marked a decisive change from the Grand Coalition's Ostpolitik. Brandt moreover acknowledged the existence of "two German states in one German nation." The Soviet comments on the speech were cautiously positive, and there was approval of the fact that, for the first time, a German chancellor had used the term German Democratic Republic without quotation marks.[30] Negotiations on the renunciation of the use of force began in December. In addition to the Chinese problem, there were reasons nearer home that prompted the USSR to accept Brandt's olive branch. Moscow may have hoped to loosen West German ties with NATO by concluding a bilateral deal, and it was trying to secure the de facto recognition of the GDR, which would enhance the USSR's and the GDR's prestige. After Bonn signed the nuclear nonproliferation treaty at the end of November, the USSR ceased to view the FRG as a potential threat in the same terms as it had previously done. Moscow did not stand to lose much by these negotiations – after all, it was Bonn that had taken the initiative and was willing to recognize the postwar boundaries without demanding any substantive concessions from the Russians as a precondition.

If Brandt's election was one of the reasons for the change in

Soviet Westpolitik, then one must also ask what the German chancellor's own motives were in reorienting West German Ostpolitik. The invasion of Czechoslovakia was as important for Brandt as it was for Brezhnev in influencing policy. The chancellor realized that bridge building and the Kiesinger policy were counterproductive and that the road to Warsaw and Prague had to lie through Moscow, while the GDR had to be afforded some form of recognition. Indeed, one of the main reasons for entering into a dialogue with the USSR was the hope that this would ultimately improve intra-German relations. The beginning of US–Soviet detente also encouraged Brandt to pursue his own rapprochement within the framework of the superpower negotiations. Brandt viewed the new Ostpolitik as a way of asserting West Germany's right to conduct a foreign policy that was more independent of U.S. control. The rapprochement with Moscow was intended to increase German security and influence through normalization of relations with the USSR.

Once the USSR and the FRG had agreed to enter into renunciation of force negotiations, the talks moved at a fairly rapid pace, although the negotiations were often acerbic and complex. Initially, in December 1969, the West German ambassador in Moscow, Helmut Allardt, began talks with Gromyko. However, these talks stalled over the questions of de jure or de facto recognition of the GDR and the inviolability of frontiers. Thereafter, to the chagrin of the German ambassador, the responsibility for the talks was transferred from the Foreign Ministry to the Federal Chancellery (*Bundeskanzleramt*). Ambassador Allardt, like a significant number of officials in the Foreign Ministry, opposed the policy of recognizing the boundaries of Eastern Europe without demanding major concessions from the USSR. The recognition of the postwar status quo was the overriding Soviet goal because this would consolidate the USSR's control over Eastern Europe.[31]

In January Brandt's special assistant, Egon Bahr, began to negotiate with Gromyko. Finally, Foreign Minister Scheel completed the negotiations in July.[32] The negotiations were complemented by a separate series of public bilateral meetings between Brandt and GDR Prime Minister Willi Stoph in Erfurt and Kassel and also by quadripartite negotiations on Berlin that began in March. The talks were complicated by many factors.

The Soviets wanted the European boundaries to be recognized as "unchangeable," whereas the Germans suggested the word "inviolable." The Russians refused to admit that their meetings with the Germans were taking place, and there was continued criticism of the FRG in the Soviet press.[33] The comments castigated the Bonn government for its refusal to recognize the GDR in international law.[34] Some commentators even suggested that the SPD was as "imperialistic" as its CDU predecessors.[35]

A more serious domestic problem for Brandt was the CDU's unrelenting opposition to Ostpolitik. Rainer Barzel, the CDU leader, refused to support any treaty with Moscow until an agreement on West Berlin had been signed.[36] In June, opponents of Brandt's Ostpolitik within the German Foreign Office leaked the substance of the sensitive, secret Bahr–Gromyko negotiations to the popular conservative paper *Bild Zeitung*. The publication of the "Bahr Paper" containing the contents of a proposed treaty caused a national scandal and almost torpedoed the talks.[37]

Finally, and no less important, was the attitude of the United States. Despite Brandt's repeated assurances of his loyalty to the Western alliance, West Germany was clearly attempting to increase its international autonomy. To some degree, the agenda had been set by the United States, since President Nixon and his special assistant for national security, Henry Kissinger, had inaugurated and developed their own detente policy. The FRG could never have pursued its Ostpolitik without the general improvement in East–West relations initiated and sanctioned by Washington. However, there is some question on the extent to which the United States was initially consulted about the Soviet–West German negotiations. According to an interview with Secretary of State William Rogers, the United States approved wholeheartedly of the German–Soviet negotiations.[38] Other sources, however, claimed that there was considerable alarm in Washington at the pace and intensity of the German–Soviet detente.[39] In a letter to Willy Brandt, President Nixon expressed confidence in Bonn's attemps to contribute to the cohesion of the Western community by attempting to reduce tensions in the East but pointedly stated, "like you, I believe the first is the indispensable condition for success in the second."[40] The delicate nature of the negotiations suggests that there were groups within the United States government that did not entirely approve of the policy and were suspicious of Germany's motives.[41] National Security Advisor Henry Kissinger was known to be uneasy about Brandt's initiatives, and more conservative specialists in German affairs, such as Acheson, Clay, and McCloy, were adamantly opposed to them.[42] The USSR had more difficulties with the GDR, but the Kremlin was ultimately able to assert its will over that of the reluctant Ulbricht. According to reports attributed to Polish leader Gomulka, Ulbricht opposed any communist rapprochement with the FRG and tried to persuade Gomulka not to go along with the USSR.[43] In Western Europe, the French said that Brandt's Ostpolitik "has come as a bombshell," and Britain was also wary of the new German policies.

Despite all these domestic and foreign difficulties, the Renunciation of Force Treaty was signed in Moscow on August 12, 1970. The treaty itself was largely symbolic. It affirmed the intention of both parties to settle all their disputes by peaceful means and asserted that the treaty would come into force only after ratification. It stated that the existing borders of each country were "inviolable" and could not be changed by force. In addition, the Germans appended a letter claiming that "this treaty does not conflict with the political objective of the Federal Republic of Germany to work for a state of peace in Europe in which the German nation will recover its unity in free self-determination."[44] The letter, which was designed partly to deflect the opposition criticism, did little to endear the CDU to the treaty. Nevertheless, it represented a major achievement on the part of the Brandt government. It was evident to the Germans that the Soviets were not motivated only by political considerations during the course of the negotiations. Economic incentives played an important part in the overall negotiations and reinforce the view that the Soviets were contemplating a change in their attitude toward the Bonn government even before Brandt was elected. This is not to diminish the significance of Brandt's and Bahr's achievements, but rather to suggest that the Soviet motivation was more complex than it might initially have appeared.

The natural gas deal: forerunner or product of Ostpolitik?

After 1968, West German–Soviet trade began to increase at an accelerating pace, and West Germany's negative balance of trade with the USSR changed to a positive one. Total German–Soviet trade grew from \$565.7 million in 1968 to \$739.9 million in 1969, and Germany's negative balance of trade of \$18.9 million in 1968 changed to a positive balance of \$71.5 million in 1969 (see Table 7). The 30 percent increase in trade in one year was due to three factors: considerable Soviet orders for sheet metal; German supplies of special machinery for the Fiat plant in Togliattigrad; and supplies of steel pipes.[45] From the Soviet side, although the USSR's total foreign trade increased by 27.7 percent from 1968 to 1969, its exports to West Germany rose by only 6.8 percent whereas its imports from Germany rose by a staggering 52 percent.[46] Germany regained its position as Moscow's most important Western trade partner. The Soviet Union remained the FRG's biggest trading partner in the socialist world.[47]

For the Russians, there seemed to be a new and promising way out of the twofold dilemma of exports and payments – energy. Although the volume of Soviet oil and natural gas reserves has been a state secret since 1947, the reserves must be considerable, because by the 1970s the USSR was the world's leading producer of oil and the second largest producer of natural gas.[48] For the Soviets, the most attractive feature of hydrocarbon exports is their hard currency-earning potential.[49] The export of gas and oil is not only important as a hard currency earner; these exports, in exchange for imports of pipes, were vital for the further development of the Soviet energy industry. Because most of the deposits of natural gas and oil are in Siberia or Central Asia, and because the largest consumption of Soviet energy is in the European part of Russia, the transportation problem is the key to the further development of both hydrocarbon exports and domestic use. The cost of transporting oil by pipeline is less than a third of the cost by rail. In the case of natural gas, capital investment and transport costs can be dramatically lowered by increasing the diameter of the pipe.[50] Of course, the Russians could theoretically have imported Western pipeline technology without exporting gas or oil, but because their payments problem was so great, the most desirable way to develop their energy sector was to couple the import of technology with the export of energy.

From the Western point of view, there were advantages in

importing Soviet energy. Since 1958, Moscow had been exporting oil to Europe and had supplied the FRG with 10 percent of
its oil needs in 1961. By 1965, exports of Soviet petroleum to the
FRG had increased sixfold.[51] One of the main attractions for the
West Germans was the price of Soviet oil. Although the price
differential between Soviet and other oil narrowed during the
sixties, there was still a competitive advantage in purchasing
Soviet oil, as the following figures show:

Average cost of oil imported into the FRG (DM per ton at border)

Year	From all sources	USSR	Difference
1960	82.7	53.5	29.2
1965	62.4	52.2	10.2
1970	60.1	50.4	9.7[52]

Although natural gas in 1968 composed only 3.2 percent of
total domestic German energy consumption, the advantageous
Soviet price for natural gas was also attractive. Indeed, some
third world countries complained that the USSR was competing
unfairly with them in the Western market by charging below
world market prices.[53] In addition, it was not only the price of
Soviet energy that made it attractive in 1969; the German steel
industry welcomed the chance to increase its exports, because
the Russians were interested in importing large-diameter pipe.

Soviet–West German trade in energy had been severely affected by the 1962 pipe embargo, and even after the embargo
was lifted at Germany's insistence in November 1966, the Soviets
did not immediately rush to conclude new pipeline deals. The
Soviets still refused to have direct dealings with any German
steel concern, but in 1968 they concluded an indirect deal with
the Austrian iron and steel concern VOEST. Thyssen and Mannesmann were to supply the Austrian company with 520,000
tonnes of 48-inch pipe, which the Russians would then purchase
from the Austrians.[54] The Soviets finally relented on the issue of
dealing directly with German firms. In April 1969, Thyssen announced the conclusion of a contract with the Soviets for the
joint construction of pipe factories in the USSR and the FRG.
The agreement, worth $25 million, envisioned the construction
of one factory in the USSR and one in the FRG, and the Russians

had initiated the contacts that had led to one and a half years of negotiations. The largest high-pressure pipelines in the USSR were 42 inches in diameter and in 1967, the USSR had inquired of Thyssen whether it was technically possible to build larger pipes, to transport natural gas from Siberia to Western Russia and Europe. Thyssen was the only company capable of building such pipes, and the pipes were to be used for transporting gas from the Tyumen Oblast to Lvov, Bratislava, Vienna, and Trieste.[55] The Thyssen deal was not only significant in its scale but was above all symbolically important, in that it signified that the Soviets had finally agreed to forget the 1962 pipe embargo.

The Thyssen deal was announced at the 1969 Hanover Fair, and it turned out to be a prelude to a much more important German–Soviet deal – the natural gas contract, which was the biggest business transaction ever concluded between the USSR and West Germany. Apparently, the USSR had been impressed by the efficiency of the German deliveries under the VOEST contract, and after concluding a natural gas deal with Austria in January 1968, it appeared that the Soviets would make similar agreements with other Western countries.[56] Soviet Foreign Trade Minister Nikolai Patolichev came to the Hanover Fair in 1969 and had a series of talks with Economics Minister Karl Schiller – the first time since Mikoyan's visit in 1958 that a German cabinet member had conducted talks with a Soviet colleague in the FRG. This visit had been carefully arranged after the USSR had expressed interest in sending a high-level delegation to Germany. It was obvious that the Russians were contemplating a major shift in their economic relations with Germany. Patolichev suggested that West Germany might consider extending the Friendship Pipeline – the Soviet pipeline supplying Eastern Europe that had supposedly led to the 1962 pipe embargo – to West Germany, which meant that the pipeline would lead directly from East to West Germany. Patolichev's other suggestion was that the FRG might be interested in importing Soviet natural gas on a large scale, in return for large-diameter pipe. Shortly thereafter, the state secretary at the Federal Economics Ministry, Klaus Dohnanyi, flew to Moscow to initiate the talks on the gas deal.[57] A series of complicated negotiations began shortly thereafter, involving the Bavarian economics minister, Ruhrgas

(Germany's largest distributor of natural gas), and various steel firms.[58]

The main issues in the negotiations were the amount of gas and the amount of pipe to be supplied, the price, and, most important, the financing of the deal. The Soviets were prepared to offer gas at a competitive price, that is, below that charged by the Dutch, and much to the chagrin of Shell, which had been the main supplier to West Germany up to that point. The negotiations were simpler than those involving broader trade agreements, because the deal was in essence barter. However, the problem of financing was crucial, and there were also technical problems involved for the steel companies.[59] The triangular deal was finally signed in Essen in February 1970. The Mannesmann Export Company (which now included Thyssen) was to supply the USSR – via Promsyroimport – with 1.2 tonnes of pipes, five feet in diameter, at a cost of $400 million. This part of the agreement was to be financed by a consortium of seventeen German Banks under the direction of the Deutsche Bank, which would supply credits for the $400 million with a maturity of twelve years. The rate of interest was not officially disclosed, but it was apparently 6.25 percent, well below the current market rate. The bank rationalized this by saying that the rate of interest was normally lower in bank-to-bank credits, and this credit was administered through the Soviet Vneshtorgbank. Only half the credit was insured by Hermes, but this was still a major departure from previous German credit policies toward the USSR.[60] It ultimately transpired that Mannesmann reimbursed the banks for the difference between the market rate of interest and that paid by the Soviets by charging a higher price for the pipe. From the Soviet side, Soyuzneftexport agreed to deliver to the German Ruhrgas 5.5 billion cubic meters of natural gas over a twenty-year period beginning October 1973. The first phase of the deal involved the construction of Soviet pipeline from Siberia to the Czech–West German border at Marktredwitz, a distance of 1,500 miles.

In their articles on the contract, the Soviets stressed the economic benefit that the deal would bring to the Germans and suggested that the Germans had their own economic motivation for concluding the agreement.[61] They also implied that the economic deal could have beneficial political effects.[62] The Soviets concluded the deal for primarily economic reasons. In addition to the improvement in Soviet energy transportation within the USSR and to the CMEA nations, the USSR stood to acquire a firm position in Western energy markets. From a purely financial point of view, the agreed-on sales value of total gas delivered – $860 million – exceeded the cost of the pipe by about $460 million, which meant that the USSR made a healthy profit from the transaction.

The question of German motivations in concluding this contract is more complex. From the Bavarian point of view, the attractive price of Soviet gas meant that there were distinct economic advantages in the deal for southern Germany.[63] Because Soviet gas deliveries would not comprise more than 10 percent of the German natural gas market and would be less than 1 percent of the total energy consumption, the question of undesirable dependence did not seem unduly important.[64] The German steel industry, in particular those firms involved in making large-diameter steel pipes, was the second most export-dependent steel industry in the world after Japan, and its share in the total world production had fallen in the sixties whereas that of Japan had risen.[65] Although the steel industry in Germany could have continued without the Soviet deal, it is indisputable that the contract was a welcome opportunity to utilize Mannesmann–Thyssen's pipemaking capacity and improve their competitive position after the pipe embargo difficulties. The German banks also did well out of the deal. Even if the deal did not immediately yield profits, the fact that it was the first long-term credit to the USSR, and that the prospects for further deals were good, meant that the long-term economic perspective for the banks was advantageous.[66]

The natural gas agreement was especially significant and a departure from traditional German deals in that it embodied a felicitous coincidence of economic and political interests. Whereas the firms and banks were attracted by the economic advantages of the deal, the government was clearly interested in its political payoffs. Previously, government and business had often been at loggerheads when it came to trade with the USSR. Here, for once, there was a perfect convergence of views that facilitated the success of the negotiations. Although the negotiations were begun before Brandt became chancellor, they were partly conducted from the German side by the Social Democrat economics minister, and Brandt was not averse to using economic incentives for his own domestic political purposes. Once elected, however, when the negotiations were still at a delicate stage, Brandt apparently gave direct encouragement to Ruhrgas. This was the first time that the German government had directly intervened to promote an economic transaction with the USSR.[67] Brandt realized that the Soviets had a strong economic interest in the deal, and he understood the utility of using economic incentives to improve German–Soviet relations. Once the deal was signed, in the middle of the Bahr–Gromyko talks, it gave added impetus for the successful conclusion of the renunciation of force negotiations.[68] Although it is conceivable that the political talks could have failed although the economic negotiations were successful, the conclusion of the deal under favorable economic conditions for the Soviets had some effect on the general climate of Soviet–German relations. Even the opposition realized that the government's interest in concluding the agreement was primarily political, although they demanded to know what political price the Soviets would pay for such a generous economic deal.[69] The natural gas agreement was a factor that contributed to the improvement of German–Soviet political relations.

The Brandt visit to Moscow

Willy Brandt's visit to Moscow in 1970 contrasted sharply to that of Konrad Adenauer in 1955 and symbolized the dramatic change in German–Soviet relations that culminated in the Renunciation of Force Treaty.[70] Adenauer had flown to Moscow amid considerable domestic criticism, and he had expected controversy in his encounters with Khrushchev. Although some complications also surrounded Brandt's visit, he arrived in Moscow anticipating cooperative, successful talks with Brezhnev. Because the Renunciation of Force Treaty had been fully worked out beforehand, there were none of the tensions and setbacks that accompanied Adenauer's visit. It was a ceremonial and symbolic summit.

There had been several points of conflict prior to the initialing of the treaty by Foreign Ministers Scheel and Gromyko that had placed the entire treaty in jeopardy. In one episode, reminiscent of the 1961 compromise on Berlin in the trade treaty, Scheel had attempted to establish a linkage between the treaty and the Berlin agreements and had read to Gromyko a statement saying: "The treaty will not be laid before the Bundestag for ratification until a satisfactory outcome of the Berlin negotiations has been reached; the Federal Government has thereby discharged its responsibility for Berlin." Scheel reread the sentence three times, received no response from Gromyko, and finally gave the piece of paper to Gromyko as he was leaving. Gromyko's only reply was that the USSR would not sign any Berlin agreement without prior ratification of the Bonn–Moscow treaty by the Bundestag. This exchange did not portend well for future negotiations, nor did the fact that the CDU, at the last moment, tried to prevent Brandt from going to Moscow until a Berlin agreement was signed. However, despite these prior complications, Brandt's trip to Moscow was a success.[71] Tass labeled the treaty "a milestone in Europe's postwar history."[72]

In the preamble to the Renunciation of Force Treaty worked out during Scheel's July negotiations, there was a reference to economic factors: "The High Contracting Parties... Desiring to lend expression in the form of a treaty, to their determination to improve and extend co-operation between them including economic relations, as well as scientific, technological and cultural contacts in the interests of both states..."[73] In his talks with Kosygin during his Moscow visit, Brandt discovered that the Soviets hoped that the signing of the treaty would give them an opportunity to increase economic links. However, Foreign Minister Scheel claimed that he had discussed the Common Market extensively with Gromyko and that the Russians had decided that they could not embark on large-scale economic projects with the FRG without first placing their political relations on a firmer footing.[74] In his discussions with Brandt, Kosygin reportedly pressed the German leader on enlarging trade and technological contacts and was eager to engage the chancellor in major substantive discussions of how economic ties could be improved.[75] A major *Pravda* article on the treaty stressed its economic benefits, although it criticized the remaining "artificial barriers" to trade.[76] However, even this article emphasized the German desire for trade rather than the Soviet interest in it.

The economic content of Soviet Westpolitik

Despite the Soviet reluctance to admit economic problems, the evidence suggests that the change in the Soviet posture toward the FRG in 1969–70 was partly motivated by economic factors. Moreover, the Soviet decision to pursue detente was partly the result of the increased salience of economic factors in determining Soviet foreign policy. Perhaps the clearest indication of this is the state of the Soviet economy in the late 1960s.

The Soviet economic reforms of the mid-1960s had not improved the performance of the Soviet economy as much as had been hoped. Although the growth rate of the Soviet economy was still respectable, it had declined in the late 1960s from 8.6 percent in 1967, to 7.5 percent in 1968, to 6.1 percent in 1969. The basic problems were lack of productivity and failure to innovate, particularly in fields of advanced technology such as electronics and computers, partly because the military sector siphoned off the USSR's most efficient economic effort. In addition, Soviet labor productivity was about half that of Western European countries. In an unpublished secret speech to the Plenum of the Central Committee on December 15, 1969, Brezhnev sharply criticized the failure of the Soviet economy to develop satisfactorily, and there was some speculation that Kosygin would be made the scapegoat for these deficiencies, because he had advocated developing light industry over heavy industry.[77] A major article in *Literaturnaia Gazeta* in February 1970 sought to answer the criticisms of the December Plenum and reasserted the viability of the Soviet economic system and the reforms, but it was clear from the article that the charges were very serious.[78] In March 1969, according to a German official, a decision was taken in the Central Committee to import large amounts of technology from the West, and the unsatisfactory performance of the Soviet economy reinforced this decision. The Kremlin hoped that importing Western technology might be a substitute for far-reaching, decentralized domestic economic reform, whose political consequences might lead to greater instability, as they had in Czechoslovakia.[79]

If we accept the premise that the Russians turned to Germany to fulfill many of their economic needs because of Germany's economic superiority, the question still remains as to why it was necessary to enter into political negotiations with them. After all, the Soviets did their utmost to separate trade and politics, because they preferred to continue economic relations regardless of the political climate. After they had concluded the natural gas deal, presumably they could have continued to seek more trade and technology deals and to disregard the political side of the relations, because improved political relations were not a necessary precondition for closer economic ties. The classic Soviet attitude toward the relation between trade and politics was expressed in an article shortly after the signing of the treaty: "The essential condition for the successful development of international trade is peace. At the same time trade – which forms the economic basis of peaceful coexistence – like other forms of economic ties between socialist and capitalist countries, plays a tremendous role in strengthening world peace."[80] Another article on the Soviet–German treaty claimed, "This political basis could promote comprehensive economic, scientific, technical and cultural cooperation."[81] Numerous interviews with Foreign Trade Minister Patolichev stressed that better political relations facilitated the development of trade.[82] It appears that the Kremlin realized that economic ties with the FRG could develop only up to a certain point if political relations remained strained.[83]

Trade would have continued without renunciation of force, but its future was strengthened by the treaty, which could act as a reinsurance that politics would not influence trade negatively. Given the German government's former opposition to trading with the USSR, and its tradition of politicizing *Osthandel* domestically, the Soviet Union perceived the connection between trade and politics in its relations with the FRG. In view of past experience, the Kremlin could reasonably expect that better political relations would facilitate more trade, if for no other reason than the fact that the FRG would have a greater stake in improved political relations if it broadened its economic relations with the USSR.

The difficulties with the Soviet economy and the need to import more Western technology coincided with a desire on the part of some, if not all, members of the Politburo to stabilize and settle the German question. Indeed, it appears that Brezhnev had justified his Westpolitik partly in terms of the economic payoffs that would result from it. Brezhnev argued in favor of detente because it could improve the performance of the Soviet economy through the import of Western technology. He also realized that the stability of his regime depended on a viable economy. It was better to ensure that political factors would not suddenly impede economic relations, as they had done in the past. Evidence suggests that there were those within the Soviet economic and political hierarchy who opposed the widening of economic contacts with the West and with the FRG in particular. Like their West German counterparts, these opponents of greater Soviet–West German trade argued from a primarily political standpoint. It was better for the USSR not to become too involved economically with the West because this might have undesirable political consequences and lead to dangerous dependencies. The flow of trade might also lead to an unwanted flow of ideas, exposing Soviet citizens to Western propaganda. These opponents of trade may well have found their spokesmen in those Soviet writers who repeatedly warned of the dangers of West German monopoly capitalism and revanchism, even after the treaty.[84]

Finally, the Eastern European countries were a factor in the decision. By improving political ties with the FRG, by ensuring that the Ostpolitik was oriented toward Moscow, the Kremlin hoped to control some of the political implications of West German trade with Eastern Europe.

The economic content of German Ostpolitik

The role of economic factors in the development of Brandt's Ostpolitik is still a controversial issue. On the one hand, analysts have echoed Brandt's view that Soviet Westpolitik was a product of economic need: "The interest of the East European states in cooperation with us rests to a large extent on a desire to make economic progress and to participate in Western technology. Economics, therefore, remains for the foreseeable future an especially important element of our policy in Eastern Europe."[85] On the other hand, some West German scholars – in agreement with various Soviet writings on the subject – have claimed that Brandt's Ostpolitik was the result of pressure from German big business, especially the export-dependent steel industry, to conquer and secure new markets in the East. In this view, Brandt's political goals were mere rationalizations of an economically determined imperialistic policy.[86]

The question of the degree to which German businessmen

encouraged the improvement of German–Soviet relations is a complex aspect of the Ostpolitik, partly because there was no overwhelming enthusiasm about the prospects for Soviet–German trade. Soviet articles stressed the West German interest in trade with the USSR and claimed that German businessmen were dissatisfied with the restrictions on trade.[87] Although applauding the German interest in trade with the USSR, they nevertheless attributed it to the industrialists' desire not to be outdone by other Western countries and to the competitive aspects of imperialist economic expansion in general.[88] Nevertheless, the imperialist aspirations of German businessmen could also be advantageous for the USSR. After all, Lenin himself had seen the benefits of utilizing the unwitting capitalists to promote Soviet economic development.

It is, however, difficult to find evidence of any great German optimism about the potential of such trade. The business newspaper *Handelsblatt* reported that businessmen felt that the Renunciation of Force Treaty could have a beneficial effect on the climate of Soviet–German economic relations. However, because one of the problems with West German–Soviet trade was the absence of a trade treaty given the unresolved issue of a Berlin clause, the crucial political negotiations for business were the Four-Power talks on Berlin. The German–Soviet treaty was useful only to the extent that it might be the first step in facilitating an agreement on Berlin. There was some optimism about the possibilities for Soviet–West German trade, but it seemed to be overshadowed by more sober calculations.[89] The right-wing German press, echoed by the right-wing French press's characterization of Ostpolitik as "s'entendre pour vendre," portrayed the business community as being eager to "subsidize" Moscow's economy – and by implication its military sector – and inveighed against any economic "assistance" to the USSR.[90]

The Ostausschuss spokesman for German business interests in the USSR, Otto Wolff von Amerongen, although welcoming the German–Soviet treaty as the first step toward concluding a new trade agreement, cautioned against any overoptimistic expectations. Trade with the USSR formed 1.4 percent of German trade, and total German trade with the East (now 4 percent) could perhaps rise to 9 percent in the future.[91] In an article written after the treaty, and representative of the views of the

BDI and its Ostausschuss, von Amerongen gave nine reasons suggesting only mild optimism about the prospects for German-Soviet trade: the differences in economic systems that limited economic exchange; the orientation of the USSR's foreign trade toward CMEA; the Soviet shortage of hard currency; the lack of sufficient Soviet goods suitable for the West; the Soviet lack of understanding of the demands of the Western market; the limited Western demand for Soviet raw materials; the impossibility of developing economic relations through joint ventures because of the Soviet system; the general problem of German credits given the Soviet inability to pay for its imports from the FRG; and the problem of interest rates for those credits that could be given to the Russians.[92]

If this series of economic arguments appeared familiar – and there has been great continuity in the attitudes of German businessmen, by and large, since 1955 – then what was significant was the call by representatives of industry not to confuse trade and politics. Von Amerongen made a major speech calling for the depoliticization of the *Osthandel*. He cautioned that the Soviet interest in steel pipes would not induce the Kremlin to make political concessions. Admitting that it was the communist countries that had initially politicized trade, he stressed that "trade policy can never be a substitute for foreign policy."[93] The BDI in its annual report pointed out that it was impossible to extract political concessions from the East in exchange for political gifts.[94]

In order to establish the extent to which Brandt's Ostpolitik was determined by economic factors, one must examine not only the economic situation within the FRG but also the relations between the government and business sectors. Soviet analysts of German society have usually expressed the view that big business controls the German government.[95] Some Western scholars have also made the argument that Brandt altered Germany's Ostpolitik because of pressure from industry.[96] Undoubtedly some German firms, such as Mannesmann and Krupp, were interested in expanding profitable relations with the USSR. However, in order to prove that their desires played a key role in Brandt's decision making, one would have to demonstrate that big business has a decisive influence on West German foreign policy – and there is little evidence that industry determines

German foreign policy, although it undoubtedly has some input in foreign policy formulation.

In any discussion of the relationship between government and business in Ostpolitik, we must remember that the government, and not private business, set the Ostpolitik agenda. On such sensitive matters as relations with the East, nongovernment actors had far less input in foreign policy making than they had on less vital issues. Brandt's main concerns in pursuing the new Ostpolitik were political. Nevertheless, Brandt, in discussing his motives for altering West German Ostpolitik when he became foreign minister, writes:

I do not disguise that I was also motivated from the outset by concrete economic considerations. Even as Foreign Minister I told the Bundestag that our policy must be focused on the problems of existence in an immediate sense as well; we had to safeguard employment and open up new fields of economic opportunity.[97]

Rather than analyzing Brandt's political goals as the product of economic determinants, one could argue that the Federal Government successfully utilized various economic incentives to encourage the USSR to enter into a dialogue. Whereas previously the German government and business had been at loggerheads over the desirability of economic relations with the USSR, under Brandt the interests of government and business coincided. The government hoped that by encouraging a favorable economic climate, it might improve the general atmosphere for the talks, from which political compromises might follow. Some members of the government expected that, following the treaty, economic ties might improve substantially, which in turn might facilitate a greater Soviet willingness to compromise on political issues and give the USSR a greater stake in maintaining good relations. However, these calculations again involved questions of tone and atmospherics rather than any explicit tradeoffs.

Ironically, at the beginning of Brandt's Ostpolitik, it appears that the German government had a more optimistic view of both the economic potential of East-West trade and the ability of trade incentives to influence political developments than did most of the business community, perhaps as a reaction to former administrations' overly negative attitude toward trade with the USSR. One should not exaggerate the role of the business sector in the development of Brandt's Ostpolitik.

The political economy of Soviet–West German detente

The success of Brandt's Ostpolitik marks a decisive change in the use of economic levers to secure political goals on the part of the German government. After 1969, the rules of the game changed. The change was greater on the German than on the Soviet side, because, as we have seen, Brandt's Ostpolitik represented a more fundamental alteration of German foreign policy goals than Brezhnev's Westpolitik of Soviet foreign policy goals. The FRG had ceased to be a revisionist power politically, and the Germans finally eschewed the use of negative economic levers in the pursuit of their foreign policy goals. From Bonn's point of view, both the means and ends of Ostpolitik had altered. The end was no longer to undo the results of World War Two, but to accept them and induce improvements in intra-German relations within the status quo. However, because the boundaries were declared inviolable instead of unchangeable, the possibility for change remained. The economic means were no longer negative, nor was there any expectation that the Soviets would make substantial political concessions in return for economic rewards. From Moscow's point of view, the means and ends of Westpolitik had altered far less. The goal of Soviet Westpolitik, which the Kremlin had consistently pursued since 1955, had been achieved. Moreover, the Bonn government now seemed to agree with a policy that avoided negative leverage. Having realized that previous administrations had failed to gain any important political concessions through the negative use of economic levers, Brandt and his successor, Schmidt, altered the interface between politics and economics in German–Soviet relations.

Despite the fact that the German government had far more power in setting the economic agenda than did the business community in setting the political agenda in Soviet–West German relations, this period reveals some paradoxes about the power of the government to utilize economic levers. It was easier for the German government in the pre-Brandt era to use economic disincentives than it was for Brandt to use economic incentives. Although they aroused domestic opposition, the Adenauer, Erhard, and Kiesinger administrations were able to intervene either to forbid trade or to circumscribe it severely.

Once Brandt decided to use economic levers to promote political improvements, it became more difficult.

The reasons for the lack of specific linkage in this era lie in the asymmetry between the political and economic stakes. Brandt's Ostpolitik involved primary political goals, core values of national survival, and prestige. Similarly, Soviet Westpolitik involved primary political goals such as its position in Eastern and Western Europe. The economic stakes were only secondary. The USSR could have survived without German trade if it had to. Brandt realized that linkage had never worked when the German government had negatively utilized economic factors of secondary importance to the Russians to extract political concessions involving core values. Thus, there was no attempt at specific linkage from the German side and none from the Soviet side. Never again would any German government attempt to change Soviet policy on the German question by denying or offering trade. However, both sides hoped that the political and economic rapprochement would reinforce each other.

8

From Moscow to Bonn: the consolidation of Ostpolitik and Westpolitik, 1970-1980

A significant shift has occurred in USSR-FRG relations on the basis of the 1970 Treaty. They have become normal - and this on the only possible basis - renunciation of efforts to demolish the existing European frontiers. Now the FRG is one of the major partners in our mutually beneficial business cooperation with the West.

Leonid Brezhnev, 1976[1]

East-West trade is an important instrument for ensuring peace. We must still strengthen the effect of this interaction.

Helmut Schmidt, 1978[2]

The Renunciation of Force Treaty was the first step in the formal resolution of the German problem. During the next three years, the SPD-FDP's Ostpolitik achieved its goal of normalizing relations with all of the FRG's Eastern neighbors, including the GDR. By 1973 the German problem had for the moment been resolved and the European postwar status quo had been ratified.[3] The period between Brandt's visit to Moscow in 1970 and Brezhnev's trip to Bonn in 1973 was a time of readjustment for both sides. The USSR and Germany became aware of the systemic economic and political limits to their bilateral detente policies. By the end of 1973, the bilateral phase of Soviet-German detente had been completed with the conclusion of the Ostpolitik treaties.

Ten years after the inauguration of the Brandt Ostpolitik, a new political equilibrium had emerged. The USSR and the FRG had achieved a modus vivendi based on the normalization of relations. While Brandt was chancellor, there was considerable enthusiasm in Bonn about the potential for improvement of relations with the USSR. After Helmut Schmidt became chancellor in 1974, German Ostpolitik became less idealistic and more

179

pragmatic. Soviet–West German relations had stabilized at a lower level of expectations by 1980. Bilateral trade grew significantly; yet the initial Soviet hopes for a dramatic increase in economic relations were not fulfilled. At the same time, German Ostpolitik after 1973 entered a new multilateral phase in which negotiations between the USSR and the FRG concerned European, rather than strictly bilateral issues. The bilateral German–Soviet relationship in time became more integrated into the growing multilateral complex of detente negotiations, which reinforced bilateral trends and built a multilevel network of ties binding the two countries economically and politically.

Ostpolitik phase 1: bilateral relations and ratification of the treaties

Between 1970 and 1973 the FRG expanded and completed the first phase of its Ostpolitik by negotiating treaties normalizing relations with Poland, the GDR, and Czechoslovakia, whereas the Four-Power Agreement resolved the status of Berlin. The significance of the Moscow treaty was that it enabled the Brandt–Scheel regime to pursue accommodation with Eastern Europe (and particularly with the GDR) without threatening Moscow's control over Eastern Europe, because the treaty in effect recognized the Kremlin's hegemony in its sphere of influence. There were three main dimensions to German–Soviet relations. First, there was the implementation and consolidation of a multilateral detente based on bilateral treaties with various key countries, the Berlin accords, and preparations for a European Security Conference. Second, there was the development of closer bilateral ties between Moscow and Bonn, largely based on personal diplomacy between Brandt and Brezhnev. Third, there was the problem of the ratification of the treaties and domestic German opposition to Ostpolitik, as well as Soviet domestic criticism of Brezhnev's Westpolitik.

The process by which Germany completed its Ostpolitik with other East European countries is a complex and lengthy story that cannot be recounted here. However, a brief summary will highlight the significance of these treaties for Soviet–German relations. The treaties resolved problems concerning prewar German territories and populations. Following almost a year of negotiations, Brandt flew to Warsaw in December 1970 to sign the German–Polish treaty. The FRG, in the Warsaw Treaty, finally recognized the Oder–Neisse boundary as the western frontier of Poland, renouncing all territorial claims on Poland and accepting the transfer of 104,000 square kilometers of prewar German territory to Poland. The treaty also pledged the Germans and Poles to settle any disputes between them by peaceful means, with a renunciation of force clause similar to that in the Moscow treaty. In a separate move, the Polish government agreed to permit the emigration of ethnic Germans from Poland.[4] There was much opposition to the treaty within Germany, both from the CDU in the Bundestag and from expellee organizations, which objected to this formal acceptance of Germany's reduced postwar territorial status.[5] For the Poles, as for the Soviets, the treaty with the FRG held the promise of increased economic cooperation.

Brandt had made it quite clear in his Moscow visit that the ratification of the Moscow and Warsaw treaties in the Bundestag was dependent on a satisfactory solution to the Berlin problem.[6] West Germany implemented a strategy of linkage (*Junktim*) by insisting that prior to any ratification of Ostpolitik, the USSR and the GDR must agree to stabilize and legitimize West Berlin's existence as an entity with ties to the FRG. The Four-Power talks on Berlin were undoubtedly the most difficult part of the Ostpolitik negotiations, involving strains between Bonn and Moscow, East Berlin and Moscow, and Bonn and its Western allies. Indeed, one reason Ulbricht fell from power in May 1971 was that he opposed the USSR's efforts to come to an accommodation over the Berlin question before the FRG had given de jure recognition to the GDR.[7]

The negotiations over Berlin began in December 1969. One of the chief sources of tension was between Ulbricht, who sought to end West Berlin's ties with Bonn, which facilitated West German access to East Germany, and Moscow, which was willing to compromise on Berlin because of deteriorating Sino–Soviet relations and the desire to strengthen detente with the United States. The Berlin talks were deadlocked in February 1971.[8] After a series of compromises and the resignation of Ulbricht, the Quadripartite Agreement was initialed on September 3, 1971. The main points of the agreement were that, in the interests of reducing tension in Berlin, the USSR would ensure unimpeded access to Berlin from West Germany, and West Berlin could maintain and develop its special ties with the FRG, although West Berlin was not a constituent part of West Germany.[9]

The Four Powers agreed to disagree on the question of West Berlin's status, because the Western powers maintained that the agreement should cover the whole city, whereas the USSR claimed it could apply only to West Berlin. However, the West gained on the question of ties between the FRG and Berlin, in that West Berliners could now visit the GDR on the same basis as citizens of the Federal Republic. Indeed, most analysts believed that the Berlin agreement represented a victory for the West because despite the diminution of Bonn's symbolic presence in West Berlin, the West gained more secure access, as well as travel to and transit to and from West Berlin, and from West Germany and West Berlin to East Germany. The real loser in this process was the GDR, whose role in Berlin matters was circumscribed.[10] Subsequently, there have been significant disagreements between the four powers on interpretations of the wording of the agreement, but in September 1971, the controversial Berlin accord was seen as a firm indication that Moscow was willing to compromise on a core political issue – the reality of West Berlin's ties to Bonn – in order to ensure the success of its Westpolitik. The real significance of the Berlin accord was that Moscow would be less likely to use West Berlin as a lever in its relations with Bonn, as Stalin and Khrushchev had.

It was during the Berlin negotiations that evidence of domestic Soviet opposition to Brezhnev's Westpolitik began to filter out. Although it is difficult to document this precisely, there is enough evidence to suggest not only domestic Soviet opposition but also links between Soviet and East German critics on this question. Following the August 1970 treaty, Brezhnev embarked on a tour of the Soviet republics, and in his speeches he criticized unnamed opponents of the Soviet–West German rapprochement. In early 1971, the Ukrainian press reported the discovery of a mass grave in the Crimea containing the bodies of Ukrainians slaughtered by Nazis. A massive anti-Nazi campaign – echoed in the GDR press – began at the time that Brezhnev was calling for improved relations with West Germany. This press compaign found no echoes elsewhere in the Soviet press and suggests some collusion between Soviet and East German opponents of Westpolitik.[11] During the Berlin negotiations, a sudden spate of rumors, assertions, and denials indicated that the Soviets were not pleased with Bonn's insistence on a Berlin settlement as a precondition to ratifying the treaty. In February 1971, reports from Washington and Stockholm indicated that Soviet diplomats were suggesting that the USSR was in no hurry to achieve either a Berlin settlement or the ratification of the treaties and was angry at Brandt for an alleged volte face in his policy toward the GDR.[12] Moreover, Bonn was accused of fermenting dissent in Poland that had led to the December 1970 Gdansk riots, after which Polish leader Gomulka was removed from power. Subsequent Soviet sources denied these charges, and Kosygin personally sent a letter to Brandt pledging the USSR's commitment to improve further relations with the FRG.[13] Whatever the truth about the Soviet reports, German observers took these contradictory statements as further evidence that some Soviet leaders were opposed to Brezhnev's Westpolitik (especially after the Gdansk riots) and were warning their colleagues.[14] The Soviet threats may also have been a veiled warning to Brandt not to push too far on the Berlin compromise. One can surmise from the ultimate outcome of the Berlin agreement that Brezhnev was able to prevail over these opponents. The Twenty-fourth Party Congress (in April 1971) reflected the consolidation of Brezhnev's personal power. He added four new members to the Politburo and increased his influence in the Central Committee.[15]

The third and most controversial treaty in the Ostpolitik was the Basic Treaty or *Grundvertrag* between East and West Germany in November 1972. The treaty normalized intra-German relations on the basis of the status quo and the signatories agreed to disagree on the question of the GDR's sovereignty. The treaty neither contained Bonn's formulation of "one German nation" nor referred specifically to the GDR's sovereignty. The West Germans had demanded "special relations" with East Germany, but the GDR insisted that their relations be those between two independent states. Finally, a compromise was reached whereby the FRG did not recognize the GDR in international law, adopting the formula of "two states in one nation" and the two countries agreed to exchange "permanent representatives" instead of ambassadors.[16] Both countries applied to join the United Nations. Some West German opposition groups challenged the treaty's legality, in view of the FRG's constitutional commitment to reunification, but the German Constitutional Court somewhat ambiguously upheld it.[17] The GDR in September 1974 formally removed from its constitution all mention of the concept of eventual reunification of the two Germanies. In March 1974 the FRG and GDR finally established permanent diplomatic missions in each other's capitals, but the West German representative dealt with the GDR Foreign Ministry, whereas the East Germans dealt with the Federal Chancellery in Bonn. The *Grundvertrag* signaled Moscow's acceptance of an intra-German rapprochement within the framework of the Moscow–Bonn detente.

Although Brandt was enlarging on and strengthening his Ostpolitik with Eastern Europe, he was also conscious of the need to continue improving the FRG's bilateral relationship with the USSR. At the Twenty-fourth Party Congress, Brezhnev had singled out the USSR's improved relations with the FRG as a hopeful sign for possibilities of peace in Europe.[18] Shortly after the conclusion of the Berlin accord, Brezhnev invited Brandt for an unprecedented private meeting in the Crimea, and Brandt accepted without consulting the United States or the FRG's other allies.[19] Although he was enthusiastic about the state of German–Soviet relations on his return, Brandt was quick to point out that this meeting did not signify another Rapallo - the ghost that West Germany, it seems, can never exorcise.[20] The final communique following the talks said that both sides had discussed a wide range of problems and had reasserted their commitment to the normalization of relations.[21] Whereas the Soviet press stressed the significance of the bilateral relations, Brandt emphasized that despite the improved political relations between the two countries, it would be incorrect to assume that the FRG and USSR were developing a special relationship: "We have not become friends of the Soviet Union or of its system, but rather have become partners in a businesslike contract, just as other Western states who are treaty partners of the Soviet Union."[22] Brandt always had to find a delicate balance between his independent Ostpolitik and the need to reassure the United States of the FRG's reliability.

The third issue in Soviet–West German relations was the internal politics of treaty ratification with the FRG. The opposition CDU had objected to every facet of Brandt's Ostpolitik and made a concerted effort to prevent the ratification of the treaty. Opposition leader Rainer Barzel hoped to use the ratification controversy to bring the Brandt government down. The first ratification debate was in the Bundesrat in December 1971. One of the supporting documents that Brandt submitted to the Bundesrat was a series of statements by Soviet Foreign Minister Gromyko designed to refute the arguments of those who claimed that the treaty sealed the division of Germany and the present borders in Europe, and that Bonn had made all the concessions.[23] The battle over Ostpolitik became more acute during the first Bundestag debate on the treaties, in February 1972. Foreign Minister Scheel, replying to opposition criticism, reaffirmed the official SPD–FDP line, which the Russians had indirectly corroborated: "If there is a way towards the unity of the nation, then it is only through a general relaxation of tension in Europe which can bear the burden of pushing in the background everything that separates us from the GDR."[24]

As the controversy continued, it appeared in March and April 1972 that the Bonn government might not obtain the necessary overall majority of 249 votes in the Bundestag for ratification. Brezhnev, in a speech to the Trade Union Congress in March, blamed "revanchist" elements in Germany for opposition to the treaties. Kosygin impressed on the German ambassador how important ratification was for the Kremlin. In the following weeks, the Kremlin took certain unprecedented steps to mollify German opposition. In April Gromyko, in a speech to the Supreme Soviet, confirmed Soviet acceptance of the "letter on German unity" appended to the 1970 treaty.[25] One of the CDU's main complaints was that the USSR had since 1957 refused to recognize the existence of the EEC, which was a vital component of Germany's economic and political security. Speaking to the trade unions, Brezhnev said: "The Soviet Union by no means ignores the situation in Western Europe, including the existence of an economic grouping of capitalist countries such as the Common Market. We are carefully observing the activity of the Common Market and of its evolution."[26] This de facto recognition of the EEC was seen in Germany as a major concession from the USSR. In April, a CDU vote of no confidence in Brandt was defeated by only two votes in the Bundestag. The treaty with the USSR was ratified on May 17 by 248 votes for, 10 against, and 238 abstentions in the Bundestag. On May 31, the Supreme Soviet unanimously ratified the treaty.[27] The controversy over the ratification had mobilized large sectors of the German population.[28] Polls indicated that 80 percent of the population supported Ostpolitik, among them every third CDU voter.[29] In the November 1972 election, the unexpectedly large victory of the SPD confirmed the overall support for Ostpolitik within the FRG. The SPD won 271 seats in the Bundestag, as opposed to 224 in 1969. The main reason Brandt was able to secure the ratification of his Ostpolitik was because of his own bargaining with other politicians. The USSR nevertheless used its own influence to try to insure passage of the treaties, showing how important this was for the Kremlin – or at least for Brezhnev and those who supported Westpolitik.

After the ratification of the treaties, Soviet–German relations continued to improve. The Soviet press, although warning against those in the FRG who opposed the normalization of relations with the USSR, began to change its coverage on West Germany in contrast to the pre-Brandt period. Gone were the constant denunciations of German imperialism and revanchism. In their place, more balanced articles stressing the predominance of reason and "businesslike" cooperation between the two countries began to appear.[30] In July 1973, Bonn and Prague finally buried the Munich Agreement in their bilateral treaty.

In Chapter 1 the four main components of the German problem were outlined. By 1973, all four areas had been dealt with in the *Ostvertraege*. The question of Germany's *geographical* location was settled in the Moscow, Warsaw, and Prague treaties. The question of the *division* of Germany was temporarily resolved in the *Grundvertrag*. The *Berlin* problem was resolved in the Four-Power Treaty. The question of Germany's integration into the Western alliance system was also settled by these treaties. The German problem was, for the time being, solved, although the long-term question of reunification remained.

The 1972 trade treaty: the end of linkage?

When Economics Minister Karl Schiller visited Moscow in September 1970, he discussed with Kosygin the renewal of talks to conclude a trade treaty with the USSR. The German government was concerned to reestablish a legal framework for economic relations. Apparently, Kosygin was receptive, but the problem of West Berlin was not resolved. The Russians also insisted on further import liberalization before the conclusion of any treaty.[31] The problem of the EEC had long complicated trade negotiations, because the Common Market had been trying to prevent the conclusion of bilateral East–West trade treaties and wanted to coordinate all its members' trade agreements with the East. However, in November 1970, Brussels agreed to allow the FRG to negotiate a five-year trade pact with the USSR.[32] When the USSR announced its ninth Five-Year Plan for 1971–75, it was clear that it was counting on a major expansion of foreign trade to make possible the realization of the plan.[33] Foreign trade was scheduled to rise by 33 percent in those five years, with computerization of the economy as one of the main Soviet goals.[34]

Against this background, the Soviets and Germans conducted negotiations on a new trade treaty from February 25 to March 5, 1971, in Bonn, the first time such negotiations had taken place since 1967. In the meantime, long-term trade treaties had been concluded between the FRG and Rumania (December 1969), Poland (October 1970), Hungary (October 1970), Czechoslovakia (December 1970), and Bulgaria (February 1971). All these agreements included an unpublished clause specifying that they were "valid for the area of the D-mark West," that is, West Berlin. This was what Bonn wanted in the Soviet treaty. In addition, however, the agreements provided for mixed commissions, one of whose functions was to proceed with liberalizing German import quotas from Eastern Europe so that 80 percent of these imports had been liberalized.[35] Because the FRG did not have a trade agreement with the USSR, no such commission existed, and there was no legal framework for monitoring trade difficulties and encouraging trade expansion by reducing quotas. Thus, German trade with the USSR was far less liberalized than with the rest of Eastern Europe. Moscow therefore had an economic interest in concluding a trade agreement, namely, increasing the volume and range of Soviet exports to the FRG and securing more guaranteed German credits.

Despite this Soviet economic motivation to conclude a trade treaty with the FRG, Moscow was still unwilling to meet the

FRG's minimal political condition for the conclusion of the trade treaty – the inclusion of West Berlin in the trade area. Moscow's political commitment to the independent status of Berlin at this stage overrode its economic self-interest. Likewise, although the Germans were interested in the agreement on trade for economic reasons, they were using it as a trial balloon to test the Russians' willingness to come to a general agreement on Berlin. The Brandt government had made it clear that there would be no ratification of the Moscow treaty without a Berlin agreement, and if the Russians would not even include Berlin in a trade treaty, then this was a bad omen for future Four-Power negotiations. Thus, both sides had economic and political stakes in the trade agreement. The German government was supported by industry in its insistence on a satisfactory Berlin solution. Otto Wolff von Amerongen, president of both the Ostausschuss and the DIHT, stressed that "a Berlin solution comes first."[36] During the ten days of negotiation, no solution was found to the Berlin question and the talks adjourned deadlocked. Moscow had given notice that it would not compromise its political principles for possible economic gain, and Bonn had likewise impressed on the Soviets how seriously it viewed their stubbornness on the Berlin issue.

In the intervening months, German hopes for the completion of trade agreements and a Soviet compromise on Berlin began to decline, and the follow-up talks on trade, originally scheduled for April, were not held. However, when the Berlin accord was initialed, the Germans took this as a signal from the Soviets that they would be willing to agree to a Berlin clause in a new trade agreement.[37] Nevertheless, the USSR refused to do this, and the talks remained stalled. The question still remains as to why they were willing to sign a Four-Power agreement guaranteeing West Berlin's political links to the FRG but were not prepared to agree to a clause reaffirming West Berlin's trade links with the FRG. It is possible that the Soviets held back so that they would still have a lever to use during the difficult ratification process in Germany. Because the Kremlin had repeatedly said that the economic and political aspects of normalization of relations were linked, it apparently did not want to compromise on the economic side until it was certain that there would be a political quid pro quo from the Germans. On the other hand, subsequent developments suggested that any Soviet acceptance of West Berlin's links with Bonn in treaties were an exception rather than a rule. In 1978, Moscow refused to sign agreements with the FRG that included West Berlin, and its stand in 1971 was consistent with its general policy of not signing Berlin clauses in treaties with Bonn.

In December 1971, Scheel met with Gromyko in Moscow to discuss the problems of ratification and of German–Soviet economic relations, and Gromyko stressed that the USSR wanted a definite sign that the Moscow treaty would be ratified before the USSR would sign a trade agreement including a Berlin clause.

However, German observers commented that the USSR was worried about the prospect of the FRG concluding a trade agreement with China, a concern that was reinforced and increased by President Nixon's visit to China and the prospects of greater U.S.–Chinese trade.[38] There is indeed a similarity between the Soviet decision to respond favorably to Brandt's Ostpolitik and the Kremlin's change of heart about the trade treaty. Both seem to have been motivated by developments within Germany and by the threat of Chinese competition. In March Brandt announced, at a crucial Bundestag Foreign Affairs Committee meeting, that the USSR was prepared to facilitate the ratification of the treaties both by accepting Foreign Minister Scheel's "letter on German unity" and by provisionally signing a new trade agreement recognizing Bonn's right to act for West Berlin in trade matters.[39] The Soviets' intervention at this time was crucial, because by agreeing to accept a Berlin clause, they enabled the SPD to portray the Soviet move as an important vindication of Brandt's Ostpolitik and a powerful argument for ratification. As an added incentive, Brezhnev agreed to permit ethnic Germans living in the USSR to emigrate if the treaty was ratified.[40]

Trade talks began on April 3, 1972, and with the removal of the Berlin obstacle, there were few outstanding economic difficulties. The trade pact was initialed on April 7 and covered trade and economic cooperation until December 31, 1974. The agreement foresaw a significant increase in exchanges of machinery, equipment, manufactures, and consumer goods. It included West Berlin explicitly, although the USSR did not make any compromise different from that in 1960.[41] It also estab-

lished a mixed commission to look into regulating trade relations.[42] Economics Minister Schiller, writing in *Handelsblatt*,
hailed the agreement in the following terms: "In our relations
with state trading nations, we cannot follow the principle that
political understanding follows trade and economic cooperation –
because of this, German industry needs a secure political basis
for its long-term trade and cooperation agreements with Soviet
enterprises."[43] The German government, although stressing the
economic importance of the agreement, used it to argue for the
ratification of the treaties. The Soviet press stressed the economic and political significance of the agreement, saying it
would help to strengthen peace in Europe.[44] However, the
Soviets made it quite clear that if the treaties were not ratified,
the trade agreement and German–Soviet economic relations in
general would be harmed. Speaking to the Foreign Affairs
Committee of the Supreme Soviet, Politburo member Mikhail
Suslov, reputed to be less supportive of detente than Brezhnev,
gave an explicit warning: "It goes without saying that, if the
treaty does not come into force, the FRG, having lost the political
confidence of other states, will lose its significance for the Soviet
Union as a serious economic partner."[45] At the first meeting of
the German–Soviet mixed economic commission, the Soviet delegation chairman, Novikov, intimated that the commission's
work would continue only if the treaties were ratified.[46] However, some German business circles were skeptical of Soviet sin-
cerity in these pronouncements. They believed that the Russians
were using the threat of breaking economic ties as a pressure
tactic to insure ratification of the treaties, and they claimed that,
even if the treaties were not ratified, the USSR would continue
to trade with the FRG at its previous level for purely economic
reasons.[47]

The USSR signed the trade agreement following the ratification of the treaties on July 5, 1972, and Soviet Foreign Trade
Minister Patolichev symbolically passed through West Berlin on
his way to the signing. The FRG reduced its import quotas on
Soviet goods from 40 to 16 percent and promised to reduce
them further.[48] Patolichev termed the agreement an "organic"
result of the Crimean talks between Brandt and Brezhnev.[49]
Soviet writers in general praised the agreement as laying a
firmer foundation for German–Soviet economic relations.

Brezhnev's 1973 visit to Bonn: from cold war to detente

Leonid Brezhnev's trip to Bonn in 1973, the first time a Soviet leader had ever set foot on West German territory, provides a sharp contrast to the first visit by a West German head of state to the USSR in the chilly cold war days. Indeed, the differences between Adenauer's trip to Moscow in 1955 and Brezhnev's Bonn visit highlight the profound changes that had taken place in German–Soviet relations over the past two decades. Ten years earlier, Khrushchev had been ousted partly because he was about to commit the cardinal sin of visiting Bonn. Now, the talk was of friendship and unlimited opportunities for economic cooperation. Brezhnev's trip also demonstrates the great importance that the Kremlin attached to its trade with the FRG and suggests the degree to which economic factors influenced Soviet foreign policy.

Before Adenauer visited Moscow, there was much speculation about whether the summit would succeed. At one point, negotiations were nearly broken off. By contrast, prior to Brezhnev's visit, both the German and Soviet presses were full of articles praising the visit and showing an expectation of harmony and success on both sides. The most difficult issue was expected to be Berlin, but because there was a Four-Power agreement, it was anticipated that there could not be serious dissension. The head of the Soviet trade mission in Cologne stressed that economic relations would be the focus of the visit, and that the USSR hoped for broadened economic contacts with Germany.[50] Both German and Soviet commentators, therefore, correctly gauged that the main goal of Brezhnev's visit was to promote economic relations, because the bilateral political agenda had been completed.

Brezhnev's arrival in Bonn from East Berlin on May 18 was emotional, with both the Soviet and West German leaders clearly moved by the historic significance of the event. Security precautions were extremely tight, and Brezhnev was isolated from the German people for most of his trip.[51] At one dinner Brezhnev reminisced about his memories of Germany invading his country in two world wars, and Finance Minister Helmut Schmidt discussed his activities on the Eastern front in the Second World War. Unlike the acerbic exchange of views between Adenauer and Molotov, however, these discussions stressed the prospects for improved relations between the two sides.[52] Significantly, the political part of the negotiations followed the economic talks. There was no political breakthrough, because both sides had achieved their goals, although general questions of European security were discussed. On the question of Berlin, the communiqué at the end of the four-day trip promised "strict adherence and full application" of the 1971 Four-Power agreement.[53] The declaration also stipulated that both parties would work toward the successful conclusion of the European Security Conference. Thus, the political negotiations represented a ratification and reiteration of the previous detente agreements.

In contrast to Adenauer's visit to Moscow, when economics was barely mentioned and political problems were paramount, economics occupied the bulk of Brezhnev's time in the FRG and produced the only concrete agreements following the summit. The main treaty was a ten-year accord on the development of economic, industrial, and technical cooperation, something that the Soviets had long wanted to negotiate. The agreement provided for the exchange of raw materials, energy technology and know-how, and industrial plant under the aegis of a joint commission for a period of ten years. The practical meaning of the treaty was that the USSR had expressed its willingness to provide Germany with oil, gas, and raw materials in exchange for industrial plant and technical advice from German business. In addition, a cultural agreement was signed and also an agreement on air traffic, permitting Lufthansa to fly to Tokyo via Moscow, which specifically mentioned West Berlin.[54]

Probably the most symbolic episode during the Brezhnev visit occurred when the leader of the Soviet Communist Party, to the horror of his security guards, enthusiastically jumped into the new Mercedes sports car presented to him by the German government and roared off alone down a hill at lightning speed. Compared to this show of enthusiasm for the products of German technology, Khrushchev's wry appreciation of Adenauer's gift of binoculars pales into insignificance. Like his predecessor, Brezhnev had great admiration for the West German economy. He referred positively to interwar German–Soviet economic cooperation and praised the German engineers who had worked at the factory where he had been employed.[55] The difference was that Brezhnev, unlike Khrushchev, was not only committed to broadening the USSR's economic links with the FRG; he also had the wherewithal to do it. Conscious of Germany's growing energy import needs, Brezhnev knew that he had something to offer the Germans in return for increased imports of German capital goods. The highlight of Brezhnev's tour was the helicopter flight over the Ruhr and his meeting with sixteen top German businessmen. Even though economic affairs are more closely controlled by politicians in the USSR than in the FRG, Soviet economic functionaries usually negotiate trade and cooperation matters. It was a sign of Brezhnev's great interest in economic ties with the FRG that he personally spent a day discussing specific projects. He also described in glowing terms the prospects of opening up Siberia and other long-term deals. It was clear that Brezhnev's main interest was not in trade but in huge cooperative ventures, and that his vision of future German–Soviet cooperation was extremely optimistic.

The irony of Brezhnev's enthusiasm over German–Soviet economic relations was that many of the German businessmen with whom he talked thought he was being unrealistic – those same businessmen who a decade before had pressed the German government to increase trade with the USSR. Brezhnev told his guests: "We are looking for new cooperation agreements for 30, 40 and 50 years. Seize those opportunities, don't wait." They thought that Brezhnev's admiration for the German economy and its potential investments in the USSR was exaggerated. For instance, he overestimated the scale on which German industry operated when he proposed the joint exploration of copper and bauxite. Brandt, in his memoirs, recalls how much Brezhnev stressed the economic component of Soviet–German relations and the possibilities of giant cooperative deals, claiming that he personally had criticized certain ministers for some of the problems in trade with the FRG at the previous plenum of the Central Committee. It was Brandt's strong impression that Brezhnev overestimated the FRG's potential for trade with the USSR.[56] Armed with offers of vast supplies of Soviet energy, Brezhnev thought that economic relations between the two countries could be transformed, both quantitatively and qualitatively.

Whereas Khrushchev had spoken of "an ocean of trade with

the East," Brezhnev took this theme a significant step further. Gone were the familiar statements made by Khrushchev in 1955 and again by Kosygin in 1971 that the USSR did not need West Germany economically.[57] Although Brezhnev did not express his desires in terms of Soviet need but rather in terms of the boundless possibilities of mutual economic ties, the message was the same: The Soviet Union definitely wanted to expand its economic relations with Germany as much as possible and as soon as possible. In his television speech in the FRG, Brezhnev had pointed out that increased economic relations would provide a firm basis for peace.[58] The German press viewed this Soviet enthusiasm as having "historical meaning" and said that there had never before been such an offer of economic relations from the USSR to any Western state.[59] A Soviet commentary on the trip stressed the other familiar theme that the Germans wanted Soviet trade, adding: "The organization of long-term economic cooperation is in the interests of both sides. It leads to the strengthening of trust between states, strengthens peaceful relations with one of the most powerful capitalist states, and permits a more rational use of international economic ties."[60]

After Brezhnev returned to Moscow, the Soviet press emphasized the economic aspects of his trip, explaining that "nothing can better contribute to the strengthening of peace than business cooperation." Rather than emphasize the German need for trade with the USSR, the Soviet media now stressed the theme of mutual advantages, although commentators admitted the economic difficulties involved in implementing specific projects.[61] Brezhnev clearly hoped that one of the main results of his Westpolitik would be a significant increase in German–Soviet trade. He also felt secure enough – having ousted two of the main opponents of Westpolitik, Ukrainian Party leader Pyotr Shelest and Gennaidi Voronov, one month before his departure for Bonn – to pursue quite unabashedly the economic aspects of his Westpolitik.[62] Moreover, because the bilateral Westpolitik had been completed, there was little more, politically, that Brezhnev could obtain from Brandt. The next phase of German–Soviet detente negotiations would be multilateral and concerned with European security, the Strategic Arms Limitation Treaty (SALT), Mutual Balanced Force Reduction (MBFR), and other strategic issues, depending more on the United States than on Germany.

In contrast to Adenauer's departure from Moscow, which was characterized more by relief than any other emotion, Brezhnev delayed his departure from Bonn by thirty-five minutes in last-minute embraces with German politicians. Commentators from both countries noted the improved political climate, yet little concrete was achieved. It was an end rather than a beginning. Brezhnev's trip symbolized the waning of the cold war and the temporary resolution of the German problem. Shortly after his departure, a new era was to begin, one in which the formal aspects of Ostpolitik and Westpolitik no longer occupied such an important position in the world arena. Bilateral detente was a legal fait accompli, and now it remained to be seen what operational meaning it had in day-to-day terms, as opposed to the theatre of summitry.

The years 1970 to 1973 marked the transition to a new period in German–Soviet relations in which the old patterns of interaction that had prevailed during the cold war were modified. Brandt's visit to the USSR and Brezhnev's trip to Bonn symbolized the passage between the two eras. The press talked of the transition from confrontation to cooperation. Nevertheless, although the political symbolism of the Brezhnev visit was significant, the fanfare attached to the economic agreement testified to the continuing abnormality of Soviet–West German trade. As one German diplomat cautioned, "Things that seem spectacular with the Soviet Union would just be taken as normal in other countries."[63]

Ostpolitik phase 2: multilateral detente between the two Brezhnev visits

The 1973 Brezhnev visit to Bonn marked the close of the bilateral phase of West German–Soviet detente. Henceforth, detente in Europe was to be a product of multilateral negotiations – which would have been impossible without the prior bilateral detente. Probably the most important of these were the negotiations for the European Security Conference. The USSR had for years called for the convening of an all-European conference on security to ratify multilaterally the boundaries of postwar Europe. After much debate, the Conference on Security and Cooperation in Europe (CSCE) of thirty-five nations opened in 1973. It would have been impossible without Brandt's Ostpolitik, because Brandt's acceptance of the boundaries of Europe and his de facto recognition of the division of Germany was a prerequisite for the conference. Initially, the USSR had sought to block U.S. participation in CSCE, stressing the incompatibility between American and European interests and presenting CSCE as a safe way for the Europeans to escape American domination. However, once they had accepted U.S. participation, the Soviets were concerned to consolidate their control over Eastern Europe during the conference.[64] The Soviet call for CSCE was greeted with considerable skepticism in the West, because it appeared to serve primarily Soviet interests in legitimizing the division of Europe. Nevertheless, the conference ultimately may have inaugurated a process of political change with unexpected and undesired consequences for the USSR. In addition, the West was able to secure Soviet agreement to begin talks on MBFR in Europe by predicating Western participation in the CSCE conference on Soviet participation in MBFR talks.

The results of the two-year CSCE negotiations that culminated in the Helsinki Final Act of August 1975 have been analyzed elsewhere.[65] Briefly, after complicated negotiations (which Brezhnev aptly described as a "useful school of international politics for the participating states"), the thirty-five signatories signed a document consisting of three "baskets," or provisions, and a fourth basket relating to a follow-up conference. The first basket concerned general political principles governing interstate relations. The West German government was intent on preventing CSCE from ratifying the division of Germany and fought to ensure that the language in basket one left open the possibility of German reunification similar to the provisions of the Bonn–Moscow treaty and the *Grundvertrag*.[66] The Soviets finally compromised on the question of the immutability of frontiers, and the declaration stated that the participating states "consider that their frontiers can be changed, in accordance with international law, by peaceful means and by agreement." Basket two, which was the least controversial, and was more important for Eastern than for Western Europe, dealt with facilitating greater economic and technological relations, asserting that economic activity would "contribute to the reinforcement of peace and security in Europe and in the world as a whole."[67] The most controversial basket was the third, dealing with "cooperation in humanitarian and other fields." The Eastern side fought against including this provision and Secretary of State Kissinger downplayed its importance, but Western Europe insisted on its inclusion. With this basket, the USSR signed a document committing it to encourage the freer flow of ideas and people within the Soviet Union in exchange for securing Western agreement to recognize the boundaries of Europe and to promote trade and technological cooperation. At the end of the conference, many viewed the Helsinki Act as a diplomatic victory for the USSR. After all, Moscow had secured public Western assent to the postwar division of Europe, and it was difficult to see what the West had achieved through this concession.

But in the two years following the Helsinki conference and prior to the first follow-up conference in Belgrade, it became clear that the Soviet Union had incurred unforeseen liabilities by signing the Final Act. Dissident groups within the USSR and Eastern Europe cited Soviet assent to basket three to legitimize their demands for more freedom of expression. Helsinki monitoring groups burgeoned throughout Eastern Europe, demanding greater freedoms consistent with the Helsinki declaration.[68] Despite Soviet insistence that it was complying with the stipulations of basket three, and despite the persecution of these monitoring groups, the Kremlin was forced to make some concessions after Helsinki, casting doubt on the assertions of Western opponents of CSCE that the USSR was the victor in this process.[69] As a West German spokesman said, "None of us believed that the Final Act would develop such an impact in this area."[70]

The CSCE process has particular significance for West Germany because of its implications for relations between the two Germanies. The FRG was careful to ensure that CSCE did not turn into an ersatz peace conference legitimizing the permanent division of Germany, which the Kremlin ideally would have liked. However, basket three has probably had more effect on intra-German relations than in any other area. The provisions regarding a freer flow of people and ideas and reunification of families have been a major reason for the GDR's willingness to permit greater emigration to the FRG and more visits from the FRG.[71] In return, the GDR has received tangible economic benefits through increased intra-German trade. CSCE has reinforced the process of intra-German normalization initiated by the *Grundvertrag*. If one attempts to draw up a balance sheet, it seems that CSCE had had more effect on intra-German relations than on West German–Soviet relations, and that what the FRG may have lost by further legitimizing the GDR's existence it has surely gained by increasing the flow of people and contacts between the two Germanies.

The West German government played an active role in linking the CSCE conference to negotiations on force reduction in Europe, but these produced fewer concrete results than did CSCE because of a variety of unresolved difficulties. The MBFR talks began in Vienna in October 1973 and were intended to increase West German security by diminishing the Warsaw Pact presence in Central Europe. However, the talks were stalled by three main issues. The first was the definition of "balanced" force reduction. Given the asymmetrical geographical proximities of the USSR and the United States to the European heartland, (defined in Vienna as Belgium, the Netherlands, Luxemburg, West and East Germany, Poland, and Czechoslovakia) it was difficult to arrive at a definition of balance that was acceptable to both sides. Second, there were persistent discrepancies between Western and Soviet estimates of the size of Warsaw Pact troop strength in Eastern Europe.[72] A third problem was the fact that whereas the talks were continuing at a snail's pace, the USSR was building up conventional Warsaw Pact troop strength in Central Europe. France's refusal to take part in the negotiations further complicated the talks.

Given the FRG's pivotal role in the NATO alliance and its geographical position facing Warsaw Pact troops, West Germany's stake in the MBFR negotiations was particularly significant. The USSR was faced with a contradictory choice. On the one hand, it wanted to reduce the American military presence in Europe; on the other hand, it did not want Bundeswehr strength to increase to compensate for the troop withdrawal. Bonn, although not necessarily endorsing growth in its own armed strength, wanted to ensure that its vulnerability to the Soviet presence was not increased through conventional troop reductions. Moreover, Bonn stressed the differing implications of MBFR for the US and the USSR, on the one hand, and for those European countries actually situated in the areas of proposed reductions, on the other. Because the FRG would be much more directly affected by troop reductions than would the US, the Germans proposed a two-stage process of troop reduction, first by the US and USSR and then by European forces, to deal with the asymmetrical situation.[73]

In the initial phase of the MBFR talks, the USSR insisted on troop cuts that would ensure Soviet predominance. However, under Western pressure, the Kremlin began to modify its policy, and when Brezhnev visited Bonn in May 1978, the joint Soviet-West German communiqué emphasized approximate parity as a negotiating principle. In addition, the USSR agreed to negotiate about medium-range missiles in the so-called gray area, such as the SS-20s, which were included neither in SALT nor in MBFR. Chancellor Schmidt expressed optimism about the future of MBFR, but by the end of 1978 it was difficult to detect significant progress on this issue.[74] The MBFR negotiations were, however, overshadowed by the bilateral US-Soviet SALT negotiations on strategic nuclear weapons. Bonn was consulted on these negotiations and publicly supported American proposals, although its main concern was with weapons that threatened Central Europe.[75] The multilateral aspects of East-West detente both reinforced bilateral German-Soviet detente and also highlighted differences within the Western alliance over policy toward the USSR.

Soviet-West German relations were affected by the change in government in Bonn. In May 1974, Willy Brandt resigned after it was revealed that one of his closest personal advisors in the Chancellery, Gunther Guillaume, was an East German spy. One of the final ironies of Brandt's career as chancellor was that the man who had done most to improve relations with the USSR and the GDR lost his position because of East German espionage. The Soviet press commented only briefly on the change in the West German government when Helmut Schmidt became chancellor, Walter Scheel president, and Hans-Dietrich Genscher foreign minister. No reason was given for Brandt's resignation.[76] Although Schmidt pledged to continue his predecessor's Ostpolitik, the Soviet leaders were somewhat wary of him, because he was known to be less emotionally committed to Ostpolitik than was Brandt.

The difference in both style and substance between the two men was evident when Schmidt visited Moscow in October 1974. It was a meeting that focused on economic questions.[77] Continuing problems over the interpretation of the Four-Power agreement on Berlin were also discussed, as well as general political issues. The tone was businesslike, and one outcome was a commitment to regularize relations by holding fairly frequent summit-level talks. Following the Schmidt visit, there were a number of high-level meetings between Bonn and Moscow prior to the 1978 Brezhnev visit to Bonn. Schmidt and Brezhnev met at the Helsinki Conference in 1975, and Brandt, in his capacity as chairman of the SPD, was invited to the USSR in 1975. Both President Scheel and Egon Bahr visited the USSR, as did FDP Foreign Minister Genscher. The Kremlin, realizing that Genscher had a more critical attitude toward Ostpolitik than his predecessor, was somewhat suspicious of him, but Soviet reports of his visit stressed the "businesslike" nature of the talks.[78] Whereas in the 1960s high-level FRG–Soviet talks were a rarity, they had now become the norm.

Because the new Ostpolitik had been a product of an SPD–FDP coalition and the CDU continued to criticize the Brandt treaties, the Kremlin was concerned about the 1976 West German election. At one point it appeared that just as Ostpolitik had given the SPD a substantial victory in 1972, it might be its downfall in 1976. The election campaign also touched on the question of economic ties with the East. Prior to the election, the Soviet government issued a number of statements about the course of Ostpolitik. The Soviet press took an active part in commenting on the 1976 election, as it had in the 1972 campaign. It stressed the role that Ostpolitik had played in increasing the FRG's political independence in the Western world, and at the Twenty-fifth Party Congress, Brezhnev singled out relations with the FRG for special mention in his general review of ties with capitalist states.[79]

In 1972, the German electorate had endorsed Ostpolitik, but by the 1976 elections, support for it had declined, not the least because of the Guillaume affair, and the CDU's campaign was a well-coordinated assault on the Brandt policy. The CDU–CSU slogan was "Freedom not Socialism," (*Freiheit statt Sozialismus*), charging that the governing coalition was succumbing to a socialist bureaucracy domestically, a tendency exacerbated by a weak policy toward the East, through which communist countries had outwitted the SPD-FDP government. CDU TV campaign films showed pictures of Brandt and Schmidt happily consorting with Kremlin leaders, juxtaposed with shots of East German refugees.[80] While two prominent CDU spokesmen on foreign affairs, Werner Marx and Alfred Dregger, were entertained by the Chinese, the CDU candidate for chancellor, Helmut Kohl, advocated the use of negative economic levers to force political concessions from the Russians, because they desperately needed Western trade. Although the FDP publicly supported Schmidt's Ostpolitik, it was known that Foreign Minister Genscher himself preferred to take a tougher line with the Soviets on some issues, particularly that of Berlin.

During the 1972 campaign, the Soviets had aided the SPD-FDP coalition by defusing tensions over West Berlin and giving de facto recognition to the EEC. In 1976, however, despite the Soviet preference for the ruling coalition over the CDU, the Kremlin appeared more ambivalent. The Soviet press criticized Schmidt's remarks after the Puerto Rico summit, in which he said that the Germans and their allies would withdraw all financial aid to Italy if communists were given cabinet posts in an Italian government.[81] About a month before the election, however, there was a discernable shift in Soviet comments on the West German election. Moscow had apparently realized that, however much it disliked the diminished SPD enthusiasm for Ostpolitik, it would be far more injurious to Soviet-West German relations if the CDU-CSU were to win. *Izvestiia* praised the ruling coalition for its Ostpolitik, based on mutually advantageous cooperation, emphasizing the positive feelings that both Soviet and West German citizens had for bilateral detente.[82] Less than two weeks before the election, the Soviet government announced that Brezhnev would visit Bonn after the election.[83] Despite Moscow's doubts about the Schmidt government, therefore, the Soviet leadership was ultimately persuaded to come out publicly in support of the ruling coalition.

The SPD-FDP coalition won the election by a narrow victory. The CDU-CSU scored a 3.8 percent gain, their best result since 1957. Moscow reacted swiftly to the SPD-FDP victory, claiming that it represented a mandate "to carry on the Eastern policy, to develop mutually advantageous ties with the USSR and other socialist countries." Despite the negative role that Ostpolitik had played in the campaign, the Soviet press could now claim that it was the success of Schmidt's detente policies that was decisive in the election.[84]

The 1978 Brezhnev visit: lowered expectations

After two years of rumors and postponements, Brezhnev traveled to Bonn in May 1978 for the second time. The visit came at a low point in West German–American relations, and there was concern that Brezhnev was hoping to utilize these tensions to his own advantage. In general, expectations for this trip were lower than they had been in 1973, and the German press questioned what could be accomplished by the visit. It was agreed that disarmament, economic cooperation, and Berlin would be the main talking points, but that no decisive agreement would be reached on any of these topics. Soviet commentators were much more enthusiastic about the forthcoming visit. Brezhnev spoke of a "qualitatively new character" in Soviet–West German relations, adding that "the state of relations between West Germany and the Soviet Union is a sensitive indicator of international detente" and stressing that the USSR had only peaceful intentions in Western Europe. The Soviet press emphasized the economic aspects of FRG–Soviet relations, pointing out that bilateral trade had developed at a consistently higher rate than the overall foreign trade of both countries and stressing the potential for further growth in trade.[85]

It is instructive that the economic dimension of these talks was stressed so much before the visit. In the years following Brandt's resignation, Soviet–West German political relations had stabilized at a level of lowered expectations. Brandt's Ostpolitik had achieved its main goal – normalization of relations – and the only area where there could be movement in bilateral Soviet–FRG relations was in economic relations. There were no major outstanding areas of political disagreement, and the signing of a new economic agreement was the one likely tangible outcome of the talks. Economic relations between the two countries had always implied a degree of normality absent from political ties in the pre-Brandt era, and in the age of more stable – or perhaps stagnant – detente they still had this function.

The 1978 Brezhnev visit was more subdued than the Soviet president's previous visit. It was businesslike, without pomp and ceremony. One reason for this less public visit was Brezhnev's health (the Soviet leader canceled a meeting with Ruhr industrialists), but it also appeared that Schmidt wanted to minimize the ceremonial aspects of the visit. Brezhnev was in the FRG from May 4 to 7, in Bonn and Hamburg. Apart from his talks with leaders of the SPD–FDP coalition, he also saw CDU leader Helmut Kohl and CSU leader Franz-Josef Strauss, the conservative politician who had long been a bête noire of the Soviet press. This meeting received great press attention in Germany. When Brezhnev saw Kohl, the meeting was reportedly rather acerbic, but the encounter with Strauss was apparently so pleasant that Brezhnev took the unprecedented step of accompanying Strauss to his car and thereby kept Communist Party leader Herbert Mies waiting.[86] Some conservative American observers saw Brezhnev's cordial reception of Strauss as a move to weaken German ties with the US, but the warmth of the talks may have represented something less sinister than this.[87] The Kremlin, anticipating that the CDU–CSU could conceivably form the next government, wanted to improve contacts with its leaders.

The political outcome of the talks was meager, beyond general declarations of friendly intent. Brezhnev publicly did not sing the GDR's praises, and he agreed to the principle of parity in MBFR negotiations. However, in the matter of Berlin there was little progress, and three German–Soviet agreements remained unsigned because of the Berlin clause. In the joint declaration issued by Brezhnev and Schmidt, there were mainly political generalities. (The Germans ruled out the Soviet proposal to use the words "friendship" and "rapprochement" in the communiqué.)[88] The two sides agreed that "detente is necessary possible, and useful," emphasized the importance of CSCE, committed themselves to military parity, resolved to "further improve the quality and level of their relations in all fields," and reaffirmed their upholding of "strict observance and full implementation of the Quadripartite Agreement."[89] Brezhnev's prerecorded (in Moscow) television address to the German people about the outcome of the talks contained only political platitudes, and the relative uninterest with which it was received was a sign of how normal relations had become. The visit by a Soviet leader to Bonn was no longer a matter for great attention.

In the Bundestag debate following the visit, the chancellor was optimistic and even the opposition was muted in its criticism. In reply to Schmidt's affirmations of solidarity with West Berlin, CDU leader Kohl reiterated his party's commitment to detente but nevertheless criticized the chancellor for not being tough enough with Brezhnev. He said the concrete results of the visit were "very meager" and regretted the absence of positive movement on the Berlin question. A CDU statement singled out the Soviet failure to sign the three agreements that included Berlin and reiterated the opposition's commitment to reunification.[90] Nevertheless, the tone of the debate was much less acerbic than previous ones on Ostpolitik. Despite their criticisms of the SPD–FDP government, the CDU–CSU had no real alternative program to Ostpolitik, and their arguments were over form more than substance. By 1978 a bipartisan consensus over the desirability of maintaining detente had emerged.

The Soviet press was uniformly positive in its evaluation of the Brezhnev visit, and according to a TASS statement during the talks, "the political barometer pointed in an ever more confident way to good." *Neues Deutschland* also praised the talks, and a week after the Brezhnev visit, following the pattern of previous visits, Gromyko went to East Berlin for talks with GDR leader Erich Honecker. The USSR and the GDR signed a new agreement on cultural and scientific cooperation, and in the communiqué released after the visit, Honecker gave his full support to the results of the FRG–USSR talks.[91]

After Brezhnev's departure, there was a change in Soviet ambassadors in Bonn. Valentin Falin, who had served as ambassador in Bonn for seven years, returned to Moscow in August 1978, to become a spokesman on foreign affairs for the Central Committee. He was succeeded by Vladimir Semyenov. Semyenov was a high-ranking diplomat with an intimate knowledge of Germany. A former ambassador to the GDR, he had negotiated the 1957–58 treaties on trade and repatriation in Bonn and had accompanied Mikoyan to Bonn in 1958. He had also served in Germany during the period of the Nazi–Soviet Pact. He had headed the Soviet delegation to SALT and was an important spokesman on Soviet foreign policy. There was some speculation about the appointment of a man who had played such a key role in Germany's postwar history and was known to have been a previous supporter of German reunification. Undoubtedly, Semyenov's appointment was a testimony to the high place occupied by Bonn in Soviet foreign policy.

If the political results of the Brezhnev visit were unsubstantial, then the economic outcome was more concrete, indicating the improvement in German–Soviet relations. Economics Minister Graf Lambsdorff held discussions with Foreign Trade Minister Patolichev and First Deputy Prime Minister Tikhonov on a variety of issues, but the main result, the twenty-five-year economic cooperation agreement, had been prepared before the summit. The Agreement on Developing and Deepening Long-term Cooperation between the Federal Republic and the Union of Soviet Socialist Republics in the Economic and Industrial Fields of May 6, 1978, was a broad agreement covering a variety of areas. The preamble said that both sides were "seeking constantly to develop and deepen the entire complex of relations between the two states," but the rest of the agreement dealt only with economic matters. The agreement stressed long-term bilateral cooperation in various fields such as energy and "the widest possible exchange of economic information in order to improve mutual marketing opportunities," the commitment to "exert efforts to grant medium-term and long-term credits within the framework of the rules existing in each state on as favorable terms as possible," and said that the agreement "will cover [West] Berlin in keeping with established procedures."[92] The framework agreement was for twenty-five years, with the initial term fixed at ten years. In view of the EEC ruling that member states could no longer conclude bilateral trade agreements with the USSR, this was called a cooperation and not a trade agreement.

In the parliamentary debate on the Brezhnev visit, Schmidt singled out the cooperation agreement for special praise. Although he admitted that there were problems in the bilateral economic relationship, caused particularly by the Soviet preference for compensation deals that were sometimes disadvantageous to both sides, he said that the Russians were aware of these problems. He continued:

But also on political grounds I am glad that we have been able to sign this agreement – the economic agreement extends far beond the range of economic affairs. It provides an orientation for the development of political relations in general, for long-term peaceful development which presupposes that the people in both countries acquire a permanent interest in one another's economic welfare.[93]

A government spokesman said that the chancellor saw the agreement as a "political act without parallel in the recent history of the world."[94] An FDP spokesman during the Bundestag debate further claimed that the twenty-five-year agreement was a "stabilizing element for the development of bilateral relations," although he warned against too much economic optimism about the results of the treaty.[95]

In a distinct change in government reasoning, it was now argued that, even if the agreement was economically problematic, its positive political effects were considerable and outweighed the economic disadvantages of Soviet-West German trade. The government espoused the view that improved economic relations could benefit political relations. The agreement ran for twenty-five years and would therefore give both sides a stake in continuing good relations. The government was now arguing that *Osthandel* was politically significant, despite economic difficulties, a claim that the Ostausschuss itself would never have made so directly.

The CDU–CSU, although supporting trade with the USSR in principle, nevertheless found a political reason for criticizing the treaty. Helmut Kohl seized on a statement that Schmidt had made, in which the chancellor had described the cooperation agreement in terms of a Soviet reinsurance treaty like that of Bismarck (in which the Iron Chancellor had allied Germany with both Austria and Russia). Kohl used the trade agreement to accuse Schmidt of introducing a *Schaukelpolitik* and of weakening Germany's loyalty to the Western alliance. A CSU statement claimed that the agreement created the danger that the FRG would become too closely entwined with the USSR economically, and that the Kremlin could use this dependence for political purposes.[96]

The Soviets attached great importance to the treaty and were more enthusiastic about it than they had ever been about any previous economic agreements. Because the agreement expressed general goals, the Germans had nothing to lose by it, but all the government could do was to establish the parameters; it was up to the business community to implement the agreement. The Economics Ministry hoped that the framework would facilitate long-range projects, but no specific deals were envisioned.

The twenty-five-year agreement demonstrated the limits of government power to promote trade with the USSR. All the Economics Ministry could do was to provide the framework; it could not force companies to engage in trade, thus limiting its use of trade as a political incentive. The business community was notably reticent about the agreement. Wolff von Amerongen, downplaying its importance, said, "It is not a historic accord. It gives German industrialists the chance to plan better and the possibility to accelerate exchanges, but they are problematical between countries with such different economic systems."[97] The difference between government and business evaluations of the significance of the agreement highlighted its symbolic political nature, because its economic content was relatively unimportant. It was the commitment to long-term cooperation that had political implications.

The twenty-five-year agreement of 1978 reflected the qualitative changes in the interface between economics and politics that had occurred since 1970. The agreement indicated that politics and economics were considered interdependent in the long term, because such a treaty could function satisfactorily for twenty-five years only if political relations remained good. Linkage, in the sense of explicitly using economic levers to promote specific changes in political behavior, was no longer perceived to be an appropriate tactic in Soviet–German relations. Instead, bilateral relations had become normalized: Economic and political ties were considered normal aspects of Soviet–West German relations, and both sides could set the agenda. The economic stakes had been raised so that there was greater – although by no means total – symmetry between the political and economic aspects of the relationship.

As economic relations became more depoliticized, however, their structural problems came into sharper focus, reinforcing the German and Soviet awareness of the limits of East–West trade.

9

Beyond Ostpolitik and Westpolitik: the economics of detente

Simply trade in the classical sense is not a foundation for an improved and lasting relationship.

Soviet official, 1975[1]

Trade with the East . . . encourages the hope that an economic rapprochement between East and West will promote political detente.

German Economics Ministry, 1972[2]

Although West German–Soviet trade has traditionally been viewed as a political issue, its economic salience has increased since detente. If Soviet–German economic relations continue in their present direction, then the economic determinants of these relations will grow. It is therefore important to discuss the economic significance of bilateral trade to both the FRG and the USSR and to analyze the systemic limits to such trade that exist independently of political developments. Naturally, inasmuch as the Soviet and German economic systems are a reflection of their respective political structures, they are ultimately politically determined. However, one can examine the way in which the two economic systems interact as a primarily *economic problem*. Only by analyzing the economic problems and potentials of German–Soviet trade can the future possibilities for political leverage in these economic relations be analyzed. For, if there are basic economic problems inherent in the bilateral German–Soviet economic relationship, then no amount of political incentives or disincentives can alter the fundamental structural problems of the economic relationship, and these problems can limit the effectiveness of leverage.

The development of West German-Soviet trade, 1970-1980

The normalization of relations between the USSR and the FRG has had a noticeable positive impact on economic relations. Total two-way trade rose from $739.9 million in 1969 to nearly $6 billion in 1979. In the decade since Brandt's Ostpolitik, therefore, there has been a sixfold increase in trade (see Table 7). Although the Germans continued to have a positive balance of trade with the Soviets, the USSR managed to reduce its trade deficit with the FRG after 1976. The USSR has become the FRG's tenth largest export market and its most important communist trading partner. In 1970, trade with the USSR comprised 32 percent of Germany's *Osthandel* (excluding the GDR); today it forms 45 percent. In 1970, trade with the USSR comprised 1.2 percent of the total German foreign trade; today the figure is 2.3 percent. The FRG remains the USSR's most important Western trading partner, representing 16 percent of Soviet trade with developed capitalist countries and 5.6 percent of total Soviet trade. However, because the German economy is more export-dependent than the Soviet economy, exports to the USSR are relatively more important for the FRG than are Soviet exports to Germany for the USSR.[3]

In 1979, the FRG's trade surplus with the USSR had been reduced to a slight deficit. By 1976, the Soviet hard currency debt to the West had risen to about $10 billion, partly because of the economic recession in the West and the drop in demand for Soviet raw materials. The Soviet debt to Germany was about $2.8 billion, and the total indebtedness of socialist countries to the FRG represented about $8 billion, or a quarter of the East's total hard currency debt of $32 billion. Realizing that the situation would not improve without a more stringent policy, the Soviet government cut back on its imports of manufactured goods from the FRG in 1976 and expanded its exports of raw materials to Germany by 50 percent.[4]

The structure of Soviet-West German trade remains complementary, despite Soviet attempts to alter this. More than 97 percent of German exports to the USSR are of finished goods such as machinery, large-diameter pipe, and chemical products. By contrast, 17.1 percent of Soviet exports to the FRG consist of

Table 7. *West German trade with the USSR, 1967–77* (*in millions of US dollars*)

Year	Imports (CIF)	Exports (FOB)	Total
1967	264,804	198,046	462,850
1968	292,289	273,370	565,659
1969	334,160	405,723	739,883
1970	341,642	422,448	764,090
1971	366,317	460,681	826,998
1972	420,674	712,208	1132,882
1973	713,005	1182,643	1895,648
1974	1222,662	1856,084	3078,746
1975	1294,953	2824,386	4119,339
1976	1701,544	2684,725	4386,269
1977	1852,874	2788,769	4641,643

Source: United Nations, *Yearbook of International Trade Statistics* (New York, 1973, 1977).

raw materials, and 62.3 percent are semifinished goods (see Table 8). Machinery makes up less than 5 percent of Russian exports, although the Soviets would like to change the situation.[5] The FRG is the USSR's biggest Western supplier of machinery and equipment, representing 9.1 percent of total Soviet imports in this category. It is also the USSR's main exporter of chemical equipment, supplying 30 percent of Soviet imports.

West Germany is the largest single Western supplier of advanced technology to the Soviet Union. In 1977, for instance, 34 percent of Soviet imports of high technology came from the FRG, as did 29 percent of its imports of manufactures. The next most important supplier was Japan, with 17 percent of high-technology imports and 20 percent of manufactures.[6]

The Soviet Union and Eastern Europe comprise the single largest export market for the West German machine-tool industry; approximately one-third of machine-tool exports from the FRG go to communist nations. The FRG imports a considerable amount of energy from Russia. The USSR earns 75 percent of its hard currency from the FRG through the sale of energy raw materials, chemical materials, wood, and cotton.[7] In the past few years, the USSR has somewhat increased its exports

Table 8. *Structure of German trade with the USSR, 1979*

Imports from USSR	Million DM	% of total
Imports (total)	7,399	100
Agricultural	70	0.9
Industrial goods:	7,269	98.2
of which		
Raw materials	1,266	17.1
Semifinished goods	4,610	62.3
Finished goods	1,393	18.8
Back supplies and replacement	60	0.9
deliveries		
Exports to USSR	Million DM	% of total
Exports (total)	6,624	100
Agricultural	129	1.9
Industrial goods	6,470	97.7
of which		
Raw materials	44	0.7
Semifinished goods	189	2.8
Finished goods	6,237	94.2
Back supplies and replacement	24	0.4
deliveries		

Source: Bundesministerium Für Wirtschaft: Der Deutscher Osthandel 1980 (Bonn, 1980).

of machinery to the FRG, and the rate of growth of Soviet machinery exports to the Federal Republic has been 1.5 times larger than the overall rate of growth of Soviet exports to West Germany.[8]

By the late 1970s, the extent of Soviet energy reserves had become controversial. For instance, the Central Intelligence Agency initially reported that the USSR would become a net importer of oil by 1985, and although it has now revised its earlier estimates, there are indications that the USSR may well face an energy shortage in the future.[9] The FRG was in principle interested in developing Siberian energy sources, but the scale of the enterprise indicated that this would be possible only within the context of a multilateral deal involving the Japanese or Americans. However, despite the potential Soviet energy problems, in the 1970s Soviet–West Germany energy trade became the most profitable part of bilateral economic relations, following the 1970 gas pipe deal.

Immediately after the trade treaty was initialed in 1972, negotiations for a $375 million credit by West German banks to finance Soviet purchases of pipe from the FRG began. The Soviets, as in previous deals, preferred to pay a higher price for the pipe than pay the market rate of interest on credit. This time the credits were fully insured by Hermes. The second triangular natural gas deal was signed in July 1972. It had the same form as the 1970 agreement. The Soviets were to increase their deliveries of natural gas to 7 billion cubic meters. In return for the gas, the Russians would purchase a further 1.2 million tonnes of steel pipe from Mannesmann and Thyssen and a consortium of German banks would finance the deal involving a credit of $500 million to run until 1983. The rate of interest was believed to be about 6 percent. According to this second agreement, by the end of the 1970s the FRG would be getting about 15 percent of its supplies of natural gas from the USSR. However, Chancellor Brandt went out of his way to stress that "no special dependence will arise from this."[10]

In October 1973 the Russians began to pipe gas into Bavaria, and in 1974 a third natural gas deal was signed. Modeled on the previous two, it provided for up to 2.5 billion cubic meters of Soviet natural gas to be delivered until the year 2000. Taken together with the previous deals, this meant that the FRG would obtain more than 8.5 billion cubic meters of Soviet gas annually after 1980.[11] A fourth contract was signed in 1975 between the FRG, the USSR, and Iran. The three-sided IGAT II deal envisioned that the USSR would sell gas to Germany, Germany would sell capital goods to Iran, and Iran would sell gas to the USSR. The negotiations between the Iranians and Soviets were difficult because the Soviets did not want to pay the price for gas that the Iranians initially demanded. However, the Russians finally conceded. Under the 1975 agreement, Iran would supply the USSR with 13 billion cubic meters of gas per year, and the USSR would export 10 billion cubic meters to Western Europe. About half of the gas reaching the FRG would be used within Germany. The price for the gas at the border was "in line with standard international prices," according to a Ruhrgas spokesman.[12] However, after the overthrow of the Shah, the deal was abandoned.

Negotiations on a huge new European gas-pipe deal began in 1980, by which a further 40 billion cubic meters of Siberian natural gas from the Yamal Peninsula would be supplied to Europe after 1984. Mannesmann was to sell pipe valued at 15 billion marks to the USSR, and a bank consortium was to provide the financing at an interest rate of 8 percent.[13] This agreement would mean that, by 1990, the FRG would be importing 28 percent of its natural gas from the USSR, representing 5 percent of its total energy supplies. In 1980, it was importing 16 percent of its gas from the USSR and 6 percent of its oil.[14] The government let it be known that if the FRG were importing 30 percent of its natural gas from the USSR, this would not constitute a dependence risk.[15]

The question of dependence on Soviet energy supplies became more controversial as the decade wore on. Following the Yom Kippur War of 1973 and the quintupling of oil prices, the Germans reoriented their energy plans and increased the role of natural gas in their total energy imports. By 1980, natural gas was to contribute 18 percent of Germany's energy needs, and although Holland was still the largest supplier of gas, the USSR was upgraded in its contribution to Germany's total energy needs.[16] Opposition groups within the FRG began to say that Germany was developing a dangerous dependence on Soviet supplies of gas, supplies that the USSR could easily cut off in a political crisis, perhaps plunging the FRG into economic and political chaos.[17] The counterargument was that despite the technical feasibility of a Soviet cutoff of the gas supply, it was in their economic interest to continue to supply gas to Germany in order to pay for purchases of technology for their own energy industry.

The question of the possible Soviet use of gas supplies as a political lever is both a technical and a political issue. On the technical side, there is the question of substitution. On the one hand, it is easier to substitute alternative hydrocarbon sources for natural gas than it is for other forms of energy. On the other hand, because of the nature of pipeline transportation, it is not necessarily easy to substitute gas suppliers. On the political side, there are those who argue that even if the USSR would be unwilling to cut off gas supplies in a crisis, it might well utilize the FRG's dependence for preemptive political purposes – that is, through the threat of a possible future termination of supplies, it would hope to modify German foreign policy toward the USSR. There are still those who maintain that the main goal of Soviet foreign trade is to create Western economic dependencies that can one day be utilized to the USSR's political advantage. The dependence debate will remain a controversial subject within the FRG as long as there is no consensus on how to quantify the statistical boundary between sensitivity and vulnerability dependence on Soviet natural gas.

Another form of energy imports from the USSR is enriched uranium. As an incentive for the FRG to sign the nuclear non-proliferation treaty, the Soviets offered to sell enriched uranium as nuclear fuel for peaceful purposes to the FRG. The first Soviet offer was made in June 1970: The West Germans would deliver uranium to the USSR for processing, and the USSR would then supply the FRG with fissionable fuel. The United States, which has hitherto had a monopoly on supplying enriched uranium to the FRG, opposed the sale, but the USSR began to supply enriched U-235. The first Soviet sale, valued at $10.5 million, broke the U.S. monopoly by charging a lower price than that charged by the Americans.[18] In reply to a question about the sale, the parliamentary secretary for scientific affairs, Dohnanyi, said that the FRG government could not interfere with commerical dealings.[19] This remark reflected the new policy of the Brandt administration, because the German government had had few qualms about interfering in the past. In 1979, 55 percent of enriched uranium used in nuclear power plants in Germany (domestically a very delicate issue) came from enrichment plants in the USSR.[20] In 1977, a high-level Soviet delegation had come to the FRG to discuss cooperation in the field of nuclear technology, particularly in high-temperature nuclear reactors, a development welcomed by German firms involved in this area.[21]

The range and extent of economic relations between the USSR and the FRG have increased so much since 1970 that it is impossible to detail their development. Yet despite this growth, one should not exaggerate the dependence of either economy on the other. For certain sectors of the German economy, exports to the USSR are more important than their relative contribution to total German exports would imply. For instance, about 40 percent of German exports of large-diameter pipe went to the USSR in 1980; in 1979, these exports formed 12 percent of FRG exports to the USSR, the largest single item.[22] Likewise, machinery imports from the FRG are important for the Soviet economy. Although these trade dependence figures for certain sectors of the German and Soviet economies are not insignificant, they do not represent a substantial dependence for either economy.

The German attitude toward trade since Brandt's Ostpolitik

Since 1970, trade with the USSR has been accepted as a normal aspect of Germany's economic life. However, within this general consensus, there are differences of opinion about the economic parameters of this trade, both within different branches of the government bureaucracy and between government and businessmen.

Since the inauguration of Brandt's Ostpolitik, there has been a change in the attitudes of German business and government toward trade with the USSR. As the head of the Ostausschuss pointed out: "The Federal Republic has in the past more than twenty years of its existence pursued a differentiated [political] policy and a relatively consistent economic policy towards the East."[23] The economic *policy* of the government may have been relatively consistent, but the expectations behind that policy have changed. A government spokesman in 1976 expressed the prevailing view that only growing trade with the East would create mutually beneficial interdependencies and have a stabilizing effect on the German economy; it also held significant potential for expansion.[24]

If there is one single document that symbolizes the general change in the German government's attitude toward trade with the USSR, it is a booklet put out by two officials in the Economics Ministry that caused a certain amount of controversy on publication at the end of 1972. In *Osthandel-Ostpolitik in der Praxis,* the authors discussed Germany's trade with the East in a positive light, stressing its advantages and potentials, with no caveats about either political or economic dangers. The booklet examined the various forms of economic contact between the two sides and emphasized that "increased trade with the East is for many reasons as much in Germany's economic interest as in the interest of her Eastern partners." The pamphlet concluded that it was primarily in Germany's economic interest to promote trade with the East, and that this trade was above all a product of economic factors.[25] This publication was typical of the views of the younger generation of civil servants in the Economics Ministry. Although admitting the beneficial effects on detente of trade with the USSR, their main concern was to point the economic advantages of doing business with the USSR.[26] This depoliticized attitude toward trade with the USSR caused some consternation in the Foreign Ministry, where those concerned with the trade felt that the new people in the Economics Ministry were taking a potentially dangerous "economic" attitude toward trade with Russia and neglecting its political dimensions.[27]

Although there is some disagreement between government spokesmen on the specifics of East-West trade, their general attitude toward linkage is fairly consistent. There is no talk of utilizing economic veto power to elicit Soviet political concessions. Rather, the general view seems to be that expressed by Foreign Minister Scheel – that the political treaty of August 1970 laid a firm basis for expanding trade. On the other hand, Economics Minister Schiller emphasized that the FRG's foreign trade policy was unideological and determined purely by economic factors.[28]

A new element in the government's position emerged during the 1976 election campaign, when the SPD–FDP administration began to utilize trade with the USSR for its own domestic political purposes. Because of the exaggerated fears about economic dependence on the USSR and the political use that the Soviets might make of this fact, the German government had previously avoided discussing questions of how many German jobs were dependent on Eastern orders. During the pipe embargo, it was the German firms, and not the government, that had linked the embargo to loss of German jobs, and this pattern continued throughout the sixties.

During the 1976 election, however, because of the growth in unemployment in Germany and the CDU–CSU assault on *Ost-*

handel, the West German government began to stress how many German jobs were dependent on East–West trade. It was the first time that the government had publicly admitted the economic utility of trade with the East in such an explicit way. A political advertisement printed shortly before the election claimed that *Osthandel* employed 300,000 people, that exports were vital for the FRG's existence, and that continued good relations with the East were necessary if trade were to continue. Thus, the government made the explicit link between Ostpolitik and the employment situation in Germany, arguing for better political relations with the USSR and justifying Ostpolitik partly on the basis of domestic economic need. This was indeed a volte face from the pre-1969 debates, when trade with the East was termed economically marginal and politically dangerous because it enhanced Soviet power.

The trend which had begun in 1969 – namely, that the business sector engaged in trade with the USSR was more skeptical about its importance to West German industry than was the government – continued during the 1970s. Otto Wolff von Amerongen publicly disagreed with the government employment estimates, and the Ostausschuss went on record as saying that trade with the USSR was no solution for unemployment problems. He argued: "If you calculate that way, you must compare the jobs which are secured through trade with the East with those that are threatened through imports from the Eastern bloc."[29] In 1978, a spokesman from the Economics Ministry was more cautious about citing exact figures on how many jobs were dependent on trade with Russia, saying only that 30 percent of Germany's machine-tool exports went to the East and 40 percent of its pipe production, but that these figures changed with time. Moreover, a study released in 1980 claimed that if one balanced jobs lost through imports from the USSR against those gained through exports to the USSR, the net effect of trade with the USSR was that it secured about 92,000 jobs in Germany.[30]

Unlike the government, the business community by and large argued with a consistency that harked back to the 1950s. It said that trade with the USSR was desirable from an economic standpoint and could have beneficial secondary political effects. However, the businessmen were always wary of overestimating the economic potential of Soviet–German trade because of the substantial economic problems involved. The BDI, which had always been cautious in its evaluation of East–West trade, emphasized that it was incorrect to believe that this trade would increase markedly as a result of the political treaties.[31] However, if the BDI in general was cautious, even negative, about the possibilities for trade, its Eastern Committee took a far more sanguine view. Perhaps this is a result of different concerns – after all, the Ostausschuss represented those firms continually engaged in trade with the East, which had a vested interest in improving trade between the FRG and the USSR.

The head of the Ostausschuss, von Amerongen, continued to express views consistent with those that his group had articulated almost since its inception twenty years prior to the Brandt era. In testimony before the United States Congress, he argued that it was "not very realistic" to expect the USSR to offer political concessions in return for economic concessions from the West. He further argued: "Finally, I would like to say that, fundamentally, trade possibilities with the state-trading countries are not only limited by their commercial policies and by their bureaucratic and legal obstacles, but most importantly by the weakness of their domestic markets. This, after all, is due to the system."[32]

The German press, although generally welcoming greater trade between the FRG and the USSR, was divided over the prospects for this trade. Not surprisingly, the more conservative papers stressed the economic pitfalls inherent in such trade, whereas papers representing business, and more liberal journals, were more optimistic. *Handelsblatt,* although discussing at great length such problems as financing Soviet imports and the lack of suitable Soviet exports, emphasized positive economic developments between the two countries and implied that political developments had facilitated the growth of trade. The conservative papers warned against assuming any automatic connection between Ostpolitik and increased trade. However, the arguments against increasing FRG–USSR economic relations were purely economic.[33]

A major study of West German–Soviet economic relations published in 1976 concluded: "Before the detente in German–Soviet relations, political factors were decisive in German–Soviet economic relations; today they are also important but not decisive."[34]

The Soviet attitude toward trade since Brezhnev's Westpolitik

Although Soviet authors have always stressed the consistency, since Lenin's time, of the USSR's views about trading with capitalist countries, there have been some modifications in Soviet views on trade with West Germany since the inauguration of Brezhnev's Westpolitik. It is also significant that more differences of opinion within the USSR about the Soviet policy for trading with the West are now being expressed in Soviet publications. For instance, a major article in *Pravda* commemorating the fiftieth anniversary of the Fourteenth Party Congress at which Trotsky's proposals for industrialization were defeated, stated that the USSR had to "ensure [its] economic independence from the world capitalist economy."[35] However, despite the recurrent articles reminding the world that the USSR may not altogether have renounced its formerly autarkic policies, the Soviets generally recognize the economic and political advantages of increased trade with the West. According to Foreign Trade Minister Nikolai Patolichev, Soviet foreign economic relations entered a "qualitatively new stage" after 1971 with a spectacular increase in trade with the West, which now accounts for 31 percent of Soviet foreign trade.[36]

In the aftermath of the Moscow treaty, there was no immediate shift in Soviet writings on the desirability of economic relations with the FRG or on their political implications. But gradually over the next few years, more and more articles about economic relations with West Germany began to appear in the Soviet press. There had always been a plethora of articles about the political dangers of a revanchist West Germany, but after August 1970 the more propagandistic writings about the FRG were deemphasized and more factual articles about economic relations between the two countries, devoid of hostile political rhetoric, increased. The Soviets, however, take pains to stress that their view of trade with the FRG has always been consistent, and that it was the Germans, and not they, who had modified their previously negative attitude toward economic relations between the two countries. Although Soviet writers stress the Russian interest in improving trade with the USSR, the Kremlin periodically reminds the Germans that its desire for greater economic contacts with the FRG is not so overwhelming that it would make any significant political compromises to secure trade. When the Soviets adopt a harder political line, they devalue the importance of trade. On the other hand, when they decided to do everything they could to facilitate the ratification in 1972, they stressed the political and economic value of trade as a stabilizing force in relations between the two countries.[37]

For the most part, however, the Soviets continued to disguise their own desires for increased trade with Germany by attributing to German businessmen an overwhelming need for enlarging their economic contacts with the USSR. At the end of 1970, an *Izvestiia* correspondent published a long article describing interviews with many prominent German businessmen, all of whom stressed the advantages of the Soviet market and welcomed the change in government policy toward the USSR. He indicated that trade would be more profitable if the remaining German restrictions on Soviet imports were removed.[38] It has always been a theme of Soviet writings that trade with the FRG was an economic necessity for Germany and was helping the German working class, and the German election debates of 1976 gave these Soviet arguments ample support.

Although continuing to emphasize the positive effects of increased trade with West Germany, much Soviet comment stressed the USSR's equal standing with the West as an advanced industrialized trading partner, to justify Soviet demands that the FRG buy more Soviet finished goods. Soviet writers went out of their way to emphasize how much the USSR had to offer to Bonn – particularly in the way of industrial goods – presumably because of the USSR's adverse balance of trade with the FRG and frequent German complaints that the Russians had little to export to Germany. One author cited the Soviet export of ships, machine tools, cameras, airplanes, and hydrofoils.[39] Other articles pointed out that the German concern about Soviet credit needs was groundless.[40] Soviet articles also discussed trade in the context of the USSR's raw materials supplies to the FRG, although the emphasis was often on Soviet manufactured exports.[41] This theme became more prominent as time wore on. An article in the scholarly *International Affairs* said: "The structure of Soviet exports to the FRG has also been substantially changed – machinery and equipment exports have also been steadily growing. Last year alone they increased by over thirty percent."[42] In an interview with *Der Spiegel,* Dzhermen Gvishiani, deputy chairman of the State Committee for Science and Technology, emphasized that German scientists could learn much from Soviet scientists in such fields as nuclear physics, metallurgy, and mathematics.[43]

In his speech to the Twenty-fifth Party Congress, Brezhnev stressed the need for "new forms of foreign economic links that go beyond the framework of conventional trade" and cited "compensation agreements" as examples of these new forms. He called for the further participation of the USSR in the international division of labor and said that the USSR "must expand the production of goods that are in demand on foreign markets and make them more competitive".[44] This theme was reiterated in a long article by a deputy minister of foreign trade, who emphasized that the USSR, if it was ever to participate fully in the international market, must produce exports of machinery and other finished goods that were truly competitive. Although the author went out of his way to emphasize the high quality of Soviet exports of machinery and finished goods, the message was clearly that the USSR must concentrate on improving these exports in order to sell them to the West.[45] The Russians deemphasized their financial problems. Although admitting that there was a Soviet hard currency debt, Soviet commentators claimed that this was nothing extraordinary and attributed the size of their debt to the West's economic crisis, which had diminished its ability to purchase goods from the USSR, and to the remaining import restriction on Soviet goods in the West.[46]

Another constant theme in Soviet writings about trade with the FRG was that the potential of their bilateral economic contacts had by no means been fully utilized. The implication was that both the FRG and the USSR would benefit by expanding their economic contacts.[47] The Soviets blamed the artificial economic barriers established during the cold war for this state of affairs.[48] This was tied to another theme in Soviet writings – that although many West German industrialists favored broadening trade contacts, there were still influential conservative businessmen who were against trade with the USSR.[44] Soviet articles claimed that the main reason for opposition to trade with the USSR was the fear that this would increase Soviet military potential. Needless to say, the Soviets dismissed these fears, pointing out that the FRG was far more dependent on foreign trade than was the USSR.[50] The main point was to blame external political forces for the difficulties in West German–Soviet trade.

The evidence since 1970 suggests that Soviet economists do not view trade with the West as a means of satisfying short-term demand but rather as an important way of improving the economy's performance. In a major article, the head of the Institute of World Economy stressed that the economic reasons for trading with the West were becoming increasingly important, although trade could also form the basis for better political relations. More specifically, he argued that if the USSR was to take fuller advantage of the international division of labor, then its purchases abroad should be oriented not so much to satisfying current needs as to raising productivity and quality throughout the economy in the long run.[51]

During the last decade, there has been a debate in the USSR over the extent to which the Soviet Union should import Western technology and the degree to which it can develop its own technology. This debate has partly been determined by domestic factors, particularly the extent to which the Kremlin feels it can admit that the socialist system needs the Western capitalist system in order to complete the scientific–technological revolution. Often, political leaders – in particular, those responsible for ideology – tend to stress the USSR's technological self-sufficiency. Economic specialists, the technical intelligentsia, and those involved in the crucial sectors such as the oil industry, however, tend to favor greater reliance on Western technology.[52]

The Soviet view of the relationship between economics and politics has remained fairly consistent. Soviet writers stressed that Ostpolitik and Westpolitik had borne out their earlier pronouncements about the interdependence of trade and politics. As one book put it:

The development of economics and economic cooperation between states can and must have an influence on world politics, just as this cooperation offers its own economic basis for a policy of peaceful coexistence. The dialectical connection and the mutual influence of the political and economic processes of detente are evident.[53]

By the mid-1970s, articles on West German–Soviet trade were overwhelmingly positive, stressing the qualitative change in economic relations between the two countries and the particular significance of the natural gas deals, the trade treaty, and agreements on scientific and technical cooperation.[54] The balance sheet of Soviet–German economic ties since the 1970 treaty was, in Moscow's eyes, very positive.[55] Although the USSR has historically tried to avoid linkage, it has also stressed the positive long-term interdependence of economics and politics.

Kursk and the credit question

The fundamental economic problems of Soviet–West German trade are those of all East–West economic interactions and have been extensively analyzed elsewhere.[56] They include the USSR's inability to participate fully in the international economic system; the inconvertibility of the ruble, necessitating bilateral trade and a Soviet preference for compensation deals; the lack of suitable Soviet exports; and the Soviet reluctance to pay Western market rates of interest on credits.[57] It is over this last point that there have been recurrent Soviet–FRG altercations, because West Germany is one of the few Western governments that does not officially subsidize interest rates on credits to the USSR.

In 1974, the question of granting subsidized credits became particularly acute because of the problems of financing the Kursk steel mill.[58] Britain, France, Italy, Japan, and the United States (through the Export–Import Bank) have mechanisms for granting state-subsidized credits to the USSR, but the FRG does not.

In 1972, it had been announced that the German firms Salzgitter and Korf had outbid their West European rivals in winning a massive contract to construct a steel mill in Kursk in the Ukraine, a project first suggested by Kosygin in 1971. The project, which envisioned joint construction, was divided into two parts. In the first part, the plant would use a new German technology for direct reduction of ore pellets, which would be used to manufacture steel. The Russians would then export the ore pellets to the FRG. The plant would operate on a far larger scale than the other two comparable plants in the world, and would be the world's largest steel plant based on the direct reduction method. For the Germans, who used a great deal of sponge iron, the project was very attractive.[59] The deal was announced two days before the German elections, in which Brandt was asking for an endorsement of his Ostpolitik. Some observers hailed the contract as a victory for his policy; others saw Soviet intervention to try to help him win the election.[60] Even if the timing of the conclusion of the deal was political, its long-term significance was economic. The $1 billion deal, the largest on record between East and West, was the biggest industrial cooperation agreement ever signed between the FRG and the USSR. It was in essence a barter deal similar to the natural gas contract, in that the Russians would export the excess pellet production to the FRG as payment and German banks would provide financing.[61]

After the initial optimism over the agreement, it became clear that negotiations were foundering on the question of credit. The Soviets reportedly were willing to pay only 6 percent interest on the credits from the German banks.[62] The Kursk deal caused a sharp disagreement between those in the German government who favored subsidized credits for the USSR and those who were against them. By 1974, there was considerable sentiment within the German cabinet, particularly on the part of Chancellor Brandt, Egon Bahr, and Foreign Minister Scheel, that the FRG should alter its policy and grant state-subsidized credits for the Kursk project. They were supported by some people within the Foreign Office, who believed that the granting of credits would improve the political climate. The economic specialists, however, in particular Helmut Schmidt, who was then finance minister, and Economics Minister Friedrichs, argued that it was economically unsound for the German economy, which had an excess export demand, to grant such credits. Many of the CDU-CSU were opposed to granting credits, and Franz-Josef Strauss called all credits to the East "reparations." Thus, on the issue of credits it seems that those representing economic interests were less willing to compromise than those representing foreign policy concerns, unlike the previous alignment, in which the Foreign Ministry was more wary of trade concessions than was the

Economics Ministry. The business community also argued against subsidizing credits for economic reasons. The export market was so healthy that there was no need to grant these credits. In addition, Defense Minister Leber argued that Bonn should not subsidize credits for Moscow as long as "the last necessary Pfennig" had not been spent on German defense.[63] The government possessed a possible means by which to grant credits that did not violate the terms of the Foreign Trade Law, namely, the Kreditanstalt fuer Wiederaufbau (Reconstruction Finance Corporation). It was 80 percent owned by the government and 20 percent by the federal states, and its original purpose had been to help with the reconstruction of postwar Germany. However, it was later used to finance projects in the Third World.[64]

After much debate and continued opposition to subsidized credits in the Bundestag, Brandt, Scheel, and Bahr conceded defeat. In the end, Bahr and the head of Krupp, Mommsen, had to go to Moscow to explain that the low rate of interest for which the Russians were pressing was unrealistic.

The Soviets agreed to drop their demands for credits at a low rate of interest and were willing to pay cash, a notable development given their former insistence on loans. Berthold Beitz of Krupp termed the deal "a turning point," and Soviet willingness to pay cash was seen as an important step on the road to normalizing East-West trade. A Soviet official explained his country's change of heart on the question of financing by saying, "We wish to work together with Germany." The Soviet ambassador to the FRG described the Kursk deal as "a normal trade deal."[65] Subsequently the project ran into difficulties and its beginning was delayed, although ancillary contracts were concluded for the Kursk-Oskol complex totaling 1.1 billion marks. It was not completed by 1980.

The current German position on credits has not altered since 1974. An Economics Ministry spokesman has said that Germany will maintain its position unless it becomes apparent that German businessmen are losing out to their West European competitors because of the lack of state-subsidized credits. Some German businessmen feel that they are at a disadvantage in terms of competing with other Western suppliers, but as long as German-Soviet trade continues to grow, this does not seem to be a particularly noticeable disability. The BDI had called for a minimum of 8 percent interest on credits to the East, with cash down payments of at least 15 percent on export orders. In 1976, an international consortium of fifteen banks, led by the German Dresdner Bank, made a loan of $600 million to Moscow's International Investment Bank, and from 1973 to 1976 German banks and companies granted a total of $4.6 billion in long-term credits to the Communist countries – more than half of which was for the USSR. In 1977, two German banks gave a $1.25 billion credit to the USSR for the purchase of a turnkey chemical plant.[66] West German commercial credit, therefore, is readily available to the USSR and is fully insured, the only problem being interest rates.

On the credit question, however, all is not as it seems. The government exercises a degree of influence on credits. The "gentlemen's agreement" on interest rates does not always work; for instance, the Federal Bank sometimes charges lower rates, thus giving de facto subsidies. In addition, the government controls the Hermes Company, which guarantees credits. Many German banks have ties to the government, particularly the *Länder* governments, so the administration can influence the rate of interest. De facto subsidies, therefore, are given, although there are no official credit subsidies. It is doubtful that the lack of subsidies substantially hinders the development of West German–Soviet trade except in a symbolic sense.

The Kaliningrad negotiations: Berlin and the limits to depoliticization of trade

After the conclusion of the Ostpolitik treaties, the status of West Berlin remained the most sensitive area in Soviet–West German relations. Despite the growing depoliticization of trade and the increasing salience of economic determinants in Soviet–West German trade, economic relations have not been immune to political influence.

In order to understand the degree to which trade remained politicized after 1970, it is important to examine the nuclear power plant project at Kaliningrad because it illustrates many themes of this book. On the one hand, it was a large-scale project with much visibility and prestige, a symbol of German–Soviet rapprochement in the political and economic fields. It also involved not only bilateral German–Soviet negotiations but also the FRG's relations with its CoCom allies and the USSR's with its CMEA partners.

At the end of 1973, the Soviets and Germans had worked out the economic aspects of a major project. The Germans were to build a nuclear power plant at Kaliningrad (Koenigsberg), from which the USSR would supply Germany with electric current. Brezhnev had suggested the deal when he visited Bonn, and it would have involved the largest nuclear power plant ever to be built in the USSR. There was considerable opposition to the plant on the part of some German industrialists, who claimed that the Soviets would gain access to German nuclear know-how and could become future competitors in this field.[67] Those in favor of the project pointed out that it was economically beneficial and that Germany would be dependent on the plant for only about 3 percent of its energy needs.[68] The most intractable problem, however, was the question of West Berlin. The FRG wanted the Soviets to supply West Berlin with electricity from the Kaliningrad plant. This would involve sending the electricity through the GDR, which would have some control over it. Thus the nuclear power plant deal involved fundamental political questions, such as the desirability of being dependent on Soviet electricity supplies, the granting of advanced technology to the USSR, and the role of West Berlin. Also involved were priorities in Soviet–GDR relations.

When Chancellor Schmidt visited Moscow in October 1974, the power plant was a major topic of discussion. Prior to Schmidt's visit, Economics Minister Friedrichs had hoped to straighten out all the details. However, when Schmidt arrived in Moscow, the Soviets insisted that electricity from the 1200-megawatt, $600 million plant could not go directly to West Berlin. The USSR suggested instead that the power line serve the GDR city of Magdeburg, from which there could be a branch line to West Berlin.[69] At the end of his talks Chancellor Schmidt said that he and Brezhnev had reached "fundamental agreement" on the power plant, which would feed West Berlin as well as the GDR and the FRG. The situation appeared to be acceptable to both sides. The USSR would acquire know-how in nuclear energy from the Germans, and West Berlin's energy requirements for the next decade would be assured.[70]

No sooner had Schmidt announced the agreement on the plan than objections were raised. These highlighted the limits to Bonn's freedom of maneuver in East–West trade because of its need to comply with multilateral CoCom export control regulations. With British support, the United States at a CoCom meeting in January 1975 raised objections to the German sale of nuclear power plants to the USSR. American officials claimed that the issue at stake was inspection of nuclear facilities by the International Atomic Agency. The Soviets had never agreed to on-site inspections as part of the nuclear nonproliferation treaty. Although this provision may have been part of a larger strategy to force signatories of the treaty to accept on-site inspections, the United States also questioned the security aspect of selling such nuclear technology to the USSR. The Germans claimed that, because the USSR already possessed several nuclear power plants, the building on this plant would hardly constitute a strategic threat to the West.

Some German businessmen raised the question of the United States's commercial motivation in utilizing the CoCom mechanism to block the German sale of the plant and pave the way for an American firm to conclude the deal instead. Westinghouse, which had already outbid the German Kraftwerk Union in reactor sales to Spain and Yugoslavia, was reportedly interested in the deal. Kraftwerk Union (jointly owned by Siemens and AEG–Telefunken) was supposed to build the plant and was particularly concerned to conclude the agreement, hoping that if the USSR purchased a nuclear power plant, it would allow its East European allies to buy them too. Foreign orders were particularly important for Kraftwerk Union. However, if CoCom had prevented the West German sale, Westinghouse too could not have sold a reactor to the USSR. Thus the FRG faced opposition to an important economic agreement from its Atlantic allies, particularly the United States.

The Soviet Union also faced some competition from its East European allies in concluding the project. The Poles were interested in having the Germans build a nuclear power plant in Poland, and Warsaw did not hesitate to discuss the supply of electricity to West Berlin.[71] The GDR was also bidding for a West German nuclear power plant and apparently was trying to pressure the USSR to reject the deal.[72] Although the USSR could impose its will on these allies, it had to balance the economic advantages of securing the plant against the possible political disadvantages of denying Eastern Europe access to German nuclear technology.

Apart from these external pressures on the allies of West Germany and the USSR, there were also internal pressures within the FRG to stop the deal. The opponents, harking back to the arguments of the 1950s, claimed that by letting the Soviets be responsible for delivering electricity to West Berlin – which faced a future power shortage – the Germans were granting the Russians undesirable leverage and creating a dangerous situation whereby West Berlin would become dependent on the USSR for its vital economic supplies. This fear was reinforced when the Soviets suggested building an East European ring-grid system from Kaliningrad to Rumania with West Berlin as a branch line. The FRG had wanted to transmit electricity from its own grid to West Berlin if, for any reason, the Soviets cut off the energy for the city, and this new proposal invalidated that plan. It was a question of who would control the electricity supply. Proponents of the plan argued, however, that if the Soviets cut off the current for West Berlin, they would also cut off the FRG, causing serious complications that might ultimately backfire on the USSR. They also claimed that the Soviets were interested in the power plant not for leverage but for supplying Soviet industry with electricity.[73]

The Kaliningrad negotiations were finally adjourned not because of Western resistance in CoCom but because of the GDR's opposition. In March 1976, the West German government announced that, owing to insuperable difficulties, the Kaliningrad project had been abandoned for the time being. According to a German spokesman, economic problems were involved, such as the failure to agree on how much the Germans should pay for their electricity from the USSR.[74] The real issue, however, was political and concerned the role of the GDR in supplying West Berlin. The East Germans objected to being used by the USSR as a transit route for electricity supplies to West Berlin, and according to one Soviet spokesman, "Just as America must sometimes take notice of West Germany, we must sometimes listen to what the GDR says."[75] The GDR therefore argued against the project for both political and economic reasons. Because it is generally agreed that one of the reasons the Kaliningrad project was shelved in 1976 was the successful East German pressure on the USSR, it is important to ask why the Soviets allowed themselves to be pressured, whereas previously they had little trouble imposing their political will on the GDR. After Ulbricht's fall, there were continued tensions between the USSR and the GDR over the extent to which Soviet–West German and intra-German relations could improve. Although Moscow could clearly impose its will on decisive questions, it apparently calculated that the Kaliningrad deal was not such an issue. Because the USSR had alternative sources of energy, it could afford to make a concession to the GDR, whereas it might not have had the issue been more important economically. In their calculation of assets and liabilities, the loss of the power plant seemed less deleterious to the Soviets than incurring the GDR's anger over the political implications of the project for West Berlin. Similarly, the West Germans, although somewhat annoyed by the long-drawn-out negotiations, received the news about the failure of the most spectacular German–Soviet economic agreement to date with equanimity. Schmidt initimated that he had not entirely given up on the contract. In June 1979, he discussed the possibility of reviving Kaliningrad with Kosygin, and Pyotr Neporozhny, Soviet minister of power and electrification, announced that the USSR was planning to link its power grid to that of the FRG, with the possibility of a branch line to West Berlin.[76]

The difficulties with the Kaliningrad project illustrate the continuity of past German–Soviet relations, namely, the importance of political influences on trade, particularly where West Berlin was concerned. Economic factors, although problematic, were not decisive, because they could have been solved. The political complications turned the balance against success. The West Germans were trying to secure Soviet assent on West Berlin's links to Bonn and its economic security. The Soviets, although they had signed the Berlin agreement, considered the refusal to include West Berlin in virtually all other agreements with the exception of the trade treaty a basic political principle. Because the amount of power to be supplied to the FRG was minimal, the

Bonn government had entered into negotiations mainly to ensure that West Berlin was furnished with Soviet electricity, whereas Kraftwerk Union was interested in sales to the USSR. This would have been an important symbolic legitimization of West Berlin's status and would also have lightened the FRG's burden of supplying West Berlin with electricity. The negotiations were adjourned in 1976, because East Germany was able to prevent the USSR from responding to West German linkage strategy.

Despite the Four-Power agreement, the Kaliningrad problems illustrate that West Berlin's position is a potential source of friction between the USSR and the FRG. The problems over the Berlin agreement concern the extent to which West Berlin is linked to Bonn and what kind of ties it can have with the FRG. The USSR interprets the language of the Four-Power agreement as stating that West Berlin is not a "part" of the FRG. The West Germans claim that the wording says it is not a "constituent part."[77] Although both sides agree that West Berlin can have "ties" with Bonn, the West Germans use the word *Bindungen* (indicating a close bond between the two), whereas the East Germans use the word *Verbindungen* (implying a looser connection). Whenever the West Germans attempt to strengthen their presence in West Berlin, the Soviets and East Germans protest. A controversial issue has been the establishment in 1975 of a Federal Agency for Environmental Protection in West Berlin, an FDP-inspired move that the Soviets claim is illegal. In addition, the USSR has objected to the German claim that Bonn's consulates in Eastern Europe have the right to represent the courts and other institutions of West Berlin as well as those of the FRG.[78]

The West Germans have also failed to secure the inclusion of West Berlin in cultural or scientific agreements. This shows that the Soviet assent to a Berlin clause in the 1972 trade treaty was indeed the exception rather than the rule. In addition, the Soviets continue to denounce any Federal Republic links with West Berlin. The Soviet ambassador to East Berlin, Pyotr Abrassimov, a hard-liner who held this position from 1962 to 1971 and again since 1975, has reiterated that the West was interpreting the Four-Power agreement in a "prejudiced manner," and that constant attempts were being made to violate the basic principle that the three western sectors of Berlin did not come under the direct jurisdiction of the FRG.[79]

Although the USSR was willing to recognize West Berlin's economic ties with the EEC, it objected to the inclusion of West Berlin in the 1979 direct elections to the European parliament.[80] Soviet criticism of the FRG's actions in Berlin was not confined to words; there were also actions. In the summer of 1976, there was a series of incidents involving traffic harassment on the route to West Berlin from West Germany and two fatal shootings along the East–West German border.[81] The Soviets claim that they are scrupulously upholding the Quadripartite Agreement and blame the FRG for violating its provisions.[82] They are also not above threatening that, if the Germans do not cease their "illegal" activities, "it is obvious that this . . . could revive the atmosphere of a 'frontline city' with all the ensuing serious consequences both for the detente in Europe and for the interests of the West Berlin population."[83]

West Berlin not only had to endure continued Soviet protests about its links with Bonn, it also began to suffer internally. As a result of the stabilizing effects of the Four-Power agreement, it no longer received the attention and money that it had when it was the vanguard city in the cold war. It had become almost a casualty of detente, and as its economy declined, the population began to leave. It remained highly dependent on Bonn for its economic survival, and the FRG paid 46 percent of the city's budget in 1977.[84] Although the United States has reiterated its commitment to Berlin's freedom, whether rhetoric would be matched with concrete support in the event of another Berlin crisis is a matter for speculation. For the time being, although Chancellor Schmidt may be correct that "today West Berlin is no longer Europe's number one breeding ground of crisis,"[85] it still remains a potential means of leverage for the USSR.

The economic experience of the last decade, therefore, shows that although economic factors play an increasingly important role in Soviet–FRG trade, political factors remain decisive.

10

Normalization and the future of Soviet-West German relations

The aspiration toward [German] unity – is no dusty, backward-looking imperial romanticism. Unity is much more a peaceful goal oriented toward the future.   Helmut Schmidt, June 17, 1980[1]

A decade after the normalization of relations, the USSR and the Federal Republic had developed a modus vivendi in which economic contacts played a significant role. By the end of the 1970s, the progress made in developing a stable institutional framework for bilateral and multilateral relations in CSCE had given the FRG a considerable stake in maintaining the dynamic of its Ostpolitik. Bonn had begun to play a more autonomous role in international affairs, and the United States had ceased to determine the agenda for West German foreign policy, although it continued to play a significant role in establishing the overall framework for East-West relations. Nevertheless, the growing independence of West German foreign policy inevitably led to conflicts between Bonn and Washington over policy toward the USSR. The Soviet Union was well aware of these developments and was not averse to utilizing intra-Western disagreements to its own advantage.

Afghanistan and the Western alliance

The Soviet invasion of Afghanistan in December 1979 brought into sharp focus the differences within the Atlantic Alliance over policy toward the USSR and highlighted the diverging perceptions in Washington and Bonn over the use of linkage, which had developed over the past decade. At the same time, West German Ostpolitik entered a third phase, whose central feature

233

was the preservation of the concrete improvements in relations with Eastern Europe that had been achieved since 1970. In the third phase of Ostpolitik, the FRG was trying to maintain the status quo, a form of political damage limitation in the face of deteriorating U.S.–Soviet relations, whereas the United States was revising its previous detente policies in response to what it perceived as a Soviet move to change the rules of the detente game. A discussion of the repercussions of Afghanistan on West German–Soviet relations highlights the achievements and limits of Ostpolitik and Westpolitik, the role of economic factors in German–Soviet relations, and the impact of normalization on perceptions of the relationship between economics and politics.

Although the FRG and the United States remained united in their main security goal of containing Soviet military power, it had become increasingly evident during the 1970s that America and Germany not only held diverse perceptions of how to deal with the USSR but had different concrete interests in relations with the Kremlin. These conflicts over means and ends cannot be recounted in detail; however, it will suffice to mention the main points of disagreement over policy toward the Soviet Union.

Washington and Bonn have disagreed over specific aspects of the evolution of NATO policy and over Europe's role in Western defense, although there is a consensus on some basic strategic questions. For instance, in 1977, the issue of whether the United States should produce and deploy enhanced radiation weapons in Europe became controversial. There was disagreement within the German government over the advisability of producing the neutron bomb.[2] When President Jimmy Carter finally announced that the United States would not deploy the weapons, much to Moscow's pleasure, there were signs that Bonn disapproved of this position, although the United States maintained that the FRG should have come out more strongly in favor of the bomb. One of Schmidt's problems was the considerable opposition within the SPD to the neutron bomb. Differences within the SPD over the nature of the Soviet military threat and appropriate responses to it were a source of concern to the United States. There were periodic reports that key SPD figures, such as parliamentary leader Herbert Wehner, Egon Bahr, as well as tank division commander General Gerd Bastian, claimed that Soviet military aims toward Europe were merely defensive, in conflict with the official NATO evaluation of offensive Soviet intentions. Although Defense Minister Apel and later Wehner contradicted this view, these developments created a predisposition in Washington to question Germany's true loyalties, particularly the extent to which the SPD had renounced the possibility of pursuing a *Schaukelpolitik*.[3]

Despite these recurrent American doubts, Chancellor Schmidt was in fact the Western European leader most committed to strengthening Western defense. In October 1979, Brezhnev, in what was seen as a major Soviet move to forestall the modernization of NATO forces and to exploit domestic political opposition to the deployment of new weapons in Europe, announced in East Berlin that the USSR would withdraw 20,000 Soviet troops and 1,000 tanks from the GDR.[4] Although Bonn was prepared to take this Soviet arms control offer more seriously than was the United States, Schmidt strongly supported the NATO decision of December 1979, which included the deployment of American medium-range Pershing missiles in Europe, to respond to Soviet SS-20 missiles. In an attempt to forestall German support for the decision, Foreign Minister Gromyko came to Bonn in November 1979 but failed to alter the German position. Gromyko denied that the USSR was trying to split Germany from America: "The Soviet Union does not seek to isolate the Federal Republic of Germany from the other NATO countries. We are trying to prove to the FRG government, to convince it of the same things that we are trying to prove to the other NATO countries."[5]

There were substantial conflicts between Bonn and Washington over the means of approaching the Soviet Union, particularly after the election of President Carter in 1976. Carter's support of human rights was a key determinant of his foreign policy, and he criticized the USSR publicly for its violations of human rights. The West German policy has been to maintain public silence on the issue. Chancellor Schmidt somewhat understated it when he said, "As regards human rights, we on this side of the Atlantic – and that includes my government – are on the whole more reserved in our approach than the United States."[6] The Germans preferred to continue with quiet, behind-the-scenes diplomacy to moderate Soviet policy, and they were joined by the French and other Europeans in this approach. Moreover, Bonn was less concerned than Washington to change Soviet domestic policy. Ostpolitik was a foreign policy matter.

The differences between U.S. and West German concepts of how to deal with the Russians on humanitarian questions were most public at the Belgrade Follow-up Conference to CSCE in 1977. The German government decided that it would be counterproductive to criticize the USSR too harshly on the implementation of basket three, because this might jeopardize the considerable improvements that had already been made. Bonn claimed that whereas human rights was a matter of high principle for the United States, for Germany it concerned the everyday lives of 17 million East Germans, and this necessitated a more pragmatic and less confrontational German policy.

In the third phase of German Ostpolitik, there was more agreement among the Europeans, particularly between France and Germany, on the need to maintain a dialogue with the Soviet Union.[7] Chancellor Schmidt went to Moscow in June 1980, an election year in the FRG, despite American misgivings, stressing the need to maintain "channels of communication with the USSR."[8] French President Valery Giscard d'Estaing had also met with Brezhnev in Warsaw a few weeks earlier. Ostpolitik phase three involved a German insistence on preserving the concrete gains achieved over the past decade, within the framework of a common European detente policy, which diverged from U.S. policy.

Another feature of the more independent Ostpolitik was the increasing divergence between U.S. and European concepts of the politics of East–West trade. Whereas the Bonn government had eschewed the use of negative economic levers to induce political concessions from the USSR, the U.S. Congress passed the Jackson–Vanik Amendment, predicating Most Favored Nation status on Jewish emigration from the Soviet Union. This, combined with the Stevenson Amendment limiting the amount of credits to be given by the Export-Import Bank to the USSR, caused the Soviets to cancel their trade treaty with the United States in 1975. The West German government specifically rejected this method of dealing with the USSR. According to a government spokesman, "a policy like the one Congress thought was right or like what our own Opposition occasionally recommends, cannot only fail to achieve the desired goal, but can even make it more difficult."[9] The German approach was different and succeeded in securing the emigration of about 10,000 ethnic Germans from the USSR per year. In 1978, 58,000 ethnic Germans from Eastern Europe emigrated to the Federal Republic – 36,000 from Poland, 12,000 from Rumania, 8,500 from the USSR, 900 from Czechoslovakia, and 500 from elsewhere. Since 1970, more than 45,000 Soviet Germans were allowed to resettle in West Germany, making them the second largest emigrant group after the Jews. Many of these emigrants came from rural areas in Central Asia, and they were permitted to emigrate under the terms of the 1958 repatriation agreement, in return for financial inducements given to the Soviet government by Germany.[10] About 300,000 out of the total population of 1.8 million ethnic Germans have applied for exit visas so far.

As a result of the cancellation of the U.S. trade bill, U.S.–Soviet trade began to stagnate. West German–Soviet trade grew, however, and the interests of the two Western allies in trade with the East continued to diverge. For the U.S. economy, this trade was marginal, but for the FRG, it was much more important. Under the Carter administration, the discussion about the political use of trade was publicly revived, and the most explicit statement of the new position was made by National Security Council Advisor Samuel Huntington: "For the Soviets, as for others, leverage works most effectively when applied in the form of a carrot rather than a stick and when exerted subtly and discreetly rather than openly and arrogantly."[11] Despite the low level of U.S.–Soviet trade, the United States still considered that these economic relations could be used to wrest political concessions from the USSR.

Conflicts between German and American attitudes over linkage politics were highlighted after the Afghanistan invasion. President Carter decided to implement a negative linkage strategy, utilizing punitive economic levers to show displeasure with Soviet actions. He announced a grain embargo, a boycott of the 1980 Moscow Olympics, and a high technology embargo, committing the United States to tighten CoCom export controls. Most Western European countries, including the FRG, were reluctant to engage in trade denial because they did not consider it an appropriate way of countering the Soviet military moves. Moreover, Bonn resisted American efforts to have the German government cease underwriting Hermes credit guarantees. As Chancellor Schmidt said in a Bundestag debate, although the FRG would not take economic advantage of the U.S. trade boycott, it considered trade with the USSR and Eastern Europe an important element of stability in Europe.[12]

Shortly after the United States announced its intention to embargo high-technology exports, the Germans began negotiations on the Yamal gas-pipe deal with the USSR. The ninth session of the joint Soviet–West German Commission for Economic, Scientific, and Technical Cooperation was held in May 1980 in Bonn, and first Deputy Prime Minister Nikolai Tikhonov met with Schmidt. Both sides explicitly stated that they did not want the current international tensions to affect their bilateral economic relations, and that long-term economic relations would promote detente.[13] The contrast between Schmidt's reaction to the U.S. embargo in 1980 and Adenauer's support of the pipe embargo in 1962 showed clearly that the FRG had developed its own East–West trade policy and would no longer accept U.S. definitions of what was permissible in this area.

Nevertheless, the FRG was the only Western European ally of the United States to participate in the Olympic boycott. Schmidt apparently calculated that Bonn had to show solidarity with Washington in some area, and that it was preferable to engage in a short-term measure such as the Olympic boycott than to jeopardize long-term relations with the USSR by cutting off supplies of high technology or abrogating economic agreements. The Soviet Union criticized the German decision, claiming, "The FRG government's decision is a strictly political one. It was adopted in deference to President Carter's arrogant stance. The FRG government's 'recommendation' on non-participation in the Moscow Olympics is an obvious Cold War relapse in West German policy."[14]

The Soviet press stressed that German businessmen had come out against a technology embargo.[15] Indeed, the business community and government were in agreement on the undesirability of utilizing negative economic leverage against the USSR. Although no West German athletes went to Moscow, German companies were prominent in providing much of the equipment for the games – from a new airport at Sheremetyevo to the silverware used by athletes in the Olympic canteen.[16]

The Soviet reaction to German–American disagreements over policy toward the USSR revealed the continuity of Soviet Westpolitik. As in past years, the Soviet press adopted simultaneously a conciliatory and a censorious attitude toward Bonn. For instance, a major article in *Literaturnaia Gazeta* warned of the "dangerous intensification of latent militarist tendencies in the FRG," and *Pravda* claimed that "H. Schmidt's support for J. Carter's line becomes almost grotesque."[17] On the other hand, many articles pointed out that the US was endangering its allies' gains from detente, and that the West German government was concerned to preserve good relations with the USSR.[18] These different media signals were perhaps the result of a conscious Soviet strategy of pursuing two policy lines at once. Alternatively, they may have been an indication of differences within the Kremlin over whether to woo Bonn in the wake of clear US–FRG differences on policy or to adopt an aggressive stance criticizing Bonn for the extent of its solidarity with the United States. In their actions, the Soviets seemed to favor the more conciliatory course of action. For instance, it was notable that the situation in Berlin not only did not deteriorate as East–West relations became more tense after Afghanistan but actually improved.

Linkage politics before and after detente

Ostpolitik phase three does not represent a qualitative change in West German–Soviet relations; rather, it is an expression of the degree to which both sides went to preserve the normalization of bilateral relations. The desire to maintain the status quo reveals the degree to which the relationship between politics and economics has altered since the decline of the cold war. As relations have become normalized, their economic and political aspects have ceased to contradict each other, as they once did. Greater economic interdependence has meant that linkage is no longer an appropriate strategy in bilateral relations.

In the period 1955–80, four different types of linkage strategies have been utilized in German–Soviet relations.

Strategy one – negative economic leverage – was the policy of successive German governments before 1969. Given Germany's greater economic bargaining power over the USSR, Adenauer, Erhard, and Kiesinger, but Adenauer in particular, tried to utilize trade denial to induce Soviet political concessions on Germany. The USSR has generally been unable to initiate such a strategy because of its weaker bargaining power and has rarely responded to negative leverage.

The German government has also implemented strategy two. It has utilized positive economic levers in the pursuit of political goals. Under Adenauer, this involved offering a trade treaty in return for the release of Germans living in Russia or a Berlin clause. Under Brandt, it meant offering general economic inducements to reinforce the inclination toward a more conciliatory Soviet Westpolitik and also linking specific issues, such as trade treaties, to Soviet political concessions. If the Germans have been able to utilize only economic levers, then the Soviets have been able to implement only those linkage strategies involving political levers.

The Soviets have occasionally used negative political levers – strategy three – to try to induce the Germans to make economic concessions. The Soviets have not pursued negative linkage strategies too often, because in general they were concerned to increase their trade with the FRG. They resorted to utilizing negative political levers only when they realized that the Germans would not yield and when the economic stakes were not so important.

The most usual form of linkage for the Soviets has been the use of positive political levers involving secondary issues. In 1958, the Russians released German prisoners of war in return for the trade treaty. In 1972, they were willing to include Berlin in the trade treaty with Germany in return for the promise of more trade.

This discussion of the differential validity of linkage strategies over time suggests that the actor who initiates the linkage will more likely utilize positive levers. It is easier to secure concessions if one utilizes positive inducements. Usually, negative linkage is pursued as a response to an agenda set by one's antagonist because one is not willing to compromise. Negative linkage was practiced during the cold war, but positive linkage has been the norm since 1969. This is because previous policies, from the German side, were a failure. Adenauer had attempted to utilize economic levers to persuade the Russians to make fundamental political concessions on the German problem, but the use of economic levers involving only secondary stakes could not produce compromises on political issues involving core values. Linkage worked only where the tradeoffs were commensurate. When Brandt became chancellor, two important changes occurred. Firstly, and most importantly, the FRG ceased to demand fundamental political concessions from the Soviets on the German question. Secondly, Brandt realized that the use of negative levers could not elicit basic political compromises from the Russians, and he eschewed this practice.

Because Soviet Westpolitik represented less of a change in foreign policy than Brandt's Ostpolitik, the Germans have altered their use of linkage more than the Soviets. The USSR has not greatly altered its rather limited use of leverage in economic matters. There has been more continuity on the Soviet side than on the German side. The Soviets have never attempted to wrest major concessions from the Germans through the use of linkage. They prefer to avoid linkage if they cannot initiate it.

Before 1969, the German government was often at loggerheads with the business community over the desirability of trade with the USSR and over linking political and economic relations. Since the SPD-FDP coalition came to power, there has been general agreement between the administration and industry over the need to depoliticize and promote East–West trade. There have also been some differences of opinion within the USSR over the advisability of economic relations with the West. Within both societies, the opponents of East–West trade have become a distinct minority over the last decade.

Bonn has learned that negative linkage has not worked, and it has come to share the Soviet view about separating politics and economics. Nevertheless, one can question the extent to which FRG–Soviet trade can ultimately be depoliticized. Although economic relations have become less politicized, Soviet–German trade is still political. It is political because for the Russians, foreign economic relations are an integral part of their foreign policy and there are no nongovernmental actors who could provide a functional separation of trade and politics. Trade remains political from the German side because as long as the German problem remains open, economic relations between the two states will continue to be a political problem. This general point is true of all East–West economic relations. Because of the asymmetry both in economic needs and in economic and political relations between East and West, Western nations will continue to believe in the efficacy of utilizing economic levers to induce political concessions from the East. However, the evidence suggests that the USSR will never make fundamental political concessions because of its need for trade. Moreover the USSR will always find alternative suppliers for its economic needs if one country practices trade denial. The 1980 US grain embargo was lifted in 1981 for precisely this reason.

Although German–Soviet trade has become less political, this does not mean that it is problem-free. The ironic result of the economization of German–Soviet trade may ultimately have been to make Germans more aware of the economic limits of this trade. In the immediate aftermath of Brandt's Ostpolitik some policy makers thought that, having eschewed the negative linkage policy of the Adenauer era, trade would flourish. This euphoria has evaporated under Schmidt, who has realized that removing political impediments can have only limited effects on promoting trade. After a certain point, all the political good will in the world cannot alter the fundamental structural problems of trade with the USSR. If anything, the removal of political obstacles to trade has increased skepticism about the future of that trade. Both businessmen and the government are beginning to realize that political rapprochement cannot obliterate the economic problems of trade; it can facilitate certain contacts, but the day-to-day details are dependent on the market, not the parliament.

The Soviet Union has, of course, welcomed the depoliticization of trade from the German side. However, it has been disappointed by the relatively slow increase in the range and quantity of economic relations with the FRG. From what the Soviets write and say, it is apparent that the USSR attributes the relative lack of progress in increasing German–Soviet trade to the reticence of the German government and business community and not to fundamental structural problems in the Soviet system of foreign trade. Since Brandt, however, it has become more difficult to attribute the problems of trade to right-wing German politicians.

In any discussion of the future of Soviet–West German trade, one must separate the possible from solutions which lie in the realm of political or economic fantasy. Changes such as making the Soviet ruble convertible, abolition of the foreign trade monopoly, or freeing of Soviet prices are clearly not feasible within the foreseeable future. However, changes in the domestic Soviet organization of foreign trade are plausible. Soviet central planners will, of course, resist any overall economic reforms that might diminish Communist Party control. At the present time, the direct involvement of the party in economic decision making and staffing is critical. However, it is possible that, if the Politburo felt that changes would leave it in control of the economic "commanding heights," it might be willing to relinquish some party control over the local details of foreign trade decision making. There is some evidence that certain top Soviet specialists have been considering a reorganization of the foreign trade structure to encourage trade with the West. According to various reports, Nikolai Inozemtsev, head of the Institute for World Economics and International Relations (IMEMO), Central Committee member, and apparently with significant influence, has advocated a more direct trading role for Soviet industry, in contrast to pronouncements on this subject by the Ministry of Foreign Trade.[19] Some Soviet academics appear to believe that if the cumbersome, overlapping foreign trade bureaucracies were streamlined and Western firms could have more direct contact with Soviet enterprises that produce for the West, some of the economic problems of Soviet foreign trade would be alleviated. Any change in the organization of Soviet foreign trade will depend on the policies of Brezhnev's successors.

Another area in which politics will continue to affect the development of economic relations, although to a limited extent in German–Soviet trade, is the link between the EEC and the CMEA. The USSR has always had a contradictory attitude toward the EEC. On the one hand, to the extent that successful political and economic integration in Europe represents an alternative to U.S. domination of Western Europe, the Soviets welcome any movement that weakens the U.S. presence there. However, the surest way to diminish American influence in Europe would be for the Europeans to develop their own independent nuclear deterrent, which the Soviets, of course, do not want. In addition, the Kremlin faces a dilemma over integration. On the one hand, the USSR condemns the idea of European integration. On the other hand, this attitude could be counterproductive for Soviet attempts to intensify Eastern European integration under Soviet control. The USSR wants the EEC to succeed to the point where it will diminish the American presence in Europe, but not to be so successful that it will increase the power of Western Europe vis-à-vis the USSR. Since Brezhnev's speech in 1972 recognizing the existence of the EEC, the Soviets have come close to a de facto dealing with the EEC. After the EEC imposed a 200-mile limit on North Sea fishing, the USSR came to Brussels to negotiate with the EEC about observing this new rule. However, the negotiations broke down because the USSR failed to include a reference to West Berlin in the agreement.[20] Trade with the EEC has been steadily growing, however (see Tables 9, 10).

The EEC has, since 1974, forbidden its members to conclude bilateral trade agreements with any member of the CMEA and is trying to coordinate its members' trade policies. Likewise, the USSR has been interested in concluding a multilateral EEC–CMEA agreement. In August 1974, the CMEA sent out feelers to the EEC to arrange a meeting, which was held in Moscow in February 1975. The talks were intended to serve as a basis for future contacts between the respective heads of Comecon and

Table 9. *EEC trade with the USSR, 1967–77 (in millions of US dollars)*

Year	Imports	Exports	Total
1967	678,659	719,770	1,398,429
1968	907,657	758,103	1,665,760
1969	1,155,555	857,444	2,012,999
1970	1,150,555	850,000	2,000,555
1971	1,245,222	1,046,778	2,292,000
1972	1,830,153	1,628,947	3,459,100
1973[a]	2,698,799	2,882,839	5,581,638
1974	4,266,198	4,435,615	8,701,813
1975	6,121,182	4,601,298	10,722,480
1976	5,955,762	6,233,084	12,188,846
1977	5,790,838	6,887,684	12,678,522

[a]After 1973, all nine EEC countries included.
Source: *United Nations Yearbook of International Trade Statistics* (New York, 1973, 1977).

Table 10. *Trade with EEC countries as a percentage of Soviet foreign trade, 1965–78*

	1965	1966	1967	1968	1969	1970	1971	1972	1973	1974	1975	1976	1977	1978
EEC total	5.7	6.5	7.7	8.3	9.1	8.3	8.8	8.9	13.2	16.1	16.7	16.2	14.75	14.4
of which														
Belgium	0.5	0.6	0.7	0.8	0.7	0.7	0.7	0.7	1.1	1.5	1.0	1.0	0.9	0.9
Great Britain	2.7	3.0	2.8	3.2	3.0	2.9	2.6	2.1	2.5	2.2	1.9	2.2	2.1	2.1
Italy	1.5	1.5	2.1	2.2	2.5	2.1	2.1	1.8	2.0	2.9	2.8	3.1	3.0	2.8
Holland	0.6	0.7	1.0	0.8	1.2	1.0	0.9	0.9	1.1	1.4	0.8	1.0	0.9	0.7
FRG														
(including Berlin)	1.7	2.0	2.0	2.3	2.6	2.6	3.0	3.3	4.0	5.7	7.6	5.3	4.7	4.7
France	1.4	1.8	1.8	2.2	2.1	1.9	2.0	2.1	2.3	2.4	2.6	3.0	2.7	2.6

Source: United Nations Yearbook of International Trade Statistics (New York, 1966–79). *Vneshniaia Torgovlia za 1965–78 god* (Moscow: Izdatel'stvo Statistika, 1967–9).

the EEC, but the West Europeans realized that the talks would be "very exploratory."[21] The EEC, although it had been trying to coordinate its members' trading policies toward Eastern Europe, had not adopted a specific position vis-à-vis the East in its common commercial policy.

There have been subsequent EEC–CMEA meetings, but so far, all have failed for political reasons, particularly because the USSR wants to conclude a multilateral agreement between both organizations, whereas the EEC as a whole would prefer to conclude bilateral agreements with individual states. If Eastern and Western Europe want to reinforce the multilateral gains of detente, then some form of EEC–CMEA cooperation would be desirable.

Any assessment of the problems of German–Soviet economic relations leads to the inescapable conclusion that there are powerful economic systemic limits to trade between the FRG and the USSR, regardless of political factors, because the German government no longer interferes with business's freedom to trade with the USSR. Indeed, it appears that in the past few years, trade between the USSR and the FRG has been determined more by Soviet economic demands than by the political climate.

In view of these economic limits, if political relations can facilitate trade, is the reverse true? Can there be "Wandel durch Handel" (change through trade)? Can more intense economic relations form a viable basis for improved political relations, as the Soviets often claim? The evidence is too meager at the moment, because although German–Soviet trade has increased sixfold since 1970, it still forms only a small percentage of the total foreign trade of both sides. The fact that Germany and the USSR have signed agreements that run until 2000 indicates an expectation of cooperation. However, politics and economics are not convertible currencies, and, unlike even the ruble, could never become convertible. Politics can help improve economic relations, but the reverse does not appear to be true. However, increased economic interdependence can give both sides a greater stake in detente.

The other side of this question is this: Because economic factors seem to be limiting the development of German–Soviet trade, irrespective of the political climate, might political relations between the two nations stagnate as a result of realizing the economic limits of trade? It seems unlikely, given the enormous political stakes involved, that the economic problems of detente would have the impact of lessening the desire for political rapprochement. It is far more likely that German and Soviet foreign policies will be determined by political and security factors. There is an asymmetry in the influences of economics and politics in West German–Soviet relations. Politics can affect economics much more than the reverse.

For the foreseeable future, therefore, it seems that, if political relations between the FRG and the USSR do not deteriorate, economic factors will increasingly determine and limit the range and intensity of Soviet–West German trade. Politics, however, will not be irrelevant, and on the margin, politics may be decisive in determining the outcome of an economic debate, particularly when the economic decision involves political factors such as the status of West Berlin. In the short run, politics will continue to make the difference. In the medium term, economic factors will remain the prime determinants of West German–Soviet trade and will exercise a restraining force on the development of that trade. In the long run, however, economics and politics will both have a decisive influence on the potential and actual state of Soviet–German trade.

Has the German problem been solved?

The normalization of Soviet–West German relations in 1970 radically altered the nature of the ties between the two countries, and despite continued problems, the expectation was that increased economic relations would remain a predictable aspect of bilateral contacts. Thus the political and economic aspects of the relationship reinforced each other. The German problem had been resolved for Moscow through the formal Western recognition of the division of Germany and of Europe. Moreover, the USSR had gained economically from the pursuit of Westpolitik.

Brandt's Ostpolitik was never intended to provide the ultimate solution to the German problem, however. It was supposed to be a provisional resolution that, accepting the postwar status quo, would leave open the question of reunification. This unanswered question will therefore continue to play a role in West German–Soviet relations. The German problem may be resolved for the USSR, but the FRG still upholds reunification as its ultimate goal.[22] Indeed, one of the main reasons for Brandt's normalization of relations with the USSR was the desire to improve intra-German relations.

The GDR has, since the completion of Brandt's Ostpolitik, been the decisive factor determining West German–Soviet political and economic relations. Prior to 1969, the GDR had also been a significant factor, but in the absence of any formal political links between the two Germanies, there was a limit to how much the FRG could affect developments there. As a result of the *Grundvertrag*, Bonn's ability to affect developments in East Berlin increased. Now that there were bilateral relations, and in view of the GDR's signature on the Helsinki Final Act, intra-German political and economic interactions greatly increased, and the possibility of influencing developments in the GDR meant that East Berlin became increasingly important for Bonn. Indeed, politics played a much more important role in intra-German trade than in FRG–Soviet economic relations. Although the trade was profitable for Bonn, the FRG's main goal in intra-German trade, which gave the GDR an especially privileged position, was to use economic incentives to secure greater political flexibility on humanitarian issues in the GDR. For instance, 8 million West Germans and West Berliners per year were visiting the GDR in the late 1970s. Similarly, although the GDR was wary of the political implications of its sizeable trade with the FRG, it needed its privileged economic access to the EEC and its technology imports from West Germany. Intra-German trade has always been more politicized than Soviet–West German trade, because the issues involved were more important for the FRG and the chances of successful leverage greater.

One can question whether German reunification has been brought any closer since 1970. To return to Egon Bahr's formula, there has definitely been *Annäherung*, but the *Wandel* has been more in domestic East German politics – in particular, the greater readiness to permit family contacts between the two Germanies – than in the relations between the two German states. Relations with the GDR continue to be the salient determinant of the FRG's Ostpolitik, largely explaining its disinclination to pursue a punitive policy toward Moscow, such as that demanded by the US after Afghanistan.

The American reaction to the West German preoccupation

with maintaining the improvements in intra-German relations
has been mixed; some spokesmen have cited this policy as one of
"Finlandization" or "self-Finlandization," implying that the FRG
was voluntarily appeasing the USSR without direct Soviet pressure. Because this charge is periodically repeated, it is worth-
while to examine it briefly.

One should first perhaps question why such a charge arises.
Finlandization refers to Finland's postwar relationship with the
USSR and implies that the FRG has modified its foreign policy
to suit Soviet preferences and that it was unnecessary for the
USSR to take over West Germany physically because it had already succeeded in controlling Bonn's foreign policy.[23] It is undeniable that Soviet–FRG relations entered a qualitatively new
phase in 1969. Because detente involved the process of normalizing East–West relations, and because West German–Soviet
relations were previously so hostile, these relations altered more
dramatically than Soviet relations with other Western European
countries. It is also true that Brandt's Ostpolitik represented
more of a change in German foreign policy than did Soviet
Westpolitik in Soviet foreign policy, because the FRG normalized relations with the USSR by accepting the status quo. However, because Bonn had previously tried to change the status
quo, one can argue that the Brandt policy merely represented an
acceptance of what already existed in Europe. By ceasing to be a
revisionist power, West Germany altered its policy more than
did the USSR, which had consistently been a status quo power.
The asymmetry in concessions gave rise to more sinister interpretations of West German goals, and yet, as the Berlin
agreement shows, the Soviets have also compromised. Bonn has
consistently refuted charges of Finlandization and reiterated its
commitment to the Atlantic Alliance. If one examines the evidence, there seems to be little basis for alleging that the West German government has lessened its commitment to NATO or to the
EEC as a result of the new Ostpolitik. Finlandization is not an
appropriate interpretation of FRG–Soviet relations.[24] The American and CDU-CSU charges that the SPD is leaning toward a strategy of neutralization largely stem from Bonn's commitment to
East–West trade and its conscious policy of dealing with the
USSR more cautiously on questions of human rights. However, this more carefully calibrated policy is the product of a

decision to maximize the economic and human gains from detente through a more conciliatory stance. In every other respect, particularly in security matters, West Germany has until now been the European pillar of the Atlantic Alliance, and its Ostpolitik is not an indication of self-Finlandization. The West German media are not muting their criticism of the USSR. The German Communist Party, unlike those of France or Italy, is insignificant electorally and anticommunism is a major force in the FRG, largely because of the division of Germany.

Nevertheless, a German Peace Movement, opposed to the 1979 NATO decision, has recently grown, and has received verbal support from the USSR and the GDR. This movement was not initiated by the USSR, and has domestic religious and political roots. It does, however, indicate the extent to which potentially neutralist tendencies exist in German society, although those in favor of neutralism form a definite, though vocal, minority.

Even if the Federal Republic shows few signs of Finlandization, one might still question Soviet goals toward Germany. Moscow's maximal goal may well be a neutralized, disarmed West Germany. However, this option is at the moment and for the foreseeable future within the realm of wishful thinking, and an analysis of realistic medium-term options for the USSR indicates that there is unlikely to be a drastic change in Soviet–West German relations in the next few years.

A more feasible option might be another Rapallo, a situation in which Germany has enough power to balance the US against the USSR and could end its dependence on the Atlantic Alliance. A new Rapallo could conceivably lead to improved intra-German ties. Yet it would require a dramatic shift in the political constellation in West Germany. However, the Soviets have realized that a dependent West Germany within NATO is probably more stable and predictable than a Germany strong enough to pursue a *Schaukelpolitik*. If the FRG did possess the power to distance itself from the United States, this would mean that German domination of Western Europe might grow and Moscow might face a more powerful West Germany with nuclear weapons – not exactly an endearing scenario for the Kremlin. The more independent the FRG becomes from the United States, the more threatening and unpredictable it is ultimately to the USSR, unless it disarms. Thus, there is little to suggest that a more intense

Soviet-FRG rapprochement is likely in the next few years. Normalization, not Finlandization, is at present the bilateral reality. Nevertheless, the German question remains open. Yet it is difficult to imagine under what circumstances reunification could take place. Neither the USSR, the United States, nor France would be willing to accept a reunified Germany. Moscow may hold the key to German reunification, but it is unlikely to use it. The only conceivable route to reunification might be through a general European rapprochement involving the dissolution of NATO and the Warsaw Pact, but it is currently inconceivable that either superpower would be willing to alter the European status quo this radically. In many ways, the United States, and USSR share the same view of detente in Europe. They would like to perpetuate the system of bipolar blocs, with half of Europe capitalist and half communist. Both fear a more autonomous Europe seeking its own identity somewhere between the two superpower antipodes. However, it is unlikely that Europe will be as compliant in an era of reduced tension as it was during the height of the cold war, and the SPD view of detente is that it may eventually facilitate more independence in both parts of Europe. The "third way" of an East-West European rapprochement may be a long-term aspiration, yet it does not represent a realistic operational policy expectation of the majority of the SPD or the Federal Republic.

As long as East-West relations remain problematic, East-West trade will continue to imply a degree of normality not reflected in political relations. The German question will not be resolved through trade, yet economic relations may continue to play a salient role in its evolution. Linkage can work, but only if the gains and losses are commensurate. A fat communist may be much easier to deal with than a thin one, but the Kremlin would prefer that its citizens continue on a permanent diet rather than forfeit their way of life in an excess of gluttony.

If this book has highlighted the futility of expecting that the Soviet Union will make major foreign policy concessions in return for trade inducements, then it has also shown that trade can be a productive lever when judiciously used. German-Soviet relations were not normalized *because* of economic factors, but neither were they irrelevant. The evidence we have examined suggests that trade will continue to play an important part in

East-West relations in the future. The economic component of detente may well increase in salience, but it cannot serve as a guarantee of the political stability of detente. The Kremlin has its hierarchy of foreign policy goals, and economic relations with the West do not appear to have top priority, although they are more important than previously. Mercury may not have usurped Mars, but the god of war is more likely to consult with the god of trade in the 1980s than he would have in the 1950s.

Notes

Chapter 1. The German problem and linkage politics

1 Walter Laqueur, *Russia and Germany: A Century of Conflict* (Boston: Little, Brown, 1965), p. 13.
2 Samuel P. Huntington, "Trade, Technology and Leverage: Economic Diplomacy," *Foreign Policy,* no. 32 (Autumn 1978), pp. 63-80.
3 Joseph Joffe, "Society and Foreign Policy in the Federal Republic: The Adenauer Era, 1949-1962" (unpublished Ph.D. dissertation, Harvard University, 1975), p. 83.
4 See Daniel Yergin, *Shattered Peace: The Origins of the Cold War and the National Security State* (Boston: Houghton Mifflin, 1977); Walter LaFeber, *America, Russia and the Cold War 1945-1975* (New York: Wiley, 1976); Adam B. Ulam, *The Rivals* (New York: Viking, 1971).
5 Joffe, *op. cit.,* pp. 121-2.
6 Adam Bruno Ulam, *Expansion and Coexistence* (New York: Praeger, 1974), p. 545.
7 Klaus Knorr, *The Power of Nations: The Political Economy of International Relations* (New York: Basic Books, 1975), p. 7.
8 Juergen Kuczynski and Grete Wittkowski, *Die deutsch-russischen Handelsbeziehungen in den letzten 150 Jahren* (Berlin: Verlag Die Wirtschaft, 1947), pp. 24, 45, 67.
9 *Vneshniaia Torgovlia za 1979-god* (Moscow: Izdatel'stvo Statistika, 1980), p. 15.
10 Laqueur, *op. cit.,* p. 44.
11 Knorr, *op. cit.,* p. 14.
12 Arnold Wolfers, *Discord and Collaboration* (Baltimore: Johns Hopkins University Press, 1962), p. 16.
13 Some Western scholars have attempted to apply interest group theory to the USSR. See H. Gordon Skilling and Franklyn Griffiths, eds., *Interest Groups in Soviet Politics* (Princeton, N.J.: Princeton University Press, 1973); Jerry F. Hough, *The Soviet Union and Social Science Theory* (Cambridge, Mass.: Harvard University Press, 1977). For a refutation of these speculations, see William Odom, "A Dissenting View on the Group Approach to Soviet Politics," *World Politics* vol. *28,* no. 4 (1976), pp. 542-67.

14 See Michael Kaser, "Soviet Trade Turns to Europe," *Foreign Policy,* no. 19 (Summer 1975), p. 132.
15 Bruce Parrott, "Technological Progress and Soviet Politics," *Survey,* vol. *23,* no. 2 (Spring 1977–78).
16 Knorr, *op. cit.,* p. 158.
17 Albert O. Hirschman, *A Bias for Hope: Essays on Development and Latin America* (New Haven, Conn., Yale University Press, 1971), p. 12.
18 I. Vajda and M. Sima, *Foreign Trade in a Planned Economy* (Cambridge University Press, 1971), p. 8.

Chapter 2. The long road to Moscow: the origins of linkage, 1955

1 Interview with Ernst Friedländer for the Northwest German Radio, June 11, 1953.
2 Because the FRG and the USSR did not recognize each other diplomatically, the chancellor had no embassy out of which to operate.
3 Thomas W. Wolfe, *Soviet Power and Europe* (Baltimore: Johns Hopkins University Press, 1970), p. 28.
4 For the text of the Soviet proposal, see United States Congress, Senate Committee on Foreign Relations, *Documents on Germany, 1944–1970* (Washington, D.C.: U.S. Government Printing Office, 1971), pp. 191–3.
5 See Marshall Shulman, *Stalin's Foreign Policy Reappraised* (Cambridge, Mass.: Harvard University Press, 1963), p. 191.
6 For the text of these exchanges, see *Documents on Germany,* pp. 191–223. For an analysis of these notes, see Shulman, *op. cit.,* pp. 191–3.
7 See Pavel A. Nikolaev, *Politika Sovetskogo Soiuza v Germanskom Voprose, 1945–1964* (*The Policy of the Soviet Union on the German Question, 1945–1964*) (Moscow: Nauka, 1966), pp. 168–185.
8 For a discussion of the "lost opportunity" thesis, see Wolfe, *op. cit.,* pp. 28–31. See also Melvin Croan, "Reality and Illusion in Soviet–German Relations," *Survey* No. 44–45 (1962), p. 18, and Walter Laqueur, "Thoughts at the Wall," *Encounter,* vol. 19, no. 2 (1962), p. 66. According to a Czech account, Mikoyan expressed the quintessence of the Soviet view that any united Germany was undesirable, whatever its political leanings. Mikoyan said, "We are watching the Germans closely; we are not forgetting what they did to us during the war." His interlocutor said he thought that a German communist would dream of hegemony in the same way as a noncommunist would. Mikoyan replied, "Does that surprise you? They are Germans, aren't they?" Hubert Ripka, *Czechoslovakia Enslaved* (London: Gollancz, 1950), p. 134. See also Victor Baras, "Stalin's German Policy after Stalin," *Slavic Review,* vol. 37, no. 2 (1978), pp. 259–67. The author argues that the USSR, in offering an eventual Soviet concession (reunification) in return for immediate Western

concessions (rejection of the EDC and recognition of the GDR), was using the 1952 note primarily as a delaying tactic.

9 See *Documents on Germany,* pp. 244–58, 261–4.
10 Adam Bruno Ulam, *Expansion and Coexistence* (New York: Praeger, 1974), p. 565; Wolfe, *op. cit.,* pp. 74–5, 79.
11 *The New York Times,* May 16, 1955.
12 Ulam, *op. cit.,* p. 565.
13 *Pravda,* September 8, 1955, p. 1.
14 James L. Richardson, *Germany and the Atlantic Alliance* (Cambridge, Mass.: Harvard University Press, 1966), p. 28.
15 William E. Griffith, *The Ostpolitik of the Federal Republic of Germany* (Cambridge, Mass.: MIT Press), 1978, pp. 14–15.
16 The preamble stated, "The entire German people is called upon to accomplish, by free self-determination, the unity and freedom of Germany." Article 146 stated, "This Basic Law shall become invalid on the day when a constitution adopted in a free decision by the German people comes into force." Alfred Grosser, *Germany in Our Time* (New York: Praeger, 1971), p. 73.
17 Adenauer's speech at a meeting in Berlin, February 23, 1954, cited in Keesing's Research Report, No. 8, *Germany and Eastern Europe since 1945* (New York: Scribner, 1973), p. 185.
18 *The New York Times,* January 17, 1955.
19 Adenauer interview in *Bulletin,* April 5, 1955, pp. 533–4.
20 *The New York Times,* June 8, 1955. Adenauer, *Erinnerungen, Vol. 2, 1953–1955* (Stuttgart: Deutsche Verlags-Anstalt), p. 494.
21 *The New York Times,* June 10, 1956; Karl Deutsch and Lewis Edinger, *Germany Rejoins the Powers: Mass Opinion, Interest Groups, and Elites in Contemporary German Foreign Policy* (Stanford: Stanford University Press, 1959), p. 113.
22 Adenauer, *op. cit.,* p. 491. *The New York Times,* September 4 and 8, 1955.
23 Adenauer interview with James Reston, *The New York Times,* June 13, 1955.
24 Grosser, *op. cit.,* p. 678. See also Martin Schnitzer, *East and West Germany: A Comparative Economic Analysis* (New York: Praeger, 1972), pp. 10–11.
25 United Nations Economic Commission for Europe, *Economic Survey of Europe* (Geneva, 1957), chap. 11, p. 32.
26 Henry C. Wallich, *Mainsprings of the German Revival* (New Haven: Yale University Press, 1955), p. 253.
27 Norman Pounds, *The Economic Pattern of Modern Germany* (London: John Murray, 1963), pp. 112–13.
28 Frederick Ford McGoldrick, "The Politics of West German Foreign Economic Policy Towards the Communist States of Eastern Europe 1955–1968" (unpublished Ph.D. dissertation, American University, 1973), p. 59; Pounds, *op. cit.,* p. 58.
29 United Nations Secretariat, *Yearbook of International Trade Statistics, 1957* (New York, 1958), p. 243.

30 *Economic Survey of Europe,* chap. 6, p. 1.
31 *Ibid.,* p. 6.
32 Walter Trautmann, *Osthandel – Ja oder Nein?* (Stuttgart: W. Kohlhammer, 1954), pp. 102–8.
33 For contrasting accounts of the strategic embargo, see Gunnar Adler-Karlsson, *Western Economic Warfare, 1947–1967* (Stockholm: Almquist and Wiksell, 1968); U.S. Congress, Office of Technology Assessment, *Technology and East–West Trade* (Washington, D.C., U.S. Government Printing Office, 1979).
34 It is debatable when the FRG assumed responsibility for control of its Eastern trade. See Robert Dean, *West German Trade with the East: The Political Dimension* (New York: Praeger, 1974), p. 105.
35 Adler-Karlsson, *op. cit.,* pp. 44–5, 71–2. Much of the dissension centered on the position of trade with the GDR.
36 *Ibid.,* pp. 73, 99. For a rather sensational but nevertheless partially accurate description of the illegal trade in these years, see Joseph Bernard Hutton, *The Traitor Trade* (London: Neville Spearman, 1963), *passim.*
37 See Thomas A. Wolf, *U.S. East–West Trade Policy* (Lexington, Mass.: Lexington Books, 1973), p. 127.
38 Klaus Knorr, *The Power of Nations: The Political Economy of International Relations* (New York: Basic Books, 1975), pp. 144–5.
39 Alec Nove, *An Economic History of the USSR,* (London: Penguin Books, 1969), p. 349.
40 Adler-Karlsson, *op. cit.,* p. 84. See also Shulman, *op. cit.,* pp. 186–7.
41 Trautmann, *op. cit.,* pp. 63–4.
42 *Ibid.,* p. 64.
43 *The New York Times,* May 27, 1953.
44 McGoldrick, *op. cit.,* p. 70.
45 Deutscher Bundestag, I. Wahlperiode 1949, *Drucksache* Nr. 2935, Bonn, December 12, 1951.
46 Adler-Karlsson, *op. cit.,* p. 72.
47 Trautmann, *op. cit.,* pp. 119–23.
48 Botschafter Freiherr von Maltzan, "Zur Frage des Ost-West-Handels," *Bulletin,* no. 152 (1954), pp. 1353–4.
49 Trautmann, *op. cit.,* pp. 37, 108.
50 *Frankfurter Allgemeine Zeitung (FAZ),* July 27, 1955; August 19, 1955. *Der Volkswirt,* July 30, 1955.
51 Heinrich von Brentano, *Germany and Europe* (New York: Praeger, 1964), p. 165; Hallstein, cited in *Der Volkswirt,* July 30, 1955.
52 See Gerhard Braunthal, *The Federation of German Industry in Politics* (Ithaca: Cornell University Press, 1965), p. 310.
53 Otto Wolff von Amerongen, who still heads the Ostausschuss, is the son of the man who led the prewar Russlandausschuss, which had similar functions but more legal power.
54 The trip had been arranged in Baden-Baden in April, following the ECE conference. The trade agreement had already been worked out, with the USSR to supply grain, timber, and oil seeds

and the Germans machinery and rolling mill products; *FAZ*, May 14, 1954; Federal Economics Ministry, *Tages-Nachrichten*, April 17, 1954.

55 *The New York Times*, June 10, 1954; *Der Kurier*, June 12, 1954; *Deutsche Zeitung und Wirtschaftszeitung*, June 16, 1954. In a speech on November 15, 1954, von Amerongen said that the trip had been "indefinitely postponed"; *Handelsblatt*, November 15, 1954. He claimed that structural changes in the Soviet economy complicated the conclusion of a trade treaty. However, Trautmann, *op. cit.*, p. 66, speculates that this may have been part of a move against the Ostausschuss and that questions of competence had to be clarified.

56 Gabriel Almond, "The Politics of German Business," in *West German Leadership and Foreign Policy*, ed. by Hans Speier and W. Phillips Davison (Evanston, Ill.: Row, Peterson, 1957), p. 237.

57 *The New York Times*, December 27, 1953.

58 *Deutsche Zeitung und Wirtschaftszeitung*, December 5, 1953; *Tägliche Rundschau*, April 9, September 5, 1954, and February 13, 1955; *Le Monde*, June 27, 1954. See also Trautmann, *op. cit.*, pp. 154–64.

59 Poll cited in Dean, *op. cit.*, p. 112.

60 *The New York Times*, May 15, 1954.

61 Braunthal, *op. cit.*, p. 295.

62 *Bulletin*, March 9, 1954.

63 *Neues Deutschland*, March 23, June 22, July 21, 1954.

64 *Soviet News*, June 20, 1955. See also the article in *Industriekurier*, August 18, 1955. German commentators stressed the importance to the Russians of the economic side of these talks.

65 *Soviet News*, September 5, 1955; *Neues Deutschland*, September 7, 1955.

66 Daniel Melnikov, "The Situation in the German Federal Republic Today," *International Affairs* (Moscow), no. 9 (1955), p. 91.

67 *Soviet News*, September 5, 1955.

68 Author's interview with Dr. Gebhardt von Walter, ambassador to Moscow, 1966–68. At the time, Dr. von Walter was working in the West German embassy in Paris and recalls that a parcel was delivered to him from the Soviet embassy in Paris, containing the invitation. The invitation was unexpected and caused a considerable amount of agitation in the German embassy.

69 *Pravda*, June 8, 1955.

70 *Dokumente zur Deutschlandpolitik* (Frankfurt: A. Metzner: Bundesministerium fuer Gesamtdeutsche Fragen, 1961), p. 123. The answer was unsigned, as was the original Soviet note, and deposited with the Soviet embassy in Paris.

71 *Pravda*, August 6, 1955.

72 *Dokumente zur Deutschlandpolitik*, p. 263.

73 *Pravda*, August 20, 1955.

74 Adenauer, *Erinnerungen*, vol. 2, *1953–1955*, pp. 489–92.

75 *New York International Herald Tribune*, September 4, 1955. See also

H. G. von Studnitz, "Der Kanzler in Moskau," *Aussenpolitik,* vol. 6, no. 9 (1950), p. 553.

76 Werner Feld, *Reunification and West German-Soviet Relations* (The Hague: Nijoff, 1963), p. 175. *The Manchester Guardian,* August 29, 1955.

77 For a full and graphic account of Adenauer's visit, see Adenauer, *Erinnerungen,* vol. 2, *1953-55,* pp. 487-551. See also Klaus Mehnert, "Der Kanzler in Moskau," *Osteuropa* no. 6 (1955), pp. 448-54. For a collection of the public speeches made during the negotiations, see *Bulletin,* Sonderausgabe, September 20, 1955.

78 Adenauer, *op. cit.,* pp. 511, 515, 542, 544, 546.

79 Nikita S. Khrushchev, *Khrushchev Remembers: The Last Testament* (Boston: Little, Brown, 1974), pp. 405-7.

80 Ambassador Bohlen was "astonished" that Adenauer had "buckled" to the Russians and agreed to establish diplomatic relations. This served "to formalize the division of Germany." On Bohlen and his disagreement with Adenauer, see Charles E. Bohlen, *Witness to History, 1929-1969* (New York: Norton, 1973), p. 387.

81 Probably the most interesting part of the stay for Adenauer was his private talk with Khrushchev, in which the first secretary confided in the chancellor his fears about China and his conviction that the Chinese would soon become the USSR's greatest enemy. Adenauer thought that Khrushchev was trying to tempt him toward a new Rapallo, but the chancellor felt that West Germany might be able to benefit from the Sino-Soviet split.

82 *Bulletin,* Sonderausgabe, September 20, 1955.

83 *Ibid.,* p. 15.

84 Adenauer, *op. cit.,* pp. 518-28.

85 *Economist,* October 22, 1955.

86 Khrushchev, *op. cit.,* p. 403.

87 *Ibid.,* pp. 405-7.

88 *Bulletin,* Sonderausgabe, September 20, 1955. The Russians did not mention the prisoner of war issue in their statement.

89 *FAZ,* September 16, 1955.

90 *Financial Times,* September 17, 1955.

91 *Economist,* October 22, 1955.

92 *FAZ,* September 21, 1955. The Soviet invitations were specifically nongovernmental. They came from Soviet foreign trade organizations and other economic institutions.

93 *FAZ,* October 31, 1955.

94 *Dokumente zur Deutschlandpolitik,* 1955, p. 407.

95 *Izvestiia,* cited in *Soviet News,* October 4, 1955.

96 "The Soviet Union and Germany," *International Affairs* (Moscow), no. 10, (1955), p. 12.

97 *Pravda,* October 21, 1955.

98 Deutsch and Edinger, *op. cit.,* p. 183. Khrushchev, as if to rub it in, signed a "Treaty of Friendship" with the GDR on September 20,

1955, granting the GDR "full sovereignty in the conduct of foreign affairs." *Dokumente zur Deutschlandpolitik*, 1955, pp. 371–4.

99 Deutscher Bundestag, *Verhandlungen*. 101. Sitzung, Bonn, September 22, 1955, p. 5647.

100 *Ibid.*, 102 Sitzung, Bonn, September 22, 1955, pp. 5668–9.

Chapter 3. From diplomacy to trade: 1955–1958

1 Deutscher Bundestag, *Verhandlungen*, 177. Sitzung, December 6, 1956, p. 9818.

2 Cited in United States Senate, *East–West Trade, Hearings before the Subcommittee on International Finance of the Committee on Banking and Currency*, 90th Congress, 2nd Session, 1968.

3 Adam Bruno Ulam, *Expansion and Coexistence* (New York: Praeger, 1974), p. 570. For the formal communications of this conference, see Senate Committee on Foreign Relations, *Documents on Germany, 1944–1970*, 92nd Congress, 1st Session, p. 285.

4 Konrad Adenauer, *Erinnerungen*, vol. 3 *1955–1959* (Stuttgart: Deutsche Verlags-Anstalt, pp. 90–1.

5 William E. Griffith, *The Ostpolitik of the Federal Republic of Germany* (Cambridge, Mass.: MIT Press, 1978), p. 75. For Brentano's comments on the disappointing outcome of the conference, see Boris Meissner, *Moskau–Bonn: Die Beziehungen Zwischen der Sowjetunion und der Bundesrepublik Deutschland 1955–1973* (Cologne: Verlag Wissenschaft und Politik, 1975), pp. 150–1.

6 Thomas Wolfe, *Soviet Power and Europe* (Baltimore: Johns Hopkins University Press, 1970), p. 81. For the Soviet accusations of the German role in provoking the Hungarian Revolution, see *Pravda*, December 5, 1956.

7 Conscription was introduced on July 6, 1956. See Alfred Grosser, *Germany in our Time* (New York: Praeger, 1971), p. 224.

8 James L. Richardson, *Germany and the Atlantic Alliance* (Cambridge, Mass.: Harvard University Press, 1966), pp. 113–14.

9 Wolfe, *op. cit.*, pp. 82–6. The main point of this policy – enunciated by Dimitri Shepilov during his brief tenure as Soviet foreign minister – was to persuade Britain and France that the United States was undermining their interests in the Middle East and trying to dominate Western Europe.

10 Ulam, *op. cit.*, p. 611. For the German reaction, see Richardson, *op. cit.*, pp. 54–5. For a discussion of the origins and development of the Rapacki Plan, see Griffith, *op. cit.*, pp. 80–3.

11 Ulam, *op. cit.*, p. 575. Interestingly enough, Adenauer was convinced that destalinization was initially intended as a move against Khrushchev by Mikoyan and Bulganin, but Khrushchev, sensing the way the tide was turning, jumped on the bandwagon and became *plus anti-Staliniste que les anti-Stalinistes*. Adenauer, *op. cit.*, p. 110.

12 On the dismissal of Molotov, Malenkov, Kaganovich, and the rest of the anti-party group, see Ulam, *op. cit.*, pp. 604–5. On the establishment of the *sovnarkhozy* – regional economic councils – see Alec Nove, *An Economic History of the USSR* (London: Penguin Books, 1969), pp. 342–4. On Khrushchev, see George Breslauer, "Khrushchev Reconsidered" *Problems of Communism*, Vol. 25, no. 5 (1976), pp. 18–33.

13 Adenauer interview with Radio Copenhagen, cited in *Der Tagesspiegel* (Berlin), May 29, 1956.

14 Interviews with Brentano, cited in *Dokumente zur Deutschlandpolitik* (Frankfurt: A. Metzner: Bundesministerium für Gesamtdeutsche Fragen, 1961), p. 750; *Industriekurier*, January 24, 1956; *Svenska Dagbladet*, February 18, 1956; *U.S. News and World Report*, February 10, 1956, pp. 86–9; Brentano in Bundestag debate in *Verhandlungen*, 155. Sitzung, Bonn, June 28, 1956, pp. 8417–18.

15 "Heavy Russian Bait," *Fortune Magazine*, May 1956, pp. 70–2. See also the article by C. L. Sulzberger, *The New York Times*, November 28, 1955.

16 For the SPD question, see *Verhandlungen*, Drucksache 2736, October 3, 1956. For the full text of the debate, see *Verhandlungen*, 177. Sitzung, December 6, 1956, pp. 9811–31.

17 *Ibid.*, pp. 9818, 9822.

18 United Nations *Yearbook of International Trade Statistics* (New York, 1957), p. 243; *The New York Times*, August 25, 1957. The increase in trade was partly due to the filling of orders from a few years back. See "Wandlungen im Russlandhandel," Berliner Handels-Gesellschaft, *Wirtschaftsdienst*, no. 118 (1957).

19 Otto Wolff von Amerongen, "Traditionelle Handelsbeziehungen verbinden uns," *Handelsblatt*, Supplement ["Europäische Volksrepubliken"], August 1957.

20 *Pravda*, February 15, 1956.

21 Nove, *op. cit.*, p. 341.

22 Hans Braeker, "Die sowjetische Wirtschaft in ihren Aussenbeziehungen," *Osteuropa-Wirtschaft*, no. 2 (1956–57), pp. 89–106.

23 "Za Razvitie Torgovli So Vsemi Stranami" ("For the Development of Trade with All Countries"), *Vneshniaia Torgovlia*, no. 4 (1956), p. 1.

24 M. V. Nesterov, "Mezhdunarodnaia Torgovlia – Vazhnyi Faktor Ukrepleniia Mira" ("International Trade – An Important Factor in the Strengthening of Peace"), *Znanie*, series 3, no. 7 (Moscow, 1956), p. 21.

25 Interview with Nikita S. Khrushchev, *Journal of Commerce*, March 22, 1958, printed in *International Affairs* (Moscow), no. 5 (1958), pp. 3–11.

26 B. Pichugin, "Western Germany's Stake in Soviet Trade," *New Times*, March 1957.

27 For a discussion of the role of ideology in Soviet foreign policy, see Alexander Dallin, ed., *Soviet Conduct in World Affairs* (New York:

Columbia University Press, 1960), *passim.* See also Seweryn Bialer, *Stalin's Successors: Leadership Stability and Change in the Soviet Union* (Cambridge University Press, 1980).

28 *Vneshniaia Torgovlia,* no. 6 (1956), pp. 14–15; *International Affairs* (Moscow), no. 2 (1956), pp. 134–6; "O Torgovle FRG so Stranami Narodnoi Demokratii" ("On the Trade of the FRG with the People's Democracies"), *Vneshniaia Torgovlia,* no. 6 (1957), p. 32. See also *Ibid.,* no. 11 (1957), pp. 77–8.

29 Interview with I. G. Kabanov in *Die Welt,* cited in *Soviet News,* September 14, 1955.

30 Soviet note of October 22, 1956, in *Documents on Germany,* p. 306. For the original German note, see *Ibid.,* pp. 288–98.

31 B. Grigorevich, "Razvitie Torgovli Neobkhodimo Dlia Ukreplenie Mira i Druzhbi Mezhdu Narodami" ("The Development of Trade Is Necessary for the Strengthening of Peace and Friendship between Nations"), *Vneshniaia Torgovlia,* no. 7 (1958), no. p. 5.

32 "Documents from the History of German–Soviet Relations," *International Affairs* (Moscow), no. 1 (1957), pp. 198–9.

33 I. Koblyakov, "Rapallo – Then and Now," *New Times,* no. 20 (1957).

34 *Neues Deutschland,* January 10, 1957.

35 See, for instance, D. E. Melnikov, *Germanskaia Federativnaia Respublika (The German Federal Republic),* Znanie, series 7, no. 3 (1956). On p. 6, the author criticizes monopoly capitalists in the FRG, but on p. 10 he praises German industrialists for comprehending the importance of trade with the USSR for their economy.

36 Author's interview with Berthold Beitz, managing director of Krupp.

37 Khrushchev interview with the *Toronto Telegram,* printed in *International Affairs* (Moscow), no. 11 (1957), p. 17.

38 *Pravda,* February 9, 1956; *Izvestiia,* February 22, 1956.

39 *Bulletin,* February 1956, pp. 343–5.

40 Bulganin's letter of February 8, 1957, in *Soviet News,* February 12, 1957. See also *NZZ,* February 13, 1957.

41 This was, according to one report, the view of the German Foreign Office; *Economist,* June 22, 1957. Adenauer confirms this view in *Erinnerungen,* vol. 3, *1955–1959,* p. 356.

42 *Manchester Guardian,* February 13, 1957. For details of the problems caused by the creation of the EEC, see United Nations Economic Commission for Europe, *Economic Survey of Europe, 1958* (Geneva, 1959), chap. 3, p. 33.

43 For details of these negotiations, see Keesing's Research Report No. 8, *Germany and Eastern Europe Since 1945* (New York: Scribner, 1973), pp. 118–29; *Izvestiia,* March 11, 1956.

44 Adenauer, *ibid.,* p. 357.

45 *Sueddeutsche Zeitung,* February 13, 1957; *NZZ,* February 27, 1957; *FAZ,* February 27, 1957.

46 Adenauer's reply of February 27 to Bulganin, in *Dokumente zur Deutschlandpolitik,* 1957 (first third), pp. 421–5.

47 See the *Manchester Guardian*, July 11, 1957, for SPD leader Ollenhauer's remarks. *Christian Science Monitor*, July 16, 1957.
48 *FAZ*, May 17, 1957. See also Sebastian Haffner, "Dim Prospects for Soviet-West German Talks," *Observer Foreign News Service*, May 27, 1957.
49 *Soviet News*, June 20, 1957.
50 *Manchester Guardian*, July 22, 1957; *FAZ*, July 22, 1957.
51 Sebastian Haffner, "Germans in Russia Dispute," *The Scotsman*, August 10, 1957; *The Times*, August 20, 1957.
52 Gromyko in *Izvestiia*, August 1, 1957.
53 Note from the FRG embassy in Moscow to the Soviet foreign minister, August 12, 1957, in *Dokumente, ibid.*, 1957, p. 1442.
54 *Pravda*, August 15, 1957.
55 *Izvestiia*, August 23, 1957.
56 Geoffrey K. Roberts, *West German Politics* (New York: Taplinger, 1972), p. 33. For the first time, the CDU received an absolute majority but a small margin.
57 For details of the repatriation negotiations, see *Bulletin*, April 26, 1958. For comments on the negotiations, see *Manchester Guardian*, April 9, 1958; *The Times*, April 11, 1958; *Economist*, April 19, 1958.
58 *FAZ*, August 27, 1957; *The New York Times*, August 27, 1957; August 29, 1957; *Tass* statement of September 5, 1957, on German-Soviet negotiations in *Dokumente*, 1957 (second third), pp. 1549-50. In the Tass statement the Russians criticized the Germans for not making more concrete proposals. See also the German government statement of September 10, 1957, in *Bulletin*, September 10, 1957.
59 Author's interview with Dr. Walter Steidle, former head of East-West section of the Economics Ministry in Bonn.
60 For a list of quotas, see *FAZ*, April 26, 1958. List A was of Soviet exports – mainly raw materials – and list B of German exports, mainly machinery and electrical goods.
61 Interview with Ambassador Rolf Lahr on Hessische Rundfunk, April 17, 1958, in *Bulletin*, April 19, 1958.
62 Jozef Wilczynski, *The Economics and Politics of East-West Trade* (New York: Praeger, 1969), p. 107; *FAZ*, April 28, 1958.
63 The deutsche mark became convertible on December 28, 1958. Before then, Soviet-West German trade was conducted in "Bekomarks," special convertible marks.
64 Lahr interview, *op. cit.*, p. 712. On the economic significance of the treaty, see Wolfgang Eggers, "Die wirtschaftliche Bedeutung der Deutsch-Sowjetischen Abkommen von 1958," *Osteuropa*, no. 6 (1958), pp. 401-5. For the text of the treaty, see Meissner, *op. cit.*, pp. 381-3.
65 *Pravda*, April 14, 1958; Daniel Melnikov, "Restoring a Tradition," *New Times*, no. 22 (1958), pp. 9-10.
66 Interview with Anastas Mikoyan published in *Vneshniaia Torgovlia*, no. 5 (1958), pp. 3-8.
67 *Pravda*, April 16, 1958.

68 Melnikov, *op. cit.*, p. 22. See also "K Podpisaniiu Soglasheni Mezhdu SSSR i FRG" ("On the Signing of the Agreement between the USSR and the FRG"), *Vneshniaia Torgovlia*, no. 5 (1958), pp. 37–8.

69 Interview with Lahr, in *Meissner, op. cit.*, pp. 374–8.

Chapter 4. Trade and the Berlin crisis: 1958–1961

1 Senate Committee on Foreign Relations, *Documents on Germany, 1944–1970*, 92nd Congress, 1st session, p. 366.

2 David Binder, *The Other German: Willy Brandt's Life and Times* (Washington: New Republic, 1975), pp. 186–7.

3 See Ulbricht's speech at the Fifth Party Congress of the SED, July 10, 1958, cited in *Dokumente zur Deutschlandpolitik*, series 111, vol. 4, part 2 (Frankfurt: A. Metzner: Bundesministerium für Gesamtdeutsche Fragen), pp. 1397f. Also see the speech by Ulbricht in Berlin, October 27, 1958, *Neues Deutschland*, October 28, 1958, cited in *ibid.*, vol. 4, part 3, pp. 1835f.

4 Nikita S. Khrushchev's speech at the Polish–Soviet friendship meeting, November 10, 1958. Cited in George D. Embree, ed., *The Soviet Union and the German Question, September 1958–June 1961* (The Hague: Nijhoff, 1963), p. 19.

5 *Documents on Germany, 1944–1970*, p. 364.

6 *Ibid.*, p. 366.

7 Philip Windsor, *City on Leave: A History of Berlin, 1946–1962* (London: Chatto and Windus, 1963), p. 202. For a discussion of the wording of the note, see *ibid.*, pp. 202–4.

8 Khrushchev's Kremlin press conference on the Berlin question, November 27, 1958, cited in Embree, *op. cit.*, p. 42. See also Nikita S. Khrushchev, *Khrushchev Remembers: The Last Testament* (Boston: Little, Brown, 1976), p. 574, for an elaboration of the cancer metaphor.

9 G. M. Akopov, *Zapadnyi Berlin: Problemy i Reshenia (West Berlin: Problems and Solutions)* (Moscow: Mezhdunarodnye Otnosheniia, 1974), p. 104.

10 N. N. Inozemtsev, ed., *Mezhdunarodnye Otnosheniia Posle Vtoroi Mirovoi Voini (International Relations Since the Second World War)*, vol. 3 (Moscow: Izdatels'tvo Politicheskoi Literatury, 1962–65), pp. 198–9.

11 P. Nikolaev, *Politika Sovetskogo Soiuza v Germanskom Voprose 1945–1964 (The Policy of the Soviet Union in the German Question)* (Moscow: Nauka, 1966), p. 270. See also B. Ponomarev, A. Gromyko, and V. Khvostov, *History of Soviet Foreign Policy 1945–1970* (Moscow: Progress Publishers 1974), p. 367. The authors write, "Of course it would have been most reasonable to return West Berlin, artificially isolated by the three Western powers, to the GDR. But for the sake of peace and the important situation in Europe, the GDR government made a major sacrifice by agreeing to West Berlin's existence as a free city."

12 Adam Bruno Ulam, *Expansion and Coexistence* (New York: Praeger, 1974), p. 619. William E. Griffith, *The Ostpolitik of the Federal Republic of Germany* (Cambridge, Mass.: MIT Press, 1978), p. 84.

13 For a comprehensive analysis of possible Soviet motives, see James L. Richardson, *Germany and the Atlantic Alliance* (Cambridge, Mass.: Harvard University Press, 1966), pp. 310–13.

14 See NATO note of December 16, 1958; *Documents on Germany*, p. 367; U.S. Department of State note, December 20, 1958; *ibid.*, pp. 368–79; Note of the FRG to the USSR, January 5, 1959, *ibid.*, pp. 382–90.

15 For an examination of the differences among the Western powers, see Richardson, *op. cit.*, pp. 314–36. Macmillan's visit to Moscow in February 1959 to try to solve the crisis was one episode that revealed the difference between the British view of the USSR's motives as being more defensive and the prevailing Western view that these moves were offensive.

16 Soviet note to the United States transmitting a draft peace treaty for Germany, January 10, 1959, *Documents on Germany*, pp. 390–411.

17 Khrushchev's speech at Tula, *Pravda*, February 18, 1959.

18 Ulam, *op. cit.*, p. 621.

19 Windsor, *op. cit.*, p. 209.

20 Thomas W. Wolfe, *Soviet Power and Europe* (Baltimore: Johns Hopkins University Press, 1970), p. 91. For a full record of Soviet and Western statements on Berlin and Germany during the Geneva Conference, see *Documents on Germany*, pp. 431–81.

21 Apparently Eisenhower told Khrushchev that he thought the situation in Berlin was "abnormal," and Khrushchev took this to mean that he might be able to exact new concessions from the West. See Richardson, *op. cit.*, p. 272. For the final communiqué between Khrushchev and Eisenhower, see *Documents on Germany*, pp. 482–3. See also *History of Soviet Foreign Policy*, p. 378.

22 Jack M. Schick, *The Berlin Crisis, 1958–1962* (Philadelphia: University of Pennsylvania Press, 1971), pp. 108–26.

23 Khrushchev's Berlin speech, May 20, 1960, cited in Embree, *op. cit.*, pp. 258–69.

24 Richardson, *op. cit.*, p. 280.

25 *Ibid.*, p. 284.

26 Ulbricht attended a secret meeting of the first secretaries of the Warsaw Pact countries in Moscow from August 3 to 5; Windsor, *op. cit.*, p. 239. See also *History of Soviet Foreign Policy*, p. 382.

27 Inozemtsev, *op. cit.*, p. 284.

28 Akopov, *op. cit.*, chap. 4. See also Khrushchev, *op. cit.*, vol. 1, p. 455. He writes, "The GDR's economic problems were considerably relieved by the establishment of border control between East and West Berlin."

29 Nikolaev, *op. cit.*, p. 290.

30 It is difficult to see what measures the West could have taken to

resist the building of the wall. The margin of uncertainty about whether a Western destruction of the wall might have escalated the crisis to the nuclear level was sufficient to justify a response of acceptance, because the Soviet stake in the survival of the GDR was greater than the Western stake in the freedom of movement between the two halves of Berlin.

31 Inozemtsev, *op. cit.*, p. 211, explains the Soviet resumption of nuclear testing by blaming NATO's war preparations and pressure on Berlin.

32 Richardson, *op. cit.*, p. 326.

33 Griffith, *op. cit.*, pp. 83–7.

34 Hans Kroll, *Lebenserinnerungen eines Botschafters* (Cologne: Kiepenheuer und Witsch, 1967), p. 445. For a description of the correspondence, see *ibid.*, pp. 442–52. Kroll's memoirs tend to exaggerate his importance and the respect in which Khrushchev held him. He may also have overemphasized the intrinsic importance of this correspondence because he played the key role in transmitting the letters. The accuracy of Kroll's memoirs has been disputed by many people, and his subsequent recall for impropriety has made them more suspect. For the text of the letters see Boris Meissner, *Moskau–Bonn: Die Beziehungen Zwischen der Sowjetunion und der Bundesrepublik Deutschland 1955–1973: Dokumentation* (Cologne: Verlag Wissenschaft und Politik, 1975), pp. 586–600, 606–10, 617–25. For Adenauer's argument against the "free city" proposal, see his letter of January 8, 1960, reprinted in *Bulletin*, February 2, 1960.

35 For an exposition of his views, see *Der Spiegel*, interview with Mayor Brandt, No. 6, 1959. On p. 19 he says quite clearly that the Russians were trying to use Berlin as a lever for settling the German question and that it was West Germany's duty to prevent any one-sided changes in the relationship. A cartoon depicted Adenauer and Brandt skating together with the caption, "On thin ice, but united." For Brandt's statements on Berlin during the crisis, see Kesing's Research Report No. 8, *Germany and Eastern Europe since 1945* (New York: Scribner, 1973), pp. 155, 157–8. For Soviet criticism of Brandt as a "rightist social democrat," see *Izvestiia*, July 13, 1961.

36 *Der Spiegel*, No. 12, (1959). For the communiqué, see Kesing, *op. cit.*, p. 160. Carola Stern, *Willy Brandt in Selbstzeugnissen und Bilddokumenten* (Reinbek bei Hamburg: Rowohlt, 1975), pp. 57–8.

37 For the March 18, 1959, SPD Reunification Plan, see *Dokumente zur Deutschlandspolitik*, series 4, vol. 1, 1958–59, pp. 1207–22. For an account of the Moscow visit, see Kesing, *op. cit.*, p. 166. The Soviets criticized the program in *MEMO*, no. 2, 1959, in an article entitled "O Proekte Programmy Zapadnoi-Germanskii Sotsial-Demokraty" ("On the Projected Program of the German Social Democrats"), pp. 67–88.

38 For the SPD Bad Godesberg program, see Alfred Grosser, *Germany in Our Time* (New York: Praeger, 1971), pp. 150–1; Bruno Fried-

rich, "Godesberger Erneuerung" *Berliner Stimme,* April 6, 1974; see also *History of Soviet Foreign Policy,* p. 373.

39 Franklyn D. Holzman and Robert Legvold, "The Economics and Politics of East–West Relations," *International Organization,* vol. 29, no. 1 (Winter 1975), p. 283.

40 United Nations Economic Commission for Europe, *Yearbook of International Trade Statistics* (New York 1963), p. 270.

41 See, for instance, Khrushchev's speech at the Leipzig Fair, March 6, 1959, *Pravda,* March 7, 1959; see also the interview with Khrushchev by A. E. Johann, *Soviet News,* September 25, 1958.

42 Khrushchev's Kremlin press conference on the Berlin question, March 14, 1959, cited in Embree, *op. cit.,* pp. 151-2.

43 A. Frumkin, "The Insolvency of Bourgeois Foreign Trade Theory," *Voprosy Ekonomiki,* no. 12 (1959), reprinted in Joint Publications Research Service, *Problems of Economics,* vol. II, no. 12, 1960, pp. 58-62.

44 See, for example, I. Yermashov, "Bonn's War Merry-go-Round," *New Times,* no. 34, 1961; Pavel Naumov, *Bonn - Sila i Bessile (Bonn - Strength and Weakness)* (Moscow: Mysl, 1965), pp. 268-9.

45 Mikoyan's speech in *Pravda,* November 6, 1958.

46 Anastas Mikoyan, "Der Handel - Heute und Morgen," *Handelsblatt,* May 1960. Supplement

47 Alec Nove, *An Economic History of the USSR* (London: Penguin Books, 1969), p. 353.

48 United Nations Economic Commission for Europe, *Economic Survey of Europe in 1959,* chap. 11 (Geneva, 1960), p. 6.

49 U.N. *Economic Survey of Europe in 1961,* chap. 11 (Geneva, 1962), p. 31.

50 See M. Nesterov, "Die Moeglichkeiten beider Seiten sind nicht ausgenutzt," in Bertrand Hommey, *Ost-West Handel* (Stuttgart: Daco Verlag, 1960), pp. 34-6.

51 When the 1958 agreement was reviewed in February 1959, further stipulations about numbers of German prisoners were made. By 1960 no new German prisoners were released. *FAZ,* October 17, 1960.

52 Leonid Matveyev, head of Exportkhleb, "Getreidehandel noch immer Sorgenkind," in *Industriekurier,* Supplement, *Handelspartner UdSSR,* October 22, 1959.

53 Interview with Berthold Beitz, *New Times,* no. 24 (1959), p. 18.

54 *Der Spiegel,* no. 27, 1958. Adenauer later denied that he had called Beitz unreliable but reiterated that Beitz had not seen fit to inform either Economics Minister Erhard or himself of the trip.

55 Author's interview with Berthold Beitz, *Der Spiegel,* no. 23, (1958); *ibid.,* no. 21, 1959.

56 The group consisted of representatives from Phoenix-Rheinrohr, Kloeckner-Humboldt-Deutz, Ruhrstahl, Mannesmann, August–Thyssen Huette and Hoesch. *NZZ,* June 25, 1958.

57 *Der Spiegel,* no. 27 (1958). Mikoyan apparently explained to the industrialists that the demonstration in Moscow was unfortunately

inevitable, given the need for reciprocity, but it was in no way intended against any of the embassy staff or guests. Kroll, *op. cit.*, p. 281.

58 During the war, Beitz, who was a young man from Pomerania, had worked for Shell in Poland, and while working in Boryslav had saved the lives of many Jews and Poles who were scheduled to be deported to concentration camps. He had subsequently been honored by the Poles for his heroism during the war and was one of the few prominent Germans whom the Poles trusted.

59 For a description of Beitz's journey and his relations with the German and Polish governments, see Hansjakob Stehle, *Nachbar Polen* (Frankfurt: S. Fischer, 1963), pp. 321–34.

60 For a more detailed discussion, see Klaus Bolz, Hermann Clement and Petra Pissulla, *Die Wirtschaftsbeziehungen zwischen der BRD und der Sowjetunion* (Hamburg: Weltarchiv, 1976), pp. 418–31.

61 See remarks made by CDU Deputy Dr. Kurt Birrenbach in the ratification debate, *Verhandlungen*, 47. Sitzung, October 29, 1958, p. 2623.

62 *Der Spiegel*, no. 52, (1960).

63 *FAZ*, September 30, 1960. Erhard thought these measures would be particularly effective against a Soviet probe in the developing nations.

64 N. Baturin, "Provokatsionnyi Shag Bonn," *Vneshniaia Torgovlia*, no. 12 (1960), pp. 26–7.

65 *The New York Times*, November 28, 1960; Robert W. Dean, *West German Trade with the East: The Political Dimension* (New York: Praeger, 1974), pp. 63–4.

66 *The New York Times*, December 6, 1960; *The New York Herald Tribune*, October 19, 1960.

67 *Daily Telegraph*, December 6, 1960; *NZZ*, December 4, 1960.

68 *The Times* (London), December 13, 1960; *FAZ*, December 14, 1960; *NZZ*, December 15, 1960. Apparently during the two and a half hours of negotiations, waiters would appear at regular intervals with what was by now rather flat champagne, only to be waved away from the door with agitated cries.

69 *Izvestiia*, December 15, 1960.

70 *Neues Deutschland*, December 17, 1960.

71 *NZZ*, December 4 and 15, 1960.

72 Windsor, *op. cit.*, p. 229.

73 *Der Spiegel*, no. 52, (1960).

74 Dean, *op. cit.*, p. 124.

75 *Sozialdemokratischer Pressedienst*, p/XV/283, 113, December 1960, cited in *Dokumente zur Deutschlandpolitik*, series 4, vol. 5, 1960, p. 590.

76 *NZZ*, December 12, 1960.

77 Dean, *op. cit.*, p. 125.

78 Author's interview with Dr. Walter Steidle, former head of the East–West Division of the Federal Economics Ministry.

79 See von Brentano's and van Scherpenberg's press conferences fol-

lowing the breakdown of the talks in *Dokumente zur Deutschlandpolitik,* series 4, vol. 5, 1960, pp. 589–95.

80 *FAZ,* December 29, 1960; *NZZ,* December 30, 1960; *Le Monde,* December 30, 1960; *Der Spiegel,* no. 2, (1961).

81 *FAZ,* December 31, 1960; *ibid.,* January 2, 1961. At the small signing ceremony, State Secretary van Scherpenberg handed Ambassador Smirnov a letter stating that there were no more differences of opinion on the execution of the agreement. The area of applicability of the agreement (*Anwendungsbereich*) would be the same as before. One press account (*NZZ,* January 3, 1961) claimed that Smirnov accepted the letter without saying anything. According to a witness, however, Smirnov threw the letter over his shoulder, and it was caught by an aide. Thus, even after a compromise had been reached, the Soviets would not recognize the letter.

82 *FAZ,* January 2, 1961; *Der Tagesspiegel,* December 30, 1960; *Le Monde,* December 30, 1960.

83 *Bulletin,* January 3, 1961.

84 *Bulletin,* January 3, 1961. For complete details of the treaty, see *Vneshniaia Torgovlia,* no. 2 (1961), Supplement.

85 *Pravda,* May 25, 1961. For the original agreement, see *Bulletin,* March 12, 1960.

86 *FAZ,* May 18, 1961.

Chapter 5. The pipe embargo: 1962–1963

1 W. W. Rostow, Memo to the Policy Planning Council, "U. S. Policy on Trade with the European Soviet Bloc," July 26, 1963, p. 4; Box 223, National Security Files, John F. Kennedy Library, Waltham, Mass.

2 Speech to voters of the Kalinin electoral district, reported in *Pravda,* February 28, 1963.

3 Rostow, *op. cit.,* pp. 2, 5.

4 The rationale for the embargo was that the USSR treated foreign trade as a political weapon and thus the United States had to respond in kind. See Gunnar Adler-Karlsson, *Western Economic Warfare, 1947–1967* (Stockholm: Almquist and Wiksell, 1968), pp. 112–13. For an interesting discussion of the validity of theories of economic warfare, see Peter Wiles, "Economic Warfare and the Soviet-type Economy," *Osteuropa-Wirtschaft,* no. 1 (1965), pp. 27–42.

5 Adler-Karlsson, *op. cit.,* pp. 92, 96.

6 For the full text of the Franco–German Treaty on Organization and Principles of Cooperation, see Senate Committee on Foreign Relations, *Documents on Germany, 1944–1970,* 92nd Congress, 1st session, pp. 620–3. For Adenauer's accounts of his discussions with de Gaulle, see Konrad Adenauer, *Erinnerungen,* vol. 4, 1959–63 (Stuttgart: Deutsche Verlags-Anstalt), pp. 198–212.

7 James L. Richardson, *Germany and the Atlantic Alliance* (Cambridge, Mass.: Harvard University Press, 1966), pp. 63-4. The author speculates that Adenauer signed the treaty partly as a protest against the Kennedy administration's manner of conducting relations with the FRG. After the Germans realized how much the Americans disapproved of their moves, they reappraised their priorities.

8 Draft Paper, "U.S. Policy Toward Europe," February 9, 1963; pp. 1, 9; Box 314, National Security Files, John F. Kennedy Library, Waltham, Mass.

9 Note from the Soviet Union to the Federal Republic of Germany Protesting Certain Provisions of the Franco-German Treaty on Organization and Principles of Cooperation, February 5, 1963, in *Documents on Germany*, pp. 623-5. "West Berlin is not a part of the territory of the FRG and cannot be one." A later Soviet book interpreted the treaty as a French attempt to turn the FRG into a "loyal ally" that failed. See N. N. Inozemtsev, ed., *Mezhdunarodnye Otnosheniia Posle Vtoroi Mirovoi Voiny (International Relations Since World War Two)*, vol. 3 (Moscow: Izdatel'stvo Politicheskoi Literatury, 1962-65), p. 437. In a note to de Gaulle, the Soviets stressed that "it follows clearly from international agreements in force that West Germany does not and cannot have any right in West Berlin."

10 "Antwortnote der deutschen Bundesregierung an die Sowjetunion vom 28. März 1963," *Europa-Archiv*, no. 9 (1963), pp. D231-2.

11 *NZZ*, January 28, 1962; *The New York Times*, January 31, 1962. There was also the suggestion that the Free Democrats were annoyed at being denied a role in foreign policy making, and they therefore proposed an opposing foreign policy platform.

12 Hans Kroll, *Lebenserinnerungen eines Botschafters* (Cologne: Kiepenheuer und Witsch, 1967), pp. 552-3. Kroll claimed that he had a "special relationship" with Khrushchev, but others denied this and pointed to his penchant for exaggeration. Author's interview with Hermann Poerzgen, *Frankfurter Allgemeine* correspondent in Moscow, 1956-76.

13 *Pravda*, November 16, 1961.

14 See the speech by Gerhard Schroeder outlining his policy: "Grundlinien der deutschen Aussenpolitik," October 4, 1962, reprinted in Boris Meissner, ed., *Die deutsche Ostpolitik 1961-1970: Kontinuität und Wandel: Dokumentation* (Cologne: Verlag Wissenschaft und Politik, 1970), p. 36.

15 William E. Griffith, *The Ostpolitik of the Federal Republic of Germany* (Cambridge, Mass.: MIT Press, 1978), pp. 112-15.

16 Robert W. Dean, *West German Trade with the East: The Political Dimension* (New York: Praeger, 1974), p. 28. Konrad Adenauer, *Erinnerungen*, vol. 4, 1959-63, p. 202.

17 United Nations, *Yearbook of International Trade Statistics*, 1963, p. 270.

18 *The New York Times*, January 1, 1962; *NZZ*, April 12, 1962.
19 Dean, *op. cit.*, p. 128.
20 Albert Feller, "Warum Roehrenembargo?" mimeograph, Bonn, 1964, p. 31.
21 Nicholas Spulber, "East–West Trade and the Paradoxes of the Strategic Embargo," in Alan Brown and Egon Neuberger, eds., *International Trade and Central Planning* (Berkeley: University of California Press, 1968), p. 121.
22 Glen Alden Smith, *Soviet Foreign Trade* (New York: Praeger, 1973), p. 23.
23 *The Guardian*, June 21, 1962.
24 Klaus Marquandt, "Die Erdoelwirtschaft der UdSSR in der Expansion," in *Industriekurier*, Supplement, *Handelspartner UdSSR*, 1961.
25 "Soviet Oil in East–West Trade." Hearing before the Subcommittee to Investigate the Administration of the Internal Security Act and Other Internal Security Laws of the Committee of the Judiciary of the United States Senate, 87th Congress, 2nd Session, July 3, 1962, p. 1.
26 *Ibid.*, p. 13. "The conclusion is inescapable that the technology of the free world is making a critical contribution toward development of the Soviet Bloc into one of the world's greatest petroleum-producing areas." pp. 19, 20, 25.
27 The High Authority of the European Coal and Steel Community, *Memorandum on Energy Policy*, Jun 25, 1962, p. 16.
28 Smith, *op. cit.*, p. 23.
29 *Vneshniaia Torgovlia Za 1963 - god*, p. 236; *Financial Times*, May 29, 1962. In 1961, German imports of Soviet oil almost reached the level of the quota allowed under the German–Soviet trade agreement for the first time.
30 *The New York Times*, January 7, 1962. The refinery was not built because the quota allowed for Soviet oil in the 1960 Trade Agreement - less than 2 million tonnes a year - did not warrant such a huge investment. However, the strenuous opposition of the US government, personified by Senator Bush, also contributed to the negative German decision. See *The New York Herald Tribune*, March 30, 1962.
31 Robert E. Ebel, *The Petroleum Industry of the Soviet Union* (New York: American Petroleum Institute, 1961), p. 142.
32 Outgoing telegram from Secretary of State Dean Rusk to Bonn, Paris, and Tokyo, December 18, 1962. Box 223, National Security Files, Kennedy Library, Waltham, Mass.
33 *Pravda*, December 11, 1962. I. S. Senin, chairman of the Budget Committee of the Council of the Union, admitted that "in 1963 there will be a certain strain in the economy's supply of . . . oil pipeline tubing." *Pravda*, December 12, 1962, p. 6, reported that A. K. Kortunov, head of the USSR Chief Gas Administration, said

that "the development of the gas industry is being retarded by a lag in the production of large-diameter pipe."

34 *Vneshniaia Torgovlia Za 1963 - god,* p. 237.
35 The quotas for the three firms were as follows: Mannesmann, 80,000 tonnes; Phoenix–Rheinrohr, 52,000; and Hoesch, 31,000 (*FAZ*, March 20, 1963). Other steel firms were involved in ancillary production.
36 Adler-Karlsson, *op. cit.,* p. 130.
37 "Large-diameter pipe," Department of State Paper, March 25, 1963. National Security Files – NATO Pipe Embargo, March 1963, Box 223, Kennedy Library, Waltham, Mass.
38 *Ibid.* The United States continuously asked Britain to revise its position so that CoCom could adopt the resolution.
39 State Department INR Research Memorandum RES-13 "Subject: Western Efforts to Prevent Large-Diameter Linepipe Exports to the Soviet Bloc," April 3, 1963, p. 3, Box 223, National Security Files, Kennedy Library, Waltham, Mass.
40 Department of State Telegram from Leddy to Rusk, Paris, January 8, 1963. Box 223, National Security Files, Kennedy Library, Waltham, Mass.
41 Telegram from Dean Rusk to Bonn, Paris, Tokyo, December 18, 1962. Box 223, National Security Files, Kennedy Library, Waltham, Mass.
42 Department of State, INR Research Memorandum RES-13, "Subject: Western Efforts to Prevent Large-Diameter Linepipe Exports to the Soviet Bloc," April 3, 1963, Box 223, National Security Files, Kennedy Library, Waltham, Mass.
43 The Friendship Pipeline was ultimately destined to extend to Italy and France. See Kurt Tudyka, "Das Roehrenembargo," *Politisches Vierteljahreschrift, Sonderheft,* no. 1 (1969), pp. 205–23. The view that US oil companies pressured the US government into imposing the embargo is accepted by Michael Kreile, *Osthandel und Ostpolitik* (Baden-Baden: Nomos Verlag, 1978), p. 60.
44 State Department telegram from Dean Rusk to US Embassy in Bonn, January 4, 1963. Box 223, National Security Files, Kennedy Library, Waltham, Mass.
45 *The Economist,* January 19, 1963. *Der Spiegel,* no. 1/2 (1963), p. 17.
46 Adler-Karlsson, *op. cit.,* p. 131. This was clause 27, paragraph 2, of the Foreign Trade Law.
47 State Department telegram from Ambassador Finletter in Paris to Dean Rusk, December 7, 1962; State Department telegram from Ambassador Emerson in Tokyo to Secretary Rusk, December 7, 1962. Box 223, National Security Files, Kennedy Library, Waltham, Mass.
48 State Department telegram from Ambassador Finletter, Paris, to Dean Rusk, January 18, 1963. Box 223, National Security Files, Kennedy Library, Waltham, Mass.

49 Telegram from Ambassador Foy Kohler, Moscow, to Dean Rusk, February 28, 1963. Box 223, National Security Files, Kennedy Library, Waltham, Mass.

50 Telegram from Ambassador Kohler, Moscow, to Dean Rusk, January 7, 1963. Box 223, National Security Files, Kennedy Library, Waltham, Mass. *Pravda,* January 9, 1963, p. 4, claimed that "the actions of the official agencies of the FRG in this matter were illegal and contrary to the agreements in force between the USSR and the FRG."

51 *Industriekurier,* January 8, 1963.

52 *Der Spiegel,* no. 1/2 (1963); interview with Willy Ochel, No. 13, (1963); Terence Prittie, "No Pipeline for Moscow," *The New Republic,* April 6, 1963.

53 Telegram from Dean Rusk to Embassy in Bonn, January 16, 1963. Box 223, National Security Files, Kennedy Library, Waltham, Mass.

54 Telegram from Ambassador Kohler, Moscow, to Dean Rusk, January 15, 1963. Box 223, National Security Files, Kennedy Library, Waltham, Mass.

55 For a full account of these maneuverings, see Kurt Tudyka, *op. cit.*

56 Deutscher Bundestag, *Verhandlungen,* 4. Wahlperiode, 68. Sitzung, Bonn, March 18, 1963, pp. 3062–77.

57 *Ibid.,* p. 3072.

58 Terence Prittie, *Adenauer – A Study in Fortitude* (Chicago: Cowles, 1971).

59 *The Economist,* March 30, 1963.

60 Karl Heinrich Herchenroeder,"So kann man keine Politik treiben," *Handelsblatt,* March 20, 1963. See also Kurt Beck, "Tricks statt Politik," *Die Welt,* March 20, 1963.

61 Some CDU Members of the Bundestag who represented industry placed party loyalty over their parochial economic interests. Examples of these were Kurt Birrenbach, a prominent CDU MdB, who was on the board of directors of Thyssen, and Hans Dichgans, a business leader and deputy chairman of the Iron and Steel Industry Association. Both were severely rebuked by industry.

62 *Die Welt,* March 20, 1963. Erhard admitted that the Bundestag decision was not an "elegant form of democratic decision-making." *NZZ,* March 20, 1963, suggested that he SPD was using the issue to try to wreck the coalition.

63 State Department INR Research Memorandum RES-13, "Subject: Western Efforts to Prevent Large-Diameter Linepipe Exports to the Soviet Bloc," April 3, 1963, p. 2. Box 233, National Security Files, Kennedy Library, Waltham, Mass.

64 Dean, *op. cit.,* p. 137.

65 Adler-Karlsson, *op. cit.,* p. 132; Prittie, *op. cit.*

66 Personal interview with Dr. Friedrich Schunder, Mannesmann.

67 INR Memorandum, *op. cit.,* p. 12.

68 *Der Spiegel,* interview with Willy Ochel, no. 13, (1963). Ochel claimed

that the functioning of Hoesch's steel plant had now been called into question. He said that public business protest against the embargo had been muted because the people would have said, "You are only the Ruhr-Bosses – the Ruhr Bosses in a bad sense, for whom money is more important than Idealism, than the Fatherland."

69 Deutscher Bundestag, *Verhandlungen*, 4. Wahlperiode, 74. Sitzung, Bonn, May 8, 1963, p. 3456.

70 INR Research Memorandum, *op. cit.*, p. 14.

71 Tudyka, *op. cit.*, p. 218.

72 *The New York Times*, June 9, 1963; *Die Welt*, May 13, 1963. *The New York Times*, June 9, 1963, reported one Ruhr steel industrialist as questioning the validity of the embargo "because it just forces the Russians and others to speed up their efforts in closing critical gaps in their production lines."

73 The businessmen included Abs (Deutsche Bank), Berg (BDI), Overbeck (Mannesmann), Beitz (Krupp), Mommsen (Phoenix-Rheinrohr), Ochel (Hoesch), Amerongen (Ostausschuss), and representatives of Siemens, AEG, August Thyssen-Huette Demag, Howaldt and Salzgitter. *NZZ*, July 20, 1963.

74 *The New York Times*, July 18, 1963.

75 Heiner Ernst, *Der Osthandel – Eine Politische Waffe?* (Stuttgart: J. Fink Verlag, 1964), p. 63. The *NZZ* suggested that the procrastinating tactics of the government might have been connected with the visit of Kennedy's special ambassador, Herter, who was discussing the Kennedy round and trade negotiations between the EEC and the United States. *Neues Deutschland* reported that the government had said that the businessmen were more interested in trade with the East than was "politically tolerable." *Neues Deutschland*, July 20, 1963.

76 Those members of the committee who were involved in trade with the East were Beitz, Mommsen, and von Amerongen. Ernst, *op. cit.*, p. 63.

77 Memorandum by Ambassador Thompson, "Large Diameter Pipe," March 25, 1963. Box 233, National Security Files, Kennedy Library, Waltham, Mass.

78 *The New York Times*, March 28, 1963. The British government contended that it agreed only to enforce the ruling "as far as possible."

79 Deutscher Bundestag, *Verhandlungen*, 69. Sitzung, Bonn, March 27, 1963, p. 3095. It was also claimed in this debate that Italian firms were acting as middlemen in supplying German pipe to the USSR.

80 *The New York Times*, March 15, 1963.

81 *Izvestiia*, March 24, 1963. See also L. Kait, "Pipes for Ninepins," *International Affairs* (Moscow), no. 7, (1963), p. 86. The statement in the text was made by Kuznetsov to Ambassador Kohler, as reported in a telegram from Kohler to Dean Rusk, March 22, 1963. Box 223, National Security Files, Kennedy Library, Waltham, Mass.

82 *Die Welt*, March 25, 1963.

83 Note of the Soviet government to the FRG on the question of the pipe embargo, April 6, 1963, reprinted in *Europa-Archiv,* no. 9 (1963), pp. D243–5.

84 Telegram from Ambassador Kohler, Moscow, to Dean Rusk, January 16, 1963, Box 223, National Security Files, Kennedy Library, Waltham, Mass.

85 German reply to the USSR, April 11, 1963, reprinted in *Europa-Archiv, op. cit.,* pp. D245–8.

86 *The New York Times,* May 21, 1963. The new pipemaking plant with the capacity for manufacturing 40-inch pipes was at Khartsyzsk. There were three other plants in the USSR that could manufacture such pipes – at Zhdanov, Cheliabinsk, and Novomoskovsk. The two pipelines for which the pipe was needed were the Bukhara–Urals gas line and the Oil Friendship line from the Volga Valley oil fields to Eastern Europe.

87 Spulber, *op. cit.,* p. 121.

88 Quote by Yadgar Nasuddinoia, president of the Uzbekistan Supreme Soviet, made to the vice-president of the FRG Bundestag, Thomas Dehler, in Tashkent. Reuters, August 22, 1963.

89 Adler-Karlsson, *op. cit.,* p. 132. However, as late as 1966, an editorial in *Pravda* (February 14) complained that a shortage of pipes was delaying the development of the gas and oil industries. For a background report on the Soviet pipeline industry, see *NZZ,* April 14, 1963.

90 E. Pletnev, "International Trade and Employment," *International Affairs* (Moscow), no. 6 (1964), p. 76; "Zapadnogermanskie Promyshlenniki Obespokoenyie" ("West German Industrialists Are Worried"), *Vneshniaia Torgovlia* no. 11 (1963), pp. 54–5.

91 M. S. Voslenskii, *"Vostochaia" Politika FRG, 1949–1966 (Bonn's Eastern Policy, 1949–1966)* (Moscow: Nauka, 1967), p. 255.

92 The fact that Beitz went to Moscow as more than a mere businessman was indicated by the fact that he met with Schroeder before leaving to discuss new directions in East–West trade; *The New York Times,* April 15, 1963. See also *New Times* (Moscow), no. 22, 1963. However, Adenauer's press secretary declared that "Mr. Beitz is not on an official mission." *Der Spiegel,* no. 23, 1963, p. 36. The US government was also concerned to ascertain whether Beitz had discussed the purchase of pipe-making machinery with Khrushchev as a way of circumventing the pipe embargo. Telegram from US Ambassador Hillenbrand, Bonn, to Dean Rusk, July 20, 1963. Box 233, National Security Files, Kennedy Library, Waltham, Mass.

93 Author's interview with Berthold Beitz. According to Mr. Beitz, the Russians were obsessed with the embargo and talked about it constantly.

94 Gerhard Braunthal, *The Federation of German Industry in Politics* (Ithaca: Cornell University Press, 1965), p. 314.

95 Thomas W. Wolfe, *Soviet Power and Europe* (Baltimore: Johns Hopkins University Press, 1970), chap. 6.

96 Boris Meissner, "Westdeutsche Ostpolitik: Die deutschsowjetischen Beziehungen," in Hans-Peter Schwarz, ed., *Handbuch der deutschen Aussenpolitik* (Munich: Piper, 1975), p. 288.
97 German Ministry of Foreign Affairs official, cited in Kreile, *op. cit.*, p. 65.
98 Auswärtiges Amt, Mitteilung an die Presse, No. 457/64, Bonn, April 16, 1964. *Financial Times*, June 24, 1964.
99 See German *aide-memoire* of April 16, 1964, in *Bulletin* (Bonn), April 17, 1964. According to *The New York Times*, July 16, 1964, the Russians said they were prepared to hold talks. In October, the negotiations were postponed because of Khrushchev's proposed visit to the FRG. *Der Spiegel*, no. 42, (1964).
100 Report by Alfred Zauberman, European Service, January 24, 1964.
101 United Nations, *Yearbook of International Trade Statistics*, 1966, p. 295.
102 Kreile, *op. cit.*, pp. 63–5.
103 *Handelsblatt*, October 22, 1963. In the first nine months of 1963, the Soviet rate of growth was 8.7 percent, as opposed to 9.5 percent in 1962. *Handelsblatt*, October 23, 1968, reported that Moscow had temporarily suspended all imports because of economic difficulties.
104 *NZZ*, January 25, 1964; *Die Welt*, January 24, 1964. In the 1960 agreement the largest single item in Soviet deliveries to West Germany was grain – 300,000 tonnes of it. In addition, Soviet imports of grain from the West had strained its balance of payments.
105 Dean, *op. cit.*, p. 144.
106 *The New York Times*, May 31, 1963.
107 *Pravda*, March 8, 1963. The Tass statement, commenting on a German report, accused the Germans of "double dealing" in their dealings with Moscow and raised the specter of a "new Hitler." Claiming that "the dangerous bacilli of revanchism are still at large in West Germany," the statement urged that "normal diplomatic relations" be established between the two German states and that the FRG reconsider its refusal to conduct a "businesslike and serious" examination of Soviet proposals on Germany.
108 However, Moscow's campaign against the MLF, although the product of genuine concerns, also served as a useful propaganda tool at a time when Bonn's Ostpolitik was making some inroads into Eastern Europe. See F. Stephen Larrabee, "The Politics of Reconciliation: Soviet Policy Towards West Germany 1964–1972" (Ph.D. dissertation, Columbia University, 1977), p. 62.
109 *The New York Times*, August 2, 1964.
110 Edwina Moreton, *East Germany and the Warsaw Alliance* (Boulder, Colo.: Westview Press, 1979), p. 27.
111 For the full text of the treaty, see *Pravda*, June 13, 1964. For a Soviet discussion of the significance of the treaty, see Pavel Nikolaev, *Politika Sovietskogo Soiuza v Germanskom Voprose, 1945–1964 (The Policy of the Soviet Union in the German Question)* (Moscow:

Nauka, 1966), pp. 320–1. For an analysis of the ambiguities of the treaty, see Wolfe, *op. cit.,* pp. 122–3.

112 *The New York Times,* June 6, 1964. The Soviet diplomat in Bonn said that the visit could produce "a significant contribution to the solution of the German question through reunification."

113 *Die Welt,* June 16, 20, 27, 1964. Erhard had planned to go to Moscow some years earlier, but Adenauer and Brentano had advised him not to go. *Der Spiegel,* no. 42, 1963.

114 *Die Welt,* June 29, 1964.

115 *The Guardian,* August 4, 1964. Adzhubei said that very good business could be done with the USSR. See also *Der Spiegel* interview with Adzhubei, no. 32, (1964). In an article in *Izvestiia,* August 9, 1964, Adzhubei depicted the Ruhr industrialists as "desperate" for more trade. In his article, Adzhubei made a plea for a "new Rapallo." This subject was also discussed in an article by M. I. Trush, "Leninskii Podkhod K Ispolzovanii Kompromissov vo Vneshnei Politike" ("The Leninist Approach to the Use of Compromises in Foreign Policy"), in *Voprosy Istorii KPSS (Problems of History of the CPSU)* June, 1964, p. 30. Moscow Radio in German for Germany, August 3, 1964, emphasized how "incomparably better" economic relations could be, were it not for "artificial barriers."

116 *German International,* August 31, 1964. According to *The New York Times,* September 4, 1964, the USSR conveyed messages to Bonn through the agency of a West German businessman, indicating its willingness to negotiate a trade agreement.

117 *The New York Times,* July 29 and August 5, 1964.

118 The Volga Germans had been deported from their homes during the war, on Stalin's orders, for alleged collaboration with the Nazis.

119 *Bulletin,* September 4, 1964. Radio Belgrade, September 21, 1964, reported that the Soviet press had not mentioned the forthcoming visit, but nevertheless, "The Soviet government attaches great importance to improving relations with West Germany."

120 *New York Herald Tribune,* September 4, 1964.

121 *Die Welt,* September 14, 15, 1964; *Handelsblatt,* September 23, 1964. The technician, Horst Schwirkmann, had discovered and removed bugging devices in the West German embassy some time before. Thus, the attack on him while he was attending a church service at Zagorsk may have been in retaliation for his discoveries.

122 *Christian Science Monitor,* October 21, 1964. The second Soviet apology was profuse: "Those who indulge in such actions are trying to undermine the good relations between our countries." See Michel Tatu, *Power in the Kremlin* (New York: Viking Press, 1969), p. 310.

123 *Christian Science Monitor,* October 21, 1964.

124 *German International,* October 31, 1964.

125 Wolfe, *op. cit.,* p. 118.

126 *Pravda,* October 7, 1964.

127 *Pravda*, October 8, 1964.
128 For a discussion of events leading to Khrushchev's fall, see Tatu, *op. cit.*, pp. 388-91, 401-3. According to Tatu, Khrushchev's attempts at a rapprochement with Germany were a great source of tension within the Politburo, especially with Suslov and Brezhnev. For an analysis of Khrushchev's agricultural policies, see Alec Nove, *An Economic History of the USSR* (London: Penguin Books, 1969), pp. 327, 339, 362-8.
129 According to Gomulka's former interpreter, Erwin Weit, Ulbricht was instrumental in supporting Khrushchev's opponents, whereas Gomulka was informed of Khrushchev's "retirement" only after the fact. See Erwin Weit, *Eyewitness* (London: André Deutsch, 1973), pp. 153-4.
130 For Erhard's initial reaction to the change in the Soviet leadership, see *Bulletin*, October 21, 1964. For his repeated invitations to Kosygin to visit, see *NZZ*, October 21, 1964, *The New York Times*, February 24, 1965, *Die Welt*, April 15, 1965.
131 *Die Welt*, October 7, 1963.
132 State Department Memorandum from Thomas Hughes to Dean Rusk, RSB-97, July 16, 1963; "Subject: Trade Expansion as a Political Lever in U.S. Relations with the USSR and Eastern Europe," p. i. Box 314, National Security Files – National Security Council Meetings, 1963, vol. 11, no. 518, part 1. Kennedy Library, Waltham, Mass.
133 Rostow Memorandum, *op. cit.*, p. 55.
134 Comments on Question 17, "U.S. Benefit from Sale to USSR of Wheat," State Department Memorandum, September 25, 1963. Box 518, National Security Files, Kennedy Library, Waltham, Mass.
135 Summary record of National Security Council meeting, October 1, 1963. "Proposed Sale of U.S. Wheat to the USSR and Soviet Satellites." Box 314, National Security Files, Kennedy Library, Waltham, Mass.
136 Letter to McGeorge Bundy from the Deputy Director for Intelligence (CIA No. 2291), National Security Files, National Security Council Meetings 1963, Vol. 11, No. 518, Part 1. September 26, 1963. Box 314 Kennedy Library, Waltham, Mass.
137 McGeorge Bundy memorandum for the Secretaries of State, Defense and Commerce, October 21, 1963. Box 310, National Security Files, Subject Trade, East-West, Kennedy Library, Waltham, Mass.
138 Letter from John F. Kennedy to Mike Mansfield, November 15, 1963. Box 314, National Security Files, Kennedy Library, Waltham, Mass.
139 In the previous three years, the FRG had exported 520,000 tonnes of flour to Eastern Europe. Dean, *op. cit.*, p. 162.
140 *The New York Herald Tribune*, October 3, 1963.
141 *The New York Times*, October 9, 1963; October 10, 1963. "The Russians must be told that in return for food they need the [Berlin]

Wall must go." Adenauer attributed the Soviet agricultural difficulties to "structural causes" and said that the whole Soviet economic structure must be altered.

142 For a description of his farewell dinner, in which Adenauer accused all the Western countries of selling wheat, "a superweapon of the economic type," to the Russians, without demanding political concessions, see *Der Spiegel*, no. 41, (1963).

143 *The New York Herald Tribune*, October 3, 1963.

144 *Der Spiegel*, no. 41, 1963. The speech by Schroeder was to the Foreign Affairs Committee of the Bundestag.

145 Dean, *op. cit.*, p. 142. *Die Welt*, October 14, 1963.

146 *Die Welt*, October 3, 10, 1963; *Der Spiegel*, no. 42, (1963).

147 Erhard's interview on *Face the Nation*, November 1, 1963, reprinted in Boris Meissner, ed., *Die deutsche Ostpolitik, 1961–1970* (Cologne: Verlag Wissenschaft und Politik, 1970), p. 67.

148 *The Times*, December 4, 1963.

Chapter 6. The failure of linkage: 1964–1968

1 Gerhard Schroeder, *Wir Brauchen eine heile Welt: Politik in und fuer Deutschland.* (Duesseldorf: Econ. Verlag, 1964), p. 230.

2 M. Voslenskii, *"Vostochnaia" Politika FRG, 1949–1966* (*The Ostpolitik of the FRG*), (Moscow: Nauka, 1967), p. 197.

3 See Ekkehart Knippendorf, "Beyond the Oder–Neisse," *Survey*, no. 61 (1966), pp. 48–9.

4 See the discussion in F. Stephen Larrabee, "The Politics of Reconciliation: Soviet Policy Towards West Germany, 1961–1972" (Ph.D. dissertation, Columbia University), pp. 66–9.

5 In 1966, an interesting *volte face* occurred. Adenauer, who had always been the staunchest advocate of an uncompromising policy toward the USSR, declared that Russia's intentions were peaceful, "because she needs peace, also peace in Europe." Erhard contradicted Adenauer by saying that there was no real indication that the USSR wanted peace. For a report of the CDU conference at which this took place, see *The New York Times*, March 23 and 24, 1966. Germany's policy of bridge building was initiated and encouraged by the United States government. See Lyndon Johnson's speech in Virginia, May 23, 1964, in which he said the United States should "build bridges – bridges of trade, travel and humanitarian assistance – across the gulf that divides us from Eastern Europe." Lyndon Baines Johnson, *The Vantage Point: Perspectives of the Presidency* (New York: Popular Library, 1971), p. 471.

6 *FAZ*, February 4, 15, March 12, 1966; *NZZ*, December 17, 1965; *Rheinischer Merkur*, May 27, 1966; *Der Spiegel*, no. 9, 1966, no. 27, 1966. Horst Groepper, German ambassador in Moscow from 1962 to 1966, had, in contrast to his controversial predecessor Hans Kroll, been retiring. His successor, Gebhardt von Walter, had

worked in the Moscow embassy from 1937 to 1941 and still had good contacts with the Soviet elite. By contrast, Andrei Smirnov, the experienced Soviet ambassador in Bonn, was replaced by Semyon Tsarapkin, a man less well versed in German affairs.

7 Gerhard Schroeder, "Germany Looks at Europe," *Foreign Affairs* vol. 44, no. 1 (1965), p. 19. See also Lawrence L. Whetten, *West Germany's Ostpolitik* (New York: Oxford University Press, 1971), p. 17.

8 Thomas W. Wolfe, *Soviet Power and Europe* (Baltimore: Johns Hopkins University Press, 1971), p. 283. In April 1965, coincident with a Bundestag session in West Berlin, Soviet and GDR agents began a campaign of harassment. See the Soviet note to the United States protesting the proposed holding of a Bundestag session in West Berlin, March 23, 1965, in Senate Committee on Foreign Relations, *Documents on Germany, 1944–1970,* 92nd Congress, 1st Session, pp. 671–2.

9 N. Vladimirov, "West German Maffia [sic] in Washington," *International Affairs* (Moscow) no. 9 (1965), pp. 33–4. In this article, the proposed MLF was the apex of the "Maffia's" activity. See also V. Mikhailov, "Bonn Between Past and Present," *International Affairs* (Moscow) no. 10 (1966), pp. 22–6, for a further elucidation of the Bonn–Washington axis. For an analysis of the development of these Soviet attitudes, see Zbigniew Brzezinski, "Moscow and the MLF: Hostility and Ambivalence," *Foreign Affairs,* vol. 43, no. 1 (1964), pp. 127–33, and Alvin Z. Rubinstein, "The Soviet Image of Western Europe," *Current History,* vol. 47, no. 279 (1964), pp. 281–5.

10 P. Kryukov and V. Novoseltsev, "Bonn: Illusions and Reality," *International Affairs* (Moscow), no. 12 (1964), p. 17. The article stressed that the aim of the FRG's Ostpolitik was to isolate the GDR by establishing diplomatic relations with Eastern Europe. See also *New Times,* no. 4 (1965), p. 16, criticizing Brandt's policy toward the East. Tass international service in English, October 22, 1965.

11 See Fritz Ermath, "Kosygin to Bonn?" Radio Free Europe Communist Area Analysis Department, February 25, 1966. For Soviet criticism of the MLF and its implications for the German acquisition of nuclear weapons, see Andrei Gromyko's speech at the United Nations concerning a NATO multilateral nuclear force and German reunification, December 7, 1964, in *Documents on Germany,* pp. 665–6.

12 For the text of the note from the Federal Republic of Germany to the United States and other powers on West German efforts to improve relations with the Soviet Union and Eastern European countries, March 25, 1966, see *Documents on Germany,* pp. 691–5.

13 Brezhnev's speech to the Twenty-third Party Congress, *Pravda,* March 30, 1966. Although the congress endorsed the familiar picture of a revanchist Germany, there was one curious note, when Gromyko praised Adenauer for recognizing that the USSR wanted

peace. See Adam Bruno Ulam, *Expansion and Coexistence* (New York: Praeger, 1974), p. 724.

14 Brezhnev's speech, *Pravda,* March 30, 1966. For the opposing view, see Voslenskii, *op. cit.,* pp. 290–1. He describes the note as showing "that the Erhard government continued Adenauer's course in the sphere of Eastern policy, or more accurately the course dictated by the ruling monopolist groups in the FRG."

15 Soviet reply to the FRG, May 17, 1966, in *Documents on Germany,* pp. 698–700. The Russians proposed an eight-point agenda for a settlement of European issues in this note. The Rumanians and Hungarians were more conciliatory in their replies.

16 For a fuller discussion of the abortive speakers' exchange, see Keesing's Research Report, No. 8, *Germany and Eastern Europe since 1945* (New York: Scribner, 1973), pp. 206–8. See also Whetten, *op. cit.,* pp. 101–6. For the West German statement on the East German cancellation of the exchange, see *Documents on Germany,* p. 703. See the *Christian Science Monitor,* June 22, 1966, for the interpretation that the Russians were the prime movers behind the cancellation. See William E. Griffith, *The Ostpolitik of the Federal Republic of Germany* (Cambridge, Mass.: MIT Press, 1978), pp. 125–6; Larrabee, *op. cit.,* pp. 91–2.

17 See Bahr's speech at the Tutzing Evangelical Academy, July 15, 1963, in Boris Meissner, *Die Deutsche Ostpolitik, 1961–1970* (Cologne: Verlag Wissenschaft und Politik, 1970), pp. 45–8.

18 For the text of Kiesinger's speech before the Bundestag, December 13, 1966, see *Documents on Germany,* pp. 711–16.

19 For the text of the Rumanian–Soviet communiqué, see Meissner, *op. cit.,* p. 181. For Moscow and East Berlin's reservations on these developments, see Wolfe, *op. cit.,* pp. 315–16.

20 For the Warsaw Pact declaration, see *Documents on Germany,* pp. 704–8. For a detailed interpretation of these appeals, see Larrabee, *op. cit.,* pp. 82–90, 102–18.

21 Edwina Moreton, *East Germany and the Warsaw Alliance* (Boulder, Colo.: Westview Press, 1979), p. 70.

22 In July 1967, private talks on the renunciation of force between Brandt and Tsarapkin began. Later on, when the Russians adopted a more hostile policy toward the FRG, they published their statements on the negotiations of October 12 and November 21, 1967, in *Izvestiia,* July 11, 1968. For the German reply to the Soviet publication of secret documents, including the German proposals, see *Bulletin,* July 10, 1968. See also *NZZ,* February 7, 1968, and *Der Spiegel,* no. 47, (1967).

23 The Kremlin rebuffed Ernst Majonica, a leading CDU foreign policy expert, when he went to Moscow in September 1967 for talks on improving relations with the USSR. See *Sueddeutsche Zeitung,* September 23, 1967.

24 Larrabee, *op. cit.,* pp. 143–4.

25 Willy Brandt, "German Policy Towards the East," *Foreign Affairs,* vol. *46,* no. 3 (1968), pp. 476–86.

26 Y. Novoseltsev, "Ideological Principles of West German Foreign Policy," *International Affairs* (Moscow), no. 1 (1967), pp. 71–8; R. Federov, "Politicheskii Mekhanizm FRG i Soiuzy Predprinimatelnei" ("The Political Ties of the FRG and the Federations of Industrialists"), *MEMO,* no. 12 (1967), pp. 67–77.

27 "Bonn's 'Eastern Policy,'" *New Times,* no. 8 (1967), pp. 5–6. The article attributed the attempt to formulate a new Eastern policy to the failure of the previous one. See also M. Voslenskii, "FRG: Pravitel'stvo Novoe – a Politika?" ("FRG: A New Administration, but Its Policies?"), *MEMO,* no. 2 (1967), pp. 96–8; L. Szulczynskii, "Kiesinger's Bonn," *New Times,* no. 12 (1967), and V. Novoseltsev, "Bonn's Eastern Policy and European Security," *International Affairs* (Moscow), no. 7 (1968), pp. 27–33, which is largely a retort to Brandt's *Foreign Affairs* article.

28 Soviet statement to the FRG government entitled "Curb the Revanchists and Neo-Nazis," *Pravda,* December 9, 1967; see also Daniil Efimovich Melnikov, *Hamburg-Bonn Miunkhen-Liudi, Politika, Propaganda* (Hamburg-Bonn-Munich-People, Politics, Propaganda) (Moscow: Mezhdunarodoye Otnosheniia, 1969), chap. 1.

29 Wolfe, *op. cit.,* pp. 316–24.

30 Gromyko's speech of June 27, 1968, in Boris Meissner, *Moskau – Bonn: Die Beziehungen Zwischen der Sowjetunion und der Bundesrepublik Deutschland, 1955–1973: Dokumentation* (Cologne: Verlag Wissenschaft und Politik, 1975), pp. 1124–26.

31 *Pravda,* August 22, 1968; *op. cit.,* p. 1142.

32 Griffith, *op. cit.,* p. 159.

33 *The New York Times,* September 15, 1968; *International Herald Tribune,* September 20, 1968. According to *Izvestiia,* September 9, 1968, the USSR had the right to intervene under the "enemy states" clause in the United Nations Charter.

34 Deutscher Bundestag, 5. Wahlperiode, *Drucksache* V/3265, September 4, 1968, pp. 7–8.

35 *Pravda,* September 17, 20, 23, 30, 1968.

36 Michael Kreile, *Osthandel und Ostpolitik* (Baden-Baden: Nomos Verlag, 1978), pp. 105–13.

37 For a discussion of the possible Soviet motivations in the invasion of Czechoslovakia, see Adam Roberts and Philip Windsor, *Czechoslovakia, 1968;* Ulam, *op. cit.,* pp. 738–44; Galia Golan, *Czech Reform Movement,* (Cambridge University Press, 1971).

38 Larrabee, *op. cit.,* pp. 151–6.

39 Bundesverband der deutschen Industrie, *Jahresbericht* (Cologne, 1964), pp. 79–80.

40 Helmut Tischner, "Der Deutsche Osthandel," *Konjunkturpolitik,* vol. *13,* no. 5–6 (1967), p. 23.

41 Subcommittee on Foreign Economic Policy of the Joint Economic

Committee of the Congress of the United States, *Soviet Economic Performance 1966-1967,* 90th Congress, 2nd session, pp. 68, 100, 104.

42 Kosygin's Report to the Twenty-third Party Congress, *Pravda,* March 31, 1966.

43 See Kosygin's Report to the Central Committee, Plenary Session, *Pravda,* September 28, 1965.

44 See Yevsei Liberman, "The Soviet Economic Reform," *Foreign Affairs,* vol. 46, no. 1 (1967), pp. 54-63; Gertrude Schroeder, "Soviet Economic Reform at an Impasse," *Problems of Communism,* vol. 20, no. 4 (1971), pp. 36-46.

45 Jozef Wilczynski, *The Economics and Politics of East-West Trade* (New York: Praeger, 1969), p. 330. See also Michael Kaser, "The East European Economic Reforms and Foreign Trade," *The World Today* (1967), pp. 512-22.

46 *Pravda,* April 6, 1966.

47 See V. I. Zolotarev, "Main Stages of Development of USSR Foreign Trade," *Voprosy Istorii,* no. 8 (1967), p. 27; N. Liubimov, "Soviet Foreign Trade Problems," *International Affairs* (Moscow) no. 8 (1965), p. 14.

48 *Vneshniaia Torgovlia,* no. 4 (1967), p. 11.

49 N. S. Kremer, "Problemy Formirovaniia Vneshnei Politiki FRG (1949-1969)" ("Problems of the Formulation of the FRG's Foreign Policy, 1949-1969") (unpublished doctoral dissertation, Institute of General History, Moscow, 1971).

50 Nicholas Spulber, "The Strategic Embargo," in Alan Brown and Egon Neuberger, eds., *International Trade and Central Planning* (Berkeley: University of California Press, 1968), p. 121. See also *NZZ,* September 9, 1966, where it was suggested that Germany's attempts to remove the strategic embargo were connected to its desire to persuade the Russians to conclude a new trade treaty. For two years, there was an acerbic exchange between the FRG government and the three steel concerns that were being sued by the Russians. According to Economics Minister Schmuecker, the government considered that it had no obligation to pay the compensation the Russians demanded. See Deutscher Bundestag, *Verhandlungen,* 4. Wahlperiode, 185. Sitzung, Bonn, May 20, 1965, p. 9282; *Der Spiegel,* no. 3 (1965).

51 Radio Free Europe dispatch, March 20, 1964; *Handelsblatt,* January 27, 1966. When Krupp was forced to close its Moscow office, the Soviets showed a film about Krupp's role in the war.

52 *Frankfurter Rundschau,* November 25, 1964. The leader of this group was Schulze Buxloh of the Rhine Steelworks, who was discussing the delivery of complete industrial installations in the field of chemistry and metallurgy.

53 *Bulletin,* November 10, 1964.

54 Kurt Birrenbach, "Lockt der rote Handel?" *Die Zeit,* November 27, 1964, cited in Dean, *op. cit.,* p. 146.

55 *The Times,* January 20, 1965; *Die Welt,* July 7, 1965.
56 *Der Spiegel,* no. 30, 1965. The extent of U.S. sensitivity to America's rights in West Berlin was demonstrated by the abortive negotiations to establish a direct air link between Bonn and Moscow. The United States objected to arrangements for a Soviet stopover in East Berlin, and the Germans were apparently irritated by the American "holier than thou" attitude over Berlin. See *The New York Times,* August 6, 1965. See also *Die Welt,* June 12, 1965.
57 *The Times,* September 14, 1965; Carstens's reply, Deutscher Bundestag, *Verhandlungen,* 5. Wahlperiode, Bonn, February 9, 1966, pp. 705-6.
58 Interview with Carstens on *Deutsche Welle,* reprinted in *Bulletin,* September 22, 1965. However, the Foreign Office made it quite clear that it held out no great expectations for the talks.
59 *FAZ,* September 22, 1965; *Der Spiegel,* no. 40 (1965). Carstens met with Deputy Foreign Trade Minister Kuzmin and with Vassily Kuznetsov at the Foreign Ministry.
60 Otto Wolff von Amerongen, cited in *FAZ,* September 23, 1965.
61 *Die Welt,* September 12, 1966; *FAZ,* July 23, 1966. The Soviets had expressed an interest in concluding a new agreement in an *aide-mémoire* of March 5, 1966.
62 *Financial Times,* October 4, 1966; *FAZ,* October 7, 1966; Radio Free Europe Report, October 3, 1966; *FAZ,* October 7, 1966; *NZZ,* October 8, 1966; *SZ,* October 13, 1966; *Der Spiegel,* no. 43 (1966); *FAZ,* October 13, 1966; *SZ,* November 27, 1966.
63 Interview with Willy Brandt for *Deutsche Welle,* reprinted in *Bulletin,* April 14, 1967; *The New York Times,* April 16, 1967.
64 *The American Review of Soviet and East European Foreign Trade,* vol. *11,* no. 3 (1966), pp. 86-7.
65 *New York Herald Tribune,* April 14, 1967.
66 Kreile, *op. cit.,* p. 92.
67 *Handelsblatt,* April 21, 1967; *NZZ,* April 7, 1967.
68 For example, at a trade fair in May, 1967, in which German businessmen did very well, a Soviet foreign trade official answered the question "Does the Federal Republic of Germany no longer carry on trade with the Soviet Union?" with the enigmatic reply, "The German Democratic Republic stands at the pinnacle of Soviet foreign trade. With the rest, the Soviet Union carries on trade as it wants." Dean, *op. cit.,* p. 154.
69 *Handelsblatt,* April 17, 1968.
70 Glen Alden Smith, *Soviet Foreign Trade* (New York: Praeger, 1973), p. 163. In 1925, the Germans granted up to two-year government guarantees on credits for up to 60 percent of the purchase value, and in 1933 the German credit terms were extended to four years.
71 Smith, *op. cit.,* p. 106.
72 *Ibid.* The 1958 British credit was for Courtaulds to build a cellulose acetate spinning mill, and the German bank credit was to the Soviet state bank to finance an order for fishing boats.

73 *The New York Times,* February 24, 1964.
74 V. Mogyshin, "Novoe v Praktike Kreditovaniia Eksporta Oborudo-vaniia" (New developments in the practice of credit arrangements for exports), *Vneshniaia Torgovlia,* no. 1 (1966), p. 15.
75 This account is taken from Samuel Pisar, *Coexistence and Commerce* (New York: McGraw-Hill, 1970), pp. 111–12.
76 US Congress, *East–West Trade,* Hearings before the Subcommittee on International Finance of the Committee on Banking and Currency, US Senate, 90th Congress, p. 1176. The USSR is considered in default of payment to the United States by the terms of a 1946 amendment to the act.
77 Gunnar Adler-Karlsson, *Western Economic Warfare, 1947–1967* (Stockholm: Almquist and Wiskell, 1968), p. 133.
78 Mogyshin, *op. cit.,* p. 13.
79 The Hermes Company is part of a syndicate consisting of Hermes, Deutsche Revisions, und Treuhandel, AG, and some private companies.
80 Dean, *op. cit.,* p. 145.
81 Wilczynski, *op. cit.,* p. 229.
82 For the text of this resolution, see *Europa-Archiv,* no. 24, (1963), pp. D601–2.
83 US Department of State, "Comments on Question 13," September 25, 1963. Box 314, National Security Files, Kennedy Library, Waltham, Mass.
84 *The Economist,* February 22, 1964.
85 Smith, *op. cit.,* p. 166; see also B. Vavagrov, "An Important Factor of International Cooperation," *International Affairs* (Moscow), no. 4 (1966), p. 24. Commenting on the British, French, and Italian credits, the author writes, "The agreement on the granting of long-term credits to the Soviet Union by several Western countries with time limits exceeding those provided for in the Berne Convention are another proof that common sense dictated by the need for wider trade between countries of differing social systems is becoming an increasingly important factor in the sphere of international relations."
86 Claus-Dieter Rohleder, *Die Osthandelspolitik der EWG – Mitgliedstaaten, Grossbritanniens und der USA gegenueber den Staatshandelslaendern Suedosteuropas* (Munich: Eigenverlag der Suedosteuropa-Gesellschaft, 1969), pp. 70–1.
87 Herman Bohle, "Europaeische Wirtschaftsgemeinschaft und Osteuropa," *Industriekurier,* Special supplement, March 27, 1965.
88 Consultative Assembly of the Council of Europe, *Report on East–West Trade,* September 10, 1965, Document 1964, p. 19. The report points out that the East European trade monopolies were in an advantageous position because they could frequently obtain long-term credits from large private manufacturers, insured by private institutional insurers over whom the government had no control.
89 *The New York Times,* November 13, 1963; *The Times,* January 27,

1964; Erhard, in a speech to the Bundestag – Deutscher Bundestag, *Verhandlungen,* 4. Wahlperiode, 106. Sitzung, Bonn, January 9, 1964.

90 Author's interview with Walter Steidle, former head of the East–West Division of the Federal Economics Ministry.

91 *The New York Times,* May 30, 1964.

92 *Financial Times,* August 28, 1964; Helmut Tischner, "Der Deutsche Osthandel," *Konjunkturpolitik,* vol. 13, no. 5–6 (1967), p. 358. Bank-to-bank credits had been permitted all along, but these credits had a time limit of 180–360 days. The new rules stipulated that 20 percent of the value of the goods had to be paid at the time of purchase.

93 Seymour Friedin, "West German Credits May Be Offered to Russia," *New York Herald Tribune,* September 8, 1964.

94 Author's interview with Walter Steidle.

95 Renata Fritsch-Bournazel, *Die Sowjetunion und die deutsche Teilung* (Opladen: Westdeutscher Verlag, 1979), p. 111.

96 On September 3, 1964, Japan had approved an eight-year credit for the sale of a fertilizer plant to the USSR.

97 Kreile, *op. cit.,* p. 85.

98 *Der Spiegel,* no. 35, 1964.

Chapter 7. Brandt's Ostpolitik and the Soviet response: 1969–1970

1 Quoted in David Binder, *The Other German: Willy Brandt's Life and Times* (Washington: New Republic, 1975), p. 114.

2 F. Stephen Larrabee, "The Politics of Reconciliation: Soviet Policy Towards West Germany, 1961–1972" (Ph.D. dissertation, Columbia University, 1977), pp. 246–7.

3 According to some specialists, Egon Bahr was primarily responsible for the theoretical breakthrough in the Ostpolitik. See Walter F. Hahn's "West Germany's Ostpolitik: The Grand Design of Egon Bahr," *Orbis* vol. 16, no. 4 (1974), pp. 859–80. However, it is generally agreed that Brandt himself played a significant role in the formulation of Ostpolitik. Hahn's critical article was very controversial, and its content has been contested by Bonn.

4 It is difficult to find an objective biography of Willy Brandt. Most biographies border on the hagiographic – for instance, those by Bolesch, *Der lange Marsch des Willy Brandt,* Alma and Edward Homze, *Willy Brandt,* and others. Some, such as the recent book by Viola Herms Drath, are iconoclastic in the extreme, by contrast. Probably the most balanced, although its accuracy has been questioned, is that by David Binder. Another useful biography is that by Carola Stern, *Willy Brandt.*

5 See Willy Brandt, *My Road to Berlin* (New York: Doubleday, 1960), and Willy Brandt, *The Ordeal of Coexistence* (Cambridge, Mass.: Harvard University Press, 1963).

6 Speech to the Norwegian parliament (Storting), April 24, 1970, Oslo, reprinted in Willy Brandt, *Reden und Interviews* (Hamburg:

Hoffman und Campe, 1973), pp. 117–24.

7 For the discussion of the various aspects of the FRG's Ostpolitik, see Lawrence L. Whetten, *West Germany's Ostpolitik* (New York: Oxford University Press, 1971), *passim;* Hahn, *op. cit.,* and Josef Korbel, "West Germany's Ostpolitik: Intra-German Relations," *Orbis,* vol. 8, no. 4 (1976), pp. 1050–71, and "West Germany's Ostpolitik: A Policy Towards the Soviet Allies," *Orbis,* vol. 14, no. 2 (1970), pp. 366–400.

8 William E. Griffith, *The Ostpolitik of the Federal Republic of Germany* (Cambridge, Mass.: MIT Press, 1978), p. 175.

9 Larrabee, *op. cit.,* p. 159. For an excellent analysis of Soviet motivation in the Westpolitik, see Larrabee, *op. cit.,* chap. 2.

10 A. Zalyotny, "FRG and Developments in Czechoslovakia," *International Affairs* (Moscow), no. 11 (1968), pp. 22–7.

11 Thomas W. Wolfe, *Soviet Power and Europe* (Baltimore: Johns Hopkins University Press, 1970), p. 418. One Soviet book claimed that Germany would not sign the nonproliferation treaty because it "would be another hindrance to the nuclear ambitions of West German imperialism"; B. Ponomarev et al. *A History of Soviet Foreign Policy 1945–1970* (Moscow: Progress Publishers, 1974), p. 535.

12 It is questionable that the "Brezhnev Doctrine" was any more than an explicit reiteration of consistent themes in Soviet foreign policy since Stalin's death. The doctrine was articulated in a note sent by the Soviet ambassador in Bonn to Chancellor Kiesinger on September 2, 1968: "The entry into Czechoslovakia was founded on the obligation which the countries of the Socialist camp had mutually undertaken for the protection of their unity." See Josef Korbel, *Detente in Europe: Real or Imaginary?* (Princeton, N.J.: Princeton University Press, 1972), p. 91.

13 For the text of the speech, see *Europa-Archiv* no. 22 (1968), pp. 552–60.

14 *Sueddeutsche Zeitung,* October 5, 1968; *NZZ,* October 11, 1968; *Der Spiegel,* no. 42, 1968. There was some confusion after the event over who had initiated the talks.

15 For a description of the talks, see Willy Brandt, *People and Politics: The Years 1960–1975* (London: Collins, 1978), pp. 190–4. At the beginning of January, contacts between Ambassador Tsarapkin and Brandt on improved political relations resumed. See *International Herald Tribune,* January 10, 1969; *Sueddeutsche Zeitung,* January 9, 1969.

16 Larrabee, *op. cit.,* p. 172.

17 Soviet government statement to the government of the FRG, *Pravda,* February 16, 1969. See also "Observer," "A Serious Warning," *New Times,* no. 8 (1969).

18 *Der Spiegel,* no. 9 (1969); no. 10 (1969), pp. 31–4; *International Herald Tribune,* February 23, 1969.

19 Gerhard Wettig, "Die Berlin-Krise 1969," *Osteuropa,* no. 9 (1969), pp. 685–97. Wolfe, *op. cit.,* p. 424.

20 *Pravda*, March 12, 16, 17, 1969.

21 *International Herald Tribune*, March 13, 1969; Larrabee, *op. cit.*, p. 192.

22 This thesis is developed by Edwina Moreton, *East Germany and the Warsaw Alliance* (Boulder, Colo.: Westview Press, 1979).

23 *Pravda*, March 18, 1969; see also Boris Meissner, "Die Sowjetunion und die Kollektive Sicherheit," *Aussenpolitik* vol. *21*, no. 7, (1970), pp. 393–405. According to Larrabee, p. 196, this communiqué was noticeable for its mild language toward Bonn.

24 *Pravda*, July 11, 1969.

25 *Kommunist*, no. 5 (1969), pp. 9, 24; *Neues Deutschland*, March 26, 1969.

26 Interview with Willy Brandt, *Sueddeutsche Zeitung*, July 10, 1969; interview with Brandt in *German International*, August 1969. See also *The New York Times*, August 4, 1968.

27 On the FDP trip, see *Washington Post*, July 25, 1969; *Der Spiegel*, no. 31, 1969. On the SPD trip, see *Washington Post*, August 26, 1969; *NZZ*, August 21, 1969; *Der Spiegel*, no. 35 (1969). According to *The New York Times*, August 26, 1969, Chancellor Kiesinger claimed to have also received an invitation from Moscow, but he declined to go.

28 For a comprehensive account of the role of the PCI, which had acted as a go-between for the SPD and SED since September 1967, see Heinz Timmermann, "Im Vorfeld der neuen Ostpolitik," *Osteuropa*, no. 6 (1971), pp. 388–99. For a discussion of other secret contacts, see Hahn, *op. cit.* See also Brandt, *People and Politics*, pp. 218–22.

29 Brandt's statement of October 28 before the *Bundestag*, reprinted in *Documents on Germany*, pp. 815–17.

30 Lev Bezymensky, "Bonn: Continuity or Renewal?" *New Times*, no. 7 (1969), pp. 17–18. See also A. Zholkver, "FRG Elections and After," *International Affairs* (Moscow) no. 11 (1969), pp. 22–8; D. Melnikov, "Brandt's First Hundred Days," *New Times*, no. 4 (1970). The Soviets claimed that "the Brandt Government accepted the Soviet proposal on the renunciation of the use of force" (*History of Soviet Foreign Policy, 1945–1970*, p. 541). However, it is clear that, after his election, Brandt himself took the initiative in these talks.

31 Author's interview with Ambassador Helmut Allardt.

32 Karl Moersch, *Kursrevision: Deutsche Politik nach Adenauer* (Frankfurt: Societäts Verlag, 1978), pp. 178–9.

33 According to the *International Herald Tribune*, December 12, 1969, the German–Soviet meetings were not reported by Tass.

34 D. Melnikov, "Issue that Cannot be Evaded," *New Times*, no. 9, (1970). A. Sverdlov, "GDR, FRG, OON" (GDR, FRG, UN), *MEMO* no. 5 (1970), pp. 79–80.

35 Albert Norden, "Lenin and Germany," *New Times*, no. 15 (1970).

36 Speech by Rainer Barzel in Bundestag, reported on Cologne Domestic Service in German, March 20, 1970.

37 For the text of the "Bahr Paper," see *Documents on Germany*, pp.

862-4. The first four paragraphs of the Bahr Paper were incorporated into the final treaty.

38 Interview with Secretary of State William Rogers, reprinted in *Documents on Germany*, pp. 844-8. Mr. Rogers said that the United States appreciated Brandt's commitment to NATO and supported the FRG's efforts at improving ties with Moscow.

39 Author's interview with Ambassador Helmut Allardt.

40 Korbel, *op. cit.*, p. 194; according to Binder, *op. cit.*, p. 266, neither Kissinger nor Sonnenfeldt approved of Brandt or Bahr, who, they alleged, "embodied insecurity in Germany." According to Viola Drath, *Willy Brandt: Prisoner of His Past* (Radnor, Pa.: Chiltern Books, 1975), p. 28, Kissinger, although publicly supporting Ostpolitik, privately complained about Brandt's lack of consultation and cooperation with the United States.

41 Immediately after the treaty had been signed, Brandt sent letters to the United States, France, and the United Kingdom, proposing a meeting between the four heads of state and reaffirming Germany's loyalty to the Atlantic Alliance. *The New York Times*, August 10, 1970.

42 Griffith, *op. cit.*, p. 187. Moersch, *op. cit.*, pp. 225-6.

43 Radio Liberty Research Paper, no. 50 (1974). Radio Free Europe Report 0570, April 24, 1970, "Continued Improvements in Soviet-West German Relations." It was only after Gromyko went to the GDR that the GDR agreed to the Erfurt meeting between Brandt and Stoph.

44 *Documents on Germany*, pp. 864-5, 865-6.

45 Alice Spettnagel, "Entwicklung der deutsch-sowjetischen Wirtschaftsbeziehungen," *Deutsche Welle Dokumentation*, September 1970; *Information ueber den West-Ost-Handel*, no. 12 (1968), p. 24.

46 Radio Free Europe Research Report, December 10, 1969, *West German-Communist Trade 1969 Compared with 1968*, p. 2.

47 *Handelsblatt*, July 31, 1970; *FAZ*, August 6, 1969.

48 Jochen Bethkenhagen, "Soviet Gas and Oil Exports to the West: Past Development and Future Potential," *Yearbook of East European Economics*, vol. 6 (Munich: G. Olzog, 1975), pp. 1, 47.

49 John P. Hardt, "Soviet Commercial Relations and Political Change," in Robert A. Bauer, ed., *The Interaction of Economics and Foreign Policy* (Charlottesville: University of Virginia Press, 1975), p. 54.

50 Iain F. Elliott, *The Soviet Energy Balance* (New York: Praeger, 1974), p. 69.

51 Michael Gehlen, "The Politics of Soviet Foreign Trade," *Western Political Quarterly* vol. 18, no. 1 (1965), p. 111; Michael von Berg, *Die Strategische Bedeutung des Ost-West Handels* (Leiden: Sijthoff, 1966), p. 105.

52 Bethkenhagen, *op. cit.*, p. 3.

53 *Jeune Afrique*, "Natural Gas: A New Soviet Weapon," April 28, 1970.

54 Michael Kreile, "Ostpolitik und Oekonomische Interessen" in Egbert Jahn and Volker Rittberger eds., *Die Ostpolitik der Bundesrepublik: Triebkraefte, Wiederstaende, Konsequenzen* (Oplanden: Westdeutscher

Verlag, 1974), p. 76. According to the author's interview with Dr. Schunder of Mannesmann, the Austrians provided the sheet metal and Mannesmann provided the pipes.

55 *International Herald Tribune,* April 30, 1969; *FAZ,* April 30, 1969; *Der Spiegel,* no. 19, 1969; Radio Free Europe Report, May 9, 1969, "Patolichev and Ulbricht to the Aid of Herr Strauss." Despite the deal, some Soviet publications continued to describe Thyssen as part of the nefariots monopoly-capitalist, expansionist network of the FRG. See Siegbert Kahn, "Monopoly Concentration in West Germany; *New Times,* no. 14 (1969).

56 Radio Free Europe Research Report, January 25, 1968, "Soviet Natural Gas for Western Europe."

57 *Financial Times,* May 6, 1969; *Deutsche Presse Agentur,* May 4, 1969; *Der Spiegel,* no. 19 (1969); *The New York Times,* May 6, 1969; *FAZ,* May 28, 1969; *Sueddeutsche Zeitung,* May 28, 1969; *Der Spiegel,* no. 33 (1969).

58 Schedt, the Bavarian economics minister, had been a pioneer in bringing energy and industry to Bavaria; *Financial Times,* December 19, 1963; *Die Welt,* May 5, 1969; *Los Angeles Times,* July 15, 1969. Bavaria was particularly interested, because it was at the end of the Dutch pipeline and had to pay relatively more for its energy than did northern Germany, where the transport costs were lower.

59 According to Mannesmann's Dr. Schunder, Mannesmann had to devise a new system of producing pipes that could withstand temperatures from +60°C to −40°C in the USSR. The quantity of pipes demanded was also a problem.

60 *The New York Times,* February 2, 1970; Karl Wangerman, "Tube for Gas: The Contract with Moscow," *Aussenpolitik,* vol. *21,* no. 2 (1970), pp. 179, 180.

61 *Soviet News,* February 10, 1970; interview with A. I. Sarokin, deputy minister of the gas industry, *Nedelia,* no. 6 (1970).

62 V. Kuznetsov, "On a Businesslike Basis," *Sotsialisticheskaia Industriia,* February 6, 1970.

63 Axel Rueckert, "Ostpolitik und Ostgeschäft," *Dokumente: Zeitschrift für übernationale Zusammenarbeit* (Cologne), 27. Jahrgang, April 1971, p. 73.

64 Wangerman, *op. cit.,* pp. 182–4.

65 Rueckert, *op. cit.,* pp. 70–1. The share of the FRG in the world's steel pipe market had fallen from 11 to 8.4 percent since 1960, whereas that of Japan had risen from 10 to 13.6 percent.

66 Rueckert, *op. cit.,* p. 72.

67 Rueckert, *op. cit.,* p. 73. Ruhrgas was in the difficult position of being both a purchaser of and a competitor for Soviet gas. The steel pipe part of the deal was concluded in August, and after this Brandt used his influence with Ruhrgas.

68 Karl Birnbaum, *East and West Germany: A Modus Vivendi* (Lexington, Mass.: Lexington Books, 1973), pp. 8, 23.

69 Rueckert, *op. cit.,* p. 76; *NZZ,* February 5, 1970.

70 For an account of the visit, see Brandt, *People and Politics,* pp. 323–45.

71 A public opinion poll of August 8, 1970, showed that 81 percent of the population in the FRG were in favor of the treaty and 78 percent thought it would lead to detente. Only 5 percent thought the treaty would lead to more economic contacts. *Bulletin,* August 12, 1970.

72 *The New York Times,* August 13, 1970; *FAZ,* August 12, 1970. For other Soviet comments, see *Pravda,* August 13, 1970, and *New Times,* no. 33 (1970). *International Affairs* (Moscow) no. 10 (1970), pp. 32–5.

73 *Documents on Germany,* p. 864.

74 *Christian Science Monitor,* August 13, 1970. The question of the EEC was particularly important because after 1974 EEC members would not be allowed to negotiate bilateral treaties with nonmember countries.

75 *The New York Times,* August 14, 1970.

76 E. Grigoriev, "Vozmozhnosti Delovogo Sotrudnichestvo" ("The Possibilities of Businesslike Cooperation"), *Pravda,* August 25, 1970.

77 Klaus Mehnert, "Der Moskauer Vertrag," *Osteuropa,* no. 12 (1970), p. 815; *Der Spiegel,* no. 34 (1970). Apparently the Brezhnev talk was circulated as a secret report from the Central Committee.

78 A. Birman, "Reform of the Five-Year Plan: Thoughts After the Plenary Session" ("Reforma God Piatiletki-Mishlenny Posle Plenuma"), *Literaturnaia Gazeta,* February 11, 1970.

79 See Philip Hanson, "Soviet Technology Imports," *Problems of Communism,* vol. 27, no. 6 (1978), pp. 20–30.

80 A. Vetrov, "Economic Ties between Socialist and Capitalist states," *International Affairs* (Moscow), no. 9 (1970), p. 11. See also B. Pichugin, "East–West Economic Relations," *International Affairs* (Moscow), no. 11 (1970), pp. 40–7.

81 O. Sayanov, "Europe and the USSR–FRG Treaty," *International Affairs* (Moscow), no. 8 (1971), p. 25.

82 See Nikolai Patolichev, *Izvestiia,* December 11, 1969; "Economic Ties Grow Stronger," *New Times,* no. 15, (1970); *New Times,* no. 50, (1970); *Pravda,* June 18, 1970.

83 The Germans appreciated this Soviet realization. According to Helmut Schmidt, "The Soviet leadership knows that the social and economic development of the country needs many years of peace." H. Schmidt, "The Future of Germany in a Changing European Context," *Adelphi Papers,* no. 33 (1967).

84 Information from private Soviet sources.

85 Brandt, *A Peace Policy for Europe* (New York: Holt, Rinehart and Winston, 1969), pp. 110–111.

86 For a representative exposition of this view, see Claudia von Braunmuehl, "Ist die 'Ostpolitik' Ostpolitik?," in Jahn and Rittberger, *op. cit.,* pp. 13–28. This theory is discussed and refuted by Michael

Kreile, in *Osthandel und Ostpolitik* (Baden-Baden: Nomos Verlag, 1978), 115–17.

87 V. Kuznetsov, "Who Is Giving the Red Light?", *Sotsialisticheskaia Industriia*, August 6, 1970; *Vneshniaia Politika SSSR (The Foreign Policy of the Soviet Union)* (Moscow: Politizdat, 1972), p. 206.

88 D. Melnikov, "Zapadnogermanskii Dogovor i Razmeshanie Politicheskikh Sil v FRG" ("The West German Treaty and the Demarcation of Political Forces in the FRG"), *MEMO*, no. 12 (1970), pp. 16–17. One Soviet book contained both assertions. In G. O. Sokol'nikov, *FRG: Sovremennye Tendenzii v Ekonomike* ("FRG: Contemporary Economic Tendencies") (Moscow: Mysl, 1971), on pp. 140–1, the new Ostpolitik is attributed to "foreign trade and the influence of West German imperialism . . . to strengthen the economic and political influence of the FRG in socialist countries." On p. 203, the August 1970 treaty is described as being an important beginning for mutually beneficial economic relations.

89 *Handelsblatt*, August 10, 14, 1970; *NZZ*, August 26, 1970.

90 For a balanced rebuttal of the claims made by the Springer press, see *Die Zeit*, September 1, 1970. Even the more moderate *FAZ*, September 14, 1970, warned of giving "development aid" to the USSR.

91 *German International*, September 1970, p. 13. These figures do not include the GDR.

92 Otto Wolff von Amerongen, "Wirtschaftsbeziehungen mit dem Osten," in Erik Boettcher, ed., *Wirtschaftsbeziehungen mit dem Osten* (Stuttgart: Kohlhammer, 1971), pp. 9–14. See also the interview with Amerongen in *Die Welt*, August 12, 1970.

93 Otto Wolff von Amerongen, "Aspects of German Trade with the East," *Aussenpolitik, 1* (1970), p. 145.

94 Bundesverband der deutschen Industrie, *Jahresbericht* (Cologne, 1969–70), p. 79.

95 For instance, Yu, M. Krasnov, in *FRG na Mirovykh Rynkakh*, claims that "under the influence of business orders, particularly the Eastern Committee of German Industrialists, the FRG government had to take the first step in the direction of weakening its discriminatory course in foreign economic ties with Socialist countries" (p. 97).

96 See Jahn and Rittberger, *op. cit.*, for a detailed account of this view.

97 Brandt, *People and Politics*, p. 169.

Chapter 8. From Moscow to Bonn: the consolidation of Ostpolitik and Westpolitik, 1970–1978

1 Leonid Brezhnev's report to the Central Committee at the Twenty-fifth Congress of the Communist Party of the Soviet Union, February 24, 1976 – cited in *New Times*, no. 9 (1976), p. 35.

2 *Bulletin*, May 9, 1978.

3 In an interview with Oriana Fallaci, Brandt said in reply to a question about whether he thought he would see the reunification of

Germany, "No, I don't think so – not even within 20 or 50 years do I anticipate an isolated answer to the German problem. I think that a change in relations between the two Germanies can only come about as a result of a change in relations between the two Europes." *New Republic,* October 6, 1973.

4 For a summary of the main issues involved in the negotiations, see Keesing's Research Report 8, *Germany and Eastern Europe since 1945* (New York: Scribner, 1973), pp. 272–85; see also, William E. Griffith, *The Ostpolitik of the Federal Republic of Germany* (Cambridge, Mass.: MIT Press, 1978), pp. 194–6.

5 *German International,* December 1970. In particular, some Germans objected to Brandt's gesture of kneeling at the memorial to the Warsaw Ghetto. Brandt explained that by his gesture "I wanted to ask pardon in the name of our people for a million-fold crime which was committed in the misused name of the German people." Keesing's Report, *op. cit.,* pp. 284–5. Brandt, *People and Politics: The Years 1960–1975* (London: Collins, 1978), pp. 398–9.

6 Griffith, *op. cit.,* p. 198.

7 According to some observers, Ulbricht disobeyed Soviet orders and conducted his own policy regarding access routes to Berlin. Although one of the main reasons Ulbricht was removed from power was his opposition to Soviet Westpolitik, it is also probable that opposition to him inside the SED was responsible for this fall. See Edwina Moreton, *East Germany and the Warsaw Alliance* (Boulder, Colo.: Westview Press, 1979), pp. 182–90. See also F. Stephen Larrabee, "The Politics of Reconciliation: Soviet Policy Towards West Germany, 1961–1972" (Ph.D. dissertation, Columbia University, 1977), chap. 4.

8 Griffith, *op. cit.,* p. 198; *The New York Times,* February 16, 1971. One of the main points of contention was Bonn's insistence that West Berlin's special links with Bonn be retained.

9 For the text of the agreement, see Presse- und Informationsamt der Bundesregierung, *Die Berlin Regelung* (1971), pp. 157–71; for a Soviet discussion of the treaty, see V. Vysotsky, *Zapadny Berlin (West Berlin)* (Moscow: Progress, 1976), pp. 208–18. See also Larrabee, *op. cit.,* p. 293.

10 Griffith, *op. cit.,* p. 209. Author's interview with chief U.S. negotiator David Anderson. Renata Fritsch-Bournazel, *Die Sowjetunion und die deutscher Teilung* (Opladen: Westdeutsche Verlag, 1979), pp. 121–2.

11 Larrabee, *op. cit.,* pp. 312–17.

12 *The Times* (London), February 6, 1971. According to this article, the Russians said that Brandt had reneged on a promise to enter into direct negotiations with the GDR on access routes to Berlin. See also *Die Welt,* February 9, 1971, for similar remarks by a Stockholm-based Soviet diplomat.

13 *The New York Times,* February 11, 1971; *Die Welt,* February 11, 1971; *Sueddeutsche Zeitung,* February 11, 1971.

14 *Die Zeit,* February 12, 1971; *The New York Times,* February 11, 1971.
15 Larrabee, *op. cit.,* pp. 318–21.
16 Griffith, *op. cit.,* pp. 218–19. The East and West German envoys were called plenipotentiaries, not ambassadors. The point was that the treaty must not imply that East and West Germany were separate states in international law, so as not to preclude reunification. For the text of the treaty, see Presse- und Informationsamt der Bundesregierung, *Dokumentation zur Entspannungspolitik* (1977), pp. 190–3.
17 For a discussion of the legality of the treaty, see Fred W. Hess, ed., *German Unity* (Kansas, Miss.: East European Monographs, 1974). The Federal Constitutional Court ruled that "Germany" meant the territory within the 1937 boundaries; Fritsch-Bournazel, *op. cit.,* pp. 127–31.
18 See Brezhnev's report to the Twenty-fourth Party Congress, *Pravda,* March 31, 1971.
19 There was some press and parliamentary criticism of Brandt's decision to undertake this journey without consulting his allies, but in his memoirs, Brandt denies that the United States ever raised such objections. See Brandt, *op. cit.,* pp. 345–6. For a report of both the foreign and domestic criticism, see *Le Monde Diplomatique,* November 1971.
20 Brandt interview in *Der Spiegel,* no. 40, 1971.
21 *Soviet News,* September 21, 1971; *Bulletin,* cited in *Dokumentation zur Deutschlandfrage,* vol. 7 (Bonn: Siegler), pp. 218–20; *Brandt, op. cit.,* pp. 348–55. One amusing vignette in these memoirs is Brandt's story of how he asked Brezhnev what the difference between communism and capitalism was. Brandt told his Soviet host that under capitalism man exploits man, but under communism the reverse is true. We do not know what his host's response was.
22 Brandt's *New York Times* interview, cited in Keesing, *op. cit.,* p. 301.
23 *The Times* (London), December 1, 1971. The statements were made in July 1970, prior to the signing of the August treaty. Gromyko said, "We have made a concession to you by dropping the concept of the recognition of the frontiers." Gromyko also stated that if the FRG and the GDR voluntarily decided to reunite and correct their borders, the USSR would accept this.
24 Scheel's speech in Deutscher Bundestag, *Verhandlungen,* 6. Wahlperiode, 171. Sitzung, Bonn, February 23, 1972, p. 9748. For the entire debate, see *ibid.,* pp. 9739–70.
25 *Pravda,* March 21, 1972; *Dokumentation zur Deutschlandfrage,* vol. 7, p. 551; *Pravda,* April 13, 1972.
26 *Pravda,* March 21, 1972.
27 *Izvestiia,* June 1, 1972.
28 For instance, there were strikes supporting the Ostpolitik, and demonstrations throughout Germany. David Binder, *The Other German: Willy Brandt's Life and Times* (Washington: New Republic, 1975), p. 292.

29 Viola Herms Drath, *Willy Brandt: Prisoner of his Past* (Radnor, Pa.: Chiltern Books, 1975).

30 See, for example, L. Zakharov, "The Soviet Union and the Federal Republic of Germany: The Policy of Strengthening Relations," *International Affairs* (Moscow) no. 6 (1973), pp. 21–7; Sh. Sanakoiev, "USSR–FRG: A Turn Towards New Relations," *International Affairs* (Moscow) no. 8 (1973), pp. 12–17; V. Rostovsev, "USSR–FRG Developing Relations," *International Affairs* (Moscow) no. 7 (1974), pp. 45–54.

31 The German government had liberalized trade with the East on August 18 by removing quotas from 4,758 items. *Bulletin,* August 25, 1970. For a discussion of the import liberalization policy, see *Handelsblatt,* March 7, 1972.

32 *The New York Times,* November 6, 1970. The EEC said that its members could continue to negotiate separate agreements with communist countries until January 1974.

33 Interview with Deputy Foreign Trade Minister Alkhimov on the Five-Year-Plan, *New Times,* no. 14, 1971. See also Otto Wolff von Amerongen, "Kooperationsprojekte ruecken staerker in den Vordergrund," *Handelsblatt,* Supplement, *Sowjetunion,* April 22–23, 1972.

34 *The New York Times,* February 16, 1971. For the Soviet reports on the ninth Five-Year Plan, see *Pravda,* February 14, 1971. According to Heinrich Machowski, "Die Aussenwirtschaft der UdSSR im Fuenfjahresplan" Richard Löwenthal and Heinrich Vogel, eds., *Sowjet-Politik in den 70er Jahre: Wandel und Beharrung* (Stuttgart: Kohlhammer, 1972), foreign trade played a smaller role in the ninth five-year plan than Soviet officials had previously indicated. The lessening role of foreign trade in Soviet economic growth was seen as a sign of the problems of Soviet foreign trade, in particular, Soviet exports.

35 *The New York Times,* February, 18, 1976.

36 *German International,* March 1971; *Handelsblatt,* February 25, 1971.

37 *FAZ,* June 17, 1971; *Handelsblatt,* August 25, 1971.

38 *Handelsblatt,* December 1, 1971; March 1, 1972; *Stuttgarter Zeitung,* February 17, 1972.

39 *International Herald Tribune,* March 17, 1972; *Sueddeutsche Zeitung,* March 17, 1972; *Christian Science Monitor,* March 18, 1972.

40 *Financial Times,* April 13, 1972.

41 *FAZ,* April 4, 1972; *Sueddeutsche Zeitung,* April 5, 1972; *Handelsblatt,* April 5, 1972; Presse- und Informationsamt der Bundesregierung, *Pressemitteilung,* April 7, 1972, no. 366/72. Author's interview with Ambassador Peter Hermes, who negotiated the treaty; *Reuters,* April 7, 1972; *The New York Times,* Apirl 7, 1972.

42 *Bulletin,* April 11, 1972.

43 *Handelsblatt,* April 21–22, 1972.

44 *New Times,* No. 16, 1972, pp. 8–9; *Pravda,* April 8, 1972.

45 Suslov's speech of April 17, 1972, reported in *Soviet News,* April 25, 1972.
46 *Krasnaia Zvezda (Red Star),* April 21, 1972; Robert Dean, *West German Trade with the East: The Political Dimension* (New York: Praeger, 1974), p. 222; *Pravda,* April 21, 1972; BMWI (Federal Economics Ministry), *Tagesnachrichten,* Bonn, April 19 and May 12, 1972.
47 *The Times* (London), May 2, 1972. The industrialists pointed to the recent opening of the first Russian-owned bank in West Germany as a sign that the Soviets were determined to increase commercial ties with Germany, irrespective of the outcome of the ratification debate. See also *Die Zeit,* May 5, 1972; *Financial Times,* May 2, 1972.
48 *Bulletin,* no. 100 (1972); BMWI *Tagesnachrichten,* July 6, 1972.
49 Interview with N. Patolichev, *New Times,* no. 31 (1972); Yu. Krasnov, *FRG Na Mirovykh Rynkakh* (Moscow: Mezhdunarodnye Otnosheniia, 1973), p. 99.
50 *Deutsche Zeitung – Christ und Welt,* May 18, 1973; *NZZ,* May 17, 1973; *Literaturnaia Gazeta,* May 18, 1973; *Handelsblatt,* April 26, 1973; *FAZ,* May 16, 1973.
51 *The New York Times, FAZ,* April 19, 1973.
52 Brandt, *op. cit.,* p. 364.
53 *Bulletin,* May 22, 1973.
54 For the text of the ten-year agreement, see *Foreign Trade* (Moscow), no. 12 (1974), pp. 54–5; for the text of the other treaties, see *Bulletin,* May 22, 1973.
55 Brandt, *op. cit.,* p. 364.
56 *Der Spiegel,* no. 32, 1973; *Handelsblatt,* May 21, 1973; *Economist,* May 26, 1973; Brandt, *op. cit.,* pp. 343, 360.
57 Kosygin, during a visit by German industrialists, denied that the USSR needed to trade with the FRG. *FAZ,* February 1, 1971.
58 Brezhnev's television speech in *Vizit Leonida Il'icha Brezhneva v Federativnuiu Respubliku Germanii (Leonid Ilyich Brezhnev's Visit to the FRG)* (Moscow: *Politizdat,* 1973), pp. 57–8.
59 *Handelsblatt,* May 22, 1973.
60 R. F. Alekseev, *SSSR–FRG–Novyi Etap Vzaimo-Otnoshenii (USSR–FRG – A New Stage of Relations), Znanie,* Series Mezhdunarodnye Otnoshenie, 91 (1973), p. 88.
61 Radio Moscow, 0700 GMT, May 24, 1973, in *Summary of World Broadcasts; Pravda,* May 31, 1973.
62 Petr Shelest, as first secretary of the Ukrainian Communist Party, had been an opponent of Westpolitik, a strong advocate of intervention in Czechoslovakia in 1968, and a supporter of the East German opposition to Westpolitik. He was relieved of his duties as first secretary in 1972, ostensibly for aiding and abetting Ukrainian nationalism. On April 27, 1973, shortly before Brezhnev's departure for Bonn, he was ousted from the Politburo, suggesting that Brezhnev's policy had prevailed.
63 *The New York Times,* April 23, 1973.

64 Karl E. Birnbaum, *East and West Germany: A Modus Vivendi* (Lexington, Mass.: Lexington Books, 1973), p. 20.

65 For the full text of the Final Act, see *New Times*, no. 32 (1975). For a critical West German evaluation, see Hans-Peter Schwarz, *Zwischenbilanz der KSZE* (Stuttgart: Seewald, 1977). For a Soviet view, see A. L. Adamishin et al., eds., *From Helsinki to Belgrade* (Moscow: Progress, 1977).

66 Richard Day, "The CSCE Summit," *The World Today*, September 1975.

67 *New Times*, no. 32, 1975.

68 The Soviet government reacted to these groups by arresting their leaders. After a series of warnings, the leader of the Soviet Helsinki Monitoring Commission, Yuri Orlov, was arrested and tried in June 1978 and sentenced to a long prison term.

69 Schwarz, *op. cit.*, p. 33. The CDU opposed the SPD–FDP government's assent to the Final Act.

70 *Der Spiegel*, no. 24, 1977.

71 For a detailed discussion of the impact of the CSCE on intra-German relations, see Schwarz, *op. cit.*, chap. 4. In the first year after Helsinki, emigration from the GDR rose by 2,000, and the number of family visits also grew. See Richard Day, "Helsinki Scoreboard," *The World Today*, August 1976.

72 In 1977, for instance, Western estimates of land force manpower stationed in the GDR, Poland, and Czechoslovakia was 962,000. The USSR claimed that the true figure was 791,000, conveniently approximate to the 850,000 NATO troops stationed in the FRG, Belgium, and Holland. *FAZ*, July 28, 1977.

73 For a detailed discussion of these proposals, see State Secretary Guenther van Well's article in *Das Parlament* no. 37 (1978), reprinted in *Bulletin* (English language version), November 8, 1978.

74 For a discussion of the chancellor's views on the MBFR, see Schmidt's report on the Brezhnev visit to the Bundestag, in Deutscher Bundestag, *Verhandlung*, 8. Wahlperiode, 90. Sitzung, May 11, 1978, pp. 7063-99. See also Schmidt's speech to the Austrian Socialist Party Conference reprinted in *Relay from Bonn*, May 18, 1978.

75 Van Well, *op. cit.*, See also Chancellor Schmidt's address, "Peace and Security within the Atlantic Alliance," to NATO, reprinted in *Bulletin* (English language version), October 11, 1978.

76 *New Times*, no. 21, 1974. The question of the Soviet involvement in the Guillaume affair remains. Privately, Soviet officials disclaimed any knowledge, and, according to one report, Brezhnev told Brandt in person in 1975 that he had known nothing about Guillaume and that it was GDR leader Honecker's fault. See *German International*, August 1975. It is difficult to understand why the Russians would have wanted Brandt removed from power; however, it is equally implausible that the USSR knew nothing about the existence of Guillaume.

77 For a detailed account of the visit, including the Soviets' preference for Brandt over Schmidt, see Klaus Mehnert, "Mit Bundeskanzler Schmidt in der UdSSR," *Osteuropa*, no. 1 (1975), pp. 3-18.

78 *Pravda*, June 15, 16, 1977. The German press stressed the difficult nature of the talks, particularly over Berlin. See *Sueddeutsche Zeitung*, June 16, 1977. In October 1976, the first West German military attaché was accredited in Moscow. See *Der Spiegel*, no. 41 (1976); *FAZ*, November 15, 1970.

79 *Pravda*, November 6, 1975; for Brezhnev's report to the Twenty-fifth Party Congress, February 24, 1976, see *New Times*, no. 9, 1976.

80 Tony Burkett, "Germany Divided: The 1976 Bundestag Election," *The World Today*, November 1976.

81 *The New York Times*, August 9, 1976. For a discussion of the SPD's attitude toward Eurocommunism, see Angela Stent Yergin, "West Germany's *Suedpolitik:* Social Democrats and Eurocommunism," *Orbis*, vol. 23, no. 1 (1979), pp. 51-71.

82 *Izvestiia*, September 4, 1976.

83 *Sovietskaia Rossiia*, September 25, 1976.

84 *Sovietskaia Rossiia*, October 5, 1976; *Literaturnaia Gazeta*, October 6, 1976.

85 *Hannoversche Allgemeine*, April 22, 1978; *Financial Times*, April 27, 1978; *Die Zeit*, April 28, 1978; Brezhnev interview in *Vorwaerts*, May 4, 1978; Karen Karagezyan and Mikhail Fyodorov, "On the Eve of the Brezhnev Visit," *New Times*, no. 18, 1978; *Izvestiia*, April 25, 1978; *Pravda*, May 3, 4, 1978.

86 *Handelsblatt*, May 8, 1978; *Le Monde*, May 9, 1978; *Neues Deutschland* on May 8, 1978, gave three lines to the Brezhnev-Kohl meeting but devoted a long paragraph to the Brezhnev-Strauss talk.

87 Rowland Evans and Robert Novak, "Brezhnev and Bonn: A Shift?" *International Herald Tribune*, July 4, 1978.

88 *NZZ*, May 9, 1978.

89 Joint Declaration of May 6, 1978, published in *Soviet News*, May 9, 1978.

90 Deutscher Bundestag, *Verhandlungen*, 8. Wahlperiode, 90. Sitzung, May 11, 1978, pp. 7064-5; CDU-Praesidium statement, May 5, 1978.

91 *Sueddeutsche Zeitung*, May 9, 1978; see also *Vizit Leonida Il'ycha Brezhneva v Federativnuiu Respubliku Germanii (The Visit of Leonid Ilyich Brezhnev in the Federal Republic of Germany)*, (Moscow: *Politizdat*, 1978); *Neues Deutschland*, May 13, 1978.

92 For the full text, see *Soviet News*, May 9, 1978.

93 Deutscher Bundestag, *Verhandlungen, op. cit.*, p. 7066.

94 *New York Times*, May 7, 1978.

95 Deutscher Bundestag, *Verhandlungen, op. cit.*, p. 7084.

96 *Ibid.*, p. 7074. For a discussion of the invalidity of the Reinsurance Treaty claim, see *Die Zeit*, May 19, 1978; CSU *Pressemitteilung*, May 11, 1978.

97 *The New York Times*, May 7, 1978.

Chapter 9. Beyond Ostpolitik and Westpolitik: the economics of detente

1 *The New York Times,* April 14, 1975.
2 Joachim Jahnke and Rainer Lucas, *Osthandel-Ostpolitik in der Praxis: vom Handel zur wirtschaftlichen Zusammenarbeit* (Bonn: BMWI Dokumentation, 1972), p. 21.
3 Deutsches Institut fuer Wirtschaftsforschung, (DIW) *Wochenbericht,* (Berlin), no. 15 (1980).
4 *Financial Times,* September 9, 1976; *Le Monde,* August 1–2, 1976; *New York Times,* August 16, 1976.
5 *Business Week,* May 1, 1978; Der Bundesminister für Wirtschaft: *Der Deutsche Osthandel zu Beginn des Jahres 1978* (Bonn, 1979), pp. 23–4.
6 J. P. Young, "Quantification of Western Exports of High Technology Products to Communist Nations," U.S. Department of Commerce (Washington: GPO, 1977), pp. 15–16.
7 Klaus Bolz, Herman Clement, and Petra Pissula, *Die Wirtschaftsbeziehungen zwischen der BRD und der Sowjetunion* (Hamburg: Weltarchiv, 1976), pp. 263–5.
8 Y. Krasnov, "SSSR–FRG: Problemy Ekonomicheskogo Sotrudnichestvo," ("USSR–FRG: Problems of Economic Cooperation"), *MEMO,* no. 5 (1975), p. 13.
9 See Central Intelligence Agency, *Prospects for Soviet Oil Production,* ER 77-10270 (Washington, DC: April 1977). For opposing views, see United Nations Economic Commission for Europe, *New Issues Affecting the Energy Economy of the ECE Region in the Medium and Long Term* (Geneva: United Nations, 1978).
10 *The New York Times,* April 11, 1972; *Muenchner Merkur,* April 7, 1972; *Financial Times,* July 7, 1972; *German International,* September 1972; Radio Free Europe, May 28, 1973.
11 *The New York Times,* October 2, 1973; *Deutsche Presse Agentur,* September 5, 1974; *Financial Times,* October 30, 1974. The amount of German pipe to be delivered in return was 950,000 tonnes.
12 *Eastwest Markets,* April 21, 1975; *The Economist,* August 24, 1974.
13 *Der Spiegel,* no. 26 (1980).
14 D.I.W. *Wochenbericht, op. cit.*
15 *Der Spiegel,* no. 26, 1980. Author's interviews with German government officials.
16 *Financial Times,* October 23, 1975.
17 Author's interview with officials in the East–West Trade Desk, German Foreign Ministry. See also *Handelsblatt,* September 9, 1974.
18 *Daily Telegraph,* November 4, 1970; *Christian Science Monitor,* April 10, 1971; *Financial Times,* April 11, 1973; *The New York Times,* May 3, October 5, 1973. The uranium was purchased for a power station at Muelheim in the Ruhr.
19 Deutscher Bundestag, *Verhandlungen,* 6. Wahlperiode, 79. Sitzung, November 12, 1970, pp. 4470–1.
20 D.I.W. *Wochenbericht, op. cit.*
21 *FAZ,* July 8, 1977; *Die Welt,* July 9, 1977.

22 D.I.W. *Wochenbericht, op. cit.*
23 Otto Wolff von Amerongen, "Wirtschaftsbeziehungen mit der Sowjetunion," *Osteuropa,* no. 1 (1974), p. 3.
24 Speech by Karl Moersch, minister of state at the German Foreign Office, "Eastern Trade in a Phase of Consolidation," *Bulletin,* June 9, 1976.
25 Jahnke and Lucas, *op. cit.,* pp. 13, 33.
26 Author's interviews with Joachim Jahnke, Federal Economics Ministry.
27 Author's interview with Frau Marianne Wannow, Foreign Ministry.
28 Walter Scheel, "Aussenpolitische Teilbilanz-Wo stehen Wir?" *Aussenpolitik,* vol. 22, no. 5 (1971), pp. 253–60; for Schiller's speech, see BMWI *Tagesnachrichten,* February 9, 1971.
29 *Wirtschaftswoche,* October 1, 1976.
30 D.I.W. *Wochenbericht,* no. 13, 1981.
31 Bundesverband der Deutschen Industrie, *Jahresbericht* (Cologne: 1972–73), pp. 165–71; 1973–74, pp. 201–9.
32 Statement of Wolff von Amerongen, president, German National Chamber of Commerce and Industry, and president, Otto Wolff A. G., in *Foreign Economic Policy for the 1970's:* Hearings before the Subcommittee on Foreign Economic Policy of the Joint Economic Committee of Congress, 91st Congress, part 6, pp. 1190–1196.
33 See, for example, *Handelsblatt,* October 28, 1970, January 23, 1973, March 15, 1973; *Ost-West Kurier,* January 22, 1972; *Deutsche-Zeitung Christ und Welt,* September 24, 1971; *FAZ,* February 28, 1971. Because the Swiss *NZZ* is very influential in the FRG, I am including it in my survey of the "German" press. See *NZZ,* April 11, 1971; February 28, 1972; August 9, 1973.
34 Bolz, *op. cit.,* pp. 397, 402, 494.
35 K. Suvorov, "Po Puti Sotsialistichekogo Industrializatsiia" ("On the Road to Socialist Industrialization"), *Pravda,* December 18, 1975. Vadim Zagladin, who is responsible for international questions on the Central Committee of the Communist Party of the Soviet Union, later claimed that the article was only discussing a *historical* debate and did not imply current policy. See interview with Zagladin, *Der Spiegel,* no. 15 (1976).
36 Jack Brougher, "USSR Foreign Trade: A Greater Role for Trade with the West," in *The Soviet Economy in a New Perspective,* a compendium of papers submitted to the Joint Economic Committee, Congress of the United States, 94th Congress, 2nd Session, October 14, 1976, p. 578.
37 "Growing Trade with West Germany," *Soviet News,* February 22, 1972.
38 S. Tosunian, "Osnova – Vzaimnaia Vygoda" ("The Basis Is Mutual Advantage"), *Izvestiia,* December 17, 1970.
39 D. A. Demin and S. B. Lavrov, *FRG Segodniia (FRG Today)* (Leningrad, 1973), p. 18.
40 Yezhov and Syrokomskii, "Svezhie Vetry Nad Reinom" ("Fresh

Breezes over the Rhine"), *Literaturnaia Gazeta,* December 9, 1970. The *NZZ,* December 13, 1970, interpreted this article – which stressed how much German industrialists wanted to trade with the USSR – as a sign of Soviet desire to increase trade. See also Y. Zakharov, "USSR–FRG: Five Years of the Moscow Treaty," *International Affairs* (Moscow), no. 9 (1975), p. 37.

41 *New Times,* no. 33 (1971); *New Times,* no. 14 (1972); *Sovietskaia Rossiia,* February 13, 1973; *Sotsialisticheskaia Industriia,* May 16, 1973.

42 Y. Krasnov, "USSR–FRG: Business Cooperation," *International Affairs* (Moscow), no. 10 (1973), p. 75.

43 Dhzermen Gvishiani interview in *Der Spiegel,* no. 19 (1972).

44 Brezhnev's report to the Twenty-fifth Party Congress, *Pravda,* February 25, 1976.

45 N. Smeliakov, "Delovye Vstrechi" ("Business Meetings"), *Novyi Mir,* no. 12 (1973), pp. 203–39. Yuri Krasnov, in "Soviet–West German Trade," *New Times,* no. 5, (1978), p. 24, denies that Soviet goods are in any way inferior to those on the German market, although he admits that "Soviet export organizations still have much to learn in the matter of marketing techniques."

46 *Sowjetunion Heute,* January 15, 1977.

47 Interviews with V. Zagladin, in *Der Spiegel,* no. 50, (1971); *Der Spiegel,* no. 46, (1973).

48 N. Shmelev, "New Horizons of Economic Relations," *MEMO,* no. 1 (1973), p. 57.

49 Lev Bezyminsky, "The Logic of Facts against the Logic of Prejudices," *New Times,* no. 12 (1971).

50 *Tass* International service in English, January 12, 1971.

51 O. Bogomolov, "Trebovanie Zhizni" ("A Demand of Life"), *Izvestiia,* February 26, 1974.

52 Bruce Parrott, "Technological Progress and Soviet Politics," *Survey,* vol. *23,* no. 2 (Spring 1977–78), pp. 39–60.

53 D. Melnikov, ed., *Mezhdunarodnye Otnosheniia v Zapadnoi Evrope (International Relations in Western Europe),* (Moscow: Mezhdunarodnye Otnosheniia, 1974), p. 73. Y. Krasnov, "SSSR–FRG: Problemy Ekonomicheskogo Sotrudnichestvo," *op. cit.,* emphasizes the dialectical connection between trade and politics; the development of political trust facilitates trade, which in turn strengthens political trust.

54 G. Sokol'nikov, "Vozmozhnosti i Problemy Sovetsko Zapadnogermanskikh Ekonomicheskikh Sviazei" ("The Possibilities and Problems of Soviet–West German Economic Relations"), *MEMO,* no. 10 (1973), pp. 17–25.

55 A. Grigoryev, "USSR–FRG: Economic Relations," *International Affairs* (Moscow), no. 10 (1974), pp. 47–53; *Izvestiia,* September 17, 1974.

56 See, for instance, Franklyn D. Holzman, *International Trade Under Communism* (New York: Basic Books, 1976); Alec Nove, "East–West Trade: Problems, Prospects, Issues" *The Washington Papers,* no. 53 (Beverly Hills and London: Sage Publishers).

57 On the problems of compensation deals, see Matthias Schmitt, *Industrille Ost-West Kooperation* (Stuttgart: Seewald Verlag, 1974).

58 For a discussion of all the aspects of German credit policy, see Rolf Steffens, *Die Praxis des Osthandels* (Hamburg: Verlag Weltarchiv, 1973), pp. 73–95; Bok, op. cit., pp. 147–59.

59 *Financial Times*, November 18, 1972; *The Economist*, May 5, 1973; *The Times* (London), October 6, 1972; *Handelsblatt*, October 4, 1972.

60 *Die Zeit*, November 24, 1972; *Financial Times*, November 18, 1972.

61 *International Herald Tribune*, November 18, 1972; *Deutsche Presse-Agentur*, May 2, 1973; *Financial Times*, November 18, 1972; *The Economist*, November 25, 1972.

62 *Der Spiegel*, no. 31 (1973); *Handelsblatt*, March 12, 1974.

63 *FAZ*, August 24, September 13, 26, October 11, December 31, 1973; *Handelsblatt*, September 26, 1973; *Sueddeutsche Zeitung*, October 11, 1973; *Financial Times*, January 24, 1974.

64 The Kreditanstalt fuer Wiederaufbau issues government export credits for the Third World. Its operations are financed out of public funds, borrowings on the capital market, and credits from various financial institutions. See Thomas A. Wolf, "East-West Trade Credit Policy: A Comparative Analysis," in Paul Marer, ed., *U.S. Financing of East-West Trade* (Bloomington: Indiana University Press, 1975), p. 155.

65 *Die Welt*, January 15, 1974; *Der Spiegel*, no. 3, (1974); *Christian Science Monitor*, March 25, 1974; *Sueddeutsche Zeitung*, March 18, 1974; *Financial Times*, March 29, 1974; *Deutsche Presse-Agentur*, April 12, 1974.

66 UPI, April 9, 1974; Business International (October 1976), *Doing Business With Eastern Europe*, Part 4, p. 12; *The New York Times*, August 16, 1976; *Financial Times*, April 26, 1977.

67 *FAZ*, July 27, 1973; *Die Welt*, January 18, 1974.

68 *Der Spiegel*, no. 5 (1974).

69 *The Economist*, October 26, 1974; *The New York Times*, October 27, 1974.

70 *The New York Times*, October 31, 1974; *The Guardian*, October 31, 1974; *NZZ*, October 31, 1974; *Handelsblatt*, November 5, 1974; Klaus Mehnert, "Mit Bundeskanzler Schmidt in der UdSSR," *Osteuropa*, no. 1 (1975), pp. 10–11.

71 *The New York Times*, January 14, 1975; *Die Zeit*, March 14, 1975; *FAZ*, January 11, 1975; *International Herald Tribune*, April 14, 1975; *Wall Street Journal*, January 27, 1975.

72 *Der Spiegel*, no. 7, 1974; no. 11 (1975); *Financial Times*, August 14, 1975.

73 *Wall Street Journal*, January 27, 1975; *Financial Times*, August 14, 1975.

74 *The New York Times*, March 31, 1976. The Germans wanted to pay 0.9 kopeks a kilowatt, and the Soviets were demanding 1.6 kopeks; *Sueddeutsche Zeitung*, April 1, 1976.

75 *FAZ*, April 1, 1976; *Financial Times*, April 1, 1976; *NZZ*, April 2,

1976; Klaus Mehnert, "Mit dem Bundespraesidenten in der UdSSR," *Osteuropa,* no. 1 (1976), p. 5.
76 *Izvestiia,* June 27, 1979; *Financial Times,* June 28, 1979.
77 Gerhard Wettig, "Die Praktische Anwendung des Berlin-Abkommens durch UdSSR und DDR (1972–1976)," Berichte des Bundesinstituts fuer ostwissenschaftliche und internationale Studien, no. 31 (1976), p. 56.
78 *The New York Times,* November 29, 1974; Y. Kotov, "An Agreement and Its Observance," *New Times,* no. 23 (1976).
79 *The New York Times,* September 5, 1976; *Der Tagesspiegel,* November 8, 1977.
80 In the communiqué issued by the Soviet Foreign Ministry, the Soviet government claimed that the inclusion of West Berlin in the elections would be a "revision of the status of that town"; *Pravda,* August 4, 1976.
81 On August 13, the East Germans refused to let a CDU youth group travel by bus to West Berlin to demonstrate on the fifteenth anniversary of the building of the Berlin Wall; in the summer an Italian communist was shot as he ran across to the GDR to collect his papers, which he had left there by mistake.
82 G. Kirillov, "West Berlin: Past and Future," *International Affairs* (Moscow), no. 7 (1975), pp. 75–80.
83 Y. Zakharov, "USSR–FRG: Five Years of the Moscow Treaty," *International Affairs* (Moscow), no. 9 (1975), p. 37.
84 *The New York Times,* March 19, 1977.
85 Speech of Chancellor Helmut Schmidt, *Bulletin* (English language version) May 4, 1976.

Chapter 10. Normalization and the future of West German–Soviet relations

1 "Erklaerung der Bundesregierung zur Deutschland- und Aussenpolitik," *Bulletin,* June 19, 1980.
2 Egon Bahr personally came out against discussing the bomb with Brezhnev, whereas Genscher wanted to use it as a bargaining tool with the Russians. *Sueddeutsche Zeitung,* April 20, 1978.
3 *International Herald Tribune,* April 10, 1979; *Frankfurter Rundschau,* May 5, 1979; *FAZ,* May 5, 1979.
4 Brezhnev speech in *Pravda,* October 7, 1979.
5 Gromyko press conference in Bonn, reprinted in *Pravda,* November 25, 1979.
6 Interview in *Die Zeit,* July 21, 1978.
7 Although the Soviets criticized the Franco–German summit of February 1980 for condemning the invasion of Afghanistan, they approvingly cited the French insistence on maintaining a dialogue with the USSR. See *Pravda,* February 8, 1980.
8 See Schmidt's declaration to the Bundestag on his return from Moscow, reprinted in Presse- und Informationsamt der Bundesregierung, *Pressemitteilung,* July 3, 1980.

9 *The New York Times,* January 18, 1975.
10 *FAZ,* December 14, 1978.
11 Samuel P. Huntington, "Trade, Technology and Leverage: Economic Diplomacy," *Foreign Policy,* no. 32 (Fall 1978), pp. 63–80.
12 Radio Free Europe special, March 20, 1980.
13 *FAZ,* May 31, 1980; *Sueddeutsche Zeitung,* May 31, 1980; *Pravda,* June 1, 1980.
14 *Pravda,* April 25, 1980.
15 Moscow Radio in German to Germany, 1109 GMT, June 9, 1980 in *Summary of World Broadcasts,* June 10, 1980, pp. G1–3.
16 For details of German business involvement in the Olympics, see *Sueddeutsche Zeitung,* June 18, 1980.
17 Nikolai Portugalov, "The Lion's Share," *Literaturnaia Gazeta,* May 14, 1980; *Pravda,* March 8, 1980.
18 *Pravda,* April 23, June 9, 1980.
19 John P. Hardt, "Soviet Commercial Relations and Political Change," in Robert A. Bauer, ed., *The Interaction of Economics and Foreign Policy* (Charlottesville: University of Virginia Press, 1975), p. 73; *The New York Times,* July 10, 1973.
20 John Pinder, "The Community and Comecon," *The World Today,* May, 1977. When Soviet Fishing Minister Alexander Ishkov was asked whether his visit meant that the USSR now recognized the existence of the EEC, he replied, "That is a difficult question." See Stephen Milligan, "What do the Soviets Want in Brussels?" *European Community* (July–August 1977), p. 5.
21 Radio Free Europe Report, December 18, 1974.
22 At the 1980 NATO meeting, the final communiqué, for the first time in eight years, supported the German desire for reunification explicitly. *Sueddeutsche Zeitung,* June 26, 1980.
23 For a definition and model of Finlandization, see George Ginsburgs and Alvin Z. Rubinstein, "Finlandization: Soviet Strategy or Geopolitical Footnote?" in George Ginsburgs and Alvin Z. Rubinstein, eds., *Soviet Foreign Policy Toward Western Europe* (New York: Praeger, 1978), pp. 3–16.
24 For a detailed discussion of this issue, see Angela Stent Yergin, "Soviet–West German Relations: Finlandization or Normalization?" in Ginsburgs and Rubinstein, *op. cit.,* pp. 102–33.

Bibliography

Archives and official documents

Press Archives

Deutsche Gesellschaft fuer Auswaertige Politik, Bonn.
Radio Liberty, Munich.
The Royal Institute of International Affairs, Chatham House, London.

Presidential Libraries

The John F. Kennedy Memorial Library, Waltham, Massachusetts (National Security Files).

Documents

Adamishin, A. L. et al, eds. *From Helsinki to Belgrade: The Soviet Union and the Final Act of the European Conference: Documents and Material.* Moscow: Progress Publishers, 1977.
Auswaertiges Amt, *Mitteilung an die Presse,* Bonn.
Bundesministerium fuer Wirtschaft. *Tagesnachrichten,* Bonn.
    Der Deutsche Osthandel zu Beginn des Jahres 1978, 1979, 1980, Bonn.
    Osthandel–Ostpolitik in der Praxis. BMWF Dokumentation No. 175, October 1972, Bonn.
Bundesverband der deutschen Industrie. *Jahresbericht,* Cologne. 1949-.
Council of Europe, Consultative Assembly. *Report on the Political Aspects of East–West Trade.* Document no. 1961. September 1965.
    Report on East–West Trade. Document no. 1964. September 1965.
Deutscher Bundestag. *Verhandlungen.* Bonn 1955-.
Deutsche Welle. *Dokumentation.* Berlin.
Dokumente zur Deutschlandpolitik: Frankfurt: A. Metzner. Bundesministerium fuer Gesamtdeutsche Fragen (after 1970 known as Bundesministerium füer innerdeutsche Beziehungen) 1961-1980.
Embree, George D., ed. *The Soviet Union and the German Question, September 1958–June 1961.* The Hague: Nijhoff, 1963.

European Coal and Steel Community. *Memorandum on Energy Policy.* June 1962.

Khrushchev, Nikita S. *Soviet Policy in the Current International Situation.* New York: Crosscurrents Press, 1960.

Keesing's Research Report No. 8. *Germany and Eastern Europe since 1945.* New York: Scribner, 1973.

Meissner, Boris, ed. *Die deutsche Ostpolitik, 1961–1970: Kontinuitaet und Wandel.* Cologne: Verlag Wissenschaft und Politik, 1970.

Moskau–Bonn: Die Beziehungen Zwischen der Sowjetunion und der Bundesrepublik Deutschland 1955–1973, Dokumentation. Cologne: Verlag Wissenschaft und Politik, 1975.

Presse-und Informationsamt der Bundesregierung. *Bulletin.* Bonn. *Mitteilung an die Presse.* Bonn.

Reference Division. Central Office of Information. *Berlin and the Problem of German Reunification.* London.

Siegler, Heinrich von, ed. *Dokumentation zur Deutschlandfrage.* Bonn: Siegler, 1961–1979.

Soviet Proposals on Germany and Berlin, November 1958–January 1959. London: 1959, Soviet booklet no. 46.

United Nations Economic Commission for Europe. *Economic Survey of Europe.* Geneva, 1947–1964, thereafter New York.

Statistical Office, *Yearbook of International Trade Statistics.* New York.

United States Congress. Joint Economic Committee. *Soviet Economic Performance, 1966–1967.* Hearings before the Subcommittee on Foreign Economic Policy. 90th Congress, 2nd Session, 1968.

Joint Economic Committee. *Soviet Economic Prospects for the Seventies. A Compendium of Papers.* 93rd Congress, 1st Session, 1973.

Joint Economic Committee. *Soviet Economy in a New Perspective. A Compendium of Papers.* 94th Congress, 2nd Session, 1976.

Office of Technology Assessment. *Technology and East-West Trade.* Washington, D.C.: U.S. Government Printing Office, 1979.

Senate Committee on Foreign Relations. *Documents on Germany 1944–1970.* 92nd Congress, 1st Session.

Senate. Subcommittee on International Finance of the Committee on Banking and Currency. *East-West Trade. Hearings before the Subcommittee on International Finance of the Committee on Banking and Currency.* 90th Congress, 2nd Session, 1968.

Senate. *Soviet Oil in East-West Trade. Hearings Before the Subcommittee to Investigate the Administration of the Internal Security Act and Other Internal Security Laws of the Committee on the Judiciary.* 87th Congress, 2nd Session.

Vizit Leonida Il'icha Brezhneva v Federativnuiu Respubliku Germanii. Moscow, Politizdat, 1973, 1978.

Newspapers and magazines

Christian Science Monitor.
Daily Telegraph.

Deutsche Zeitung – Christ und Welt.
Deutsche Zeitung und Wirtschaftszeitung.
The Economist.
Financial Times.
Fortune.
Frankfurter Allgemeine Zeitung (FAZ)
Frankfurter Rundschau.
German International.
Handelsblatt.
Industriekurier.
Izvestiia.
Literaturnaia Gazeta.
Manchester Guardian.
Muenchner Merkur.
Le Monde.
Neue Zuercher Zeitung (NZZ).
Neues Deutschland.
The New Republic.
New Times (Moscow).
New York Herald Tribune (later *International Herald Tribune*).
The New York Times.
Observer.
Pravda.
Sotsialisticheskaia Industriia.
Soviet News.
Der Spiegel.
Sueddeutsche Zeitung.
Taegliche Rundschau.
Der Tagesspiegel (Berlin).
The Times (London).
Trud.
U.S. News and World Report.
Der Volkswirt.
Wall Street Journal.
Washington Post.
Die Welt.
Die Zeit.

News agency dispatches

Deutsche Presse-Agentur.
Reuters.
Tass.

Periodicals and specialist journals

Aussenpolitik (English and German editions).
Current Digest of the Soviet Press.

Current History.
Eastwest Markets.
Encounter.
Europa-Archiv.
Foreign Affairs.
Foreign Policy.
Foreign Trade (Moscow).
International Affairs (Moscow).
International Journal.
International Organization.
Journal of Common Market Studies.
Konjunkturpolitik.
Mirovaia Ekonomika i Mezhdunarodnye Otnosheniia (MEMO).
Novy Mir.
Orbis.
Osteuropa.
Osteuropa Wirtschaft.
Petroleum Economist.
Politische Vierteljahresschrift.
Problems of Communism.
Survey.
Vneshniaia Torgovlia.
Voprosy Ekonomiki.
Western Political Quarterly.
World Marxist Review.
World Politics.
World Today.
Znanie (Pamphlet Series).

Unpublished materials

Alekseev, R. F. "Ustanovlenie Diplomaticheskikh Otnoshenii i razvitie ekonomicheskikh i kulturnykh sviazei mezhdu SSSR i FRG (1955-1963)." Candidate's dissertation, Moscow University, 1973.

Arbatov, G. A. "Ideologicheskaia Borba v Sovremennykh Mezhdunarodnykh Otnosheniakh." Doctor's dissertation, Moscow University, 1965.

Buriakov, A. "Germanskaia Problema Segodnia." Candidate's dissertation, Alma-Ata, 1965.

Feller, Albert. "Warum Roehrenembargo?" Mimeograph, Bonn, 1964.

Joffe, Josef. "Society and Foreign Policy in the Federal Republic: The Adenauer Era, 1949-1962." Ph.D. dissertation, Harvard University, 1975.

Kremer, N. S. "Problemy Formirovaniia Vneshnei Politiki FRG 1949-1969." Doctor's dissertation, Moscow University, 1971.

Larrabee, F. Stephen. "The Politics of Reconciliation: Soviet Policy towards West Germany, 1961-1972." Ph.D. dissertation, Columbia University, 1977.

Marer, Paul. "Soviet Economic Relations with Eastern Europe and Their Impact on East–West and US–USSR Trade." Mimeograph. Harvard Russian Research Center, 1975.

Mueller, Friedemann. "Die Rolle der Abhaengigkeit in der Wirtschaftlichen Ost–West Zusammenarbeit." Stiftung Wissenschaft und Politik. Ebenhausen, 1975.

McGoldrick, Frederick Ford. "The Politics of West German Foreign Economic Policy towards the Communist States of Eastern Europe, 1955–1968." Ph.D. dissertation, American University, 1973.

Memoirs and books by political actors

Adenauer, Konrad. *Erinnerungen.* Vols. 1–4. Stuttgart: Deutsche Verlags-Anstalt, 1965–1968. Vol. 1, 1945–53; Vol. 2. 1953–55; Vol. 3, 1955–59; Vol. 4, 1959–63.

Allardt, Helmut, *Moskauer Tagebuch.* Duesseldorf: Econ Verlag, 1973.

Bohlen, Charles E. *Witness to History, 1929–1969.* New York: Norton, 1973.

Brandt, Willy. *Begegnungen und Einsichten: Die Jahre 1960–1975.* Hamburg: Hoffmann und Campe, 1975.

    My Road to Berlin. New York: Doubleday, 1960.

    The Ordeal of Coexistence. Cambridge, Mass.: Harvard University Press, 1963.

    A Peace Policy for Europe. New York: Holt, 1969.

    People and Politics: The Years 1960–1975. London: Collins, 1978.

    Reden und Interviews. Hamburg: Hoffman und Campe, 1973.

Brentano, Heinrich von. *Germany and Europe: Reflections on German Foreign Policy.* New York: Praeger, 1964.

Eden, Anthony. *Full Circle.* London: Cassell, 1960.

Erhard, Ludwig. *Germany's Comeback in the World Market.* London: Allen & Unwin, 1954.

    The Economics of Success. London: Thames & Hudson, 1963.

Johnson, Lyndon Baines. *The Vantage Point: Perspectives of the Presidency.* New York: Popular Library, 1971.

Khrushchev, Nikita S. *Khrushchev Remembers: The Last Testament.* Boston: Little, Brown, 1976.

Kroll, Hans. *Lebenserinnerungen eines Botschafters.* Cologne: Kiepenheuer und Witsch, 1967.

Leonhard, Wolfgang. *Child of the Revolution.* Chicago: Henry Regnery, 1958.

Moersch, Karl. *Kursrevision: Deutsche Politik nach Adenauer.* Frankfurt: Societäts Verlag, 1978.

Patolichev, Nikolai. *Foreign Trade.* Moscow: Novosti.

Penkovskiy, Oleg. *The Penkovskiy Papers.* New York: Doubleday, 1965.

Schroeder, Gerhard. *Wir Brauchen eine heile Welt: Politik in und fuer Deutschland.* Duesseldorf: Econ Verlag, 1964.

Stalin, J. V. *Economic Problems of Socialism in the USSR.* Stanford: The Hoover Institution, 1967.

Weit, Erwin. *Eyewitness.* London: André Deutsch, 1973.

Books

Adler-Karlsson, Gunnar. *Western Economic Warfare, 1947–1967*. Stockholm: Almquist and Wiksell, 1968.

Allen, Robert Loring. *Soviet Economic Warfare*. Washington: Public Affairs Press, 1961.

Akopov, G. M. *Zapadnyi Berlin: Problemy i Resheniia (West Berlin: Problems and Solutions)*. Moscow: Mezhdunarodnye Otnosheniia, 1974.

Aussenpolitische Perspektiven des Westdeutschen Staates. Teilband III: Der Zwang zur Partnerschaft. Munich: R. Oldenbourg, 1972.

Bauer, Robert A., ed. *The Interaction of Economics and Foreign Policy*. Charlottesville: University of Virginia Press, 1975.

Berg, Michael von. *Die Strategische Bedeutung des Ost–West Handels*. Leiden: Sijthoff, 1966.

Bergsten, C. Fred, ed. *The Future of the International Economic Order: An Agenda for Research*. Lexington, Mass.: Lexington Books, 1973.

Bergsten, C. Fred, and Lawrence B. Kraus, eds. *World Politics and International Economics*. Washington: The Brookings Institution, 1975.

Binder, David. *The Other German: Willy Brandt's Life and Times*. Washington: New Republic, 1975.

Birnbaum, Karl. *East and West Germany: A Modus Vivendi*. Lexington, Mass.: Lexington Books, 1973.

Bolesch, Hermann, *Der Lange Marsch des Willy Brandt*. Tübingen: H. Erdmann, 1970.

Boettcher, Erik, ed. *Wirtschaftsbeziehungen mit dem Osten*. Stuttgart: Kohlhammer, 1971.

Bolz, Klaus, and Peter Plotz. *Erfahrungen aus der Ost–West Kooperation*. Hamburg: Weltarchiv, 1974.

Bolz, Klaus, and Bernd Kunze. *Wirtschaftsbeziehungen Zwischen Ost und West. Handel und Kooperation*. Bonn: Europaunion Verlag, 1972.

Bolz, Klaus, Herman Clemennt, and Petra Pissulla. *Die Wirtschaftsbeziehungen zwischen der BRD und der Sowjetunion*. Hamburg: Weltarchiv, 1976.

Braunthal, Gerhard. *The Federation of German Industry in Politics*. Ithaca: Cornell University Press, 1965.

Brown, Alan, and Egon Neuberger, eds. *International Trade and Central Planning*. Berkeley: University of California Press, 1968.

Brzezinski, Zbigniew K. *Alternative to Partition*. New York: Council on Foreign Relations, 1965.

The Soviet Bloc: Unity and Conflict. Cambridge, Mass.: Harvard University Press, 1967.

Bykov, Alexander. *Untapped Reserves of World Trade*. Moscow: Novosti, 1968.

Carr, Edward Hallett. *The Twenty Years Crisis*. New York: Harper & Row, 1964.

Charles, Max. *Berlin Blockade*. London: Allen Wingate, 1959.

Collier, David, and Kurt Glaser, eds. *Berlin and the Future of Eastern Europe*. Chicago: Henry Regnery, 1963.

Clabaugh, Samuel F. *Trading with the Communists*. Washington: Georgetown University Press, 1968.

Dallin, Alexander, *Soviet Conduct in World Affairs*. New York: Columbia University Press, 1960.

Dean, Robert. *West German Trade with the East: The Political Dimension*. New York: Praeger, 1974.

Demin, D. A., and S. B. Lavrov. *FRG Segodnia (FRG Today)*. Leningrad, 1973.

Deuerlein, Ernst. *Deutschland Wie Chrushtschow es Will*. Bonn: Berto Verlag, 1961.

Deutsch, Karl W., and Lewis J. Edinger. *Germany Rejoins the Powers: Mass Opinion, Interest Groups and Elites in Contemporary German Foreign Policy*. Stanford: Stanford University Press, 1959.

Doing Business with the USSR. New York: Business International, 1971.

Drath, Viola Herms. *Willy Brandt: Prisoner of His Past*. Radnor. Pa.: Chiltern Books, 1975.

Dutoit, Bernard. *L'Union Sovietique Face a l'Integration Européene*. Lausanne: Centre de Recherches Europeens, 1968.

Ebel, Robert E. *The Petroleum Industry of the Soviet Union*. New York: American Petroleum Institute, 1961.

Elliott, Iain F. *The Soviet Energy Balance*. New York: Praeger, 1974.

Engels, Friedrich. *The Role of Force in History*. New York: International, 1968.

Erfurt, Werner. *Die Sowjetrussische Deutschland-Politik*. Esslingen: Bechtle Verlag, 1959.

Ernst, Heiner. *Der Osthandel – Eine Politische Waffe?* Stuttgart: J. Fink Verlag, 1964.

Feld, Werner. *Reunification and West German–Soviet Relations*. The Hague: Nijhoff, 1963.

Friesen, Connie M. *The Political Economy of East–West Trade*. New York: Praeger, 1976.

Fokin, D., ed. *Vneshniaia Torgovlia SSSR 1946–1963*. Moscow: Mezhdunarodnye Otnosheniia, 1964.

Fritsch-Bournazel, Renata. *Die Sowjetunion und die deutsche Teilung*. Opladen: Westdeutscher Verlag, 1979.

Gablentz, O. M. von der. *The Berlin Question and Its Relation to World Politics*. Munich: R. Oldenburg, 1964.

Germanskaia Vostochnaia Politika v Novoe i Noveishee Vremia. Problemy Istorii i Istoriografii. Moscow: Nauka, 1974.

Ginsburgs, George, and Alvin Z. Rubinstein, eds. *Soviet Foreign Policy Toward Western Europe*. New York: Praeger, 1978.

Golan, Galia. *The Czech Reform Movement*. Cambridge University Press, bridge University Press, 1971.

Goldman, Marshall I. *Detente and Dollars*. New York: Basic Books, 1975.

Griffith, William E. *The Ostpolitik of the Federal Republic of Germany*. Cambridge, Mass.: MIT Press, 1978.

Gromyko, A. A., S. A. Golunskii, and V. M. Khvostov, eds. *Diplomaticheskii Slovar'*. Moscow: Politicheskoi Literatury, 1960, 1971.

Grosser, Alfred. *Germany in Our Time*. New York: Praeger, 1971.

Hartl, Hans, and Werner Marx. *Fuenfzig Jahre Sowjetische Deutschlandpolitik*. Boppard am Rhein: Boldt Verlag, 1967.

Hassner, Pierre. *Change and Security in Europe*. London: Adelphi Papers No. 45, 49, 1968.

Herman, Leon, ed. *A Background Study on East-West Trade*. Washington: U.S. Government Printing Office, 1965.

Hess, Fred W. *German Unity*. Kansas, Miss.: East European Monographs, 1974.

Hirschman, Albert O. *National Power and the Structure of Foreign Trade*. Berkeley: University of California Press, 1945.

A Bias for Hope: Essays on Development and Latin America. New Haven, Conn.: Yale University Press, 1971.

Hobson, J. A. *Imperialism*. London: James Nisbet, 1902.

Holzman, Franklyn. *International Trade Under Communism*. New York: Basic Books, 1976.

Homze, Alma, and Edward Homze. *Willy Brandt*. Nashville: Thomas Nelson, 1974.

Hough, Jerry F. *The Soviet Union and Social Science Theory*, Cambridge Mass.: Harvard University Press, 1977.

Hutchings, Raymond. *Soviet Economic Development*. Oxford: Basis Blackwell, 1971.

Hutton, Joseph Bernard. *The Traitor Trade*. London: Neville Spearman, 1963.

Imperializm FRG. Moscow: Politicheskoi Literatury, 1973.

Inozemtsev, N. N., ed. *Mezhdunarodyne Otnosheniia Posle Vtoroi Mirovoi Voiny (International Relations Since the Second World War)*. Moscow: Politicheskoi Literatury, 1962–5.

Jacobsen, Hans-Adolf. *Mistrauische Nachbarn*. Duesseldorf: Droste, 1970.

Jacobsen, Hans-Adolf, and Otto Stenzl, eds. *Deutschland und die Welt*. Munich: Deutsche Taschenbuch Verlag, 1964.

Jahn, Egbert, and Volker Rittberger, eds. *Die Ostpolitik der Bundesrepublik: Triebkraefte, Widerstaende, Konsequenzen*. Opladen: Westdeutscher Verlag, 1974.

Kadyshev, V. P. *SSSR na Vneshnikh Rynkakh*. Moscow: Vneshtorgizdat, 1964.

Kaiser, Karl. *German Foreign Policy in Transition: Bonn between East and West*. Oxford: Oxford University Press, 1968.

Kapelinskii, Yu. I. *Na Vzaimovygodnoi Osnove: Torgovlia SSSR s Kapitalisticheskimi Stranami*. Moscow: Mezhdunarodnye Otnosheniia, 1975.

Keohane, Robert O., and Joseph S. Nye. *Power and Interdependence*. Boston: Little, Brown, 1977.

Knorr, Klaus. *The Power of Nations: The Political Economy of International Relations*. New York: Basic Books, 1975.

Koort, F. *Soviet Industry and Foreign Trade*. London: Soviet News Booklet No. 13, 1957.

312 Bibliography

Korbel, Josef. *Detente in Europe: Real or Imaginary?* Princeton, N.J.: Princeton University Press, 1972.

Krasnov, Yu. M. *FRG na Mirovikh Rynkakh*. Moscow: Mezhdunarodnye Otnosheniia, 1973.

Kreile, Michael. *Osthandel und Ostpolitik*. Baden-Baden: Nomos Verlag, 1978.

Krengel, Rolf. *Die Bedeutung des Ost-West Handels fuer die Ost-West Beziehungen*. Goettingen: Vandenhoeck and Ruprecht, 1967.

Kuczynski, Juergen, and Grete Wittkowski. *Die deutsch-russischen Handelsbeziehungen in der letzten 150 Jahren*. Berlin: Verlag Die Wirtschaft, 1947.

LaFeber, Walter. *America, Russia and the Cold War 1945-1975*. New York: Wiley, 1976.

Laqueur, Walter. *Russia and Germany: A Century of Conflict*. Boston: Little, Brown, 1965.

Lenin, V. I. *Imperialism, the Highest Stage of Capitalism*. New York: Bantam, 1966.

Liubimov, N. N., ed. *Sovremennye Mezhdunarodnye Ekonomicheskie Otnosheniia* Moscow: Mezhdunarodnye Otnosheniia, 1964.

Loewenthal, Richard. *Vom Kalten Krieg zur Ostpolitik*. Stuttgart: Seewald, 1974.

Loewenthal, Richard and Heinrich Vogel. *Sowjetpolitik in der 70er Jahre Wandel und Beharrung*. Stuttgart: Kohlhammer, 1972.

Ludz, Peter Christian. *The German Democratic Republic from the Sixties to the Seventies*. Cambridge, Mass.: Harvard Center for International Affairs occasional paper no. 26, 1970.

Mackintosh, John M. *Strategy and Tactics of Soviet Foreign Policy*. London: Oxford University Press, 1963.

Marer, Paul. *Postwar Pricing and Price Patterns in Socialist Foreign Trade 1946-1971*. Ind.: International Development Research Report no. 1, 1972.

——— ed. *U.S. Financing of East-West Trade: The Political Economy of Government Credits and the National Interest*. Bloomington: Indiana University Press, 1975.

Marx, Karl. *Selected Works*. Moscow: Foreign Language Publishing House, 1962.

Melnikov, Daniil Efimovich. *Hamburg-Bonn-Miunkhen-Liudi, Politika, Propaganda*. Moscow: Mezhdunarodnye Otnosheniia, 1969.

Germanskii Vopros. Moscow: Politicheskoi Literatury, 1955.

——— ed. *Mezhdunarodnye Otnosheniia v Zapadnoi Evrope (International Relations in Western Europe)*. Moscow: Mezhdunarodyne Otnosheniia, 1974.

Mezhdunarodnye Otnosheniia i Vneshniaia Politika SSSR, 1950-1959. Moscow: Nauka, 1977.

Mill, John Stuart. *Principles of Political Economy*. London: Longmans, 1929.

Montesquieu, Baron de. *De L'Esprit des Lois*. New York: Hafner, 1949.

Moreton, Edwina. *East Germany and the Warsaw Alliance.* Boulder, Colo.: Westview Press, 1979.

Morgan, Roger. *West European Politics since 1945.* New York: Capricorn Books, 1973.

Naumov, Pavel. *Bonn – Sila i Bessile (Bonn – Strength and Weakness).* Moscow: Mysl, 1965.

Nikolaev, Pavel A. *Politika Sovetskogo Soiuza v Germanskom Voprose, 1945–1964 (The Policy of the Soviet Union in the German Question).* Moscow: Nauka, 1966.

Nove, Alec. *An Economic History of the USSR.* London: Penguin Books, 1969.

Osten, Walter. *Die Aussenpolitik der DDR.* Opladen: Leske Verlag, 1969.

Pipes, Richard, ed. *Soviet Strategy in Europe.* New York: Crane and Russak, 1976.

Pisar, Samuel. *Coexistence and Commerce.* New York: McGraw-Hill, 1970.

Ponomarev, B., A. Gromyko, and V. Khvostov. *History of Soviet Foreign Policy 1945–1970.* Moscow: Progress Publishers, 1974.

Pounds, Norman. *The Economic Pattern of Modern Germany.* London: John Murray, 1963.

Prittie, Terence. *Adenauer – A Study in Fortitude.* Chicago: Cowles, 1971.

Pryor, Frederick L. *The Communist Foreign Trade System.* Cambridge, Mass.: Harvard University Press, 1966.

Richardson, James L. *Germany and the Atlantic Alliance.* Cambridge, Mass.: Harvard University Press, 1966.

Ripka, Hubert. *Czechoslovakia Enslaved.* London: Gollancz, 1950.

Roberts, Adam and Philip Windsor. *Czechoslovakia 1968: Reform, Repression, and Resistance.* London: Chatto and Windus, 1969.

Roberts, Geoffrey K. *West German Politics.* New York: Taplinger, 1972.

Rohleder, Claus-Dieter, *Die Osthandelspolitik der EWG – Mitgliedstaaten, Grossbritanniens und der USA gegenueber den Staatshandelslaendern suedosteuropas.* Munich: Eigenverlag der Suedosteuropa-Gesellschaft, 1969.

Schick, Jack M. *The Berlin Crisis, 1958–1962.* Philadelphia: University of Pennsylvania Press, 1971.

Schmid, Günther. *Entscheidung in Bonn.* Cologne: Verlag Wissenschaft und Politik, 1979.

Schmitt, Matthias, *Industrielle Ost–West Kooperation.* Stuttgart: Seewald Verlag, 1974.

Osthandel auf Neuen Wegen. Hamburg: Hoffmann und Campe, 1968.

Schnitzer, Martin. *East and West Germany: A Comparative Economic Analysis.* New York: Praeger, 1972.

Schulz, Eberhard. *Moskau und die europaeische Integration.* Munich: R. Oldenbourg Verlag, 1975.

Schwarz, Haus-Peter, *Handbuch der deutschen Aussenpolitik.* Munich: Piper, 1975.

Schwarz, Hans-Peter. *Zwischenbilanz der KSZE.* Stuttgart: Seewald, 1977.

314   Bibliography

Seidenzahl, Fritz. *Geschaefte mit dem Osten.* Duesseldorf: Econ Verlag, 1957.

Seleznev, G. *Trade, a Key to Peace and Progress.* Moscow, Progress 1966.

Shulman, Marshall D. *Stalin's Foreign Policy Reappraised.* Cambridge, Mass.: Harvard University Press, 1963.

Skilling, H. Gordon and Franklyn Griffiths, eds. *Interest Groups in Soviet Politics.* Princeton, N.J.: Princeton University Press, 1971.

Slusser, Robert M. *The Berlin Crisis of 1961: Soviet–American Relations and the Struggle for Power in the Kremlin.* Baltimore: Johns Hopkins University Press, 1973.

ed. *Soviet Economic Policy in Postwar Germany.* New York: Research Program on the USSR, 1953.

Smith, Glen Alden. *Soviet Foreign Trade.* New York: Praeger, 1973.

Sokol'nikov, G. D. *FRG: Sovremennye Tendenzii V Ekonomike.* Moscow, Mysl 1971.

Sontheimer, Kurt. *The Government and Politics of West Germany.* London: Hutchinson University Library, 1972.

Soviet Foreign Policy: A Brief Review. Moscow: Progress, 1967.

Speier, Hans, and W. Phillips Davison, eds. *West German Leadership and Foreign Policy.* Evanston, Ill: Row, Peterson, 1957.

Standke, Klaus-Heinrich. *Der Handel mit dem Osten.* Baden-Baden: Nomos Verlagsgesellschaft, 1968.

Steffens, Rolf. *Die Praxis des Osthandels.* Hamburg: Verlag Weltarchiv, 1973.

Stehle, Hansjakob. *Nachbar Polen.* Frankfurt: S. Fischer, 1963.

Stern, Carola. *Willy Brandt in Selbstzeugnissen und Bilddokumente.* Hamburg: Rowohlt, 1975.

Stolper, Gustav. *The German Economy, 1870 to the Present.* New York: Harcourt Brace and World, 1967.

Tatu, Michel. *Power in the Kremlin.* New York: Viking Press, 1969.

Trautmann, Walter. *Osthandel – Ja oder Nein?* Stuttgart: W. Kohlhammer, 1954.

Ulam, Adam Bruno. *Expansion and Coexistence.* New York: Praeger, 1974.

Uren, Philip. *East–West Trade: A Symposium.* Toronto: Canadian Institute of International Affairs, 1967.

Vneshniaia Politika SSSR. Moscow: Politicheskoi Literatury, 1972.

Voslenskii, M. S. *"Vostochnaia" Politika FRG, 1949–1966 (The Ostpolitik of the FRG).* Moscow: Nauka, 1967.

Vysotsky, V. *Zapadny Berlin (West Berlin).* Moscow: Progress, 1976.

Wallich, Henry C. *Mainsprings of the German Revival.* New Haven: Yale University Press, 1955.

Wasowski, Stanislaus, ed. *East–West Trade and the Technology Gap.* New York: Praeger, 1970.

Wettig, Gerhard. *Die Praktische Anwendung des Berlin-Abkommens durch UdSSR and DDR, 1972–1976.* Cologne: Berichte des Bundesinstituts fuer Ostwissenschaftliche und internationale Studien, No. 31, 1976.

Whetten, Lawrence L. *West Germany's Ostpolitik.* New York: Oxford University Press, 1971.

Wilczynski, Jozef. *The Economics and Politics of East-West Trade.* New York: Praeger, 1969.

Wiles, Peter. *Communist International Economics.* Oxford: Basil Blackwell, 1968.

Windsor, Philip. *City on Leave: A History of Berlin, 1945-1962.* London: Chatto and Windus, 1963.

Germany and the Management of Detente. New York: Praeger, 1971.

Wolf, Thomas A. *US East-West Trade Policy.* Lexington, Mass.: Lexington Books, 1973.

Wolfe, Thomas W. *Soviet Power and Europe.* Baltimore: Johns Hopkins University Press, 1970.

Wolfers, Arnold. *Discord and Collaboration.* Baltimore: Johns Hopkins University Press, 1962.

Worzliczek, Adalbert. *"Bonn-Moskau": Die Ostpolitik Adenauers.* Munich: Isar Buecherei, 1957.

Yergin, Daniel. *Shattered Peace: The Origins of the Cold War and the Price of the National Security State.* Boston: Houghton Mifflin, 1977.

Zimmerman, William. *Soviet Perspectives on International Relations, 1956-1967.* Princeton, N.J.: Princeton University Press, 1964.

Index